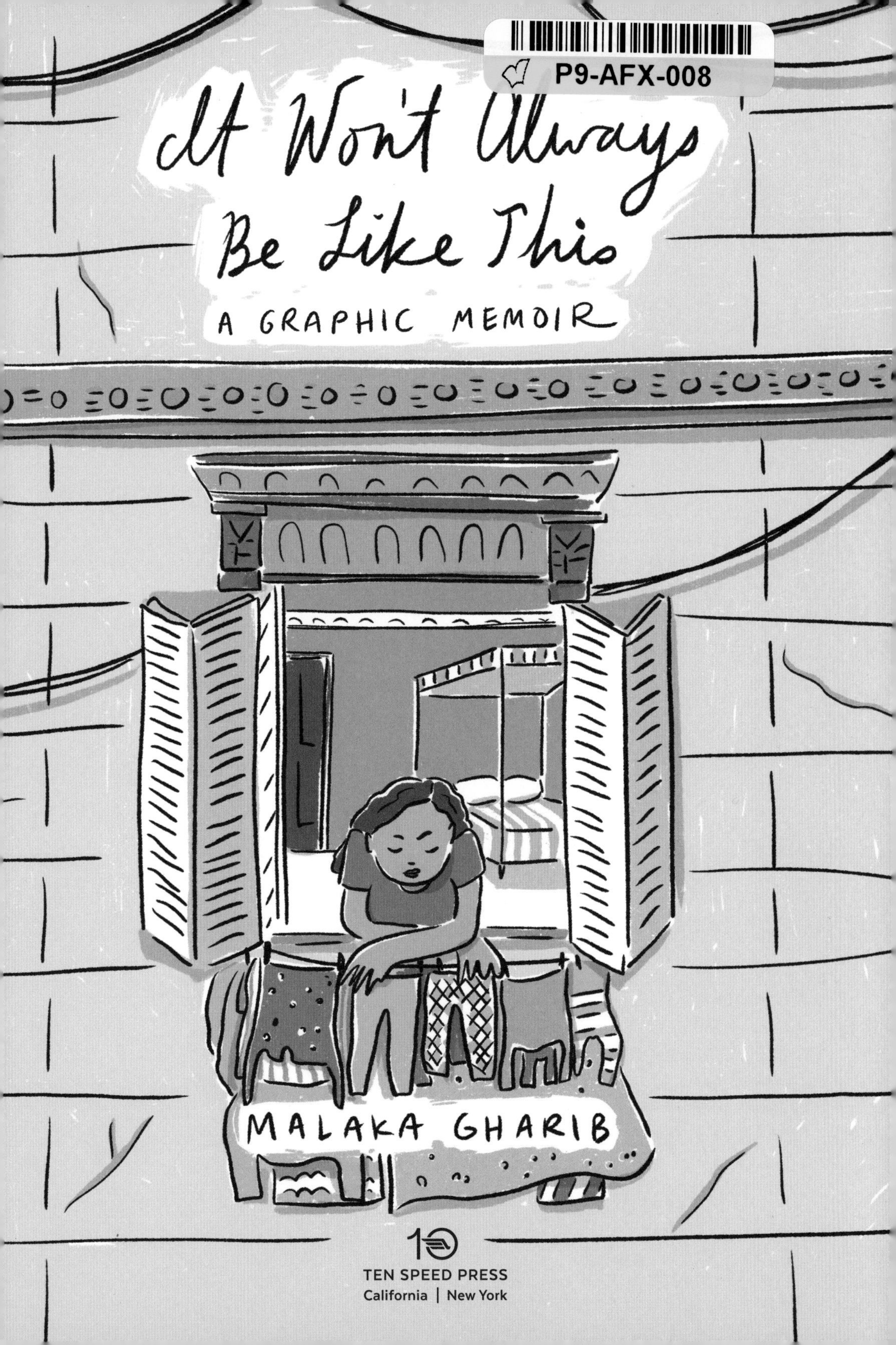
It Won't Always Be Like This
A GRAPHIC MEMOIR
MALAKA GHARIB
TEN SPEED PRESS
California | New York

Published in the United States by Ten Speed Press, an imprint of
Random House, a division of Penguin Random House LLC, New York.
TenSpeed.com
RandomHouseBooks.com

Typefaces: Malaka Gharib by Malaka Gharib and TT Norms by Ivan Gladkikh

Library of Congress Cataloging-in-Publication Data
Names: Gharib, Malaka, author, illustrator.
Title: It won't always be like this : a graphic memoir / Malaka Gharib.
Other titles: It will not always be like this
Description: First edition. | California ; New York : Ten Speed Press, [2022]
Identifiers: LCCN 2022003823 | ISBN 9781984860293 (trade paperback) |
ISBN 9781984860309 (ebook)
Subjects: LCSH: Gharib, Malaka–Comic books, strips, etc. | Immigrants–United
States–Biography–Comic books, strips, etc. | Cartoonists–United States–
Biography–Comic books, strips, etc. | Egyptian Americans–Biography–Comic
books, strips, etc. | LCGFT: Autobiographical comics. | Graphic novels.
Classification: LCC PN6727.G5 Z46 2022 | DDC 741.5/973 [B]–dc23/
eng/20220304 | LC record available at https://lccn.loc.gov/2022003823

Trade Paperback ISBN: 978-1-9848-6029-3
eBook ISBN: 978-1-9848-6030-9

Printed in China

Editor: Sara Neville | Production editor: Sohayla Farman
Art director: Chloe Rawlins | Designer: Lisa Bieser
Production designer: Claudia Sanchez
Production manager: Dan Myers
Colorist: Toby Leigh
Copyeditor: Patrick Barb | Proofreader: Kate Bolen
Publicist: Felix Cruz | Marketer: Monica Stanton

10 9 8 7 6 5 4 3 2 1

First Edition

FOR HALA

إهداء إلى حالة

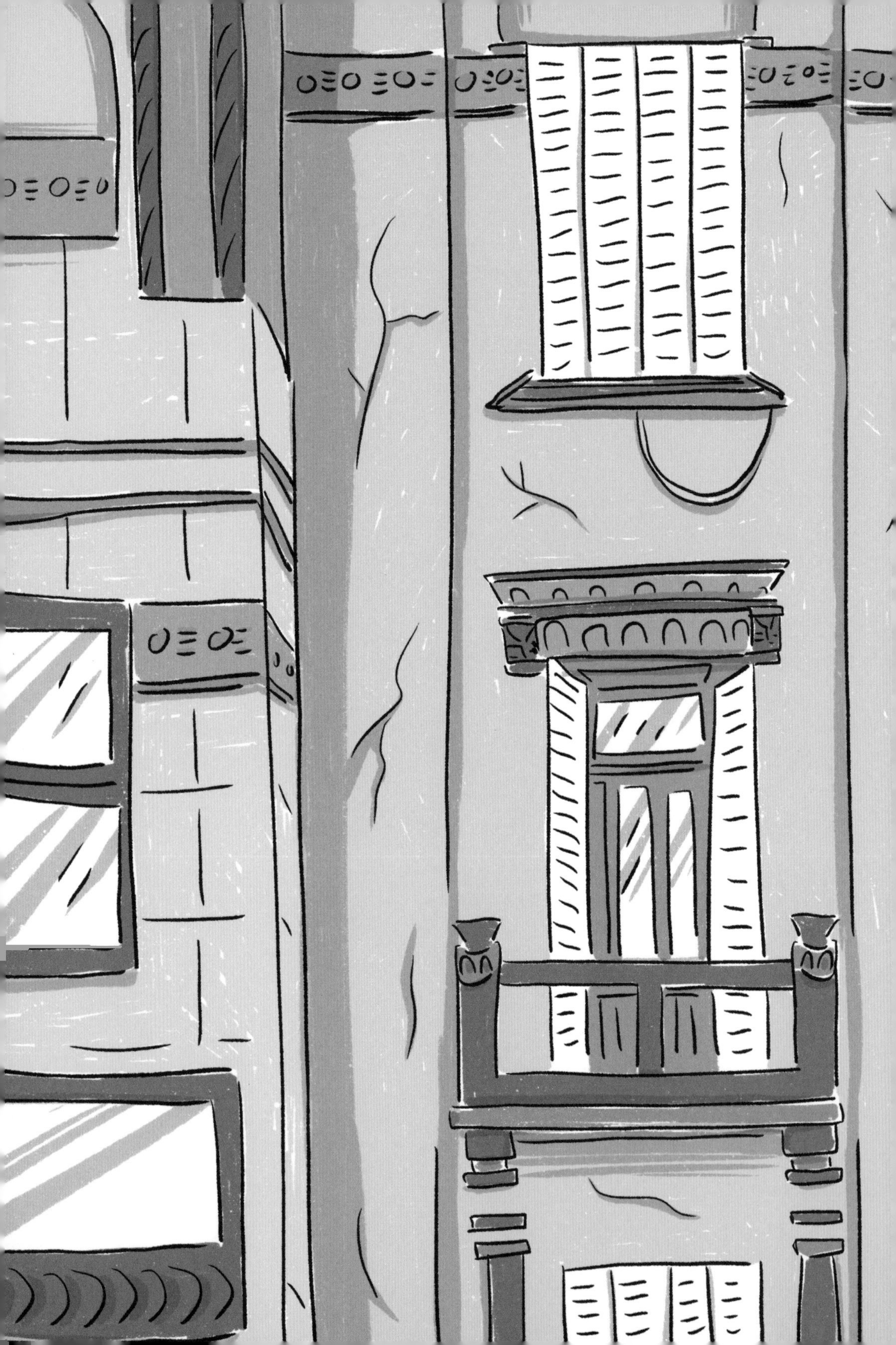

PROLOGUE

The Rock

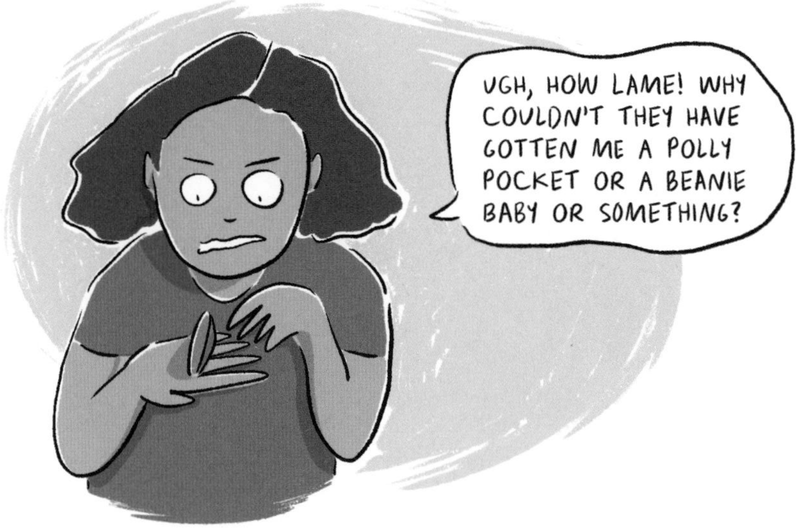
UGH, HOW LAME! WHY COULDN'T THEY HAVE GOTTEN ME A POLLY POCKET OR A BEANIE BABY OR SOMETHING?

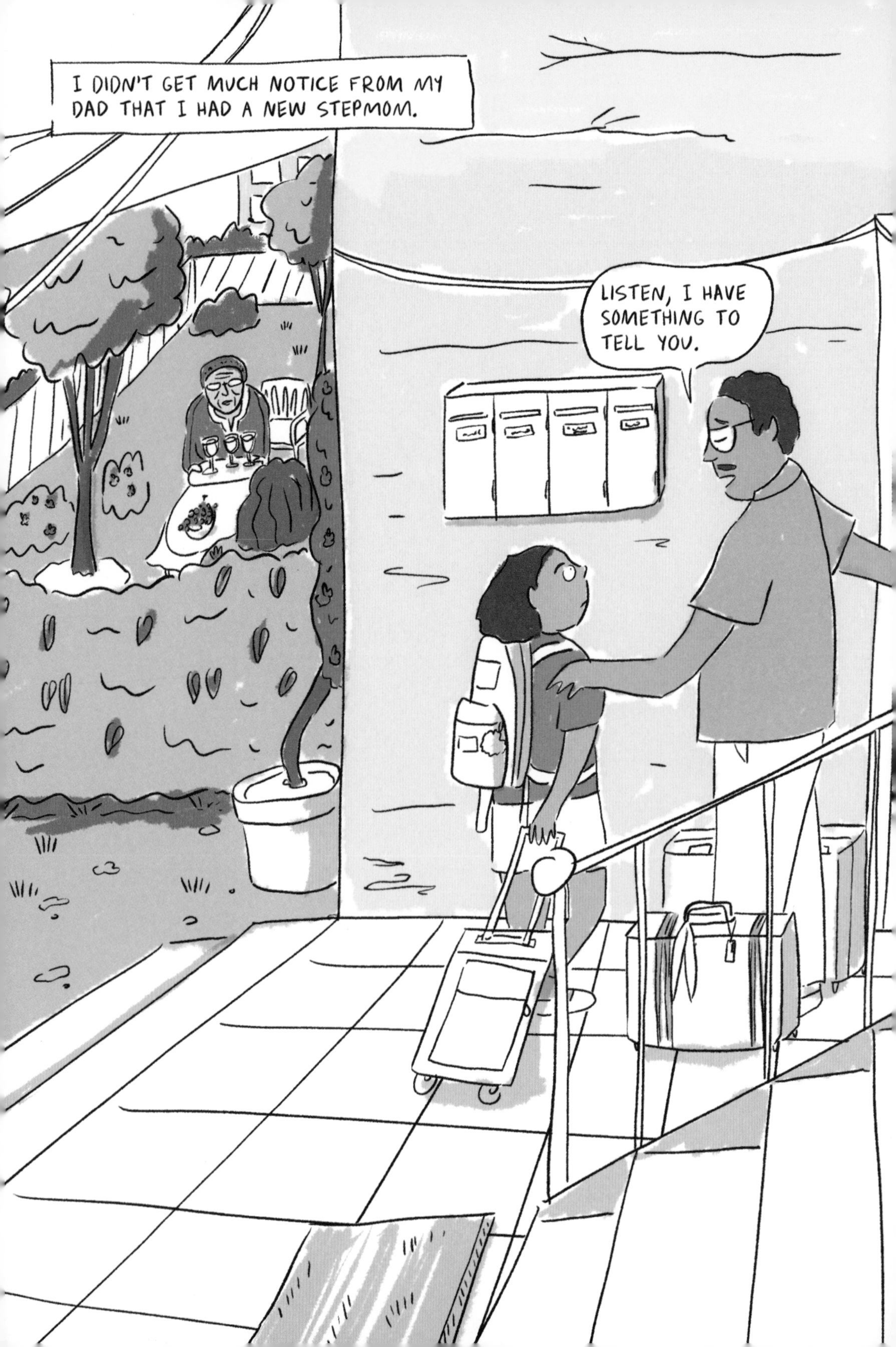
I DIDN'T GET MUCH NOTICE FROM MY DAD THAT I HAD A NEW STEPMOM.
LISTEN, I HAVE SOMETHING TO TELL YOU.

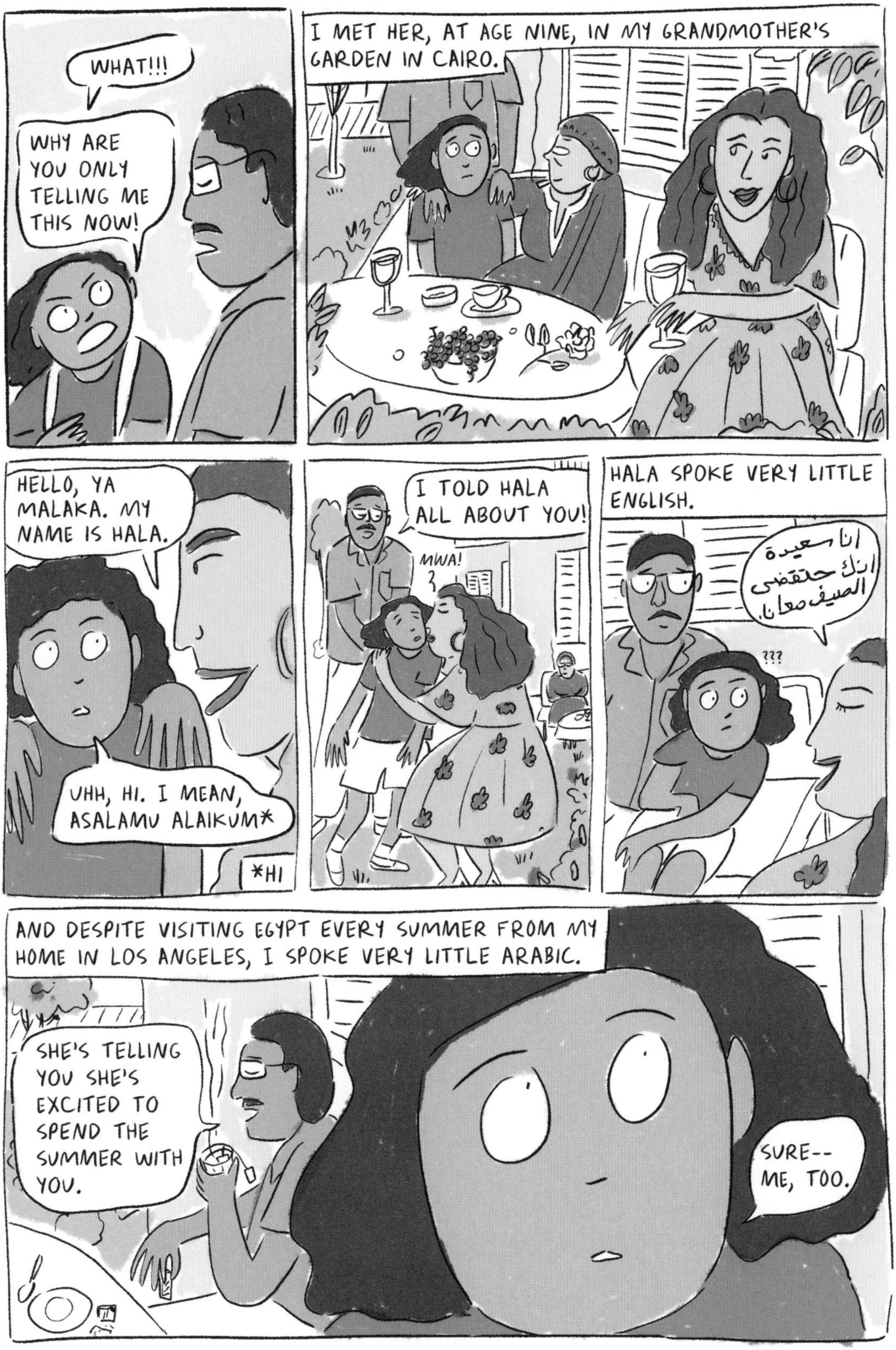

WHAT!!!
WHY ARE YOU ONLY TELLING ME THIS NOW!
I MET HER, AT AGE NINE, IN MY GRANDMOTHER'S GARDEN IN CAIRO.
HELLO, YA MALAKA. MY NAME IS HALA.
UHH, HI. I MEAN, ASALAMU ALAIKUM*
*HI
I TOLD HALA ALL ABOUT YOU!
MWA!
HALA SPOKE VERY LITTLE ENGLISH.
انا سعيدة انك حتقضى الصيف معانا.
???
AND DESPITE VISITING EGYPT EVERY SUMMER FROM MY HOME IN LOS ANGELES, I SPOKE VERY LITTLE ARABIC.
SHE'S TELLING YOU SHE'S EXCITED TO SPEND THE SUMMER WITH YOU.
SURE-- ME, TOO.

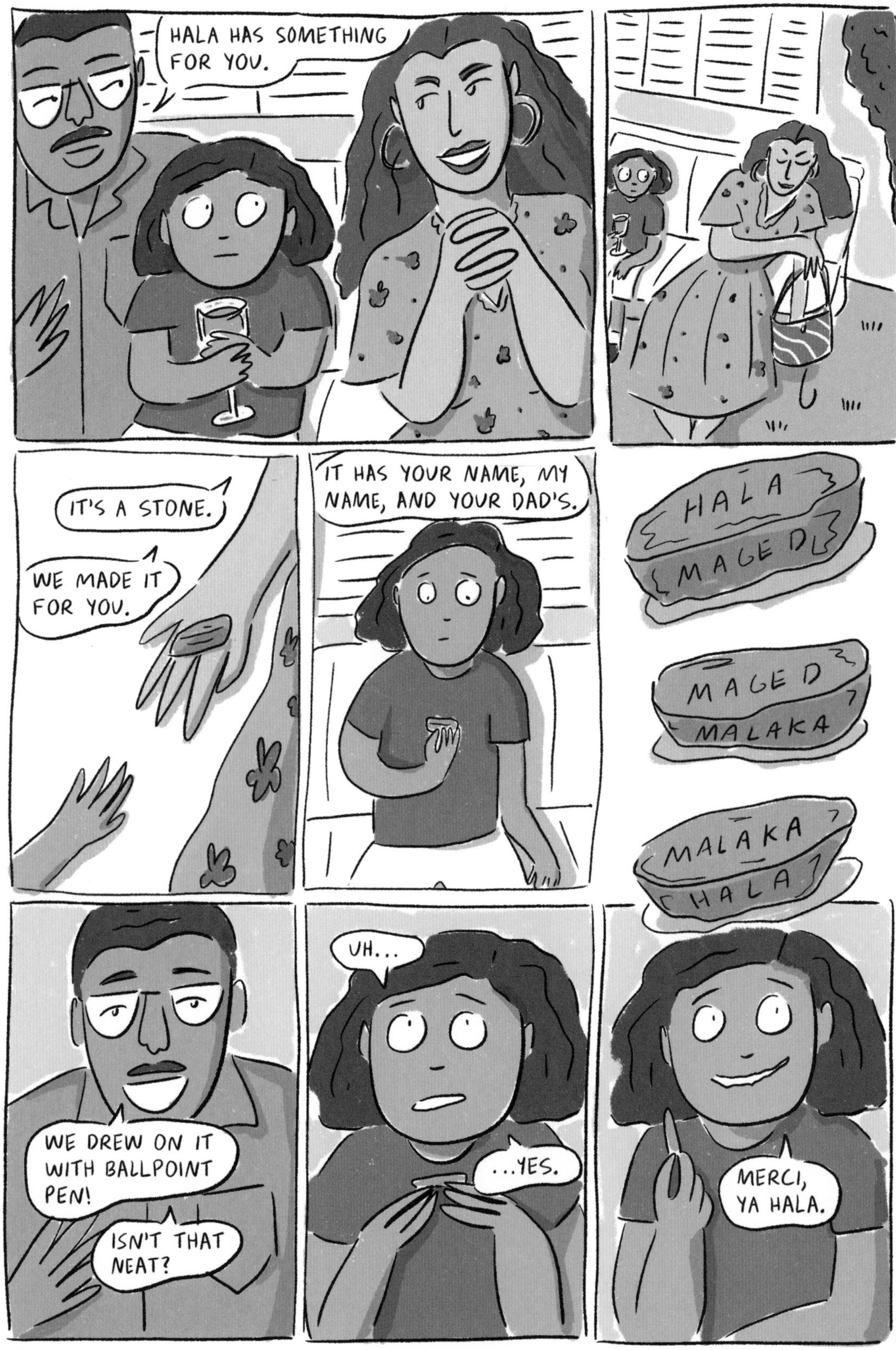

HALA HAS SOMETHING FOR YOU.
IT'S A STONE.
WE MADE IT FOR YOU.
IT HAS YOUR NAME, MY NAME, AND YOUR DAD'S.
HALA
MAGED
MAGED
MALAKA
MALAKA
HALA
WE DREW ON IT WITH BALLPOINT PEN!
ISN'T THAT NEAT?
UH...
...YES.
MERCI, YA HALA.

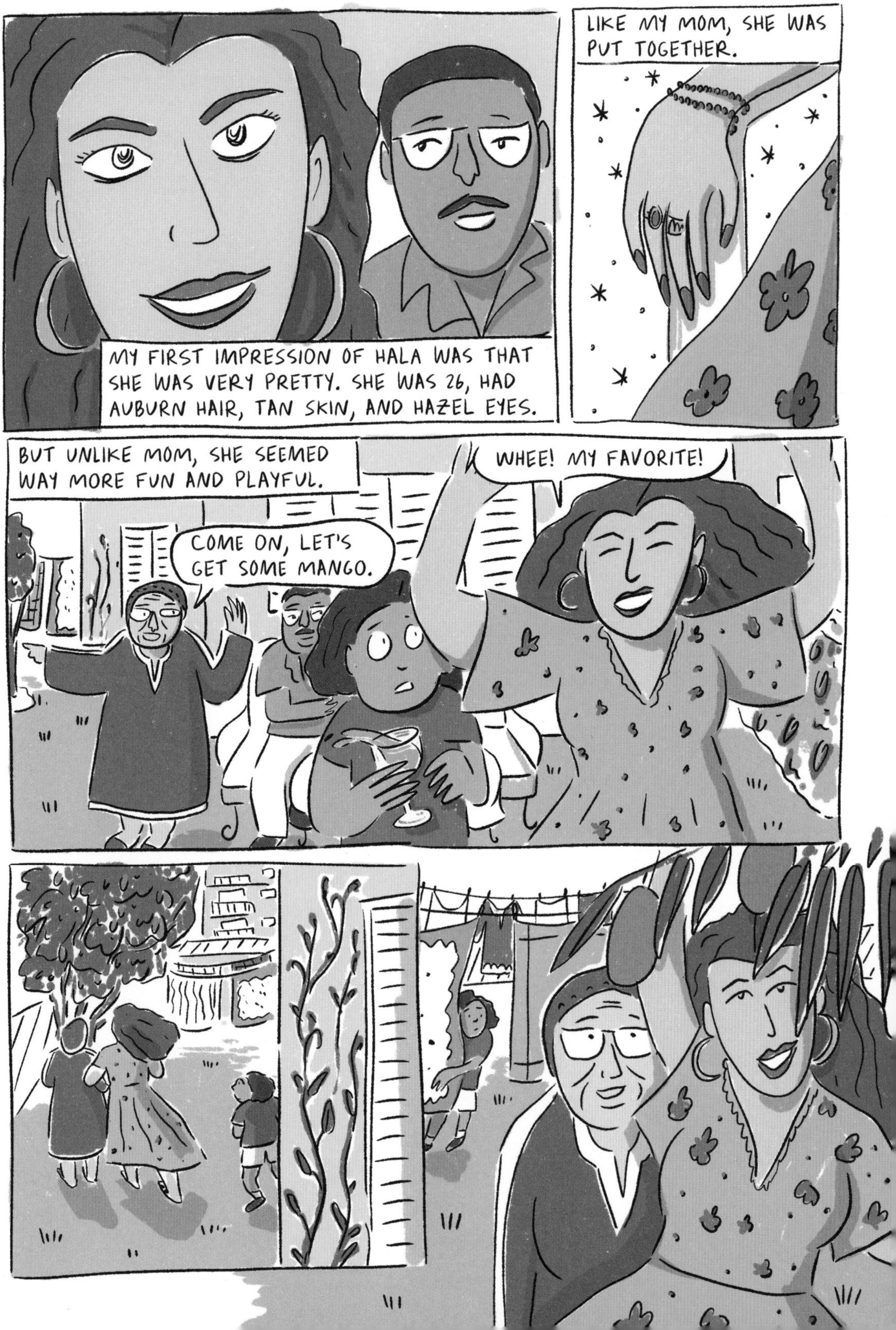
MY FIRST IMPRESSION OF HALA WAS THAT SHE WAS VERY PRETTY. SHE WAS 26, HAD AUBURN HAIR, TAN SKIN, AND HAZEL EYES.
LIKE MY MOM, SHE WAS PUT TOGETHER.
BUT UNLIKE MOM, SHE SEEMED WAY MORE FUN AND PLAYFUL.
WHEE! MY FAVORITE!
COME ON, LET'S GET SOME MANGO.

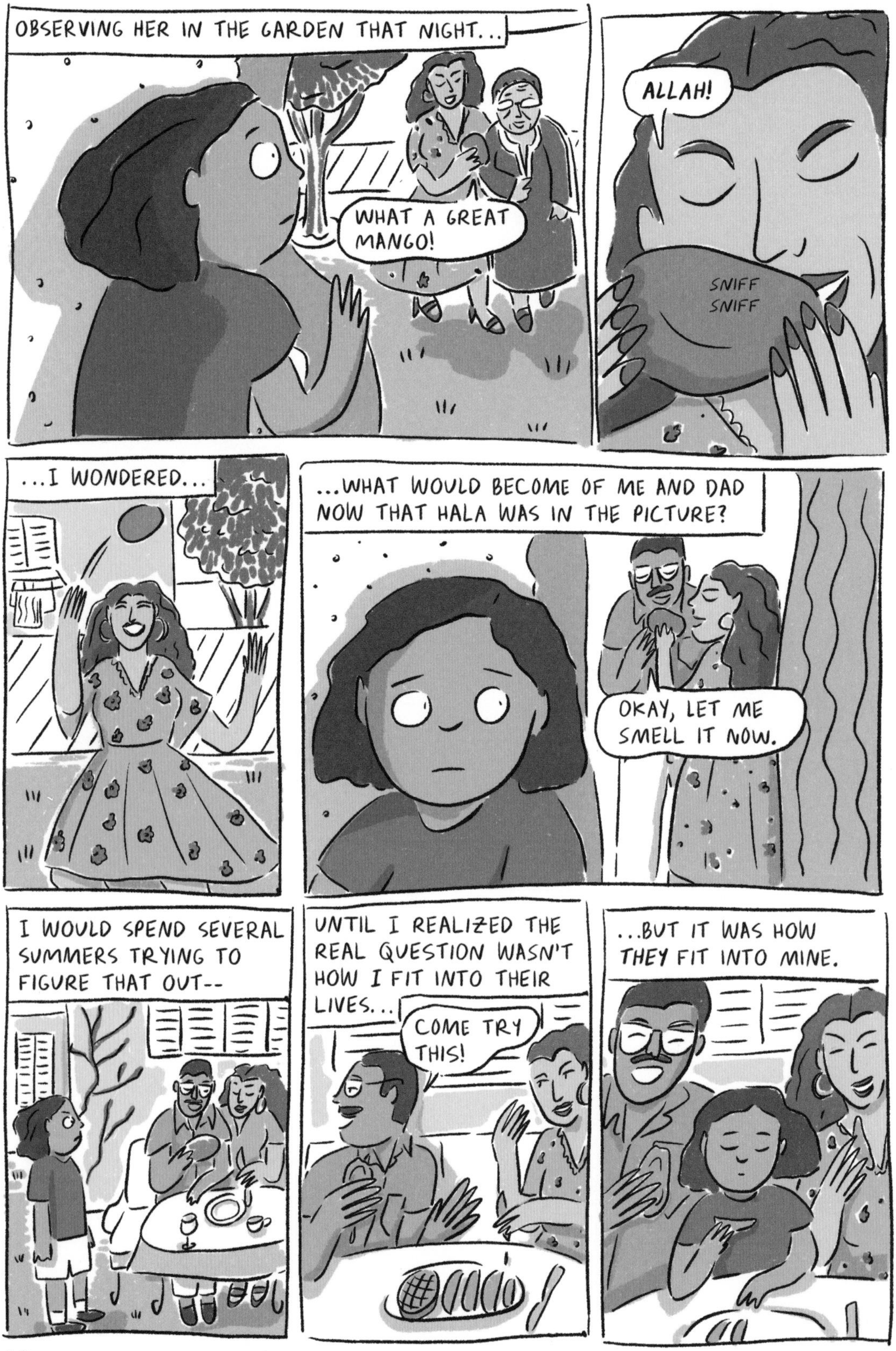
OBSERVING HER IN THE GARDEN THAT NIGHT...
WHAT A GREAT MANGO!
ALLAH!
SNIFF SNIFF
...I WONDERED...
...WHAT WOULD BECOME OF ME AND DAD NOW THAT HALA WAS IN THE PICTURE?
OKAY, LET ME SMELL IT NOW.
I WOULD SPEND SEVERAL SUMMERS TRYING TO FIGURE THAT OUT--
UNTIL I REALIZED THE REAL QUESTION WASN'T HOW I FIT INTO THEIR LIVES...
COME TRY THIS!
...BUT IT WAS HOW THEY FIT INTO MINE.

CHAPTER 1

Lisa Loeb in the Sinai

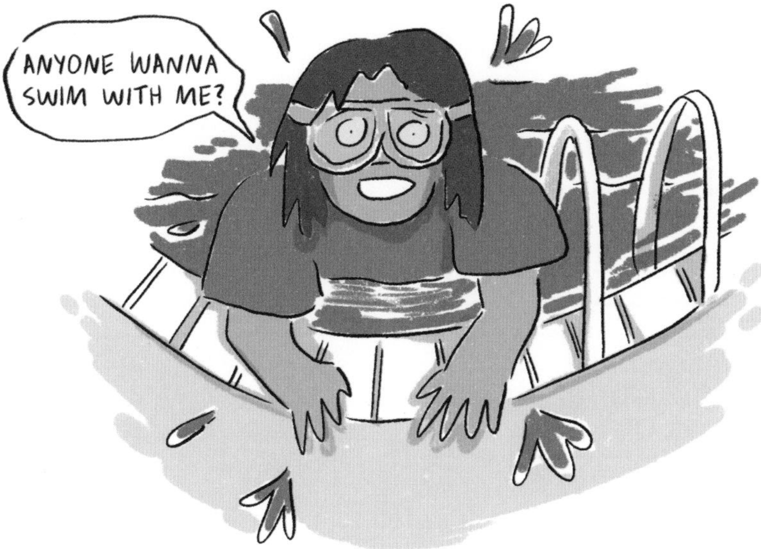
ANYONE WANNA SWIM WITH ME?

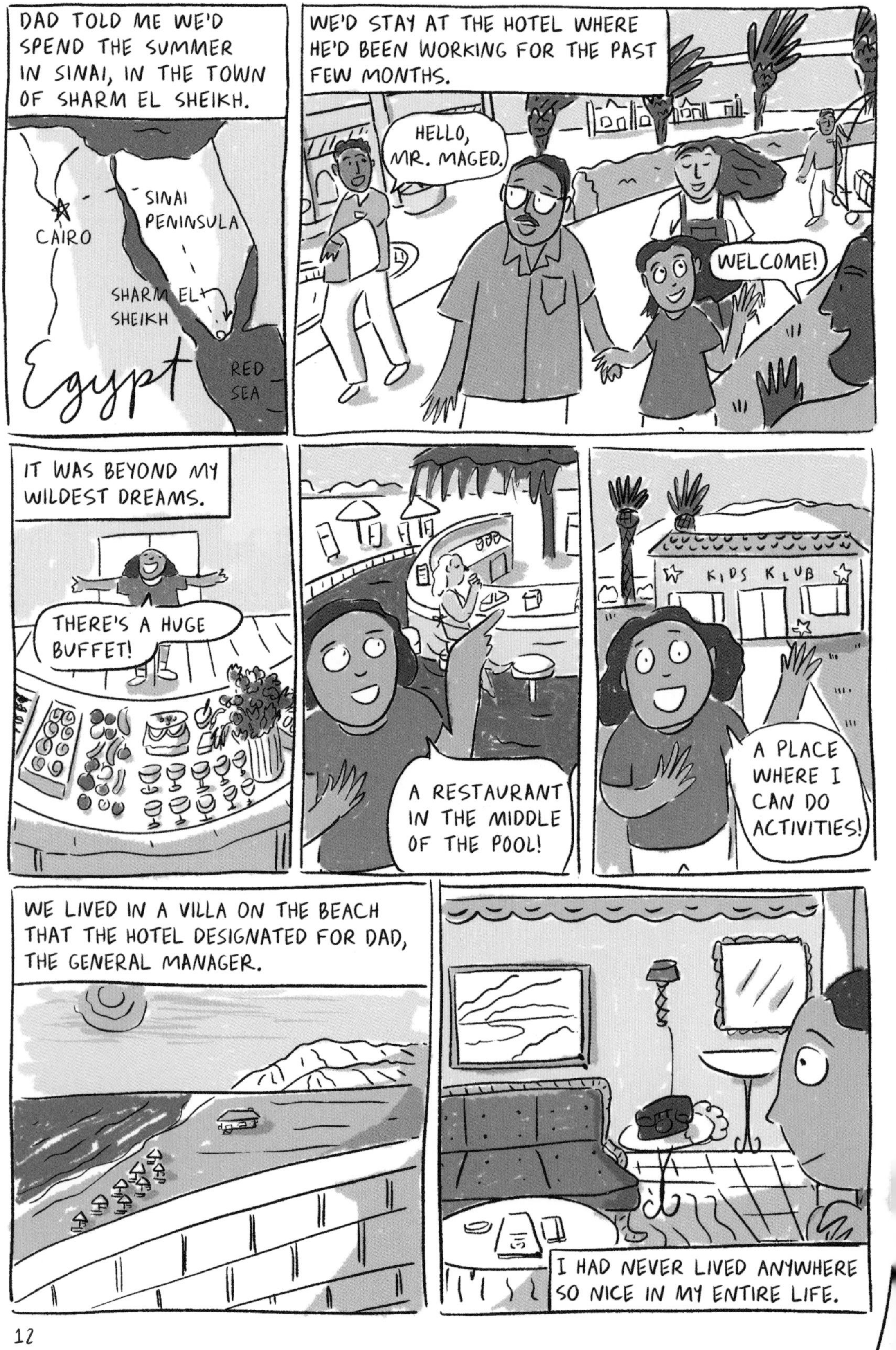
DAD TOLD ME WE'D SPEND THE SUMMER IN SINAI, IN THE TOWN OF SHARM EL SHEIKH.
CAIRO
SINAI PENINSULA
SHARM EL SHEIKH
Egypt
RED SEA
WE'D STAY AT THE HOTEL WHERE HE'D BEEN WORKING FOR THE PAST FEW MONTHS.
HELLO, MR. MAGED.
WELCOME!
IT WAS BEYOND MY WILDEST DREAMS.
THERE'S A HUGE BUFFET!
A RESTAURANT IN THE MIDDLE OF THE POOL!
KIDS KLUB
A PLACE WHERE I CAN DO ACTIVITIES!
WE LIVED IN A VILLA ON THE BEACH THAT THE HOTEL DESIGNATED FOR DAD, THE GENERAL MANAGER.
I HAD NEVER LIVED ANYWHERE SO NICE IN MY ENTIRE LIFE.

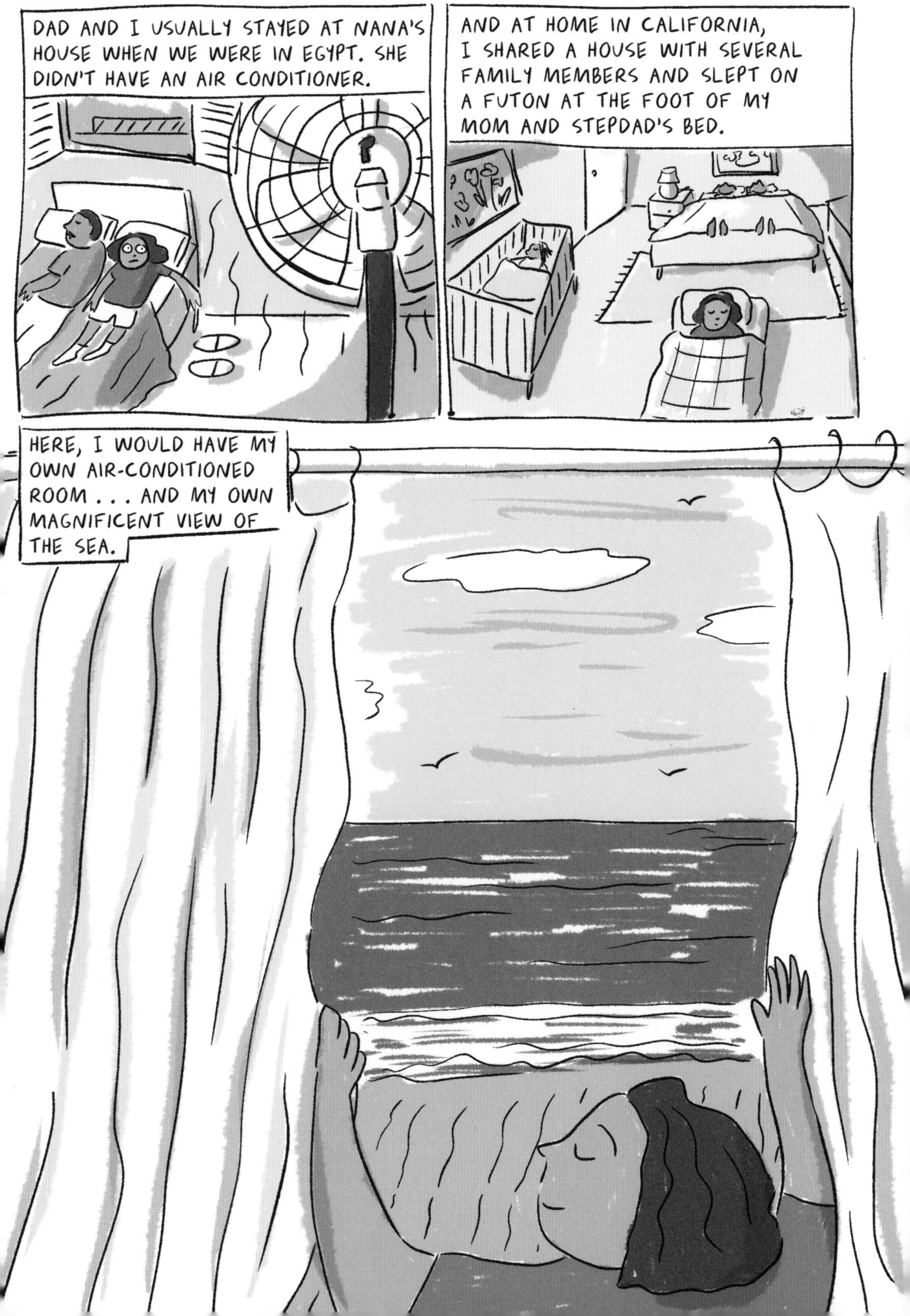
DAD AND I USUALLY STAYED AT NANA'S HOUSE WHEN WE WERE IN EGYPT. SHE DIDN'T HAVE AN AIR CONDITIONER.
AND AT HOME IN CALIFORNIA, I SHARED A HOUSE WITH SEVERAL FAMILY MEMBERS AND SLEPT ON A FUTON AT THE FOOT OF MY MOM AND STEPDAD'S BED.
HERE, I WOULD HAVE MY OWN AIR-CONDITIONED ROOM . . . AND MY OWN MAGNIFICENT VIEW OF THE SEA.

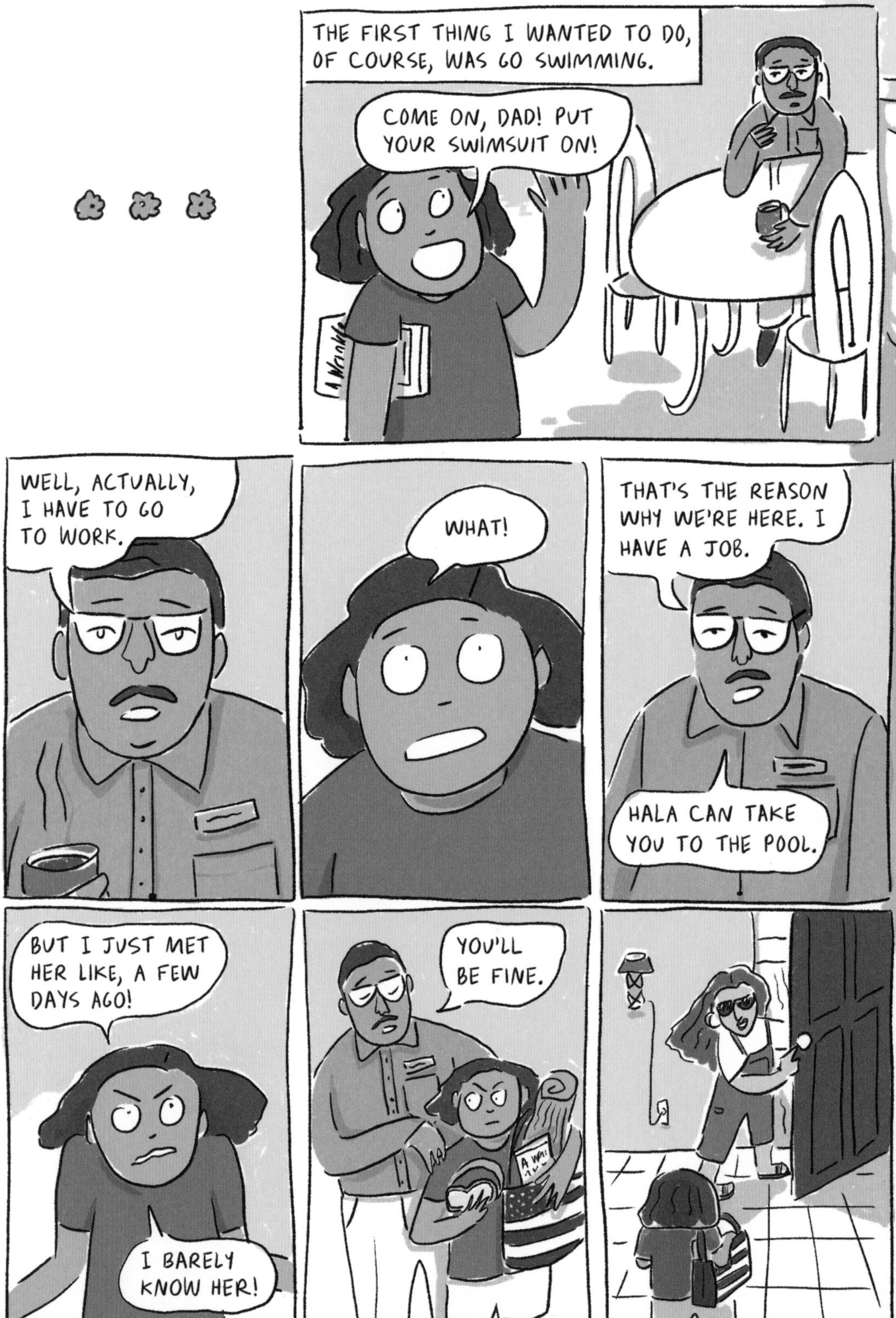
THE FIRST THING I WANTED TO DO, OF COURSE, WAS GO SWIMMING.
COME ON, DAD! PUT YOUR SWIMSUIT ON!
WELL, ACTUALLY, I HAVE TO GO TO WORK.
WHAT!
THAT'S THE REASON WHY WE'RE HERE. I HAVE A JOB.
HALA CAN TAKE YOU TO THE POOL.
BUT I JUST MET HER LIKE, A FEW DAYS AGO!
I BARELY KNOW HER!
YOU'LL BE FINE.

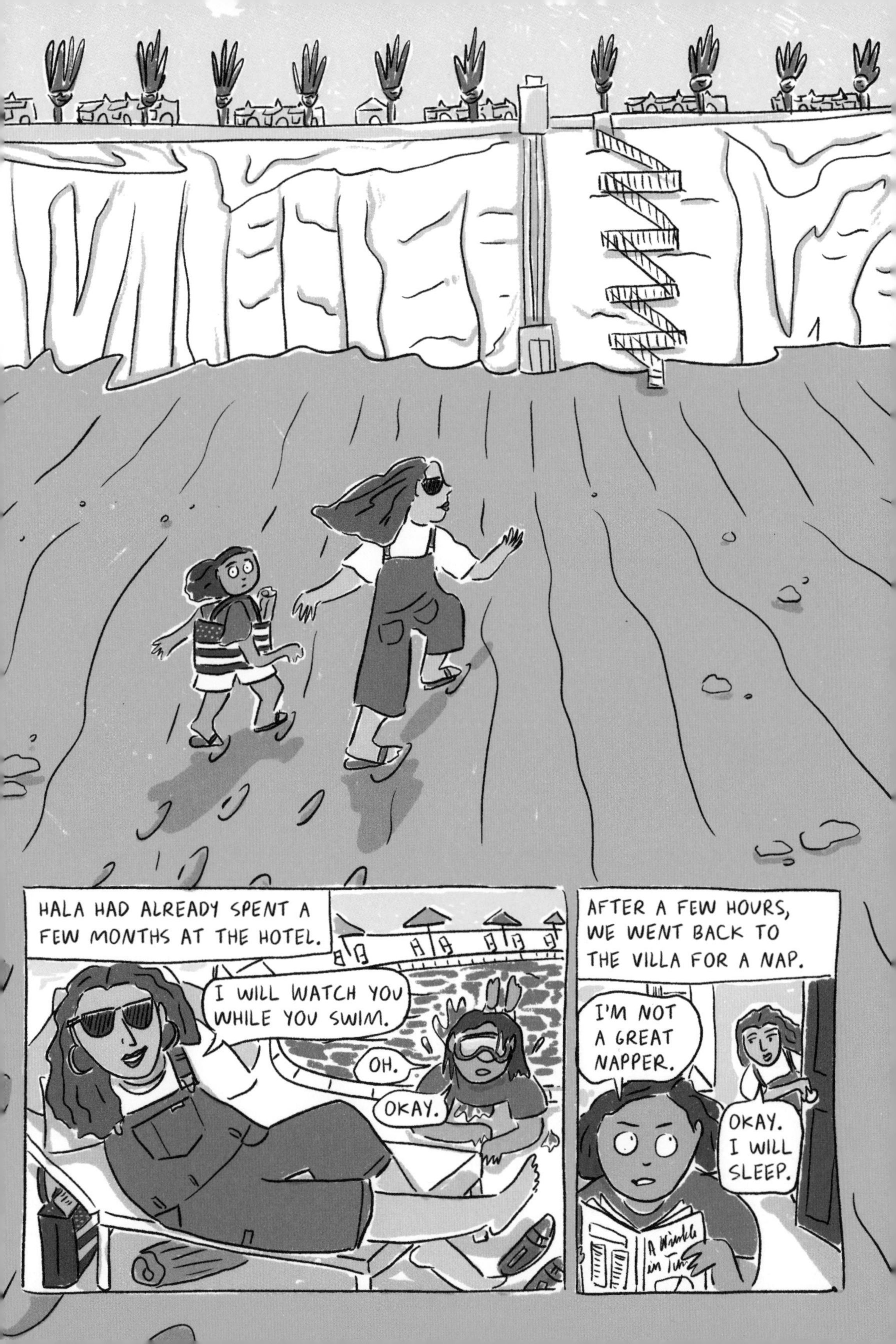
HALA HAD ALREADY SPENT A FEW MONTHS AT THE HOTEL.
I WILL WATCH YOU WHILE YOU SWIM.
OH.
OKAY.
AFTER A FEW HOURS, WE WENT BACK TO THE VILLA FOR A NAP.
I'M NOT A GREAT NAPPER.
OKAY. I WILL SLEEP.

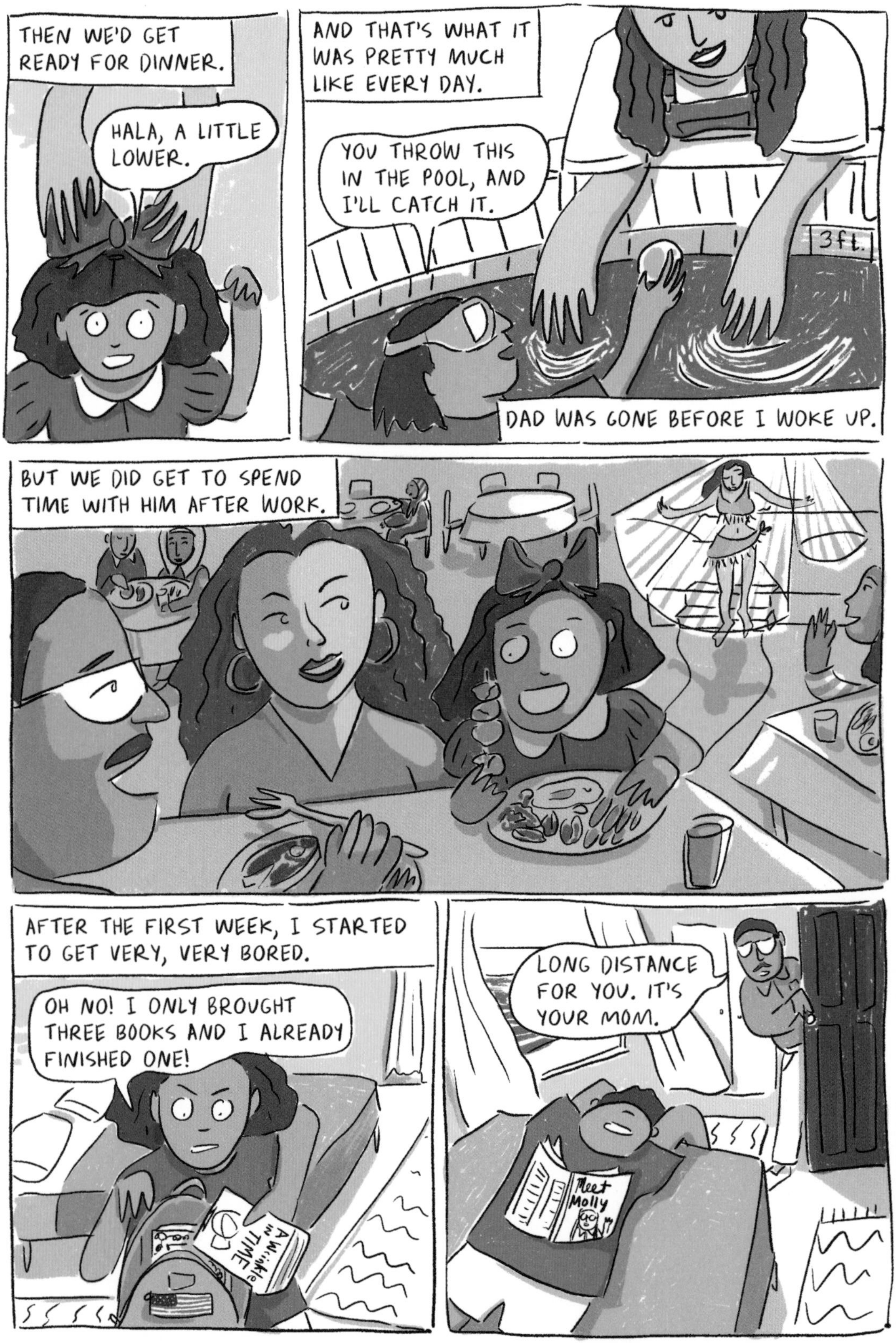
THEN WE'D GET READY FOR DINNER.
HALA, A LITTLE LOWER.
AND THAT'S WHAT IT WAS PRETTY MUCH LIKE EVERY DAY.
YOU THROW THIS IN THE POOL, AND I'LL CATCH IT.
3ft.
DAD WAS GONE BEFORE I WOKE UP.
BUT WE DID GET TO SPEND TIME WITH HIM AFTER WORK.
AFTER THE FIRST WEEK, I STARTED TO GET VERY, VERY BORED.
OH NO! I ONLY BROUGHT THREE BOOKS AND I ALREADY FINISHED ONE!
A Wrinkle in TIME
LONG DISTANCE FOR YOU. IT'S YOUR MOM.
Meet Molly

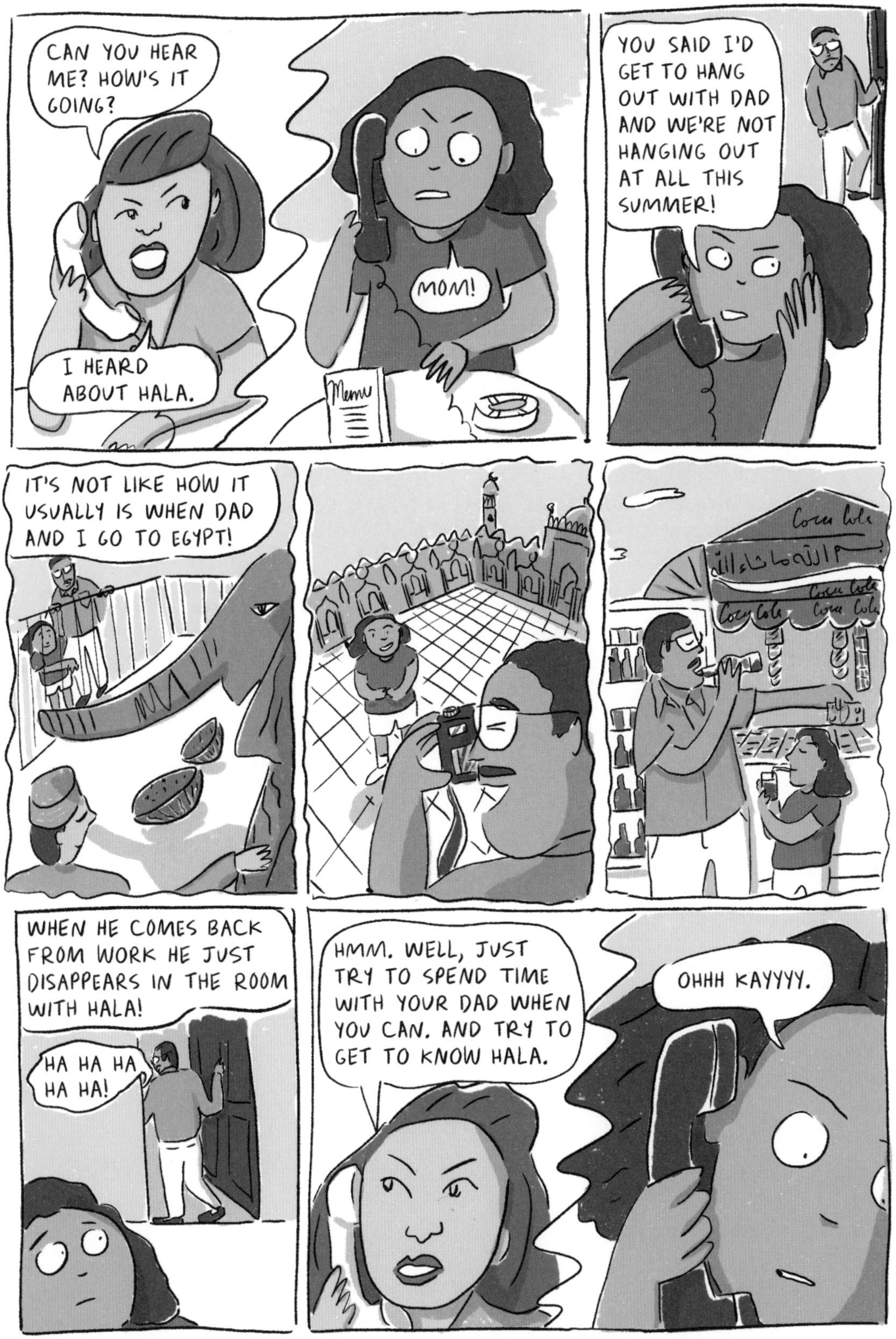

CAN YOU HEAR ME? HOW'S IT GOING?
I HEARD ABOUT HALA.
MOM!
Menu
YOU SAID I'D GET TO HANG OUT WITH DAD AND WE'RE NOT HANGING OUT AT ALL THIS SUMMER!
IT'S NOT LIKE HOW IT USUALLY IS WHEN DAD AND I GO TO EGYPT!
Coca Cola
Coca Cola
Coca Cola
Coca Cola
WHEN HE COMES BACK FROM WORK HE JUST DISAPPEARS IN THE ROOM WITH HALA!
HA HA HA HA HA!
HMM. WELL, JUST TRY TO SPEND TIME WITH YOUR DAD WHEN YOU CAN. AND TRY TO GET TO KNOW HALA.
OHHH KAYYYY.

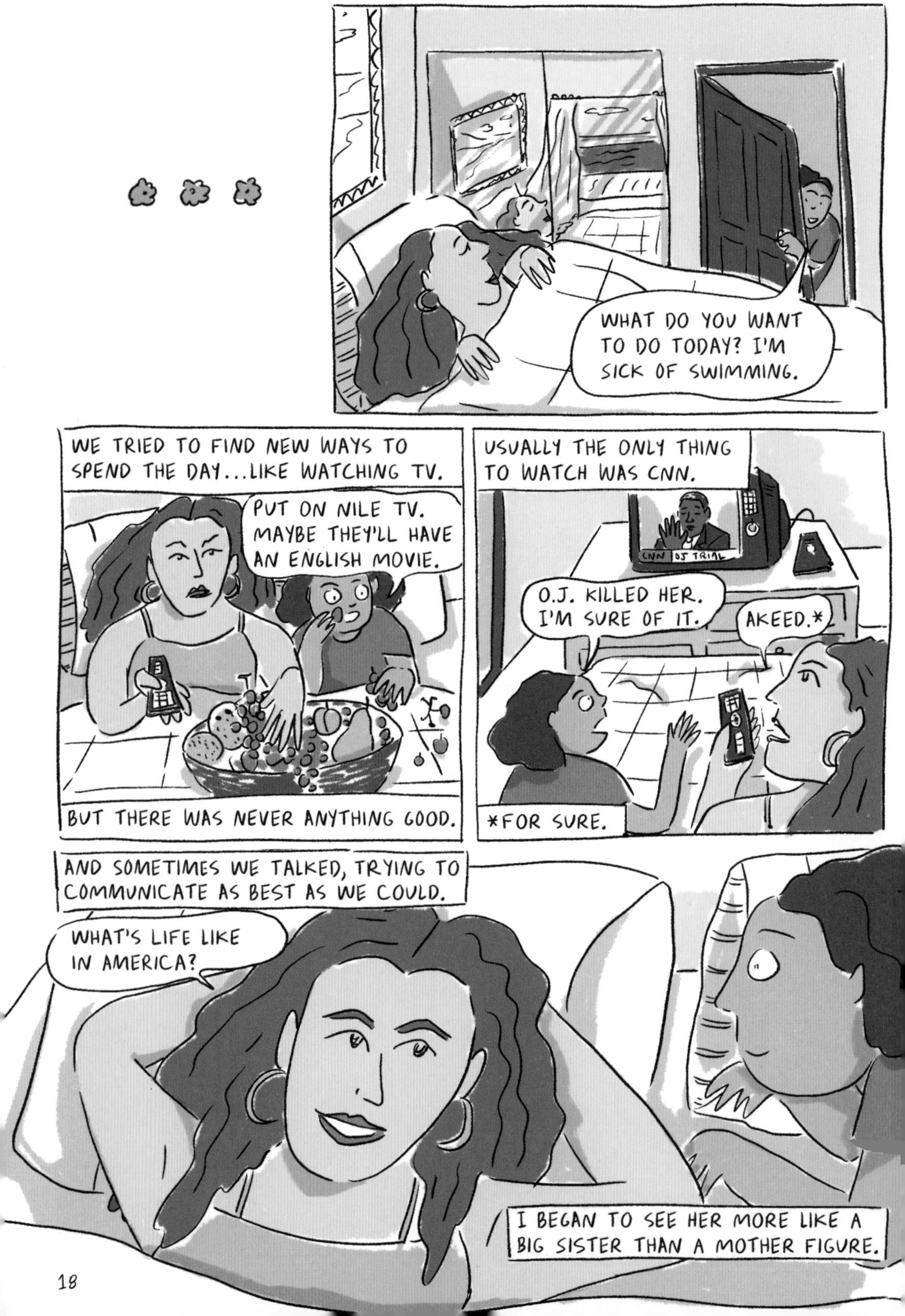
WHAT DO YOU WANT TO DO TODAY? I'M SICK OF SWIMMING.
WE TRIED TO FIND NEW WAYS TO SPEND THE DAY...LIKE WATCHING TV.
PUT ON NILE TV. MAYBE THEY'LL HAVE AN ENGLISH MOVIE.
BUT THERE WAS NEVER ANYTHING GOOD.
USUALLY THE ONLY THING TO WATCH WAS CNN.
CNN
OJ TRIAL
O.J. KILLED HER. I'M SURE OF IT.
AKEED.*
*FOR SURE.
AND SOMETIMES WE TALKED, TRYING TO COMMUNICATE AS BEST AS WE COULD.
WHAT'S LIFE LIKE IN AMERICA?
I BEGAN TO SEE HER MORE LIKE A BIG SISTER THAN A MOTHER FIGURE.

THE STORES ARE BIGGER THAN ANYTHING IN EGYPT!

YOU KNOW HOW IN EGYPT YOU HAVE TO GO TO A DIFFERENT STORE JUST TO GET LIKE, MEAT, OR A LIGHT BULB?

IN AMERICA, EVERYTHING IS IN ONE PLACE.

WE HAVE A STORE CALLED COSTCO AND THEY HAVE ROWS OF **EVERYTHING** AND FREE SAMPLES AND EVERYTHING IS CHEAP.

IT'S MY FAVORITE PLACE!

MAYBE I CAN GO THERE SOMEDAY.

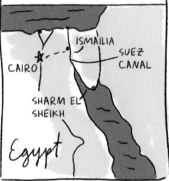

SHE TOLD ME ABOUT HERSELF. SHE GREW UP IN A SMALLER CITY CALLED ISMAILIA ON THE SUEZ CANAL.

ISMAILIA

SUEZ CANAL

CAIRO

SHARM EL SHEIKH

Egypt

SHE HAD TWO BROTHERS.

WHEN SHE WAS IN HIGH SCHOOL, SHE GOT TO TAKE PART IN A STUDENT EXCHANGE PROGRAM IN GERMANY.

SHE WENT TO COLLEGE, BUT SHE DIDN'T WORK.

I STUDIED FINANCE.

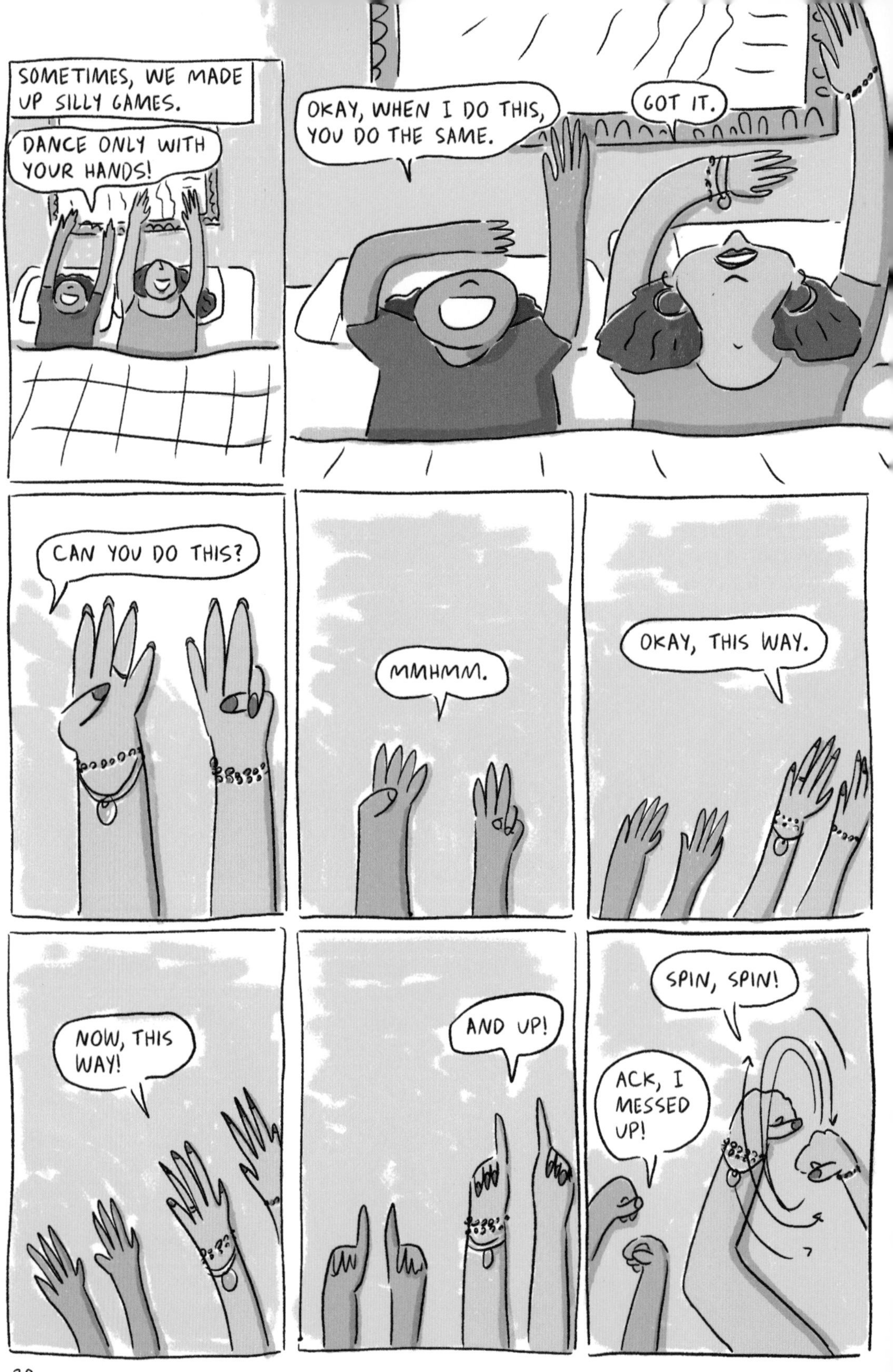
SOMETIMES, WE MADE UP SILLY GAMES.
DANCE ONLY WITH YOUR HANDS!
OKAY, WHEN I DO THIS, YOU DO THE SAME.
GOT IT.
CAN YOU DO THIS?
MMHMM.
OKAY, THIS WAY.
NOW, THIS WAY!
AND UP!
SPIN, SPIN!
ACK, I MESSED UP!

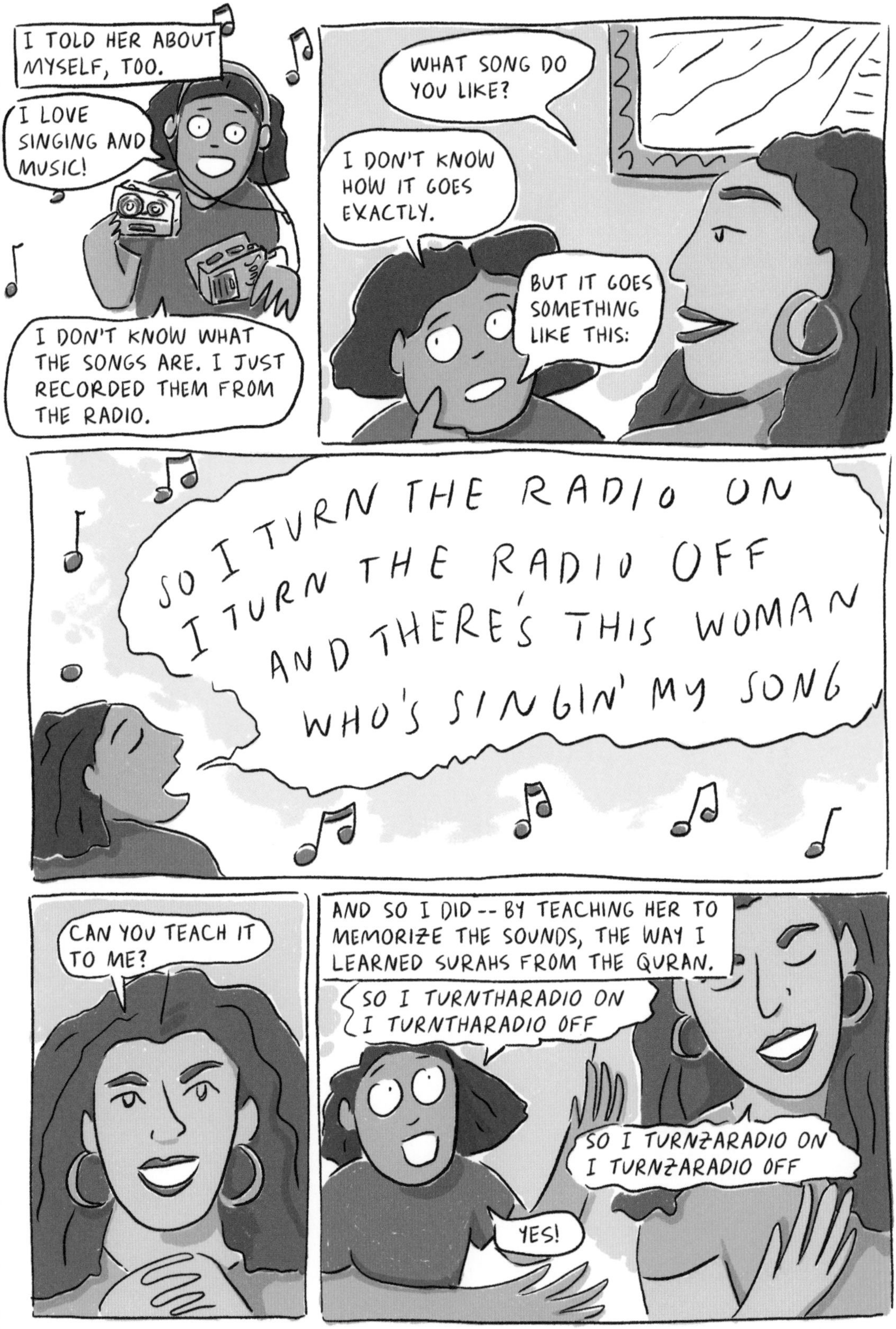
I TOLD HER ABOUT MYSELF, TOO.
I LOVE SINGING AND MUSIC!
I DON'T KNOW WHAT THE SONGS ARE. I JUST RECORDED THEM FROM THE RADIO.
WHAT SONG DO YOU LIKE?
I DON'T KNOW HOW IT GOES EXACTLY.
BUT IT GOES SOMETHING LIKE THIS:
SO I TURN THE RADIO ON
I TURN THE RADIO OFF
AND THERE'S THIS WOMAN
WHO'S SINGIN' MY SONG
CAN YOU TEACH IT TO ME?
AND SO I DID -- BY TEACHING HER TO MEMORIZE THE SOUNDS, THE WAY I LEARNED SURAHS FROM THE QURAN.
SO I TURNTHARADIO ON
I TURNTHARADIO OFF
SO I TURNZARADIO ON
I TURNZARADIO OFF
YES!

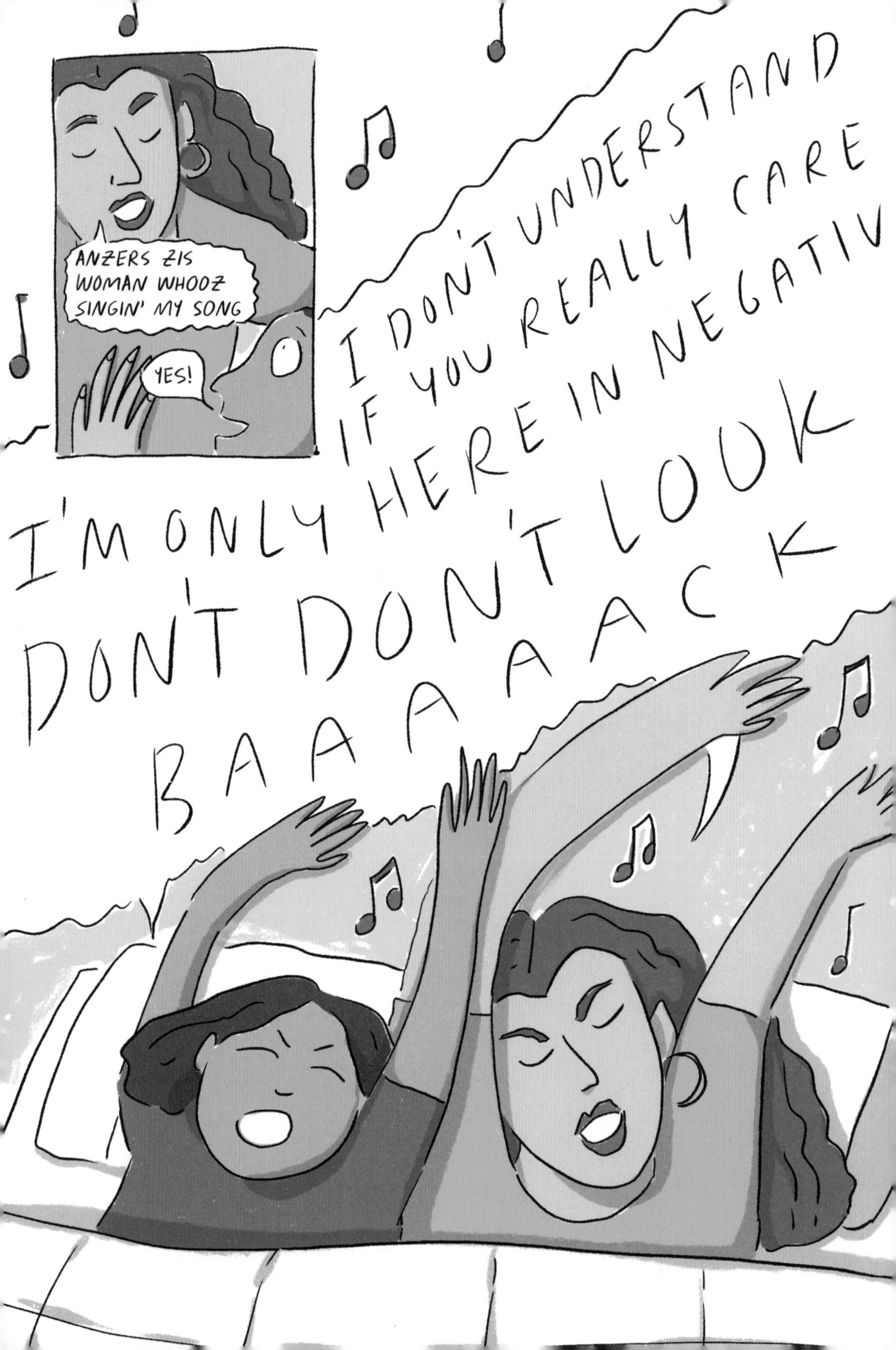
ANZERS ZIS WOMAN WHOOZ SINGIN' MY SONG
YES!
I DON'T UNDERSTAND
IF YOU REALLY CARE
I'M ONLY HERE IN NEGATIV
DON'T DON'T LOOK
BAAAAACK

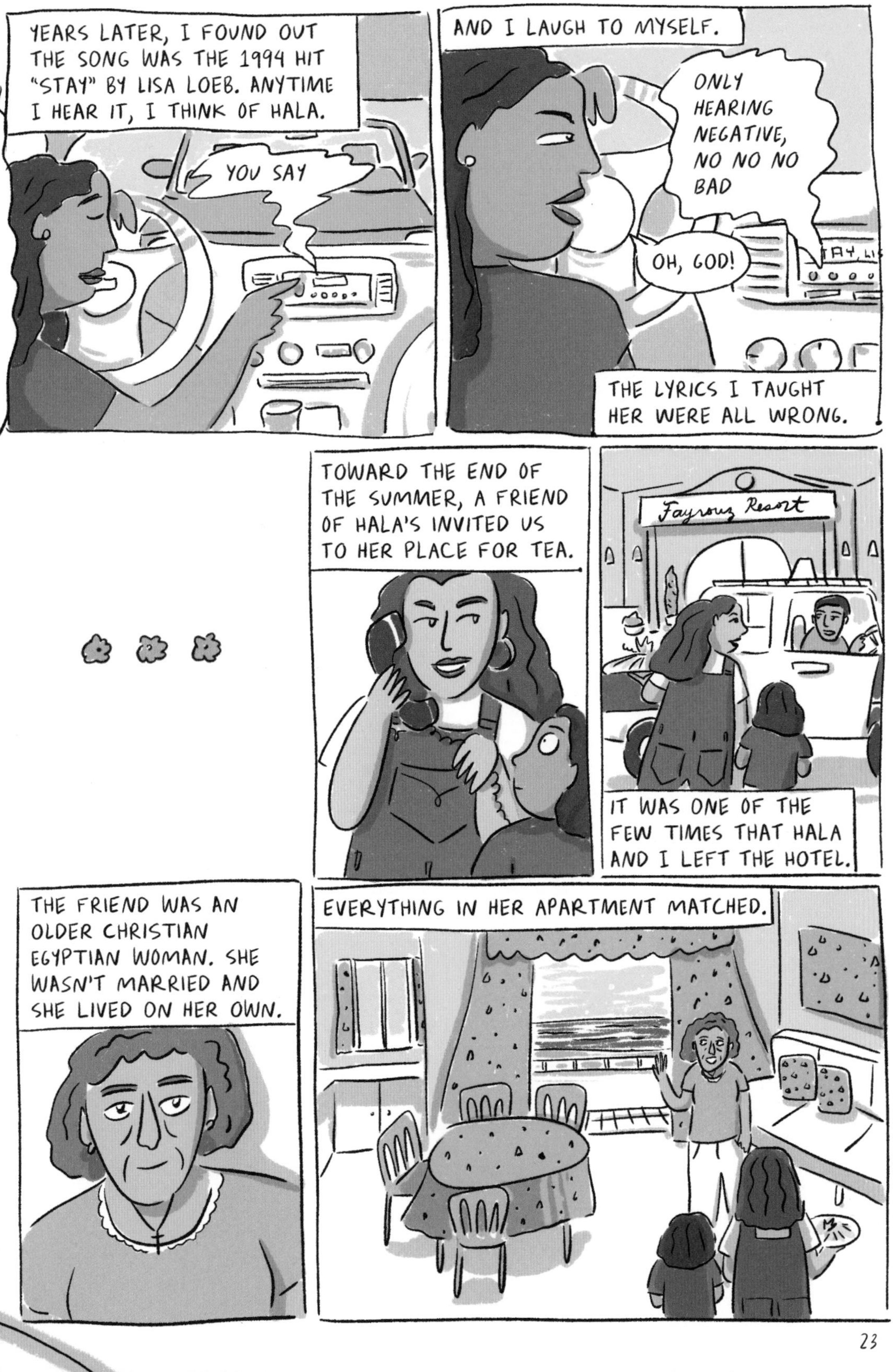
YEARS LATER, I FOUND OUT THE SONG WAS THE 1994 HIT "STAY" BY LISA LOEB. ANYTIME I HEAR IT, I THINK OF HALA.
YOU SAY
AND I LAUGH TO MYSELF.
ONLY HEARING NEGATIVE, NO NO NO BAD
OH, GOD!
THE LYRICS I TAUGHT HER WERE ALL WRONG.
TOWARD THE END OF THE SUMMER, A FRIEND OF HALA'S INVITED US TO HER PLACE FOR TEA.
Fayrouz Resort
IT WAS ONE OF THE FEW TIMES THAT HALA AND I LEFT THE HOTEL.
THE FRIEND WAS AN OLDER CHRISTIAN EGYPTIAN WOMAN. SHE WASN'T MARRIED AND SHE LIVED ON HER OWN.
EVERYTHING IN HER APARTMENT MATCHED.

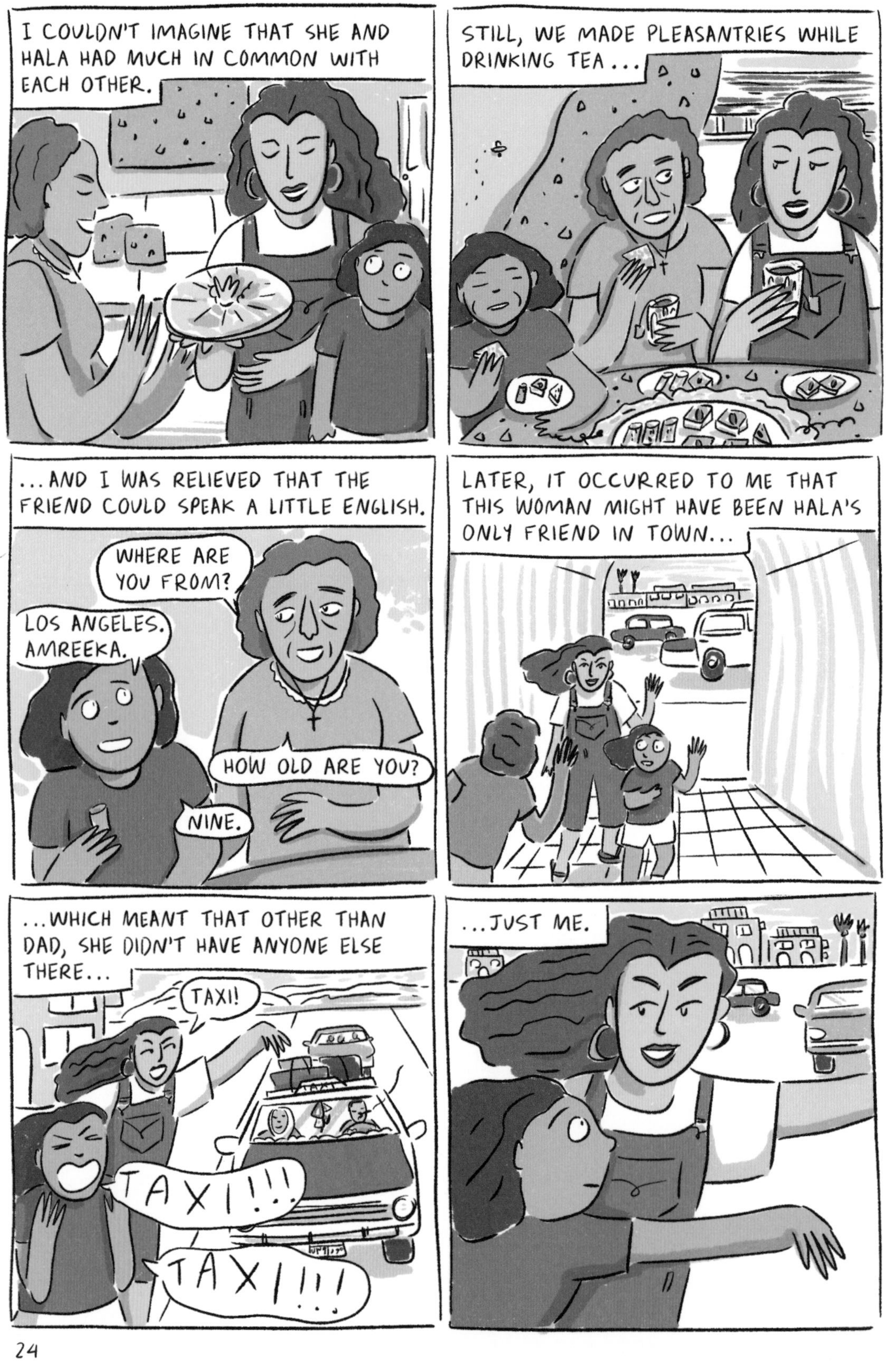
I COULDN'T IMAGINE THAT SHE AND HALA HAD MUCH IN COMMON WITH EACH OTHER.
STILL, WE MADE PLEASANTRIES WHILE DRINKING TEA...
...AND I WAS RELIEVED THAT THE FRIEND COULD SPEAK A LITTLE ENGLISH.
WHERE ARE YOU FROM?
LOS ANGELES. AMREEKA.
HOW OLD ARE YOU?
NINE.
LATER, IT OCCURRED TO ME THAT THIS WOMAN MIGHT HAVE BEEN HALA'S ONLY FRIEND IN TOWN...
...WHICH MEANT THAT OTHER THAN DAD, SHE DIDN'T HAVE ANYONE ELSE THERE...
TAXI!
TAXI!!!
TAXI!!!
...JUST ME.

CHAPTER 2

The American

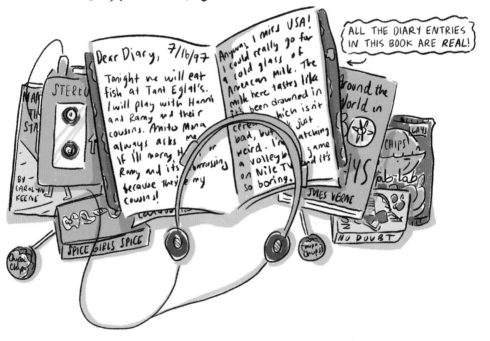

ALL THE DIARY ENTRIES IN THIS BOOK ARE REAL!
Dear Diary, 7/16/97
Tonight we will eat fish at Tant Eglal's. I will play with Hanni and Ramy and their cousins. Amito Mona always asks me if I'll marry H or Ramy and its barrassing because they're my cousins!
Anyways I miss USA! I could really go for a cold glass of American milk. The milk here tastes like it's been drowned in hich is not cerea just bad, but atching weird. I'm game a volleyb on Nile TV and it's so boring.
STEREO
BY CAROLYN KEENE
SPICE GIRLS SPICE
Around the World in
JULES VERNE
NO DOUBT
CHIPS
LAYS
Chupa Chups

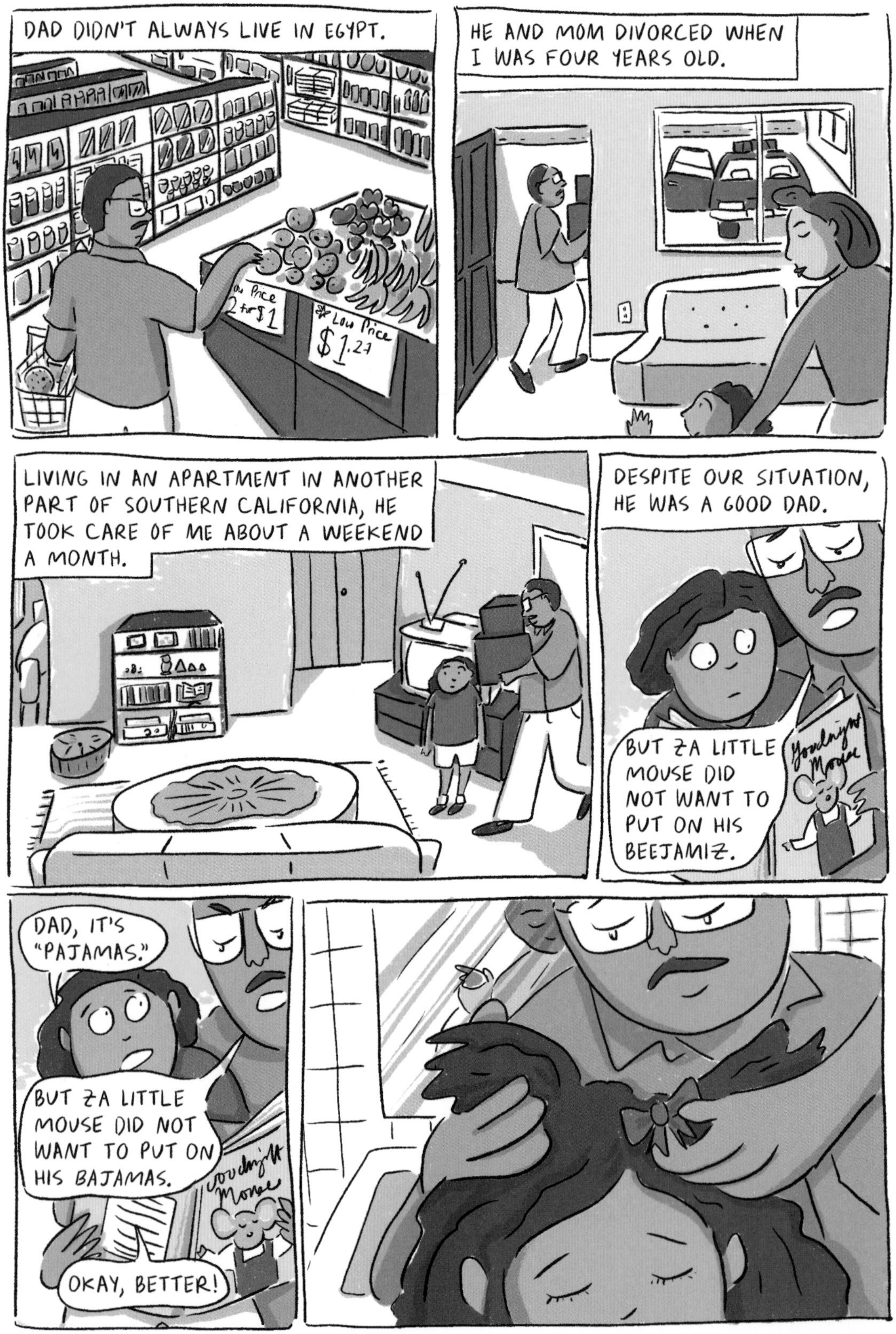
DAD DIDN'T ALWAYS LIVE IN EGYPT.
Low Price 2 for $1
Low Price $1.27
HE AND MOM DIVORCED WHEN I WAS FOUR YEARS OLD.
LIVING IN AN APARTMENT IN ANOTHER PART OF SOUTHERN CALIFORNIA, HE TOOK CARE OF ME ABOUT A WEEKEND A MONTH.
DESPITE OUR SITUATION, HE WAS A GOOD DAD.
BUT ZA LITTLE MOUSE DID NOT WANT TO PUT ON HIS BEEJAMIZ.
DAD, IT'S "PAJAMAS."
BUT ZA LITTLE MOUSE DID NOT WANT TO PUT ON HIS BAJAMAS.
OKAY, BETTER!

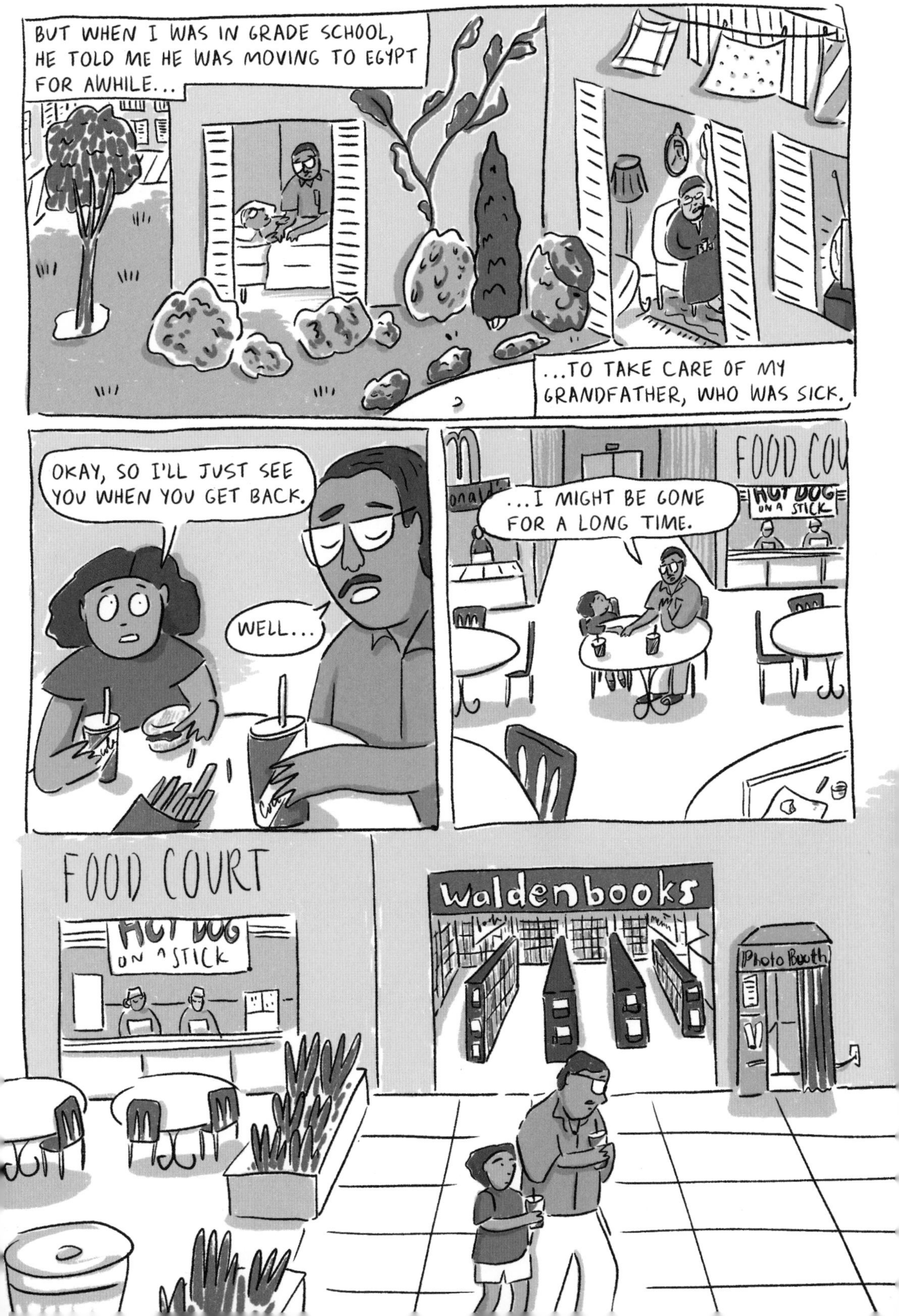

BUT WHEN I WAS IN GRADE SCHOOL, HE TOLD ME HE WAS MOVING TO EGYPT FOR AWHILE...
...TO TAKE CARE OF MY GRANDFATHER, WHO WAS SICK.
OKAY, SO I'LL JUST SEE YOU WHEN YOU GET BACK.
WELL...
FOOD COU
HOT DOG ON A STICK
...I MIGHT BE GONE FOR A LONG TIME.
FOOD COURT
HOT DOG ON A STICK
waldenbooks
Photo Booth

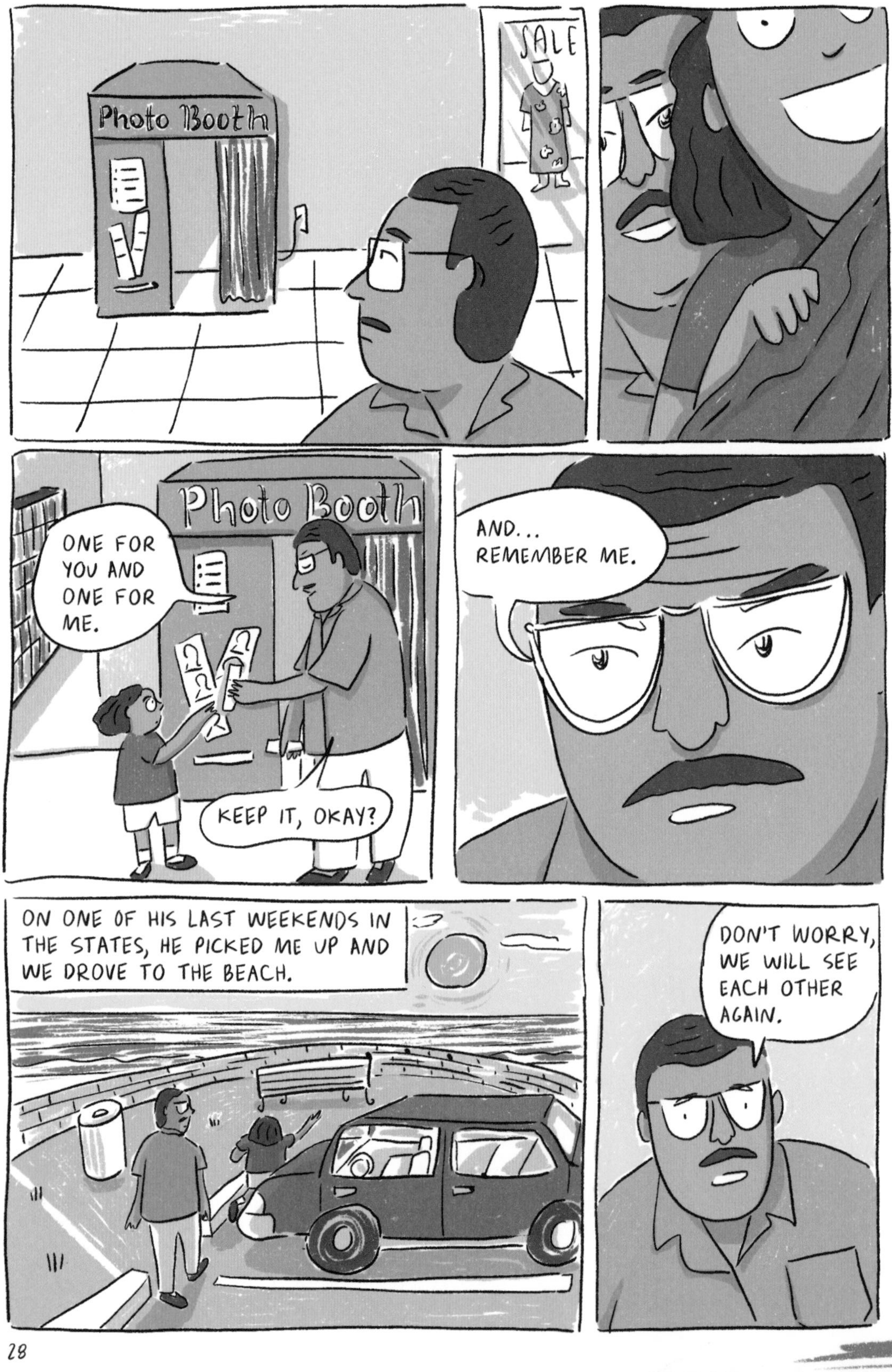
SALE
Photo Booth
Photo Booth
ONE FOR YOU AND ONE FOR ME.
KEEP IT, OKAY?
AND... REMEMBER ME.
ON ONE OF HIS LAST WEEKENDS IN THE STATES, HE PICKED ME UP AND WE DROVE TO THE BEACH.
DON'T WORRY, WE WILL SEE EACH OTHER AGAIN.

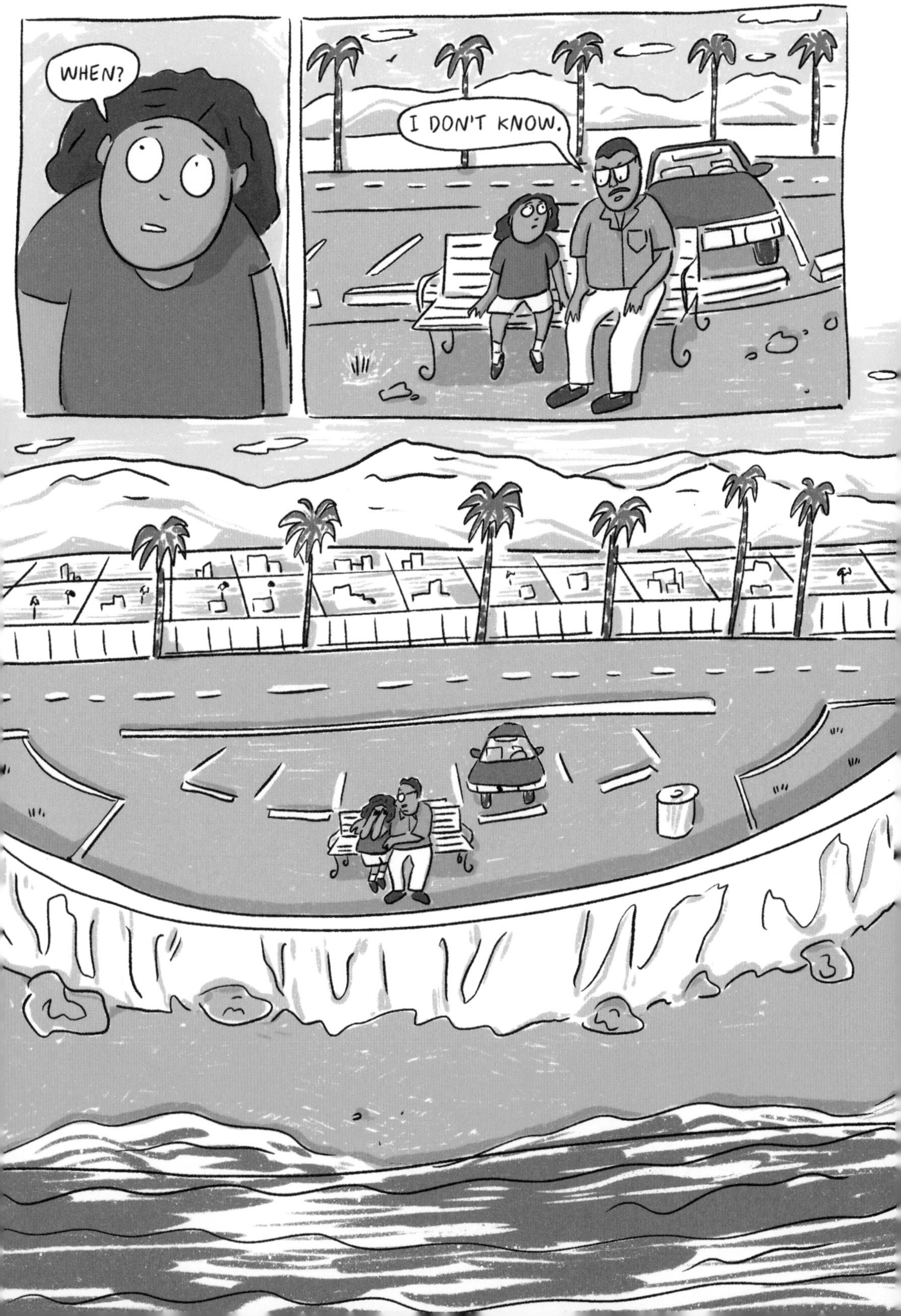

WHEN?
I DON'T KNOW.

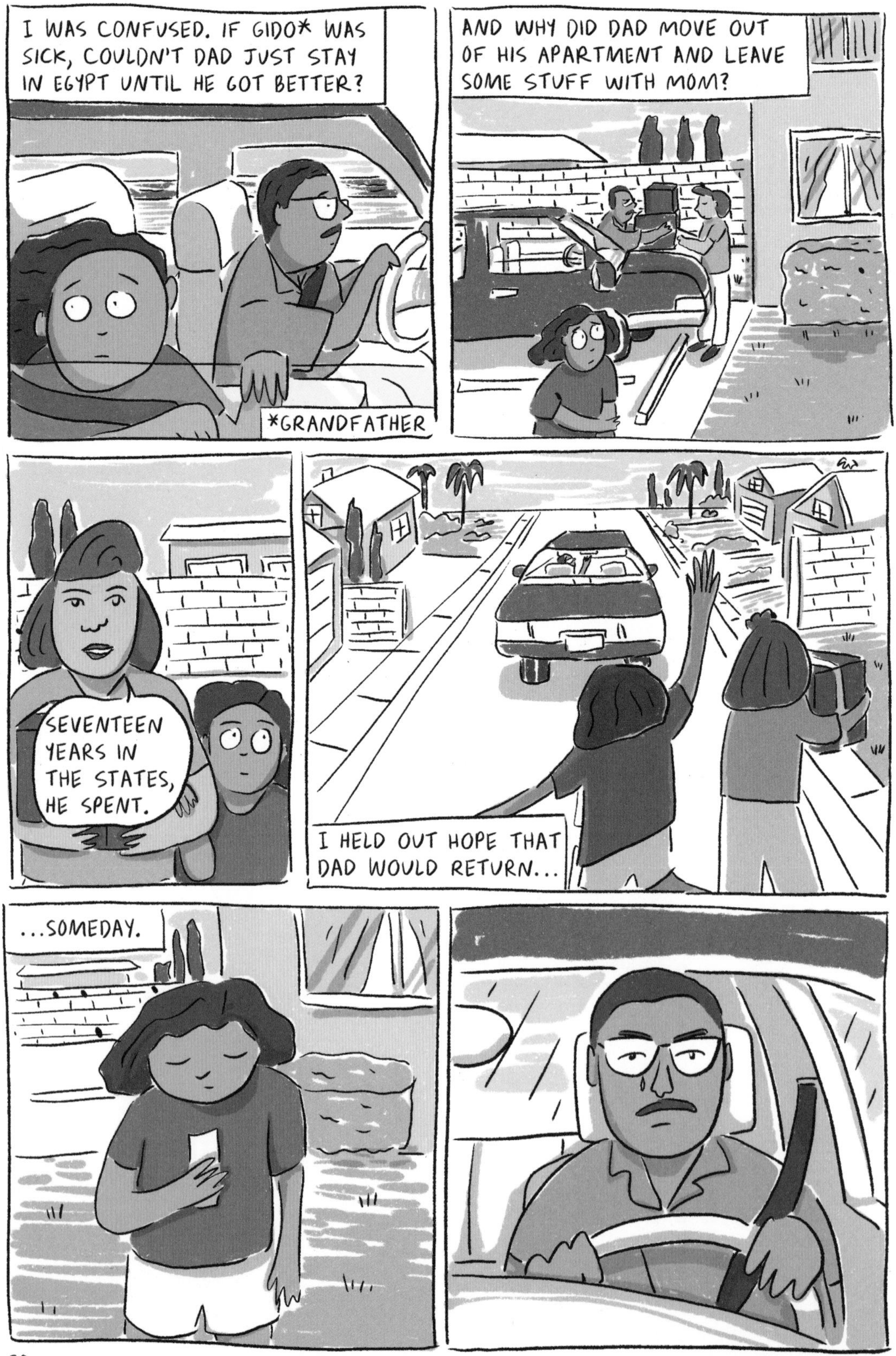
I WAS CONFUSED. IF GIDO* WAS SICK, COULDN'T DAD JUST STAY IN EGYPT UNTIL HE GOT BETTER?
*GRANDFATHER
AND WHY DID DAD MOVE OUT OF HIS APARTMENT AND LEAVE SOME STUFF WITH MOM?
SEVENTEEN YEARS IN THE STATES, HE SPENT.
I HELD OUT HOPE THAT DAD WOULD RETURN...
...SOMEDAY.

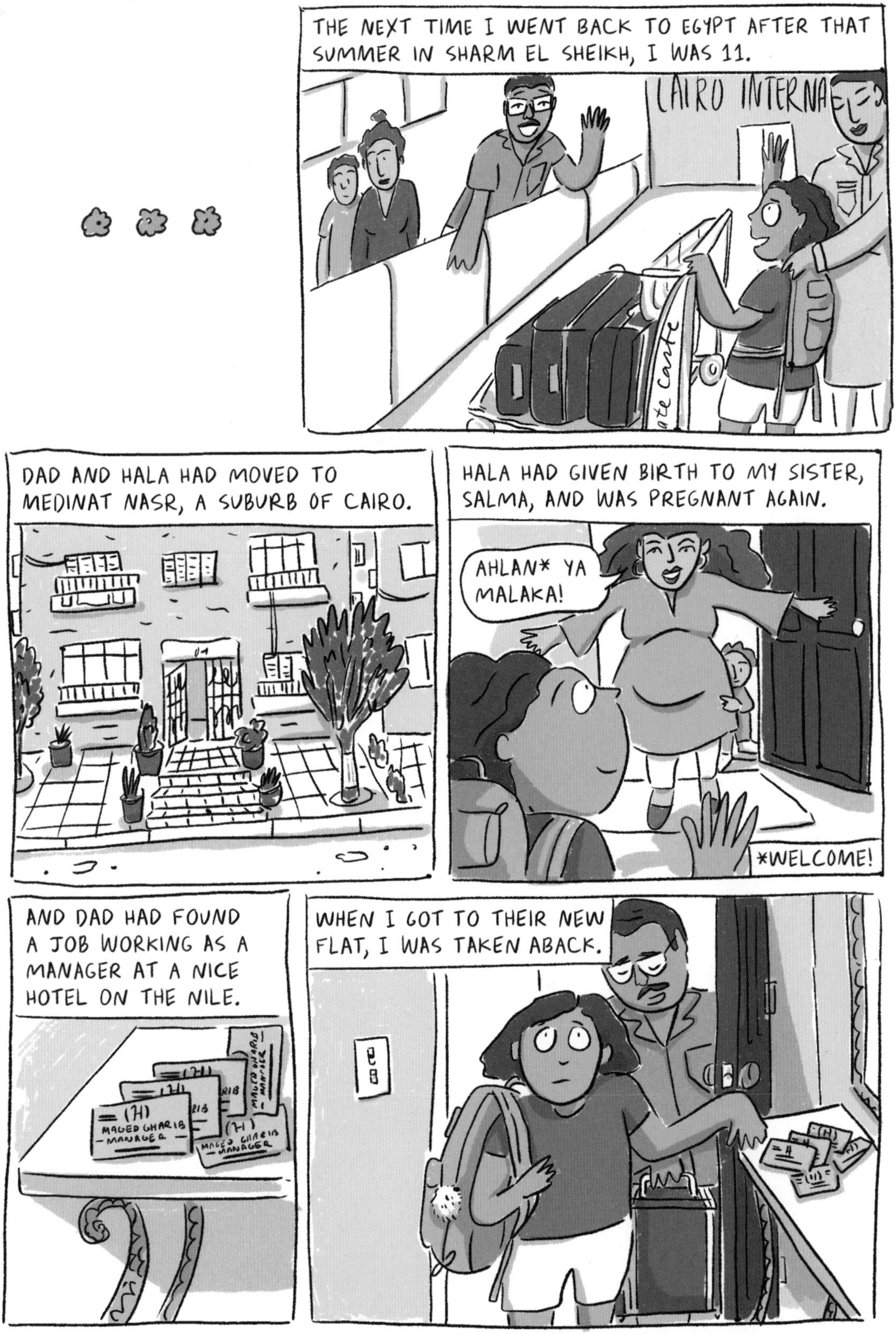
THE NEXT TIME I WENT BACK TO EGYPT AFTER THAT SUMMER IN SHARM EL SHEIKH, I WAS 11.
CAIRO INTERNA
DAD AND HALA HAD MOVED TO MEDINAT NASR, A SUBURB OF CAIRO.
HALA HAD GIVEN BIRTH TO MY SISTER, SALMA, AND WAS PREGNANT AGAIN.
AHLAN* YA MALAKA!
*WELCOME!
AND DAD HAD FOUND A JOB WORKING AS A MANAGER AT A NICE HOTEL ON THE NILE.
MAGED GHARIB
MANAGER
WHEN I GOT TO THEIR NEW FLAT, I WAS TAKEN ABACK.

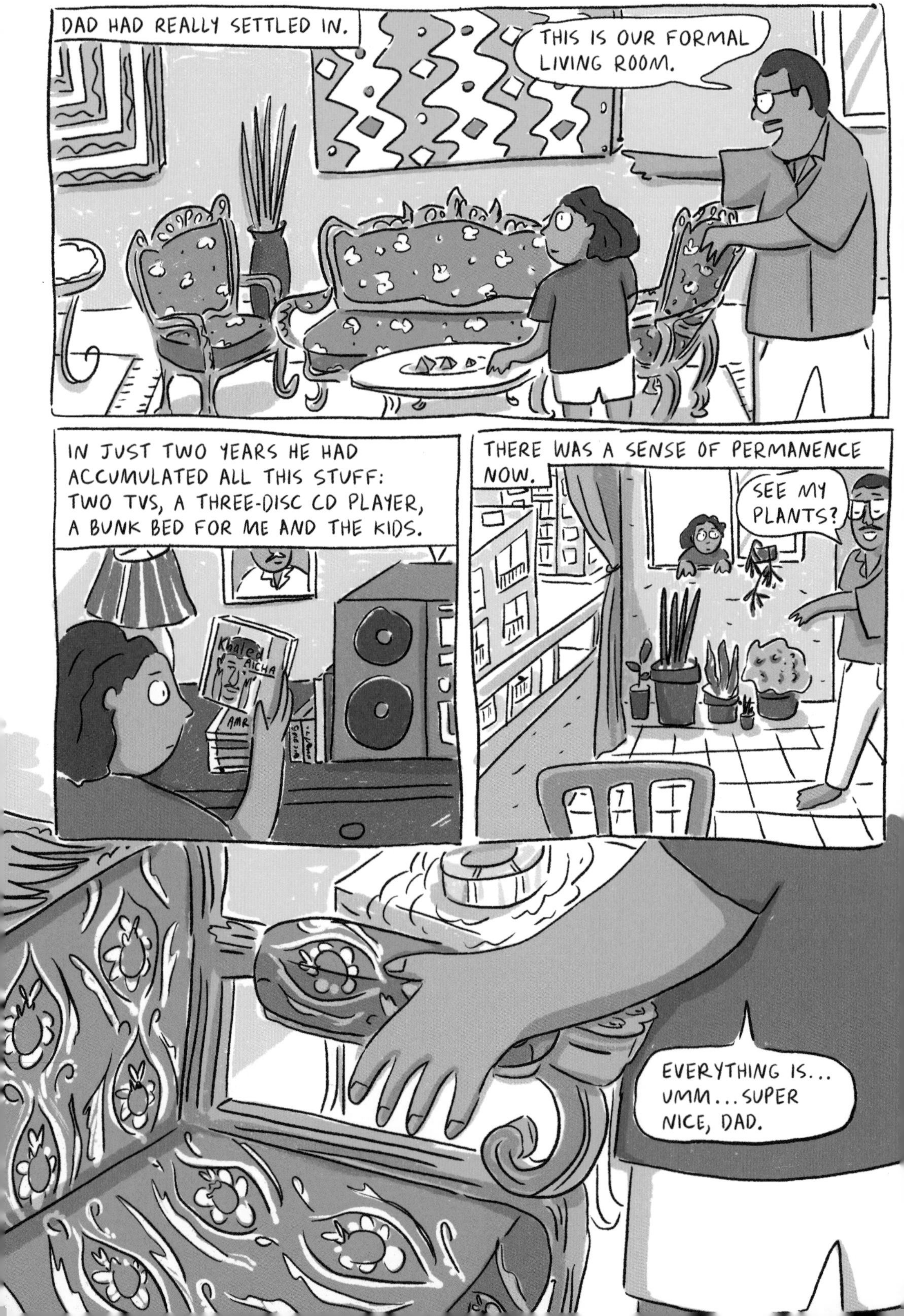
DAD HAD REALLY SETTLED IN.
THIS IS OUR FORMAL LIVING ROOM.
IN JUST TWO YEARS HE HAD ACCUMULATED ALL THIS STUFF: TWO TVS, A THREE-DISC CD PLAYER, A BUNK BED FOR ME AND THE KIDS.
Khaled
AICHA
AMR
THERE WAS A SENSE OF PERMANENCE NOW.
SEE MY PLANTS?
EVERYTHING IS... UMM...SUPER NICE, DAD.

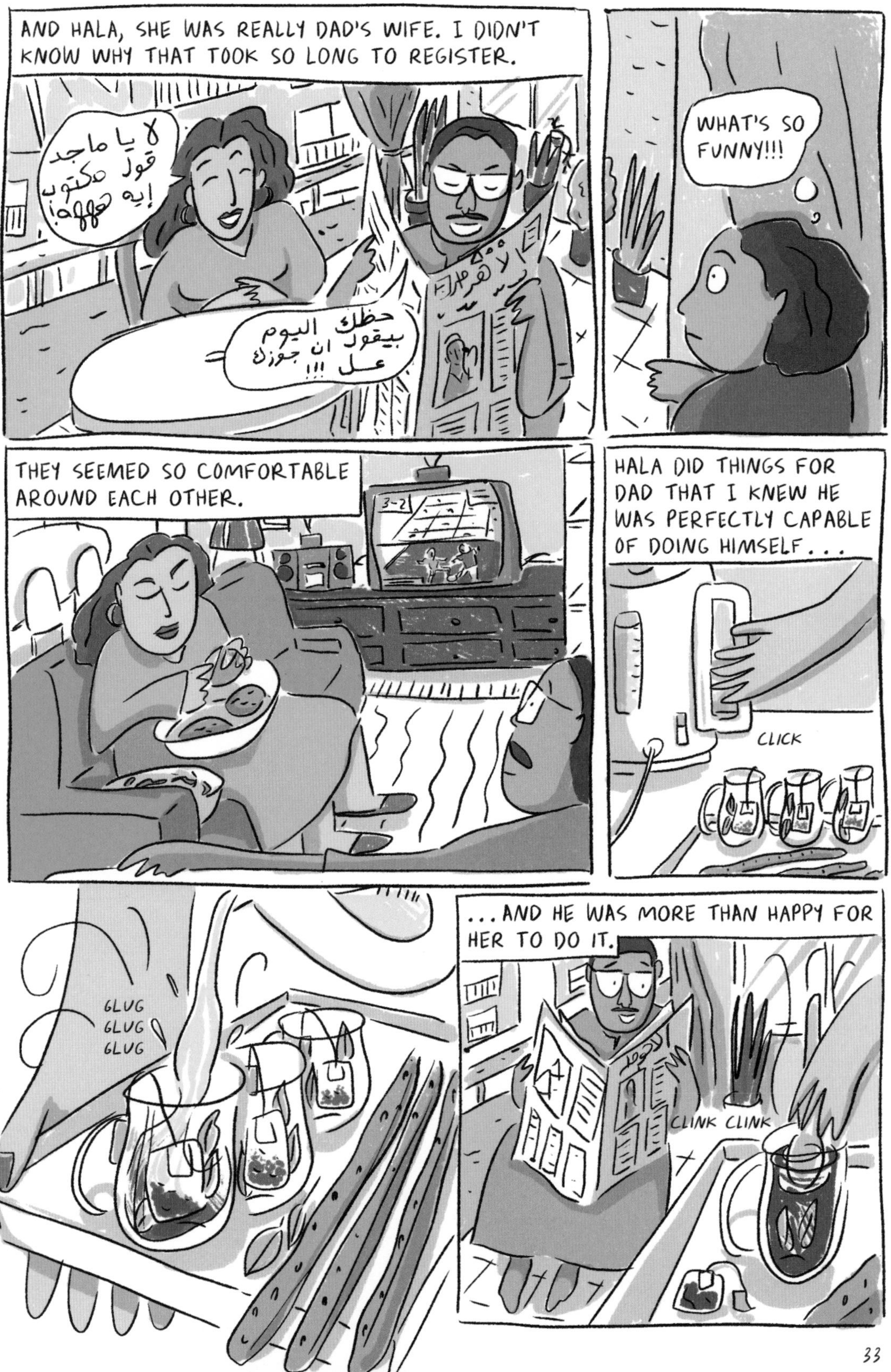
AND HALA, SHE WAS REALLY DAD'S WIFE. I DIDN'T KNOW WHY THAT TOOK SO LONG TO REGISTER.
لا يا ماجد قول مكتوب إيه ههههه!
حظك اليوم بيقول ان جوزك عسل !!!
WHAT'S SO FUNNY!!!
THEY SEEMED SO COMFORTABLE AROUND EACH OTHER.
3-2
HALA DID THINGS FOR DAD THAT I KNEW HE WAS PERFECTLY CAPABLE OF DOING HIMSELF...
CLICK
GLUG GLUG GLUG
...AND HE WAS MORE THAN HAPPY FOR HER TO DO IT.
CLINK CLINK

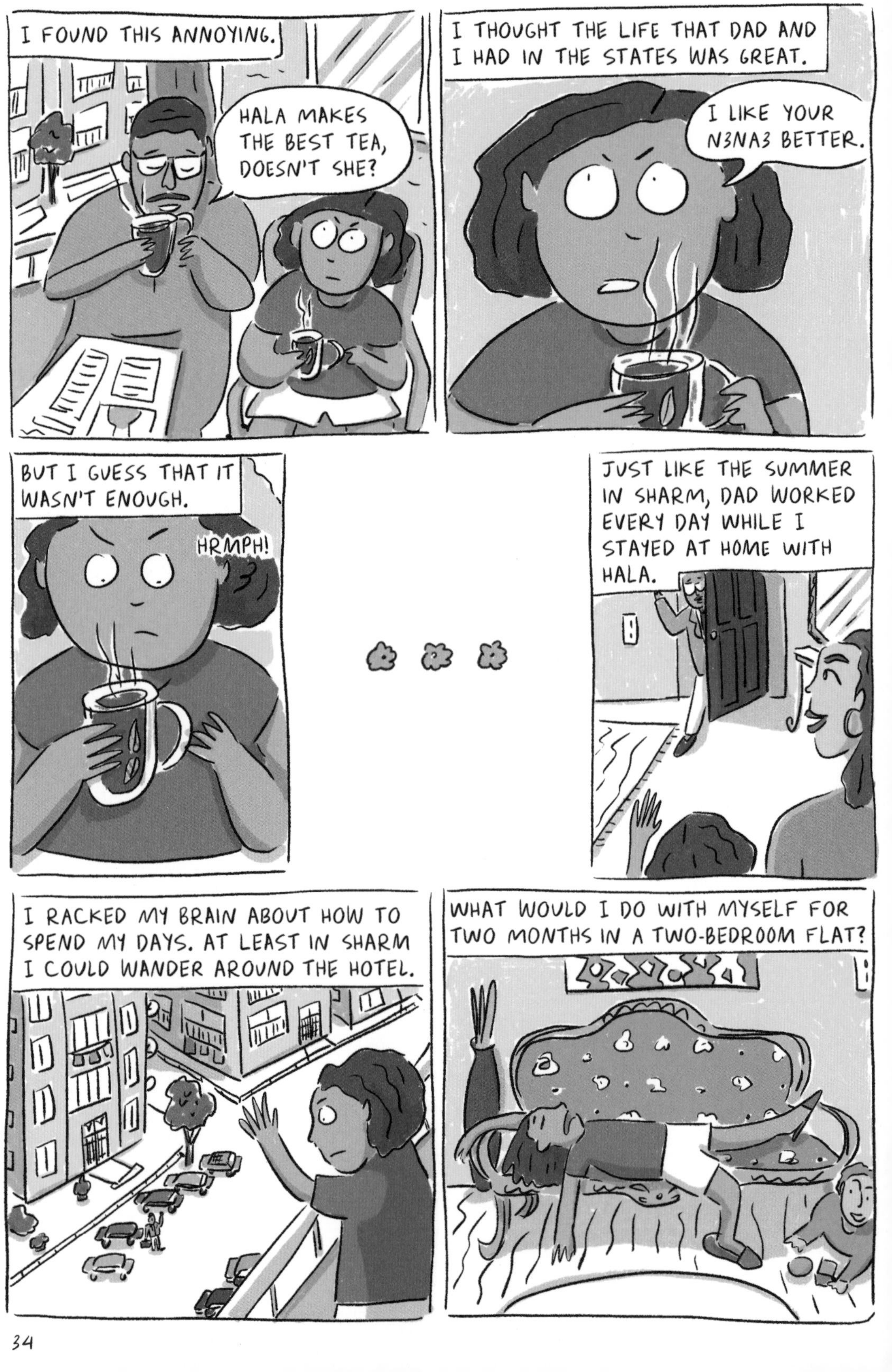
I FOUND THIS ANNOYING.
HALA MAKES THE BEST TEA, DOESN'T SHE?
I THOUGHT THE LIFE THAT DAD AND I HAD IN THE STATES WAS GREAT.
I LIKE YOUR N3NA3 BETTER.
BUT I GUESS THAT IT WASN'T ENOUGH.
HRMPH!
JUST LIKE THE SUMMER IN SHARM, DAD WORKED EVERY DAY WHILE I STAYED AT HOME WITH HALA.
I RACKED MY BRAIN ABOUT HOW TO SPEND MY DAYS. AT LEAST IN SHARM I COULD WANDER AROUND THE HOTEL.
WHAT WOULD I DO WITH MYSELF FOR TWO MONTHS IN A TWO-BEDROOM FLAT?

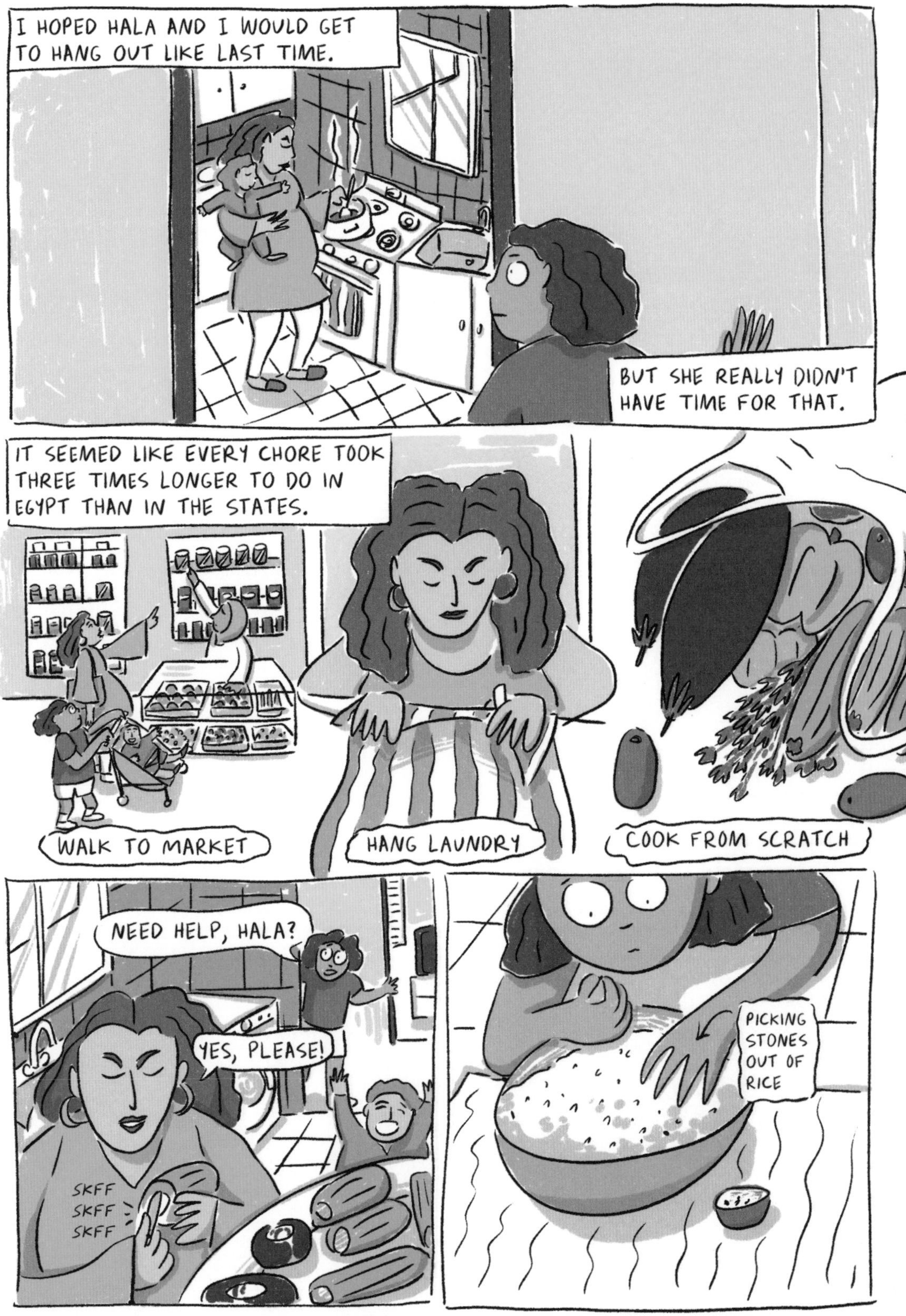
I HOPED HALA AND I WOULD GET TO HANG OUT LIKE LAST TIME.
BUT SHE REALLY DIDN'T HAVE TIME FOR THAT.
IT SEEMED LIKE EVERY CHORE TOOK THREE TIMES LONGER TO DO IN EGYPT THAN IN THE STATES.
WALK TO MARKET
HANG LAUNDRY
COOK FROM SCRATCH
NEED HELP, HALA?
YES, PLEASE!
SKFF
SKFF
SKFF
PICKING STONES OUT OF RICE

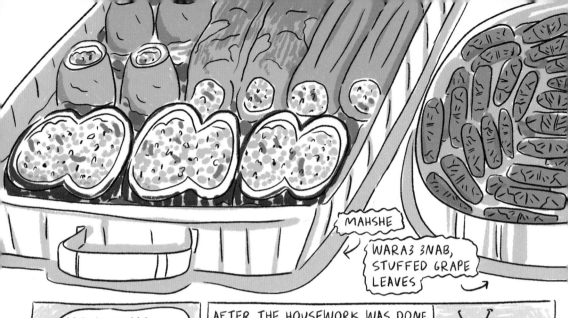

MAHSHE

WARA3 3NAB, STUFFED GRAPE LEAVES

OOF, YA MALAKA I AM TIRED.

AFTER THE HOUSEWORK WAS DONE, HALA WATCHED HER SOAP OPERA.

THEN, TOOK A NAP.

THAT'S WHEN I WAS ON MY OWN.

SOMETIMES I READ.

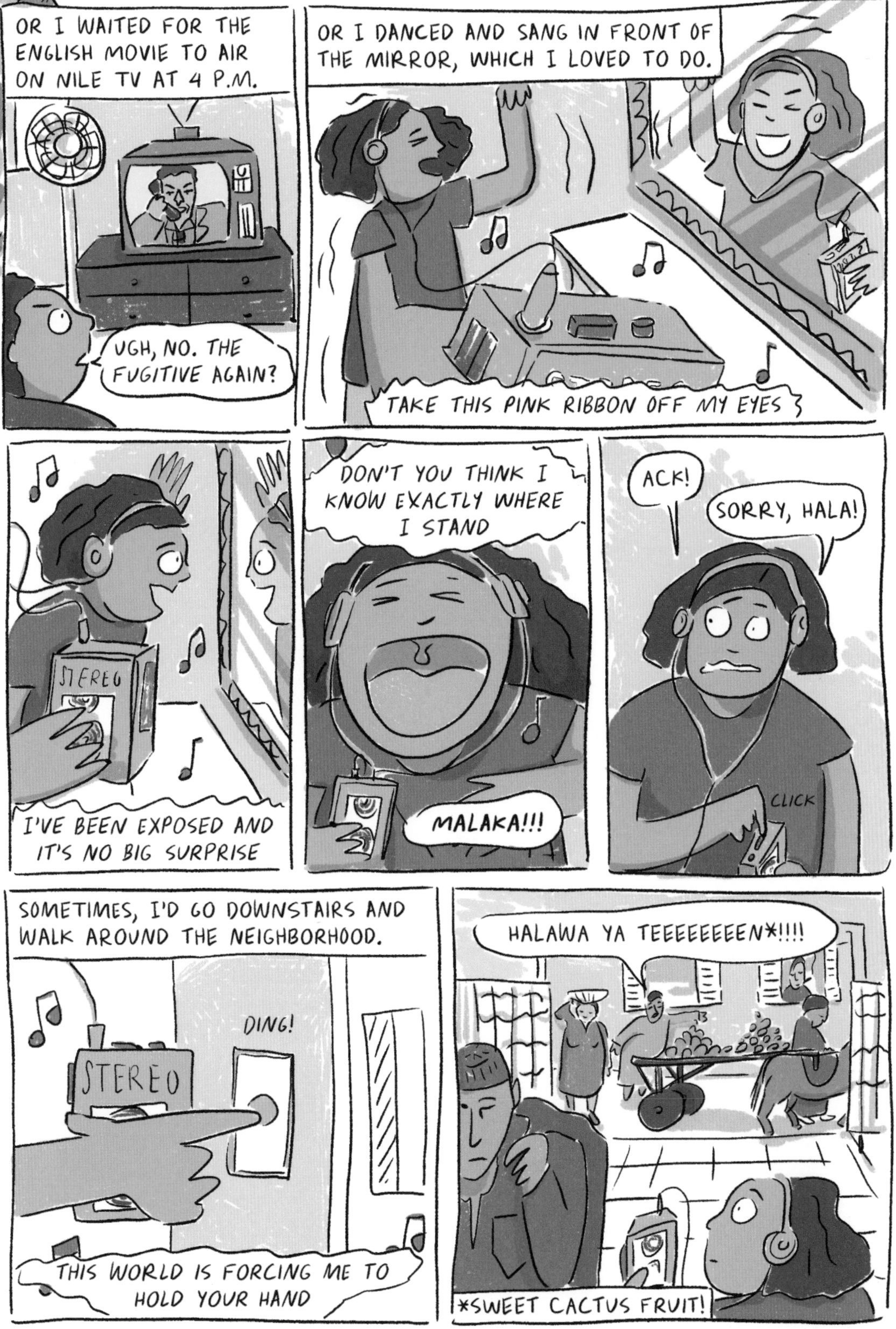

OR I WAITED FOR THE ENGLISH MOVIE TO AIR ON NILE TV AT 4 P.M.
UGH, NO. THE FUGITIVE AGAIN?
OR I DANCED AND SANG IN FRONT OF THE MIRROR, WHICH I LOVED TO DO.
TAKE THIS PINK RIBBON OFF MY EYES
STEREO
I'VE BEEN EXPOSED AND IT'S NO BIG SURPRISE
DON'T YOU THINK I KNOW EXACTLY WHERE I STAND
MALAKA!!!
ACK!
SORRY, HALA!
CLICK
SOMETIMES, I'D GO DOWNSTAIRS AND WALK AROUND THE NEIGHBORHOOD.
STEREO
DING!
THIS WORLD IS FORCING ME TO HOLD YOUR HAND
HALAWA YA TEEEEEEEEN*!!!!
*SWEET CACTUS FRUIT!

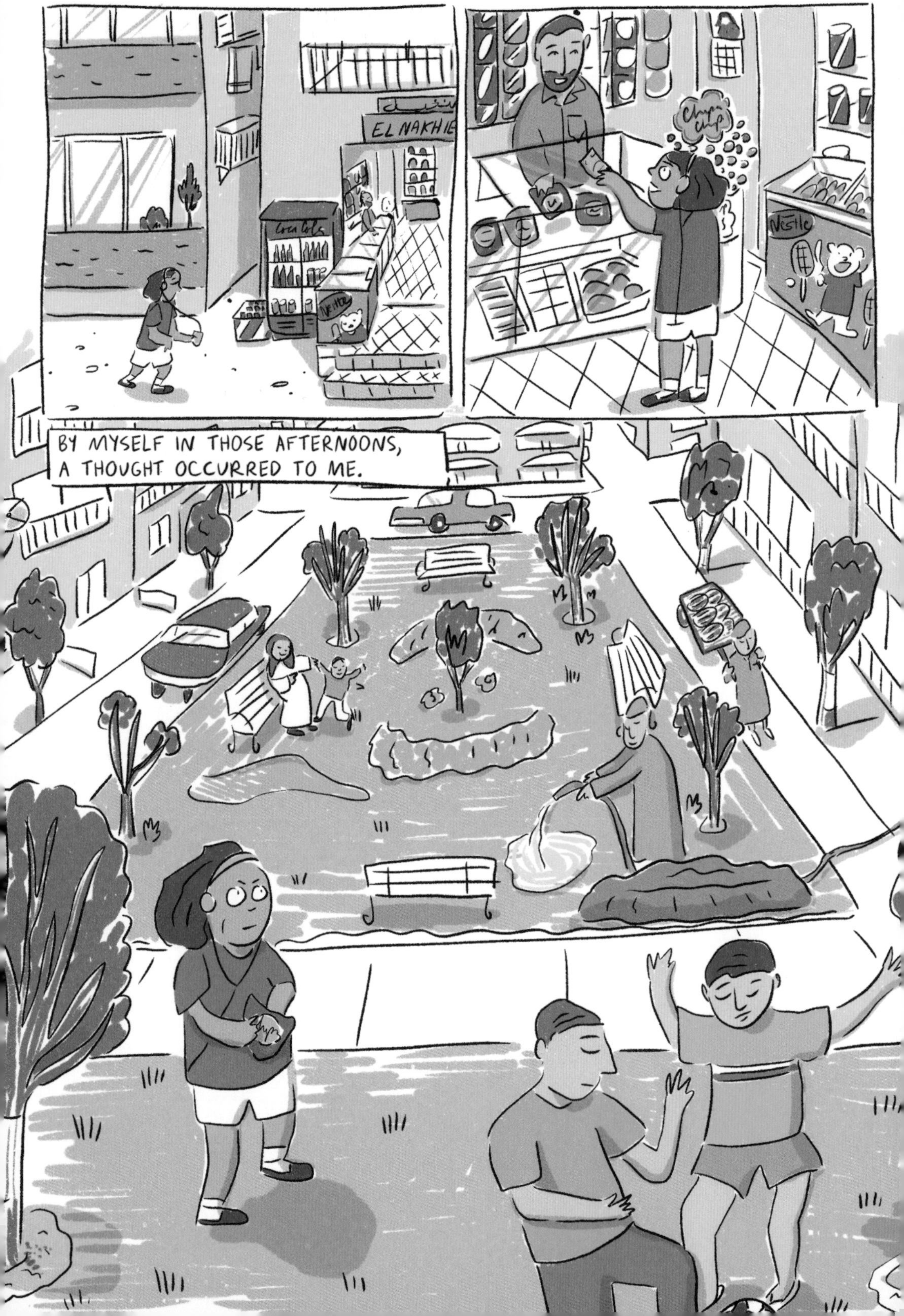
EL NAKHIE
Nestle
BY MYSELF IN THOSE AFTERNOONS,
A THOUGHT OCCURRED TO ME.

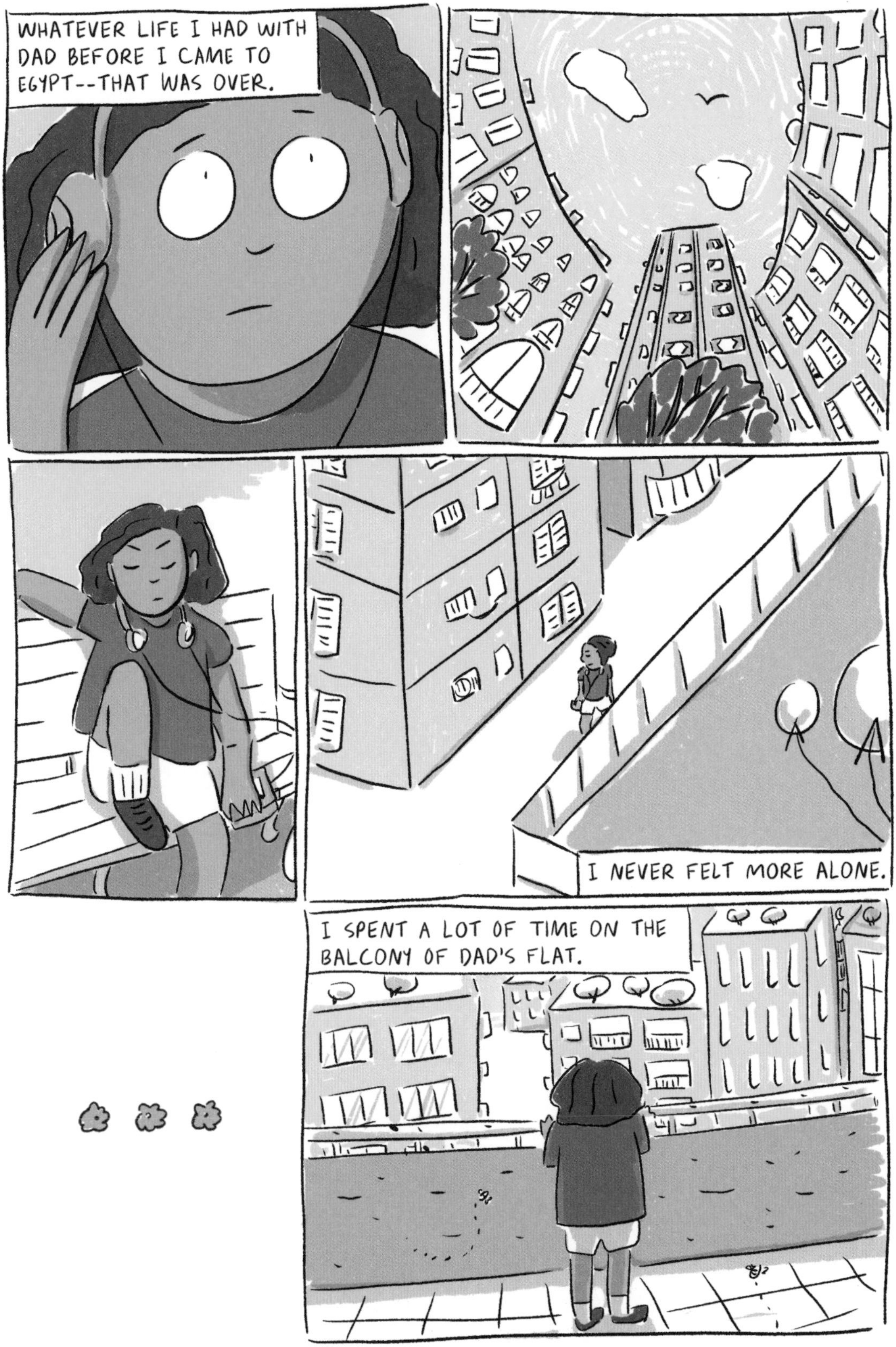
WHATEVER LIFE I HAD WITH DAD BEFORE I CAME TO EGYPT--THAT WAS OVER.
I NEVER FELT MORE ALONE.
I SPENT A LOT OF TIME ON THE BALCONY OF DAD'S FLAT.

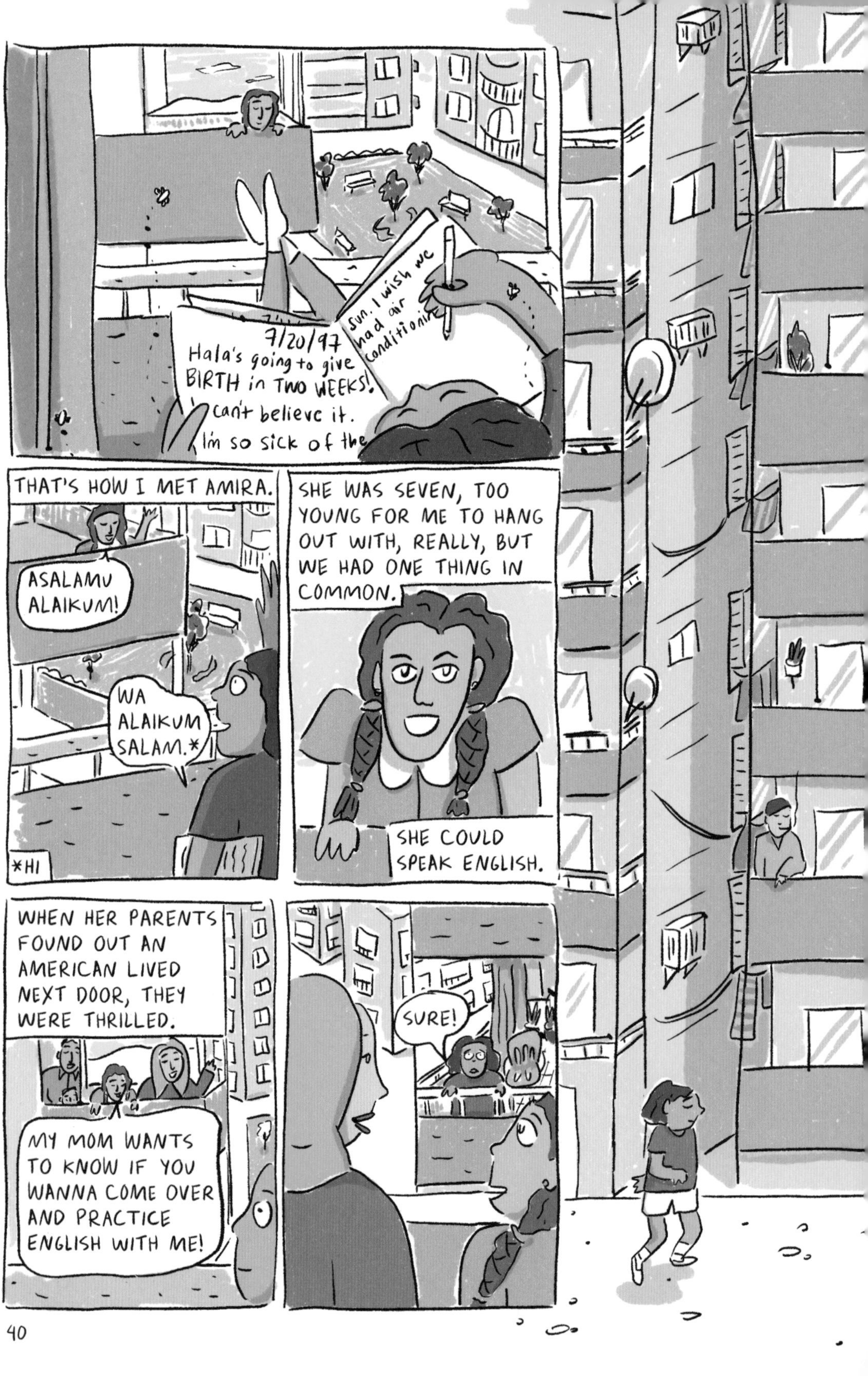
7/20/97
Hala's going to give BIRTH in TWO WEEKS! I can't believe it. I'm so sick of the
Sun. I wish we had air conditioning
THAT'S HOW I MET AMIRA.
ASALAMU ALAIKUM!
WA ALAIKUM SALAM.*
*HI
SHE WAS SEVEN, TOO YOUNG FOR ME TO HANG OUT WITH, REALLY, BUT WE HAD ONE THING IN COMMON.
SHE COULD SPEAK ENGLISH.
WHEN HER PARENTS FOUND OUT AN AMERICAN LIVED NEXT DOOR, THEY WERE THRILLED.
MY MOM WANTS TO KNOW IF YOU WANNA COME OVER AND PRACTICE ENGLISH WITH ME!
SURE!

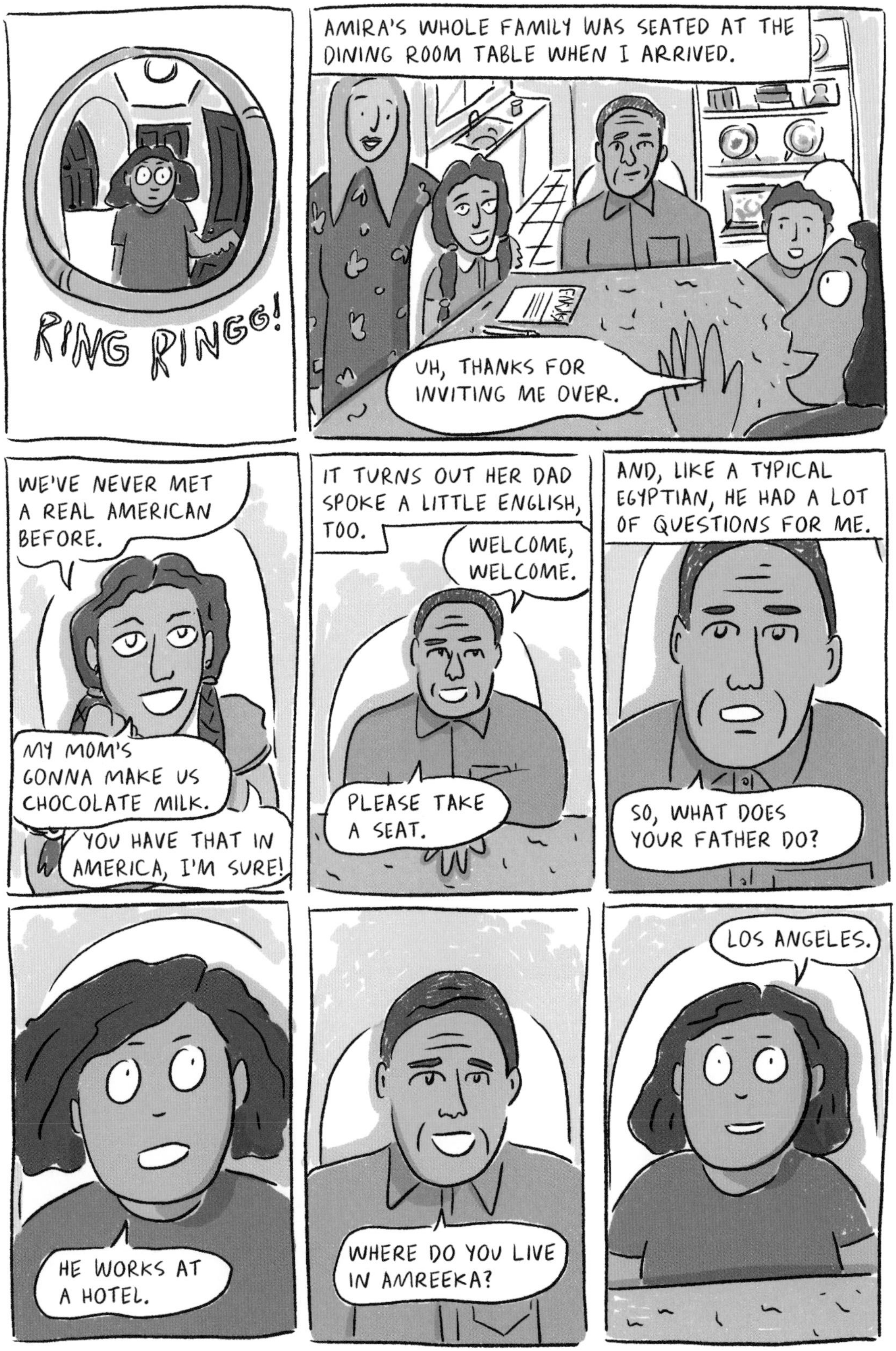
RING RINGG!
AMIRA'S WHOLE FAMILY WAS SEATED AT THE DINING ROOM TABLE WHEN I ARRIVED.
UH, THANKS FOR INVITING ME OVER.
WE'VE NEVER MET A REAL AMERICAN BEFORE.
MY MOM'S GONNA MAKE US CHOCOLATE MILK.
YOU HAVE THAT IN AMERICA, I'M SURE!
IT TURNS OUT HER DAD SPOKE A LITTLE ENGLISH, TOO.
WELCOME, WELCOME.
PLEASE TAKE A SEAT.
AND, LIKE A TYPICAL EGYPTIAN, HE HAD A LOT OF QUESTIONS FOR ME.
SO, WHAT DOES YOUR FATHER DO?
HE WORKS AT A HOTEL.
WHERE DO YOU LIVE IN AMREEKA?
LOS ANGELES.

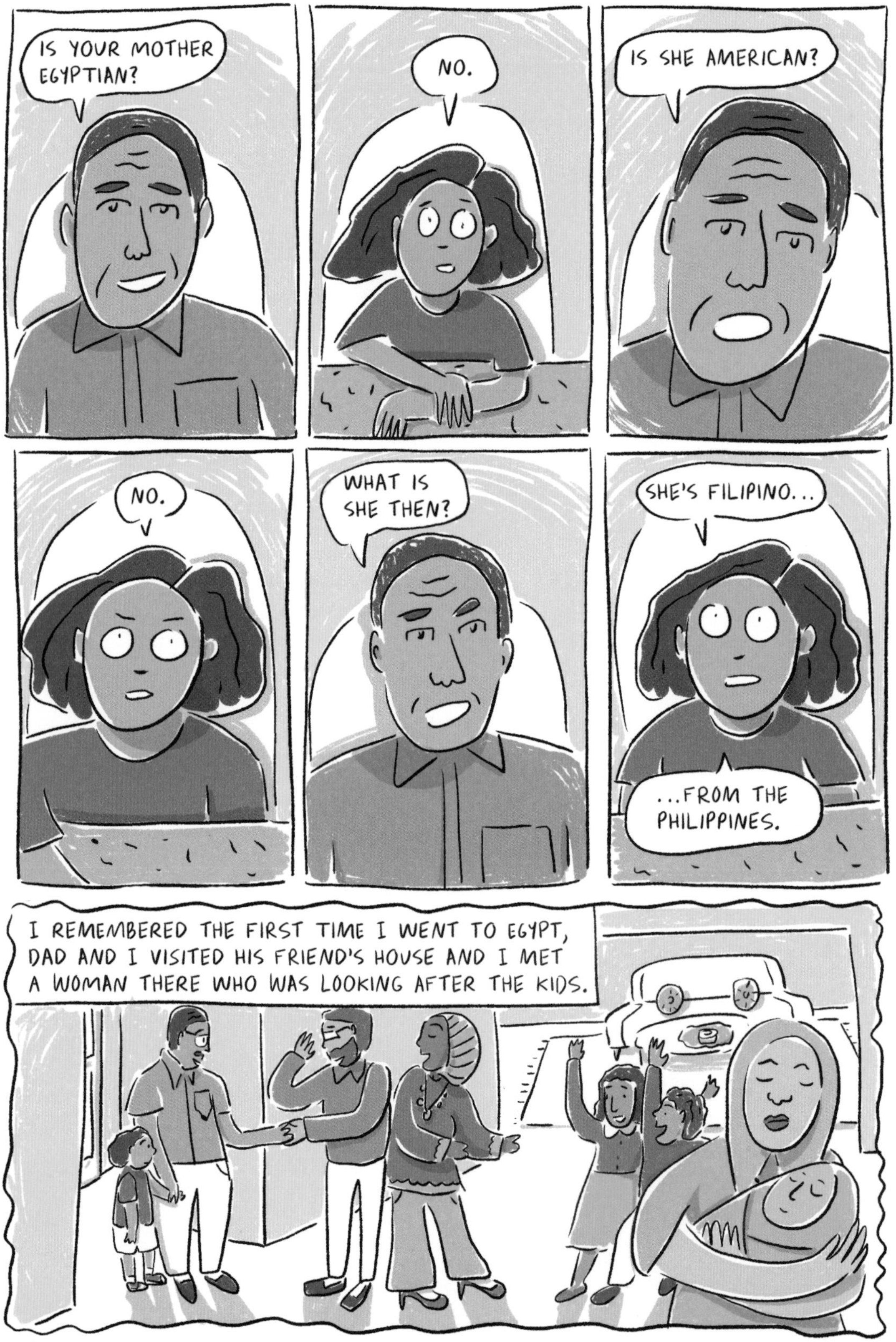
IS YOUR MOTHER EGYPTIAN?
NO.
IS SHE AMERICAN?
NO.
WHAT IS SHE THEN?
SHE'S FILIPINO...
...FROM THE PHILIPPINES.
I REMEMBERED THE FIRST TIME I WENT TO EGYPT, DAD AND I VISITED HIS FRIEND'S HOUSE AND I MET A WOMAN THERE WHO WAS LOOKING AFTER THE KIDS.

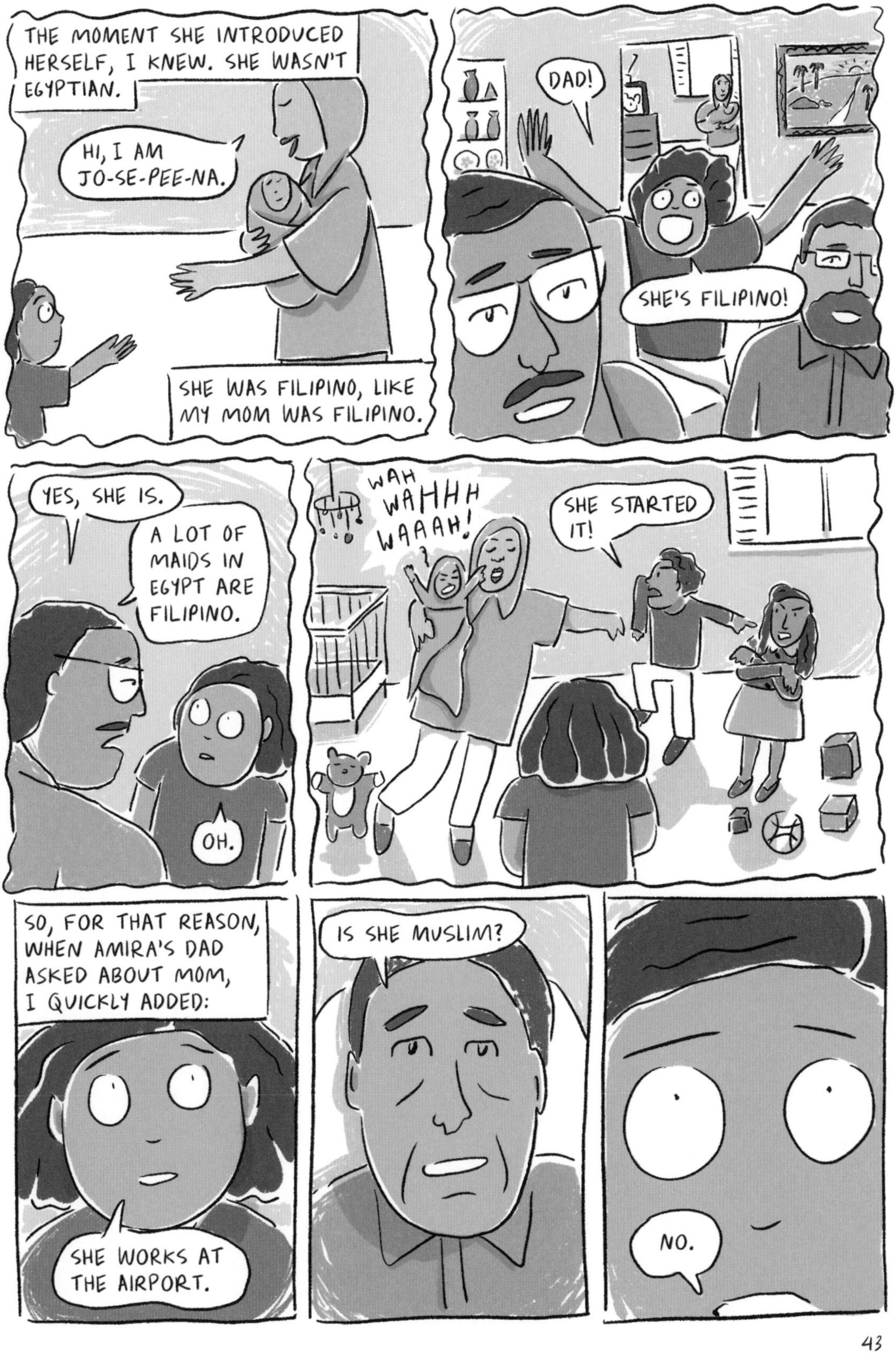
THE MOMENT SHE INTRODUCED HERSELF, I KNEW. SHE WASN'T EGYPTIAN.
HI, I AM JO-SE-PEE-NA.
SHE WAS FILIPINO, LIKE MY MOM WAS FILIPINO.
DAD!
SHE'S FILIPINO!
YES, SHE IS.
A LOT OF MAIDS IN EGYPT ARE FILIPINO.
OH.
WAH WAHHH WAAAH!
SHE STARTED IT!
SO, FOR THAT REASON, WHEN AMIRA'S DAD ASKED ABOUT MOM, I QUICKLY ADDED:
SHE WORKS AT THE AIRPORT.
IS SHE MUSLIM?
NO.

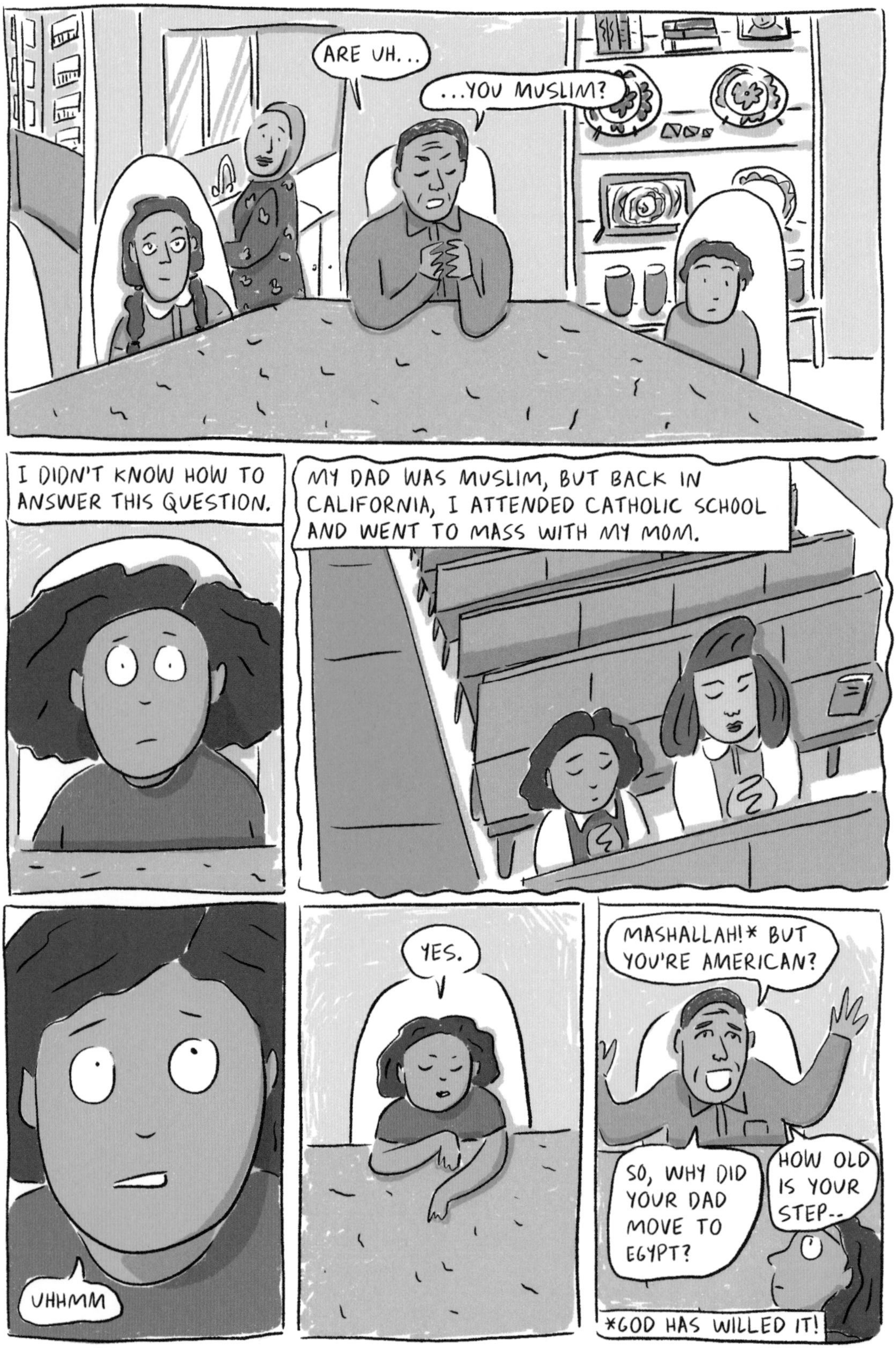
ARE UH...
...YOU MUSLIM?
I DIDN'T KNOW HOW TO ANSWER THIS QUESTION.
MY DAD WAS MUSLIM, BUT BACK IN CALIFORNIA, I ATTENDED CATHOLIC SCHOOL AND WENT TO MASS WITH MY MOM.
UHHMM
YES.
MASHALLAH!* BUT YOU'RE AMERICAN?
SO, WHY DID YOUR DAD MOVE TO EGYPT?
HOW OLD IS YOUR STEP--
*GOD HAS WILLED IT!

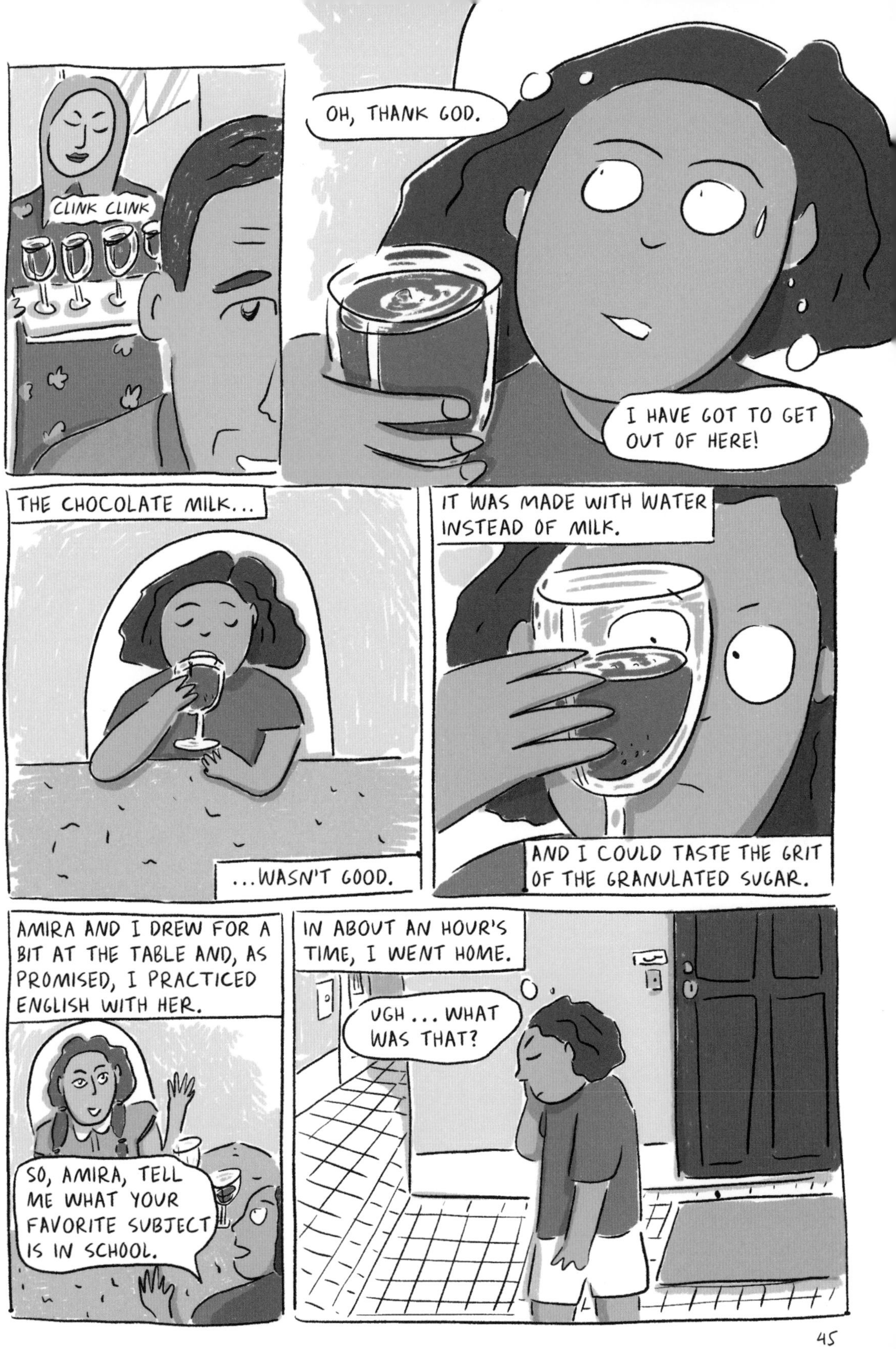
CLINK CLINK
OH, THANK GOD.
I HAVE GOT TO GET OUT OF HERE!
THE CHOCOLATE MILK...
...WASN'T GOOD.
IT WAS MADE WITH WATER INSTEAD OF MILK.
AND I COULD TASTE THE GRIT OF THE GRANULATED SUGAR.
AMIRA AND I DREW FOR A BIT AT THE TABLE AND, AS PROMISED, I PRACTICED ENGLISH WITH HER.
SO, AMIRA, TELL ME WHAT YOUR FAVORITE SUBJECT IS IN SCHOOL.
IN ABOUT AN HOUR'S TIME, I WENT HOME.
UGH... WHAT WAS THAT?

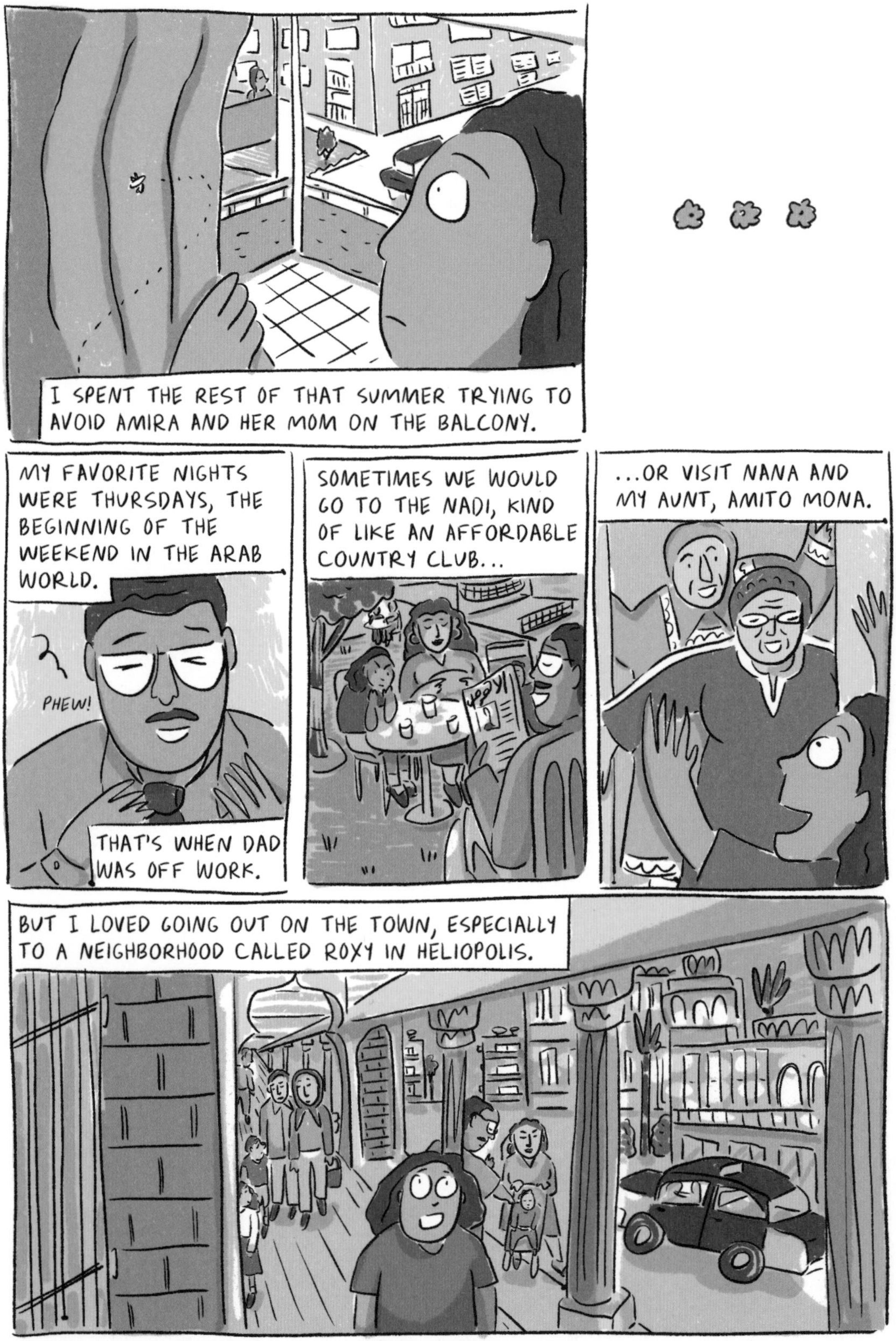
I SPENT THE REST OF THAT SUMMER TRYING TO AVOID AMIRA AND HER MOM ON THE BALCONY.
MY FAVORITE NIGHTS WERE THURSDAYS, THE BEGINNING OF THE WEEKEND IN THE ARAB WORLD.
PHEW!
THAT'S WHEN DAD WAS OFF WORK.
SOMETIMES WE WOULD GO TO THE NADI, KIND OF LIKE AN AFFORDABLE COUNTRY CLUB...
...OR VISIT NANA AND MY AUNT, AMITO MONA.
BUT I LOVED GOING OUT ON THE TOWN, ESPECIALLY TO A NEIGHBORHOOD CALLED ROXY IN HELIOPOLIS.

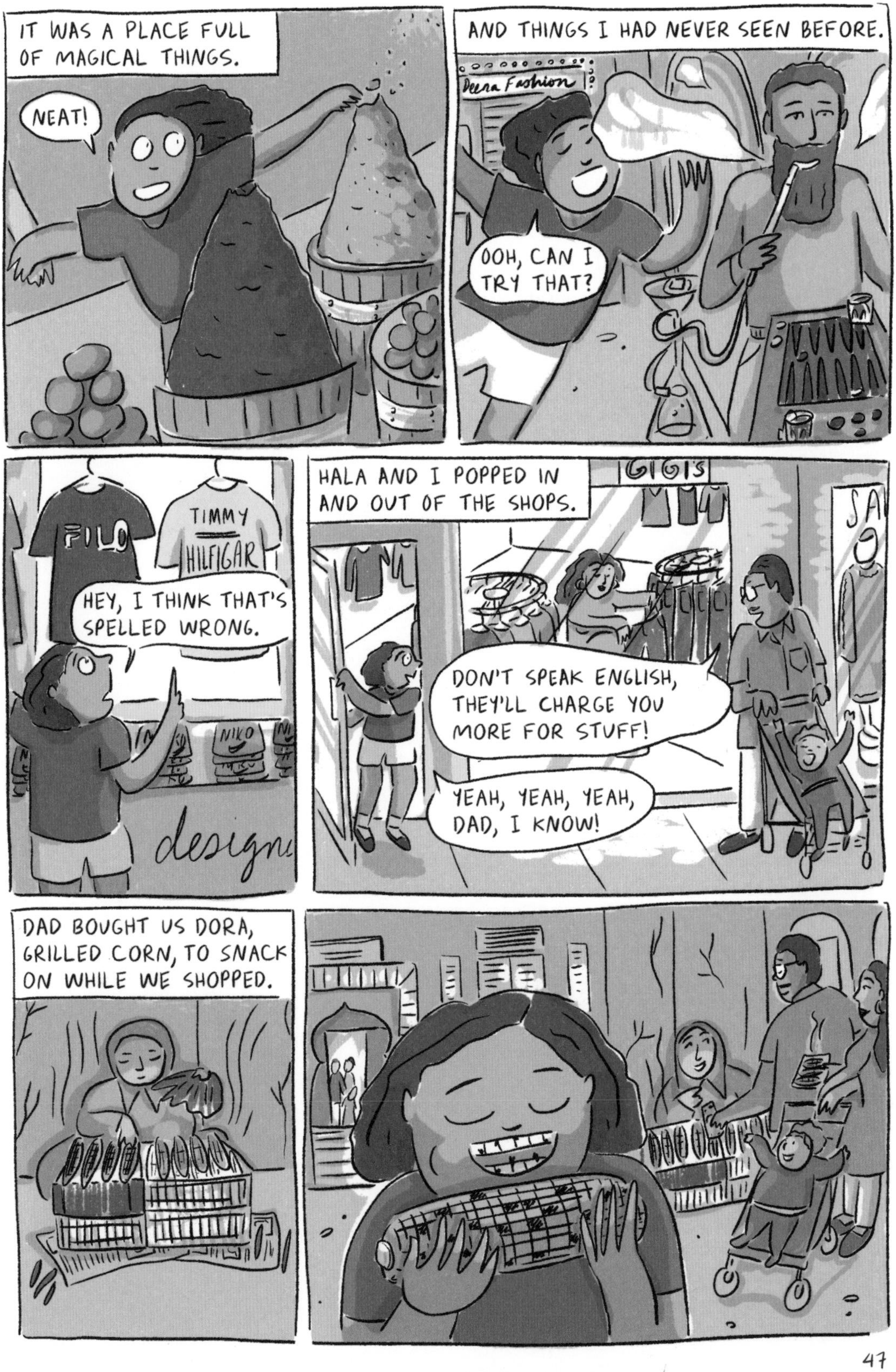
IT WAS A PLACE FULL OF MAGICAL THINGS.
NEAT!
AND THINGS I HAD NEVER SEEN BEFORE.
Deena Fashion
OOH, CAN I TRY THAT?
FILO
TIMMY HILFIGAR
HEY, I THINK THAT'S SPELLED WRONG.
NIKO
design
HALA AND I POPPED IN AND OUT OF THE SHOPS.
GIGI'S
DON'T SPEAK ENGLISH, THEY'LL CHARGE YOU MORE FOR STUFF!
YEAH, YEAH, YEAH, DAD, I KNOW!
DAD BOUGHT US DORA, GRILLED CORN, TO SNACK ON WHILE WE SHOPPED.

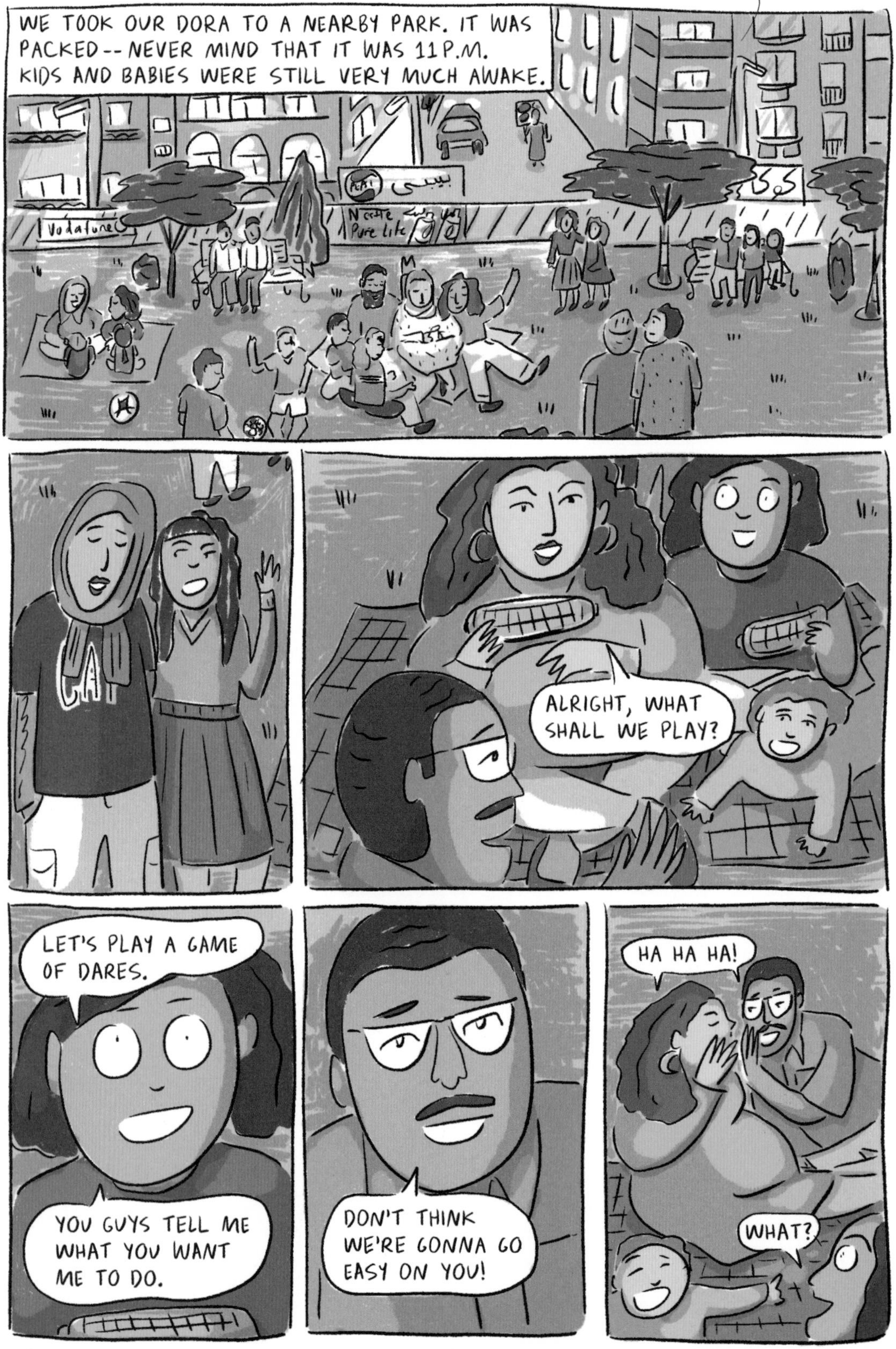
WE TOOK OUR DORA TO A NEARBY PARK. IT WAS PACKED-- NEVER MIND THAT IT WAS 11 P.M. KIDS AND BABIES WERE STILL VERY MUCH AWAKE.
Vodafone
Pure Life
ALRIGHT, WHAT SHALL WE PLAY?
LET'S PLAY A GAME OF DARES.
YOU GUYS TELL ME WHAT YOU WANT ME TO DO.
DON'T THINK WE'RE GONNA GO EASY ON YOU!
HA HA HA!
WHAT?

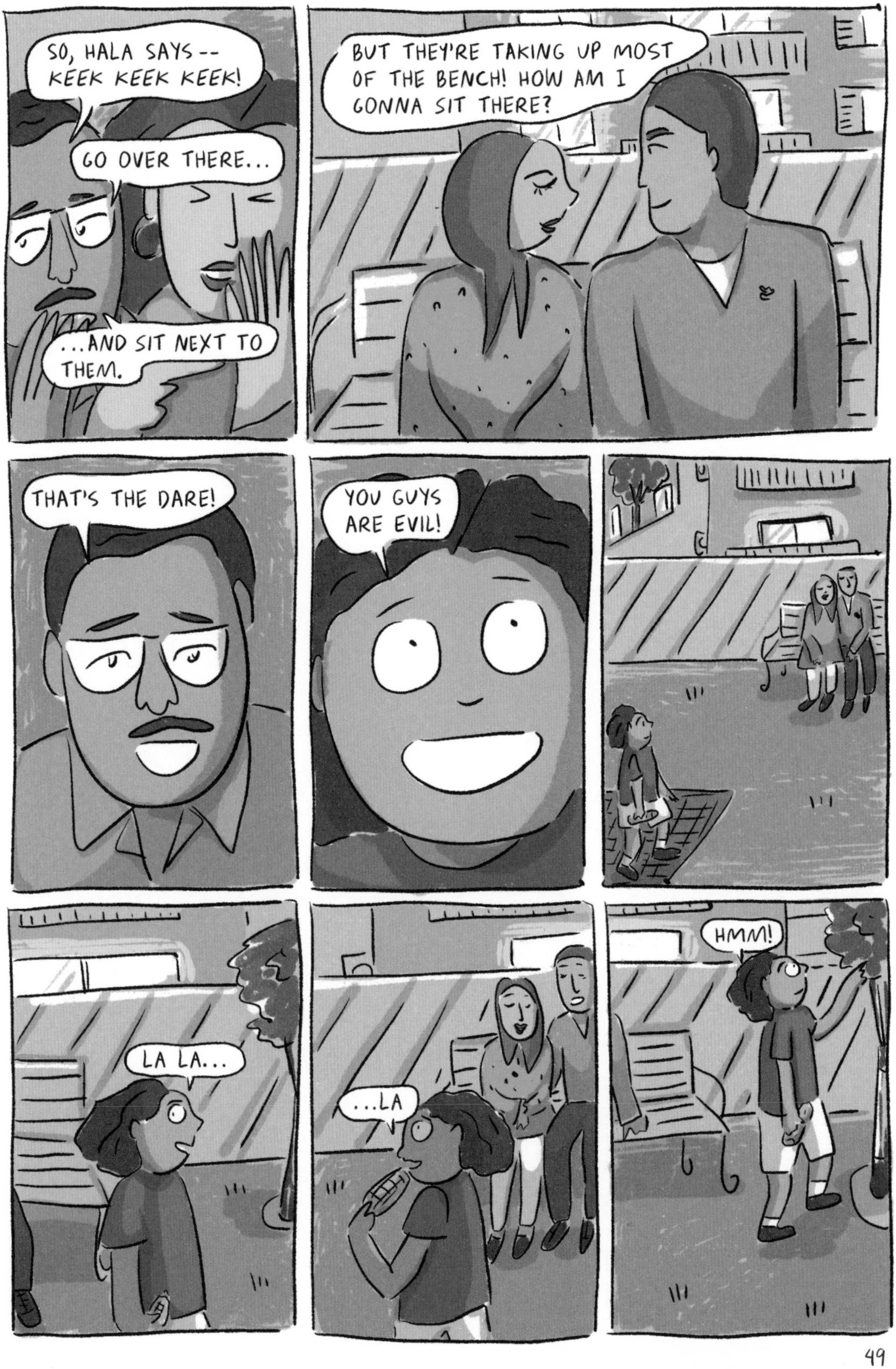
SO, HALA SAYS --
KEEK KEEK KEEK!
GO OVER THERE...
...AND SIT NEXT TO THEM.
BUT THEY'RE TAKING UP MOST OF THE BENCH! HOW AM I GONNA SIT THERE?
THAT'S THE DARE!
YOU GUYS ARE EVIL!
LA LA...
...LA
HMM!

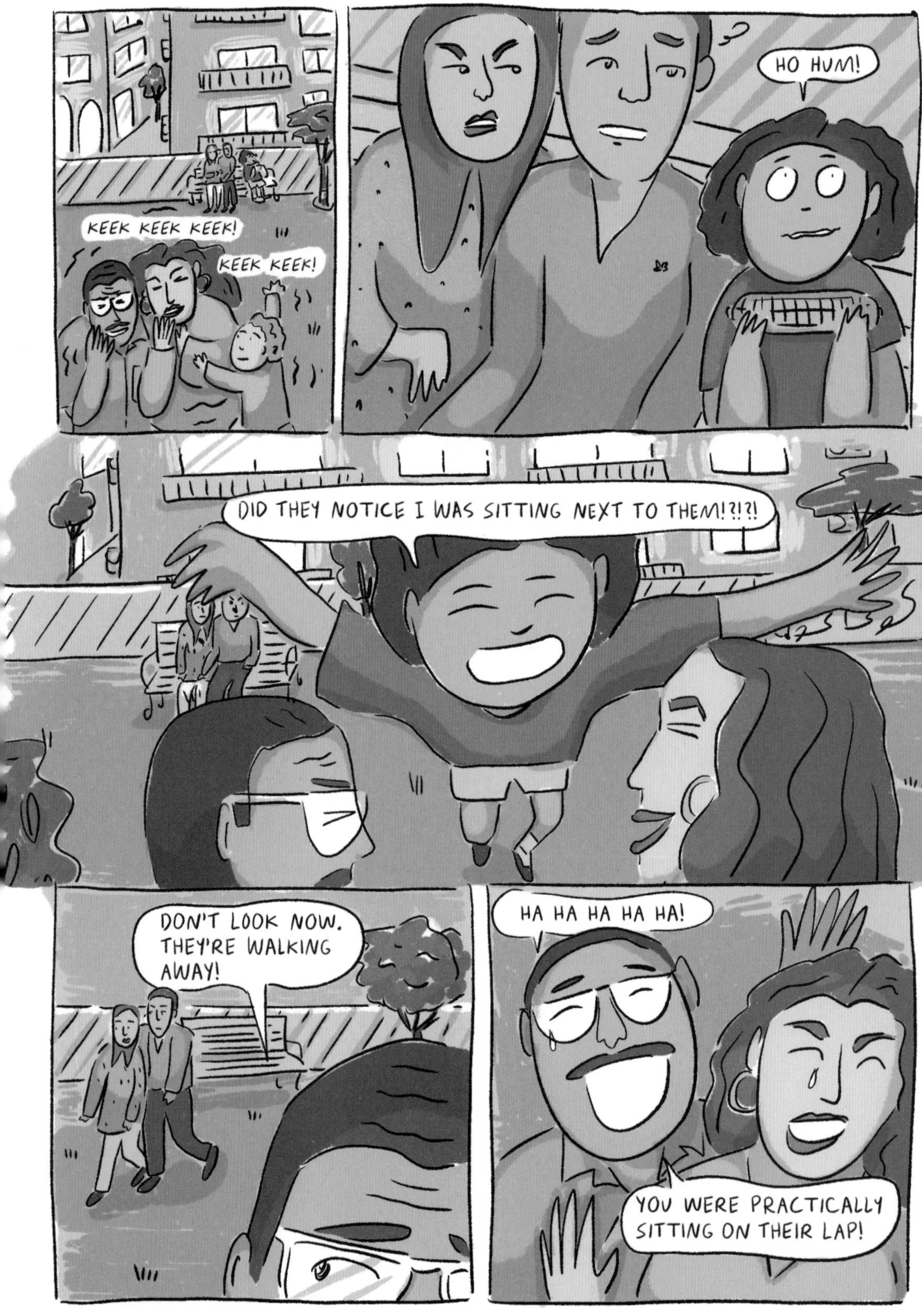
KEEK KEEK KEEK!
KEEK KEEK!
HO HUM!
DID THEY NOTICE I WAS SITTING NEXT TO THEM!?!?!
DON'T LOOK NOW. THEY'RE WALKING AWAY!
HA HA HA HA HA!
YOU WERE PRACTICALLY SITTING ON THEIR LAP!

CHAPTER 3

I Love You, Yasso

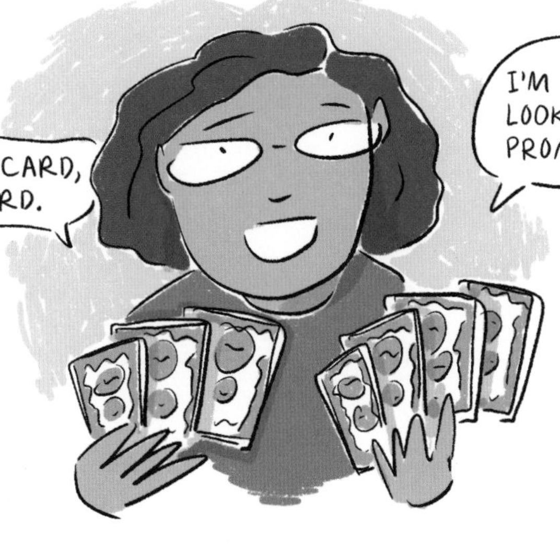
PICK A CARD, ANY CARD.
I'M NOT LOOKING, I PROMISE.

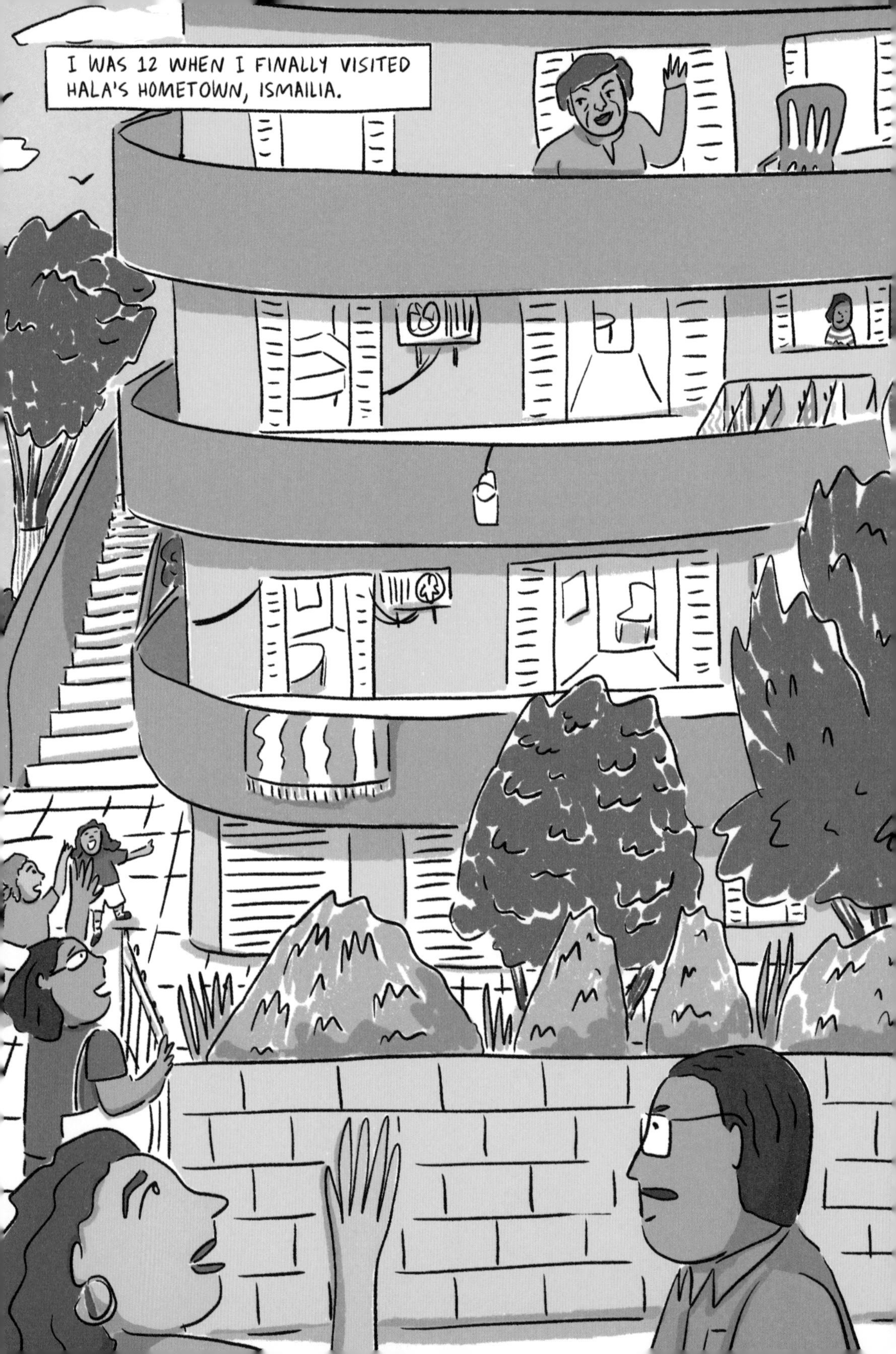
I WAS 12 WHEN I FINALLY VISITED HALA'S HOMETOWN, ISMAILIA.

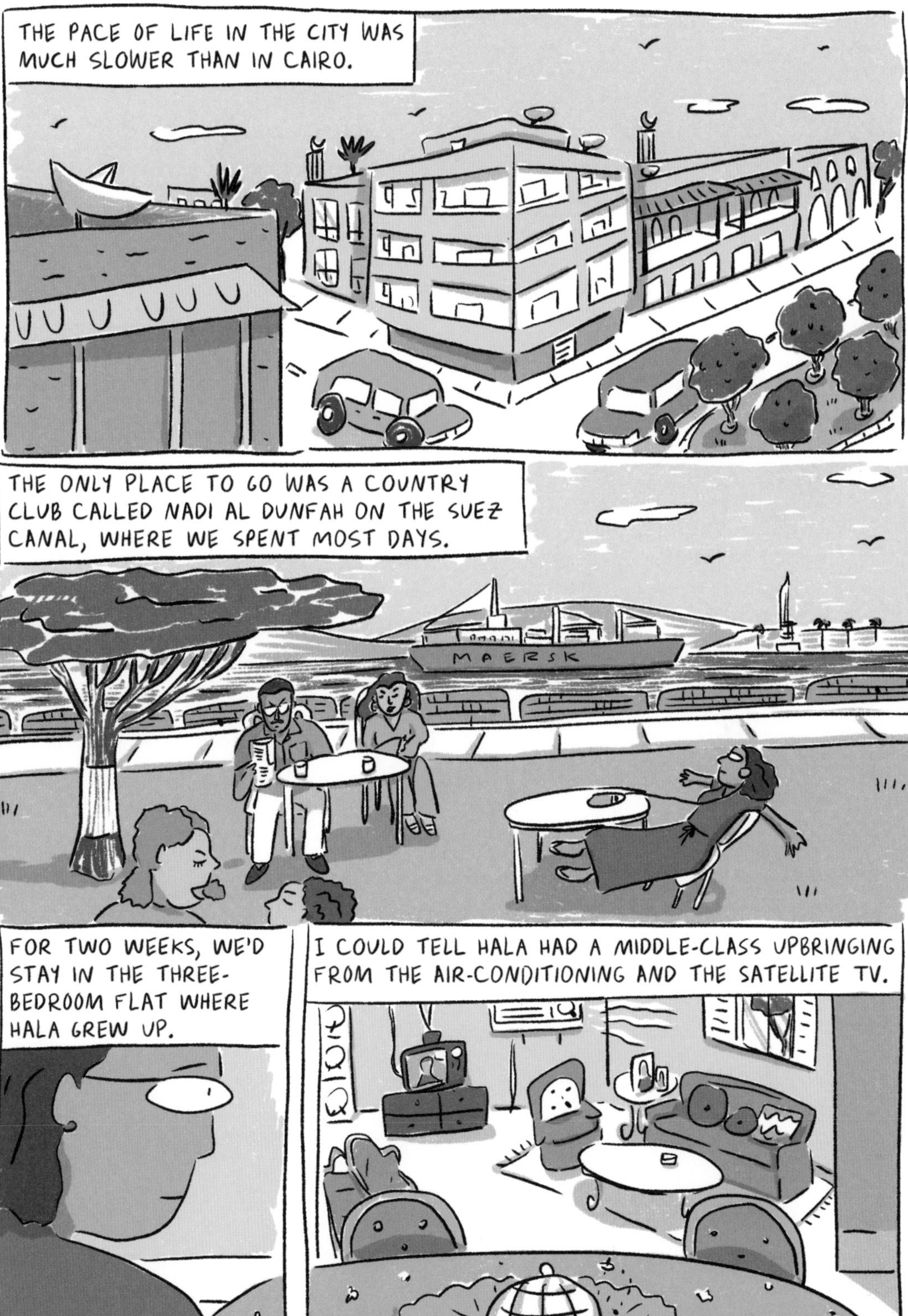
THE PACE OF LIFE IN THE CITY WAS MUCH SLOWER THAN IN CAIRO.
THE ONLY PLACE TO GO WAS A COUNTRY CLUB CALLED NADI AL DUNFAH ON THE SUEZ CANAL, WHERE WE SPENT MOST DAYS.
MAERSK
FOR TWO WEEKS, WE'D STAY IN THE THREE-BEDROOM FLAT WHERE HALA GREW UP.
I COULD TELL HALA HAD A MIDDLE-CLASS UPBRINGING FROM THE AIR-CONDITIONING AND THE SATELLITE TV.

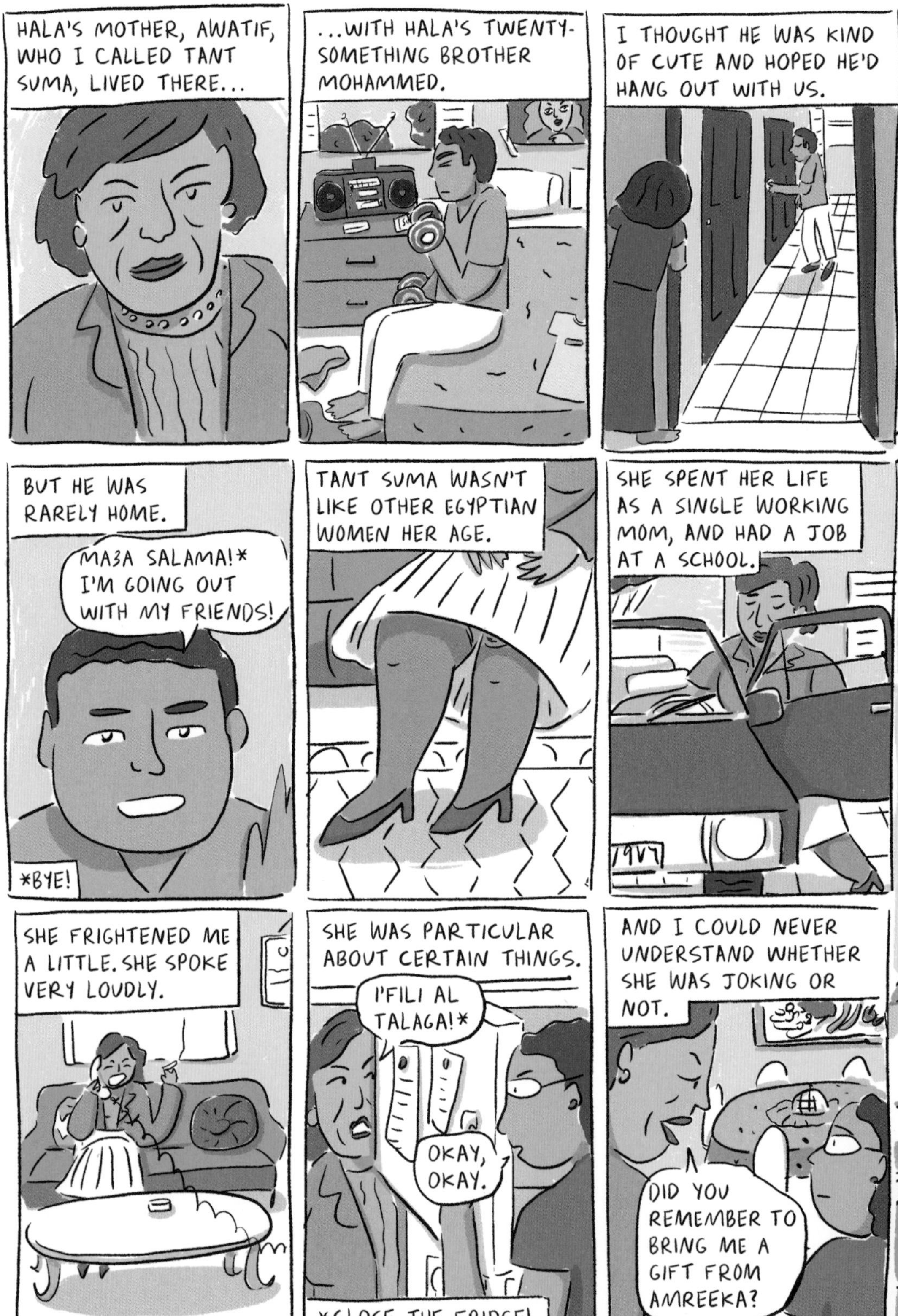
HALA'S MOTHER, AWATIF, WHO I CALLED TANT SUMA, LIVED THERE...
...WITH HALA'S TWENTY-SOMETHING BROTHER MOHAMMED.
I THOUGHT HE WAS KIND OF CUTE AND HOPED HE'D HANG OUT WITH US.
BUT HE WAS RARELY HOME.
MA3A SALAMA!* I'M GOING OUT WITH MY FRIENDS!
*BYE!
TANT SUMA WASN'T LIKE OTHER EGYPTIAN WOMEN HER AGE.
SHE SPENT HER LIFE AS A SINGLE WORKING MOM, AND HAD A JOB AT A SCHOOL.
SHE FRIGHTENED ME A LITTLE. SHE SPOKE VERY LOUDLY.
SHE WAS PARTICULAR ABOUT CERTAIN THINGS.
I'FILI AL TALAGA!*
OKAY, OKAY.
*CLOSE THE FRIDGE!
AND I COULD NEVER UNDERSTAND WHETHER SHE WAS JOKING OR NOT.
DID YOU REMEMBER TO BRING ME A GIFT FROM AMREEKA?

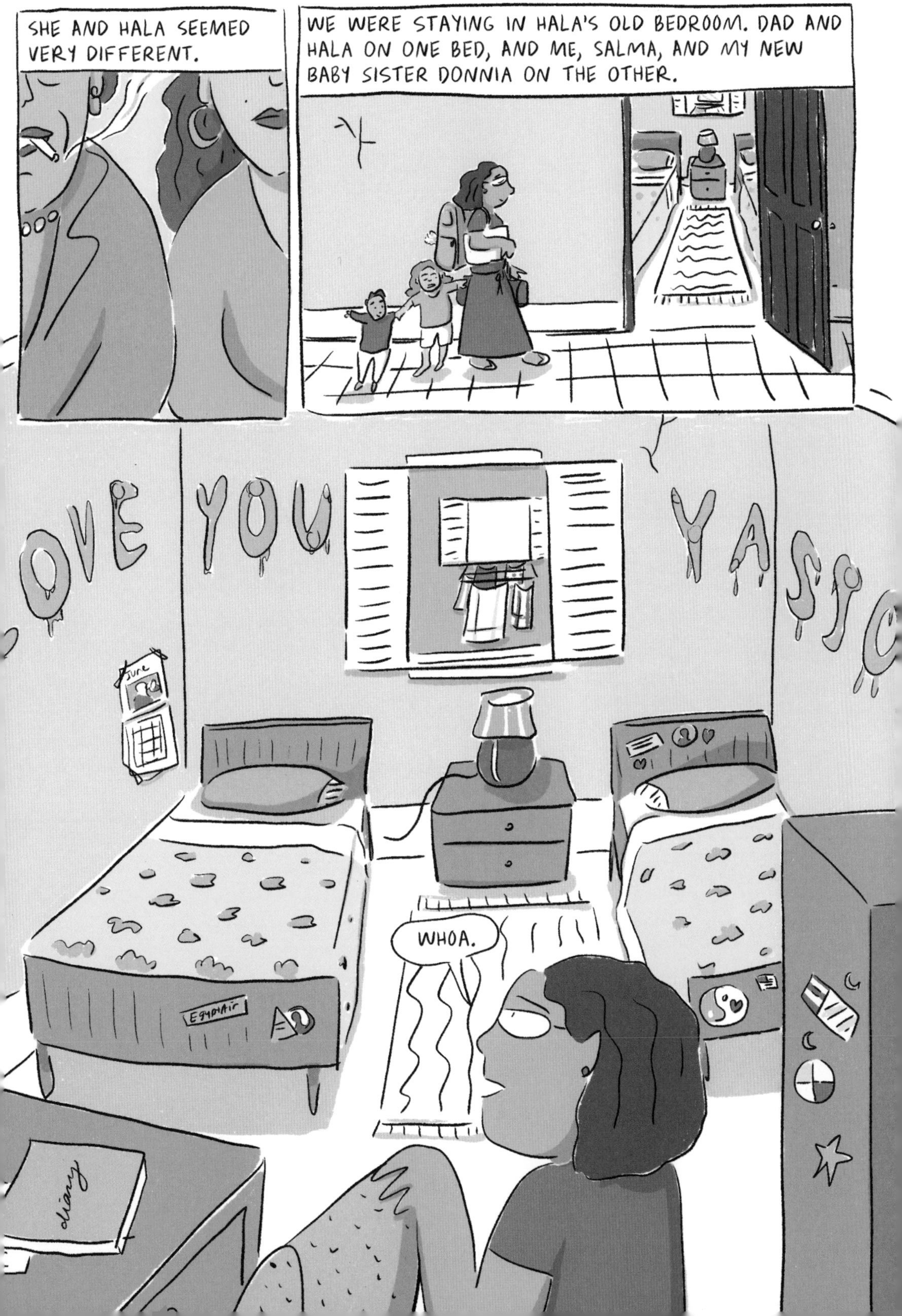
SHE AND HALA SEEMED VERY DIFFERENT.
WE WERE STAYING IN HALA'S OLD BEDROOM. DAD AND HALA ON ONE BED, AND ME, SALMA, AND MY NEW BABY SISTER DONNIA ON THE OTHER.
June
EgyptAir
WHOA.
diary

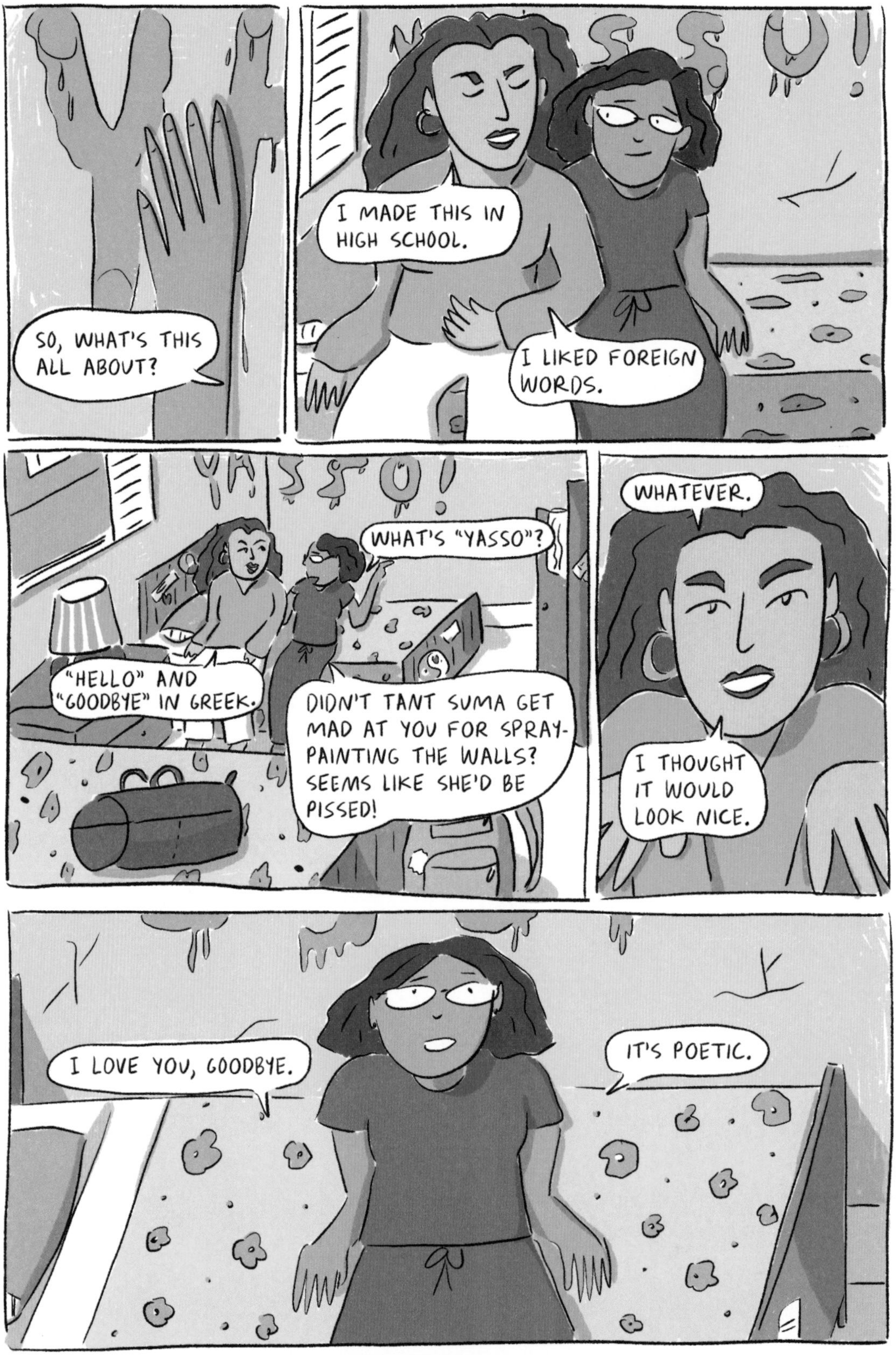
SO, WHAT'S THIS ALL ABOUT?
I MADE THIS IN HIGH SCHOOL.
I LIKED FOREIGN WORDS.
WHAT'S "YASSO"?
"HELLO" AND "GOODBYE" IN GREEK.
DIDN'T TANT SUMA GET MAD AT YOU FOR SPRAY-PAINTING THE WALLS? SEEMS LIKE SHE'D BE PISSED!
WHATEVER.
I THOUGHT IT WOULD LOOK NICE.
I LOVE YOU, GOODBYE.
IT'S POETIC.

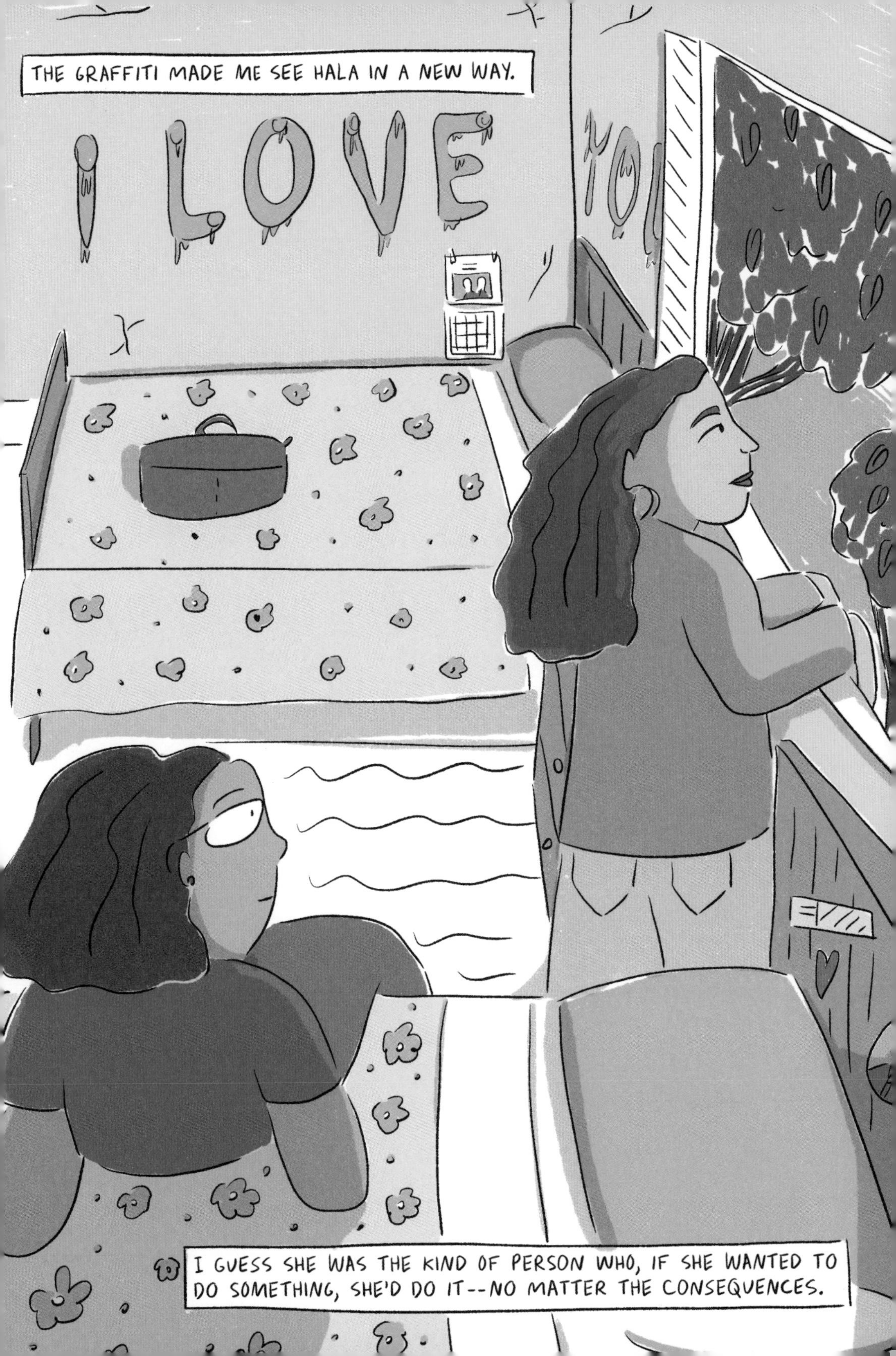

THE GRAFFITI MADE ME SEE HALA IN A NEW WAY.
I LOVE
I GUESS SHE WAS THE KIND OF PERSON WHO, IF SHE WANTED TO DO SOMETHING, SHE'D DO IT--NO MATTER THE CONSEQUENCES.

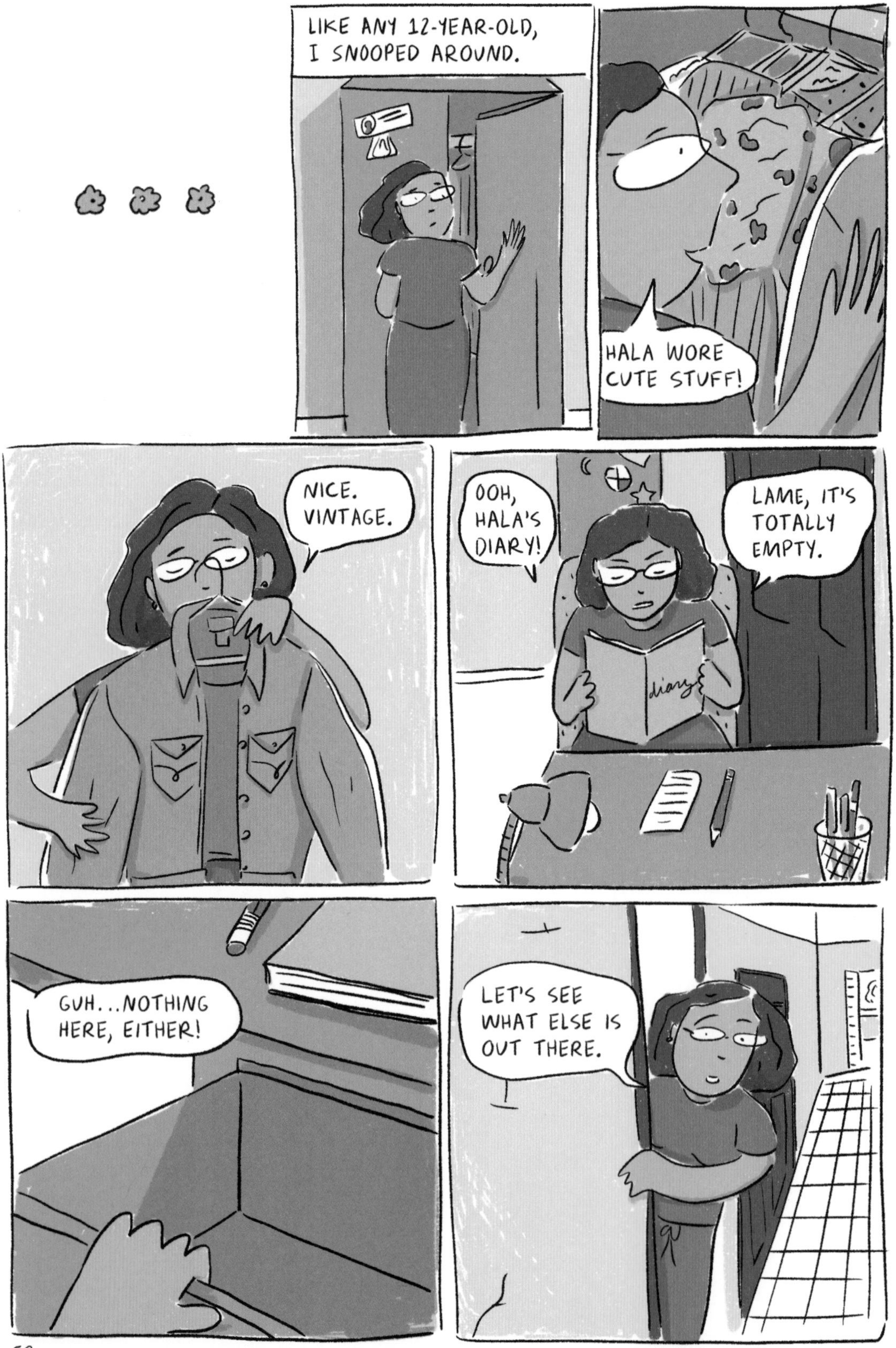
LIKE ANY 12-YEAR-OLD, I SNOOPED AROUND.
HALA WORE CUTE STUFF!
NICE. VINTAGE.
OOH, HALA'S DIARY!
diary
LAME, IT'S TOTALLY EMPTY.
GUH...NOTHING HERE, EITHER!
LET'S SEE WHAT ELSE IS OUT THERE.

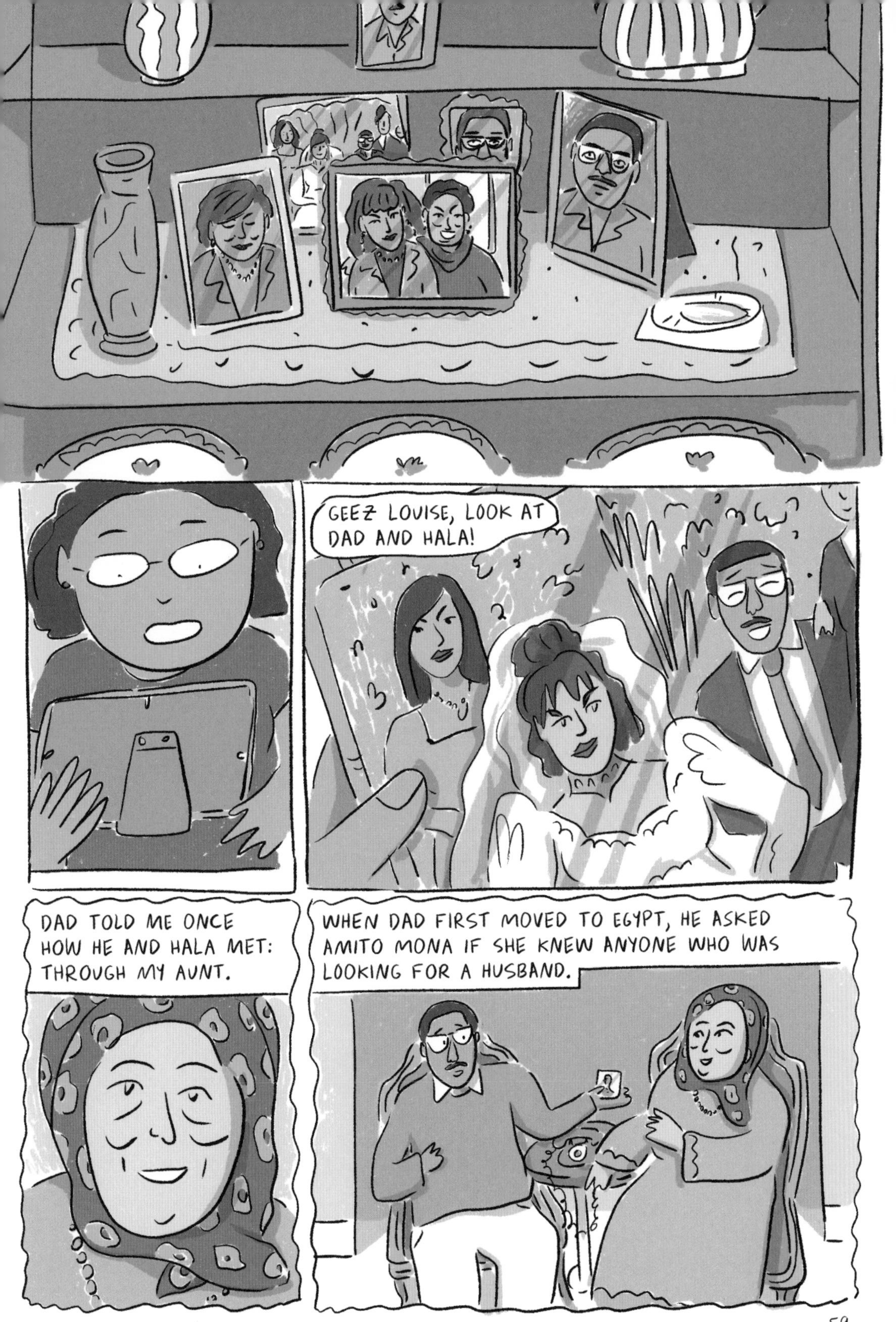
GEEZ LOUISE, LOOK AT DAD AND HALA!
DAD TOLD ME ONCE HOW HE AND HALA MET: THROUGH MY AUNT.
WHEN DAD FIRST MOVED TO EGYPT, HE ASKED AMITO MONA IF SHE KNEW ANYONE WHO WAS LOOKING FOR A HUSBAND.

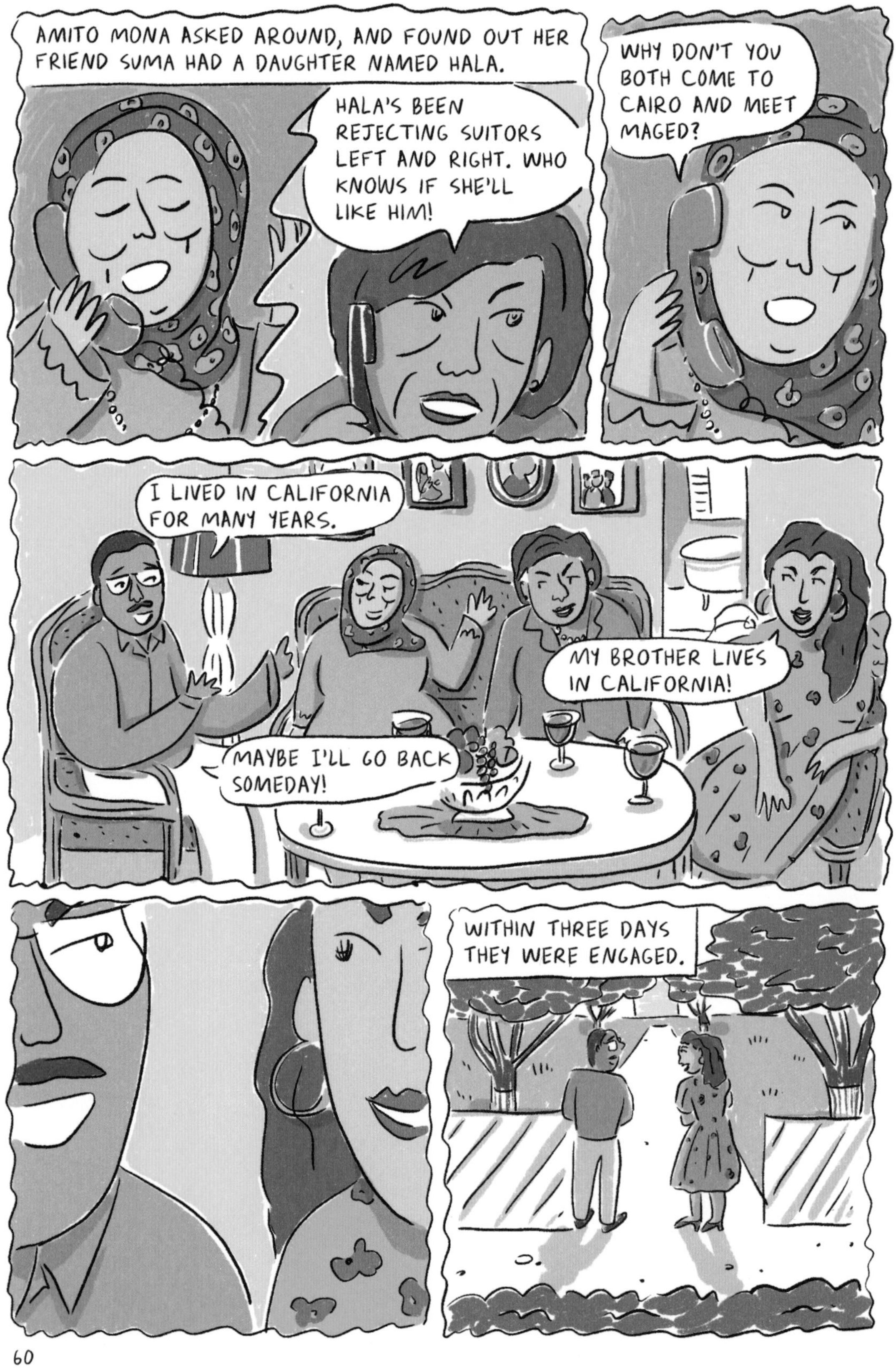
AMITO MONA ASKED AROUND, AND FOUND OUT HER FRIEND SUMA HAD A DAUGHTER NAMED HALA.
HALA'S BEEN REJECTING SUITORS LEFT AND RIGHT. WHO KNOWS IF SHE'LL LIKE HIM!
WHY DON'T YOU BOTH COME TO CAIRO AND MEET MAGED?
I LIVED IN CALIFORNIA FOR MANY YEARS.
MY BROTHER LIVES IN CALIFORNIA!
MAYBE I'LL GO BACK SOMEDAY!
WITHIN THREE DAYS THEY WERE ENGAGED.

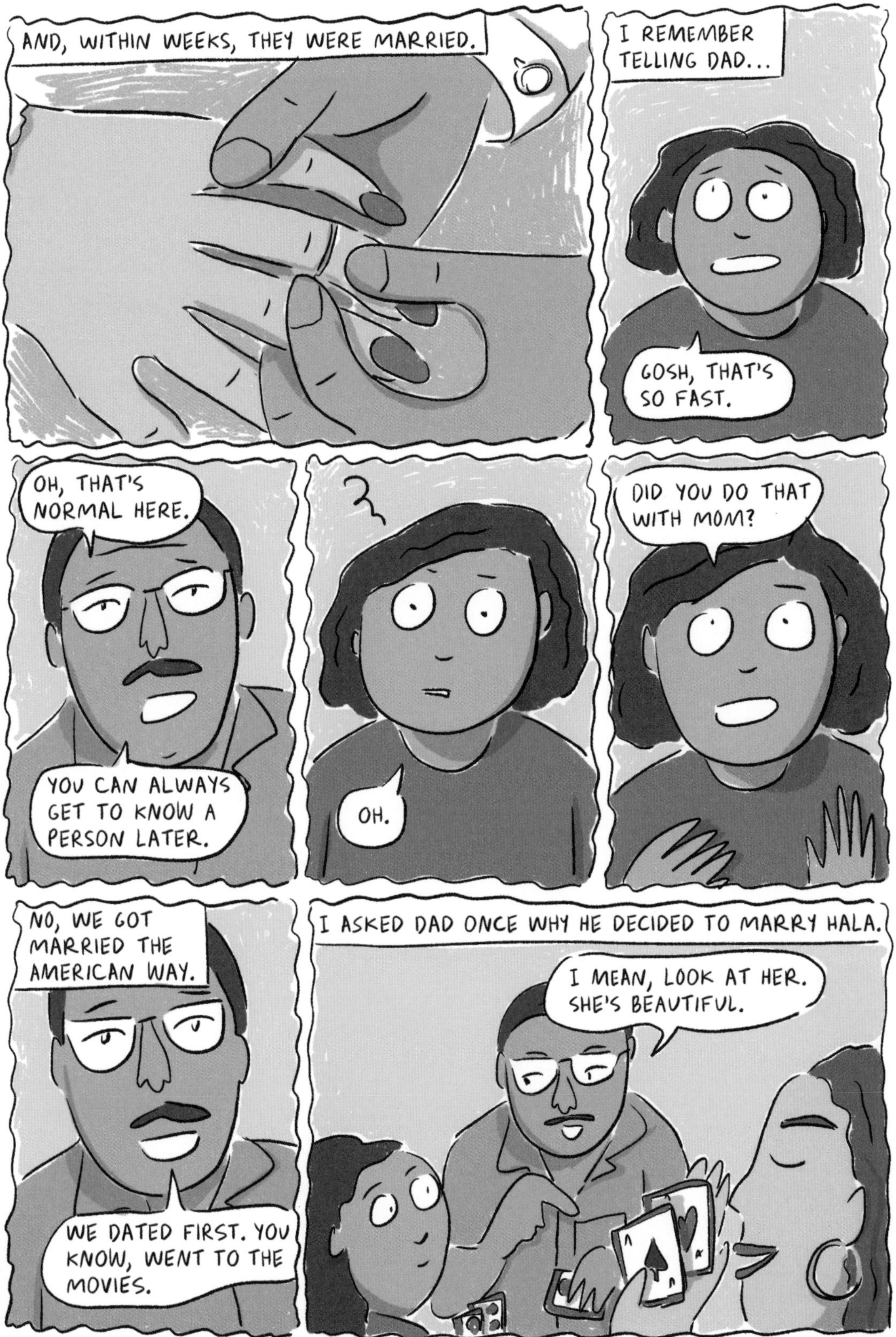
AND, WITHIN WEEKS, THEY WERE MARRIED.
I REMEMBER TELLING DAD...
GOSH, THAT'S SO FAST.
OH, THAT'S NORMAL HERE.
YOU CAN ALWAYS GET TO KNOW A PERSON LATER.
OH.
DID YOU DO THAT WITH MOM?
NO, WE GOT MARRIED THE AMERICAN WAY.
WE DATED FIRST. YOU KNOW, WENT TO THE MOVIES.
I ASKED DAD ONCE WHY HE DECIDED TO MARRY HALA.
I MEAN, LOOK AT HER. SHE'S BEAUTIFUL.

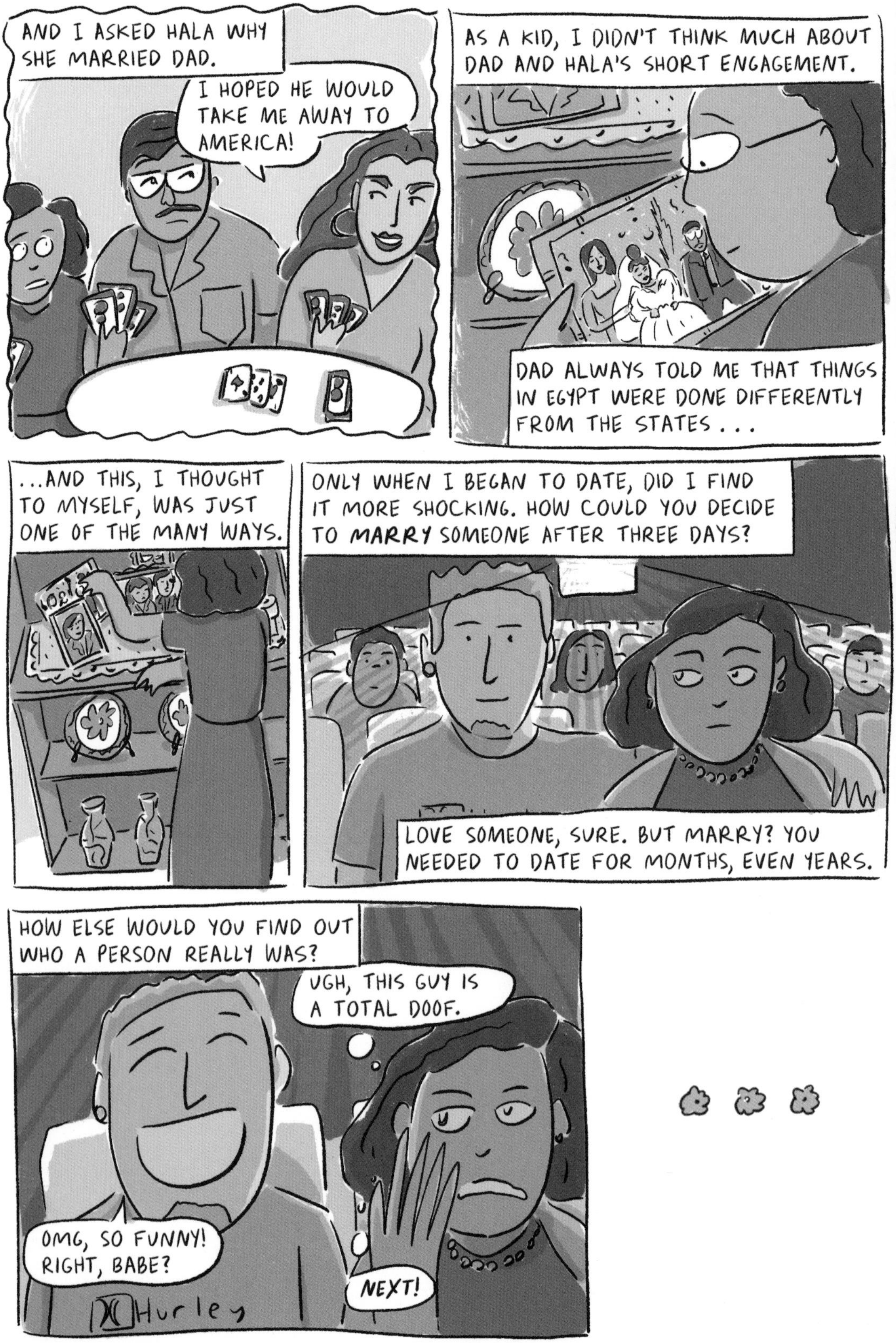

AND I ASKED HALA WHY SHE MARRIED DAD.
I HOPED HE WOULD TAKE ME AWAY TO AMERICA!
AS A KID, I DIDN'T THINK MUCH ABOUT DAD AND HALA'S SHORT ENGAGEMENT.
DAD ALWAYS TOLD ME THAT THINGS IN EGYPT WERE DONE DIFFERENTLY FROM THE STATES . . .
...AND THIS, I THOUGHT TO MYSELF, WAS JUST ONE OF THE MANY WAYS.
ONLY WHEN I BEGAN TO DATE, DID I FIND IT MORE SHOCKING. HOW COULD YOU DECIDE TO **MARRY** SOMEONE AFTER THREE DAYS?
LOVE SOMEONE, SURE. BUT MARRY? YOU NEEDED TO DATE FOR MONTHS, EVEN YEARS.
HOW ELSE WOULD YOU FIND OUT WHO A PERSON REALLY WAS?
UGH, THIS GUY IS A TOTAL DOOF.
OMG, SO FUNNY! RIGHT, BABE?
Hurley
NEXT!

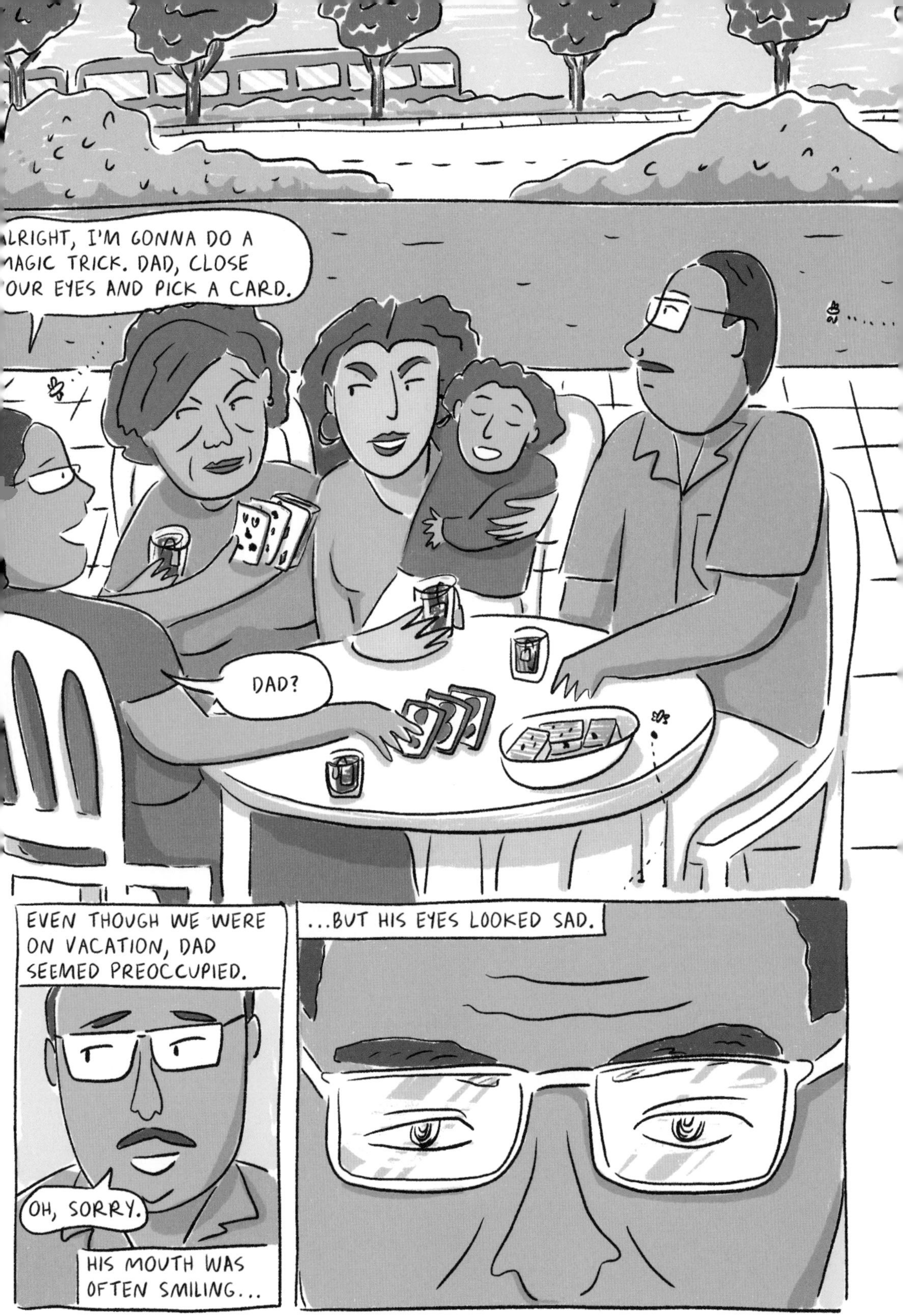
ALRIGHT, I'M GONNA DO A MAGIC TRICK. DAD, CLOSE YOUR EYES AND PICK A CARD.
DAD?
EVEN THOUGH WE WERE ON VACATION, DAD SEEMED PREOCCUPIED.
OH, SORRY.
HIS MOUTH WAS OFTEN SMILING...
...BUT HIS EYES LOOKED SAD.

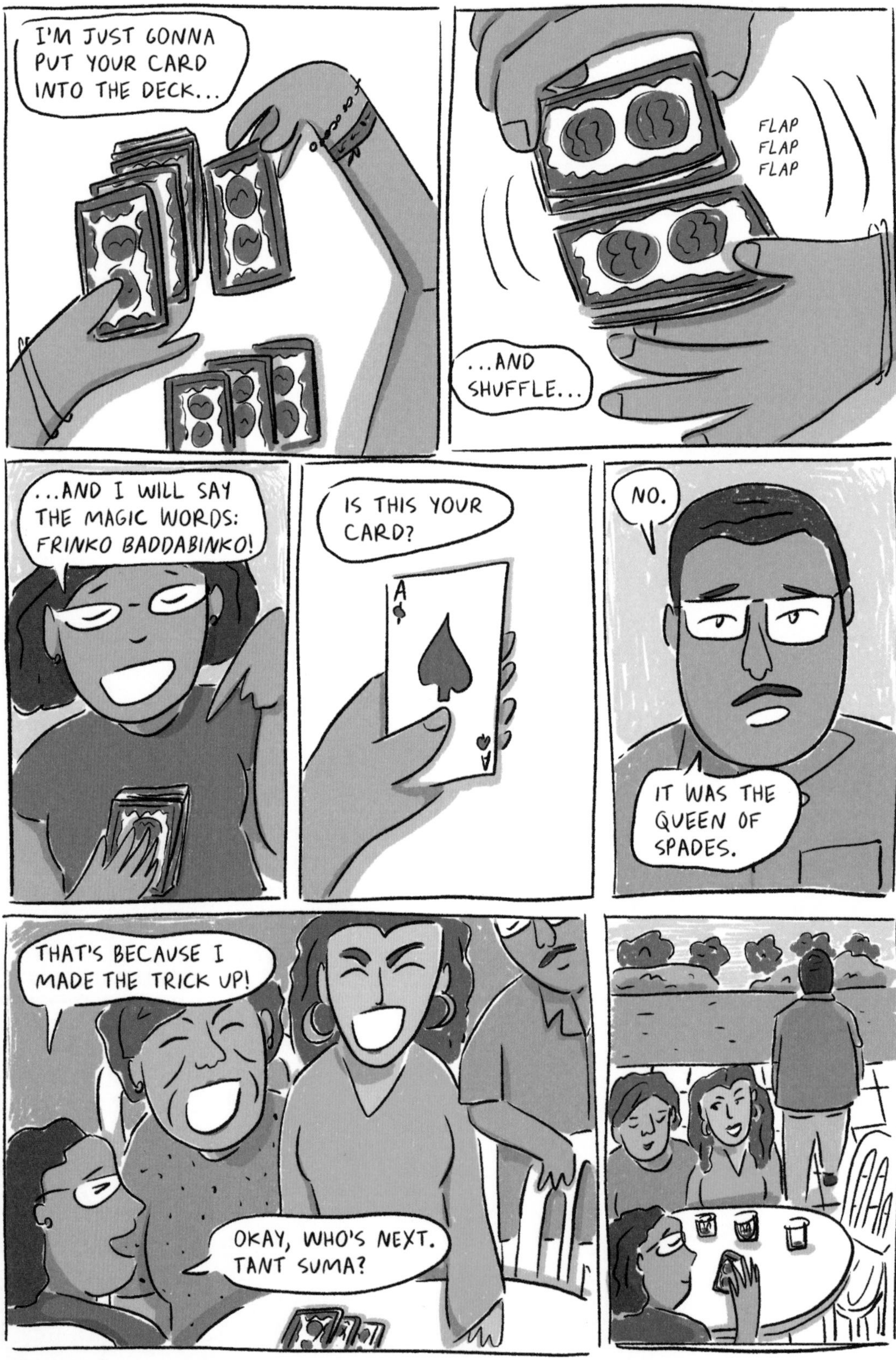
I'M JUST GONNA PUT YOUR CARD INTO THE DECK...
FLAP FLAP FLAP
...AND SHUFFLE...
...AND I WILL SAY THE MAGIC WORDS: FRINKO BADDABINKO!
IS THIS YOUR CARD?
A
A
NO.
IT WAS THE QUEEN OF SPADES.
THAT'S BECAUSE I MADE THE TRICK UP!
OKAY, WHO'S NEXT. TANT SUMA?

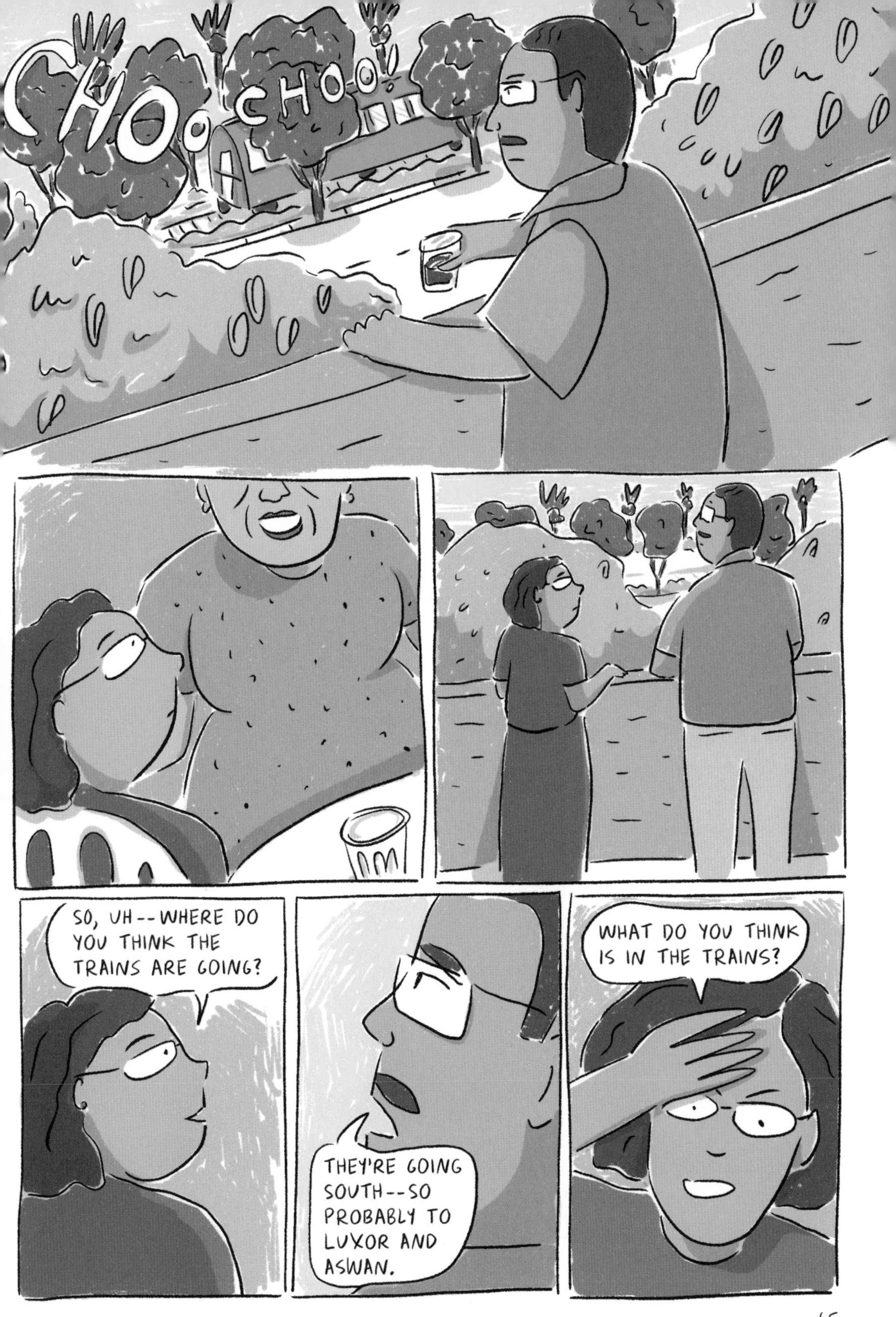
CHOO CHOO
SO, UH--WHERE DO YOU THINK THE TRAINS ARE GOING?
THEY'RE GOING SOUTH--SO PROBABLY TO LUXOR AND ASWAN.
WHAT DO YOU THINK IS IN THE TRAINS?

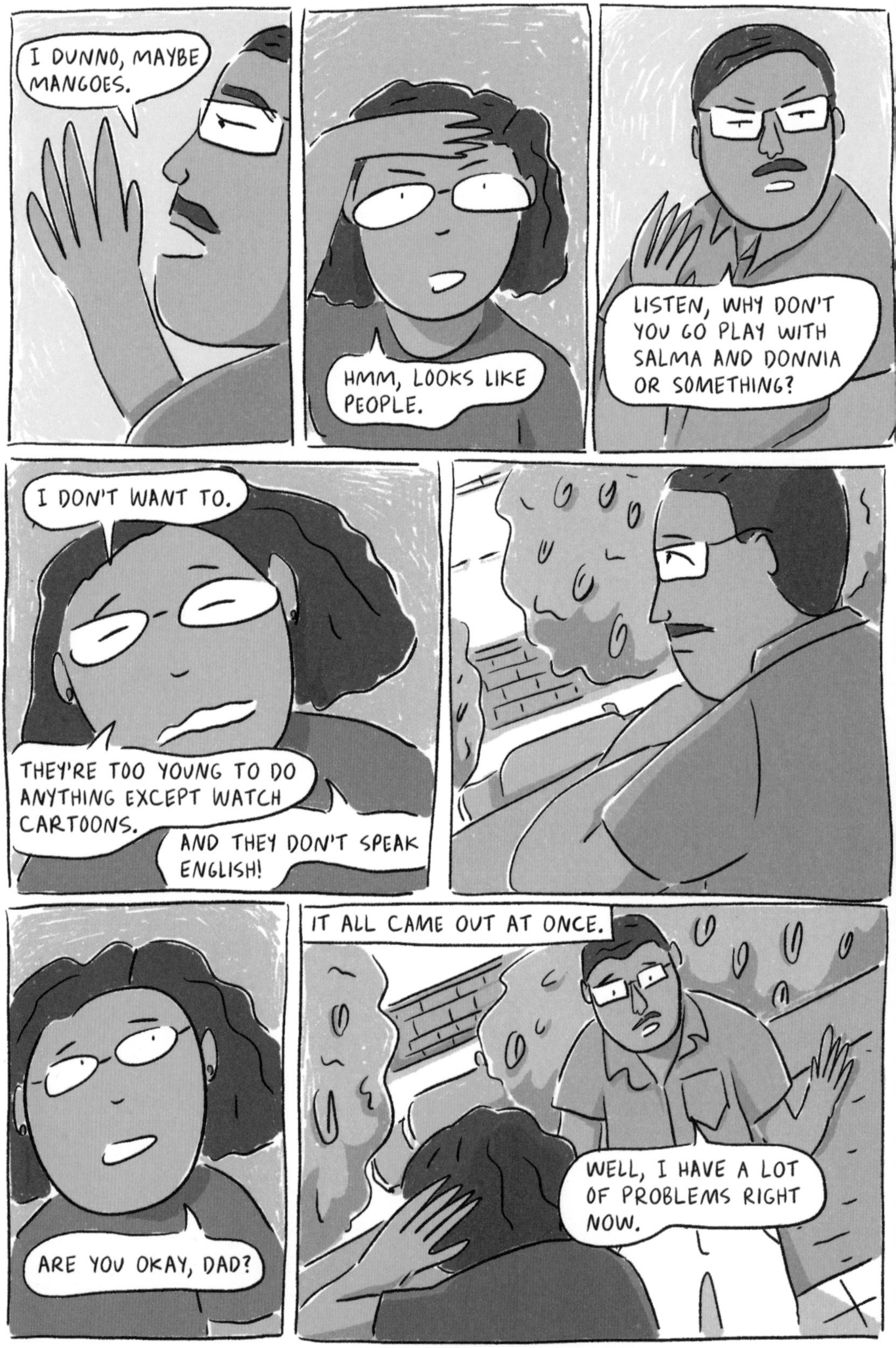
I DUNNO, MAYBE MANGOES.
HMM, LOOKS LIKE PEOPLE.
LISTEN, WHY DON'T YOU GO PLAY WITH SALMA AND DONNIA OR SOMETHING?
I DON'T WANT TO.
THEY'RE TOO YOUNG TO DO ANYTHING EXCEPT WATCH CARTOONS.
AND THEY DON'T SPEAK ENGLISH!
ARE YOU OKAY, DAD?
IT ALL CAME OUT AT ONCE.
WELL, I HAVE A LOT OF PROBLEMS RIGHT NOW.

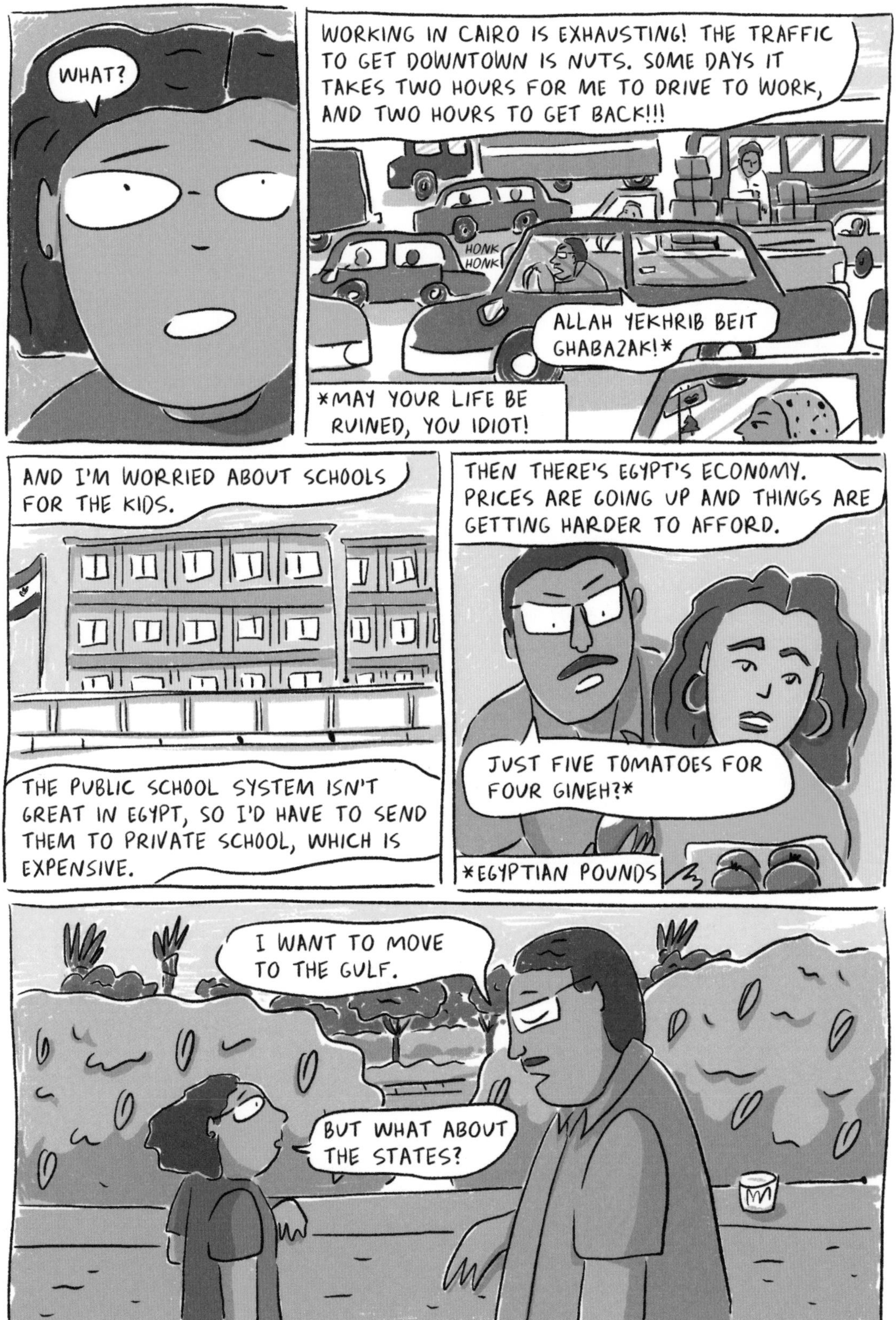
WHAT?
WORKING IN CAIRO IS EXHAUSTING! THE TRAFFIC TO GET DOWNTOWN IS NUTS. SOME DAYS IT TAKES TWO HOURS FOR ME TO DRIVE TO WORK, AND TWO HOURS TO GET BACK!!!
HONK HONK
ALLAH YEKHRIB BEIT GHABAZAK!*
*MAY YOUR LIFE BE RUINED, YOU IDIOT!
AND I'M WORRIED ABOUT SCHOOLS FOR THE KIDS.
THE PUBLIC SCHOOL SYSTEM ISN'T GREAT IN EGYPT, SO I'D HAVE TO SEND THEM TO PRIVATE SCHOOL, WHICH IS EXPENSIVE.
THEN THERE'S EGYPT'S ECONOMY. PRICES ARE GOING UP AND THINGS ARE GETTING HARDER TO AFFORD.
JUST FIVE TOMATOES FOR FOUR GINEH?*
*EGYPTIAN POUNDS
I WANT TO MOVE TO THE GULF.
BUT WHAT ABOUT THE STATES?

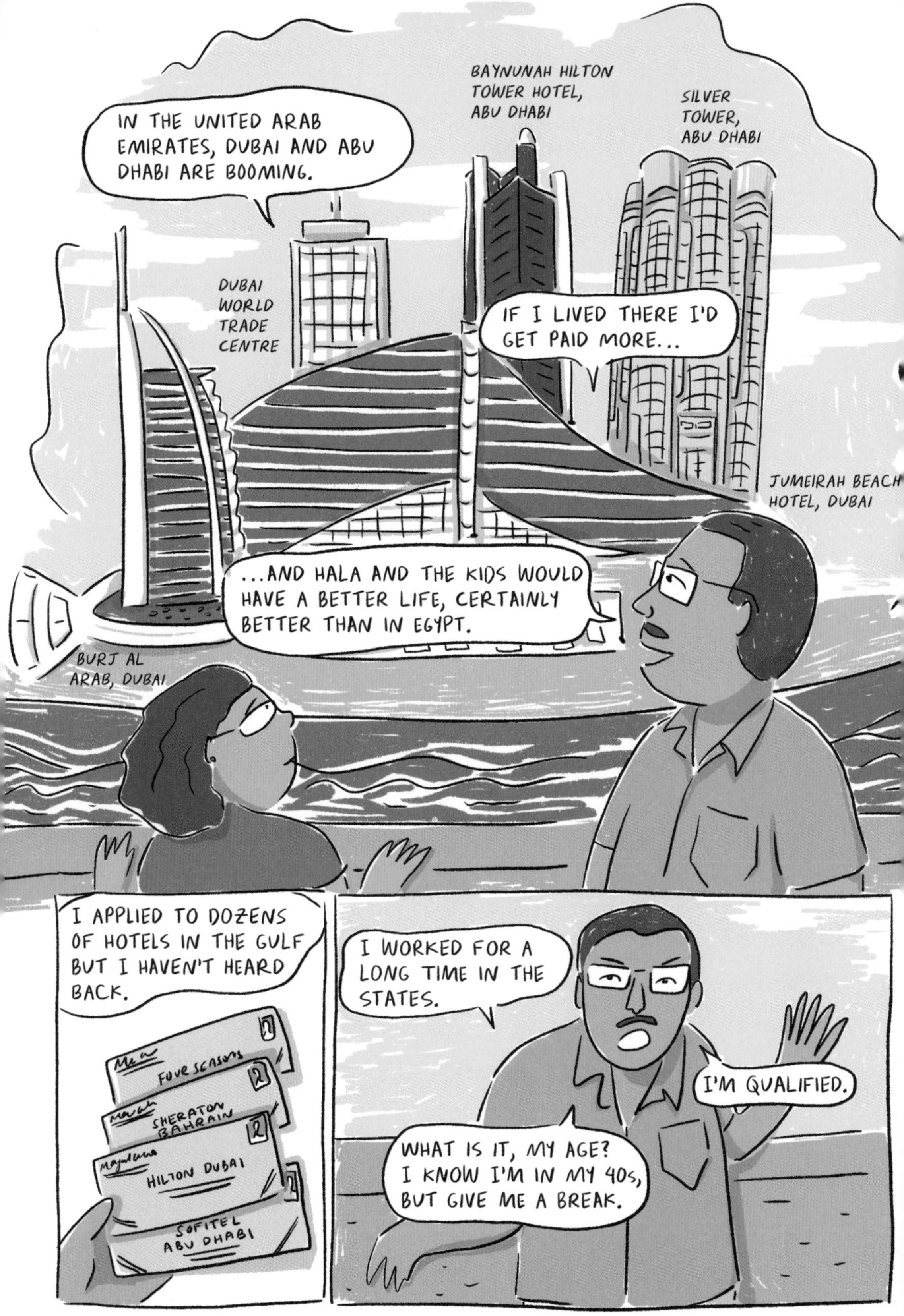
IN THE UNITED ARAB EMIRATES, DUBAI AND ABU DHABI ARE BOOMING.
BAYNUNAH HILTON TOWER HOTEL, ABU DHABI
SILVER TOWER, ABU DHABI
DUBAI WORLD TRADE CENTRE
IF I LIVED THERE I'D GET PAID MORE...
JUMEIRAH BEACH HOTEL, DUBAI
...AND HALA AND THE KIDS WOULD HAVE A BETTER LIFE, CERTAINLY BETTER THAN IN EGYPT.
BURJ AL ARAB, DUBAI
I APPLIED TO DOZENS OF HOTELS IN THE GULF BUT I HAVEN'T HEARD BACK.
FOUR SEASONS
SHERATON BAHRAIN
HILTON DUBAI
SOFITEL ABU DHABI
I WORKED FOR A LONG TIME IN THE STATES.
I'M QUALIFIED.
WHAT IS IT, MY AGE? I KNOW I'M IN MY 40s, BUT GIVE ME A BREAK.

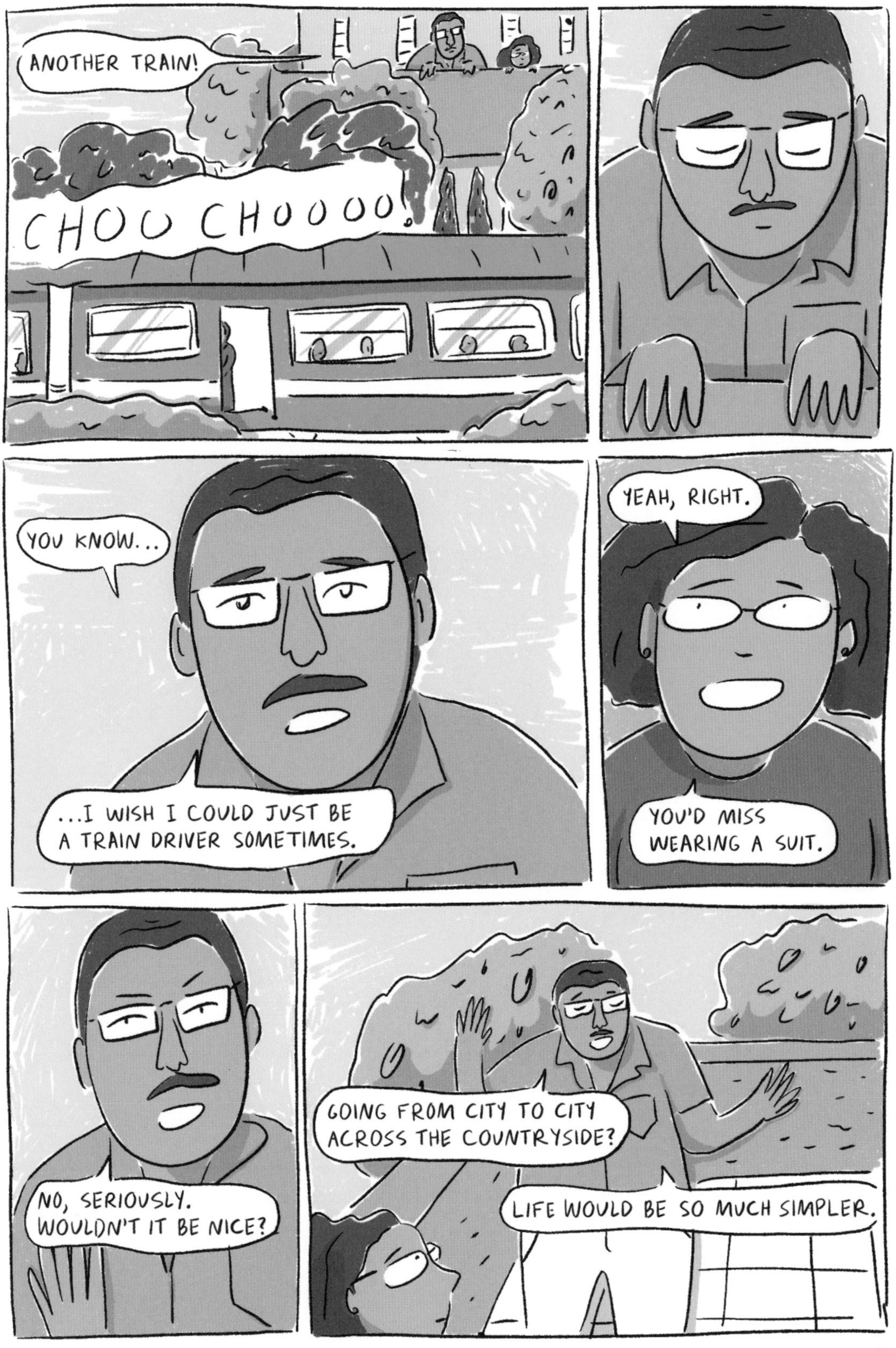
ANOTHER TRAIN!
CHOO CHOOOOO!
YOU KNOW...
...I WISH I COULD JUST BE A TRAIN DRIVER SOMETIMES.
YEAH, RIGHT.
YOU'D MISS WEARING A SUIT.
NO, SERIOUSLY. WOULDN'T IT BE NICE?
GOING FROM CITY TO CITY ACROSS THE COUNTRYSIDE?
LIFE WOULD BE SO MUCH SIMPLER.

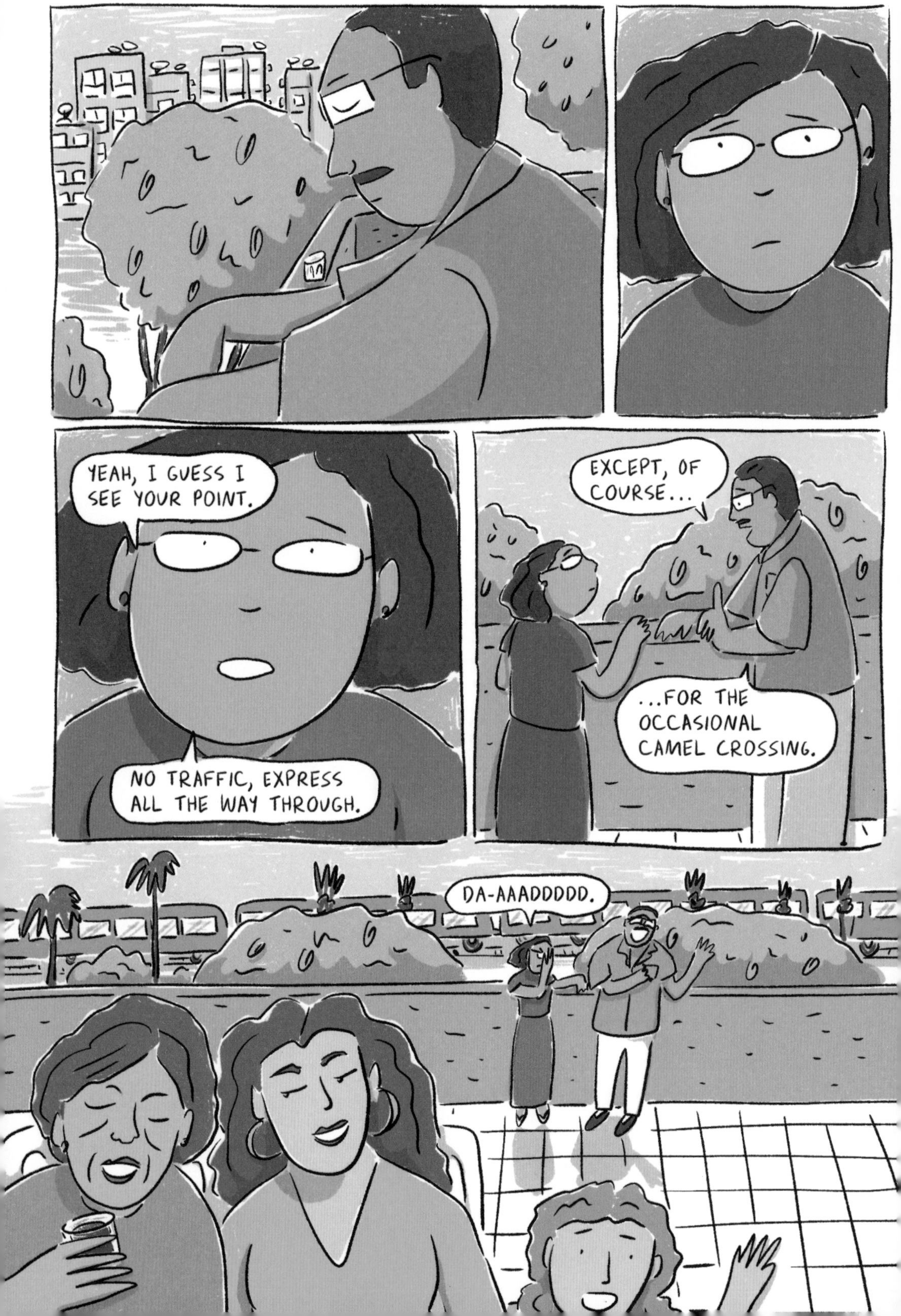
YEAH, I GUESS I SEE YOUR POINT.
NO TRAFFIC, EXPRESS ALL THE WAY THROUGH.
EXCEPT, OF COURSE...
...FOR THE OCCASIONAL CAMEL CROSSING.
DA-AAADDDDD.

CHAPTER 4

Amoora

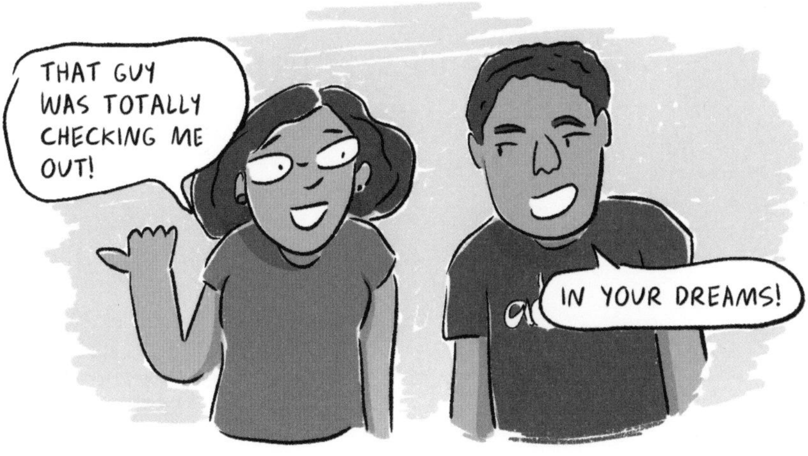
THAT GUY WAS TOTALLY CHECKING ME OUT!
IN YOUR DREAMS!

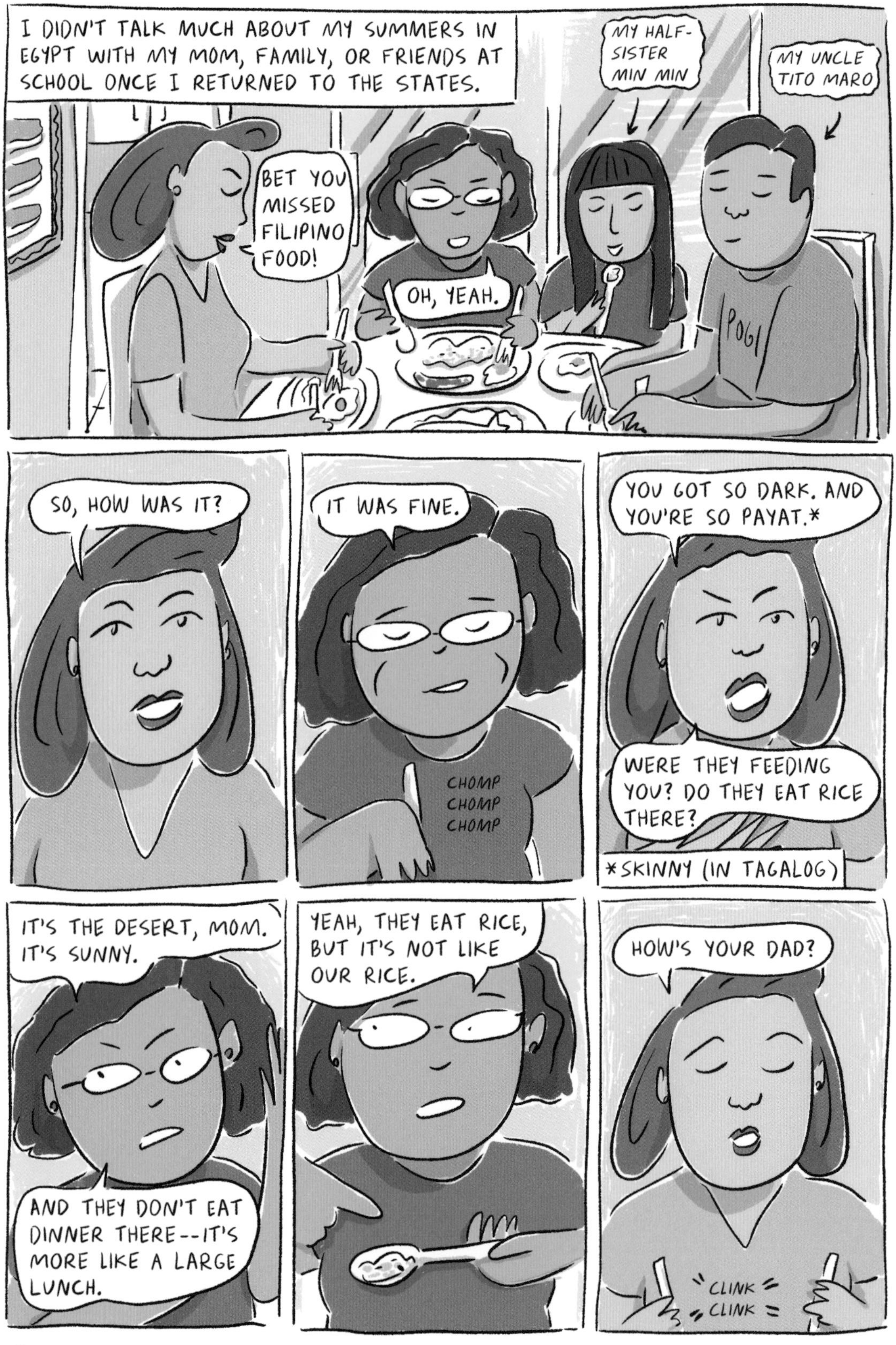
I DIDN'T TALK MUCH ABOUT MY SUMMERS IN EGYPT WITH MY MOM, FAMILY, OR FRIENDS AT SCHOOL ONCE I RETURNED TO THE STATES.
MY HALF-SISTER MIN MIN
MY UNCLE TITO MARO
BET YOU MISSED FILIPINO FOOD!
OH, YEAH.
POGI
SO, HOW WAS IT?
IT WAS FINE.
CHOMP CHOMP CHOMP
YOU GOT SO DARK. AND YOU'RE SO PAYAT.*
WERE THEY FEEDING YOU? DO THEY EAT RICE THERE?
*SKINNY (IN TAGALOG)
IT'S THE DESERT, MOM. IT'S SUNNY.
AND THEY DON'T EAT DINNER THERE--IT'S MORE LIKE A LARGE LUNCH.
YEAH, THEY EAT RICE, BUT IT'S NOT LIKE OUR RICE.
HOW'S YOUR DAD?
CLINK CLINK

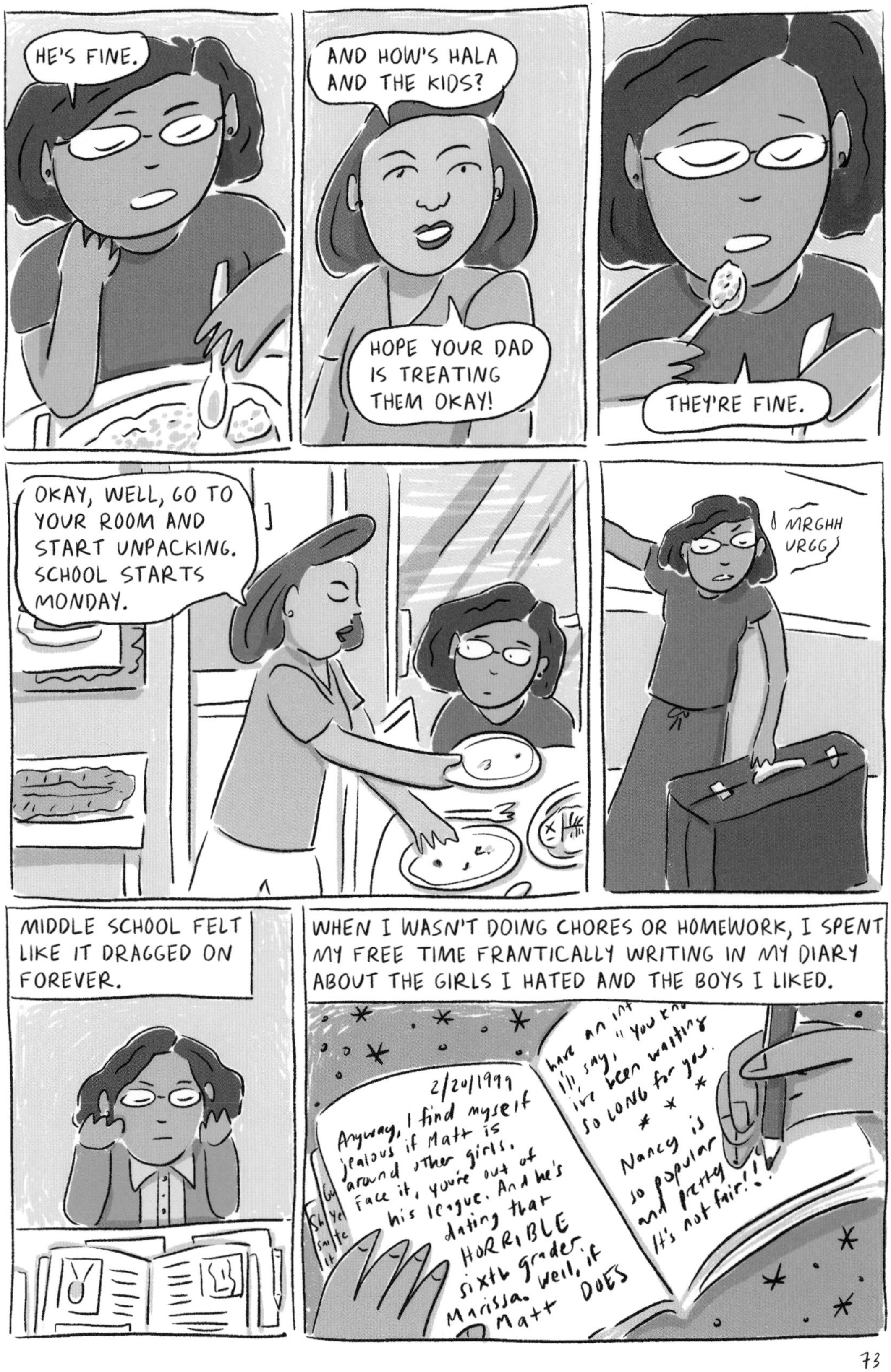

HE'S FINE.
AND HOW'S HALA AND THE KIDS?
HOPE YOUR DAD IS TREATING THEM OKAY!
THEY'RE FINE.
OKAY, WELL, GO TO YOUR ROOM AND START UNPACKING. SCHOOL STARTS MONDAY.
MRGHH URGG
MIDDLE SCHOOL FELT LIKE IT DRAGGED ON FOREVER.
WHEN I WASN'T DOING CHORES OR HOMEWORK, I SPENT MY FREE TIME FRANTICALLY WRITING IN MY DIARY ABOUT THE GIRLS I HATED AND THE BOYS I LIKED.
2/20/1999
Anyway, I find myself jealous if Matt is around other girls. Face it, you're out of his league. And he's dating that HORRIBLE sixth grader Marissa. Well, if Matt DOES
have an int
I'll say, "You kno
I've been waiting
so long for you."
Nancy is so popular and pretty. It's not fair!!!

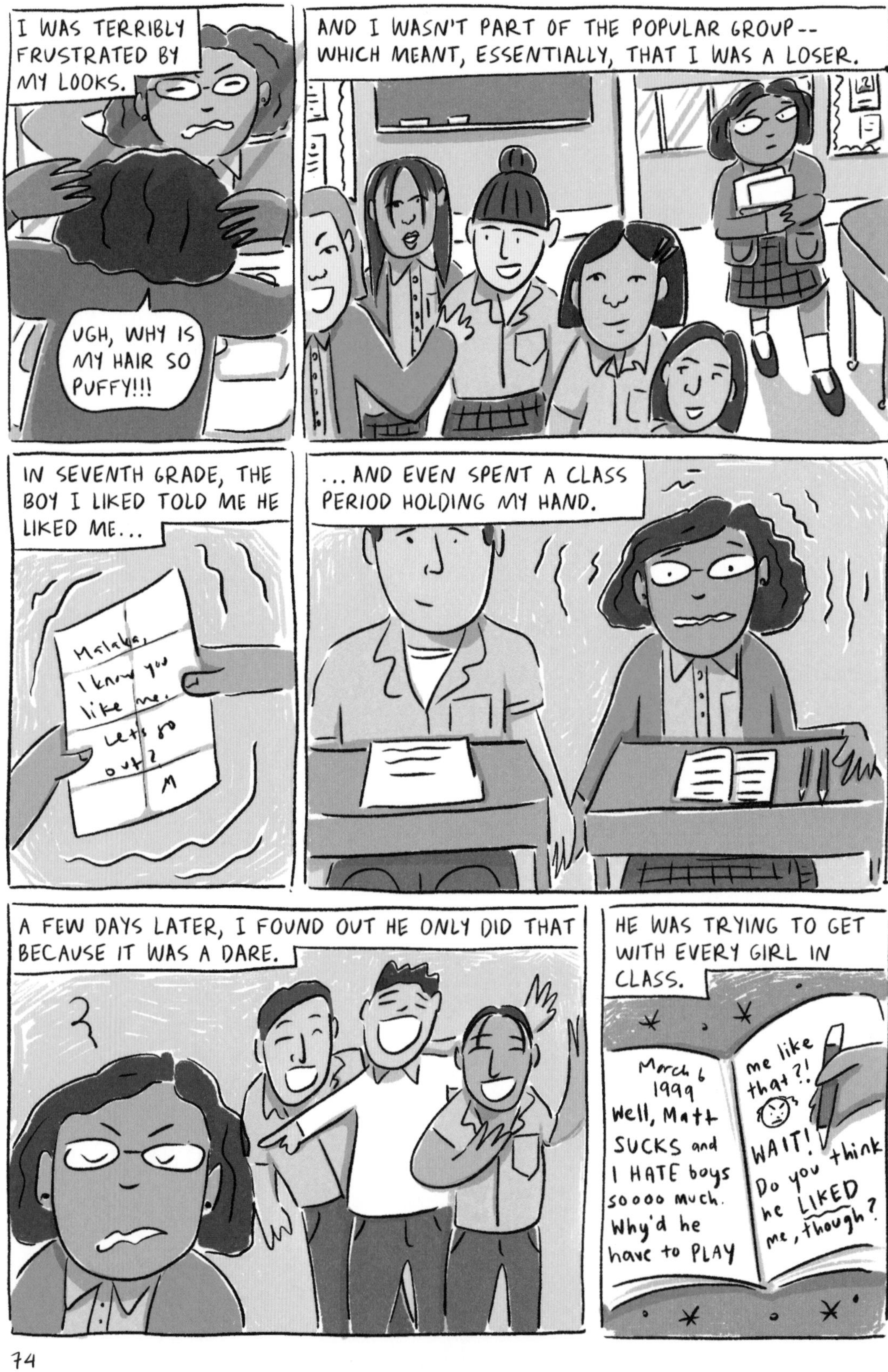
I WAS TERRIBLY FRUSTRATED BY MY LOOKS.
UGH, WHY IS MY HAIR SO PUFFY!!!
AND I WASN'T PART OF THE POPULAR GROUP-- WHICH MEANT, ESSENTIALLY, THAT I WAS A LOSER.
IN SEVENTH GRADE, THE BOY I LIKED TOLD ME HE LIKED ME...
Malaka, I know you like me. Let's go out? M
...AND EVEN SPENT A CLASS PERIOD HOLDING MY HAND.
A FEW DAYS LATER, I FOUND OUT HE ONLY DID THAT BECAUSE IT WAS A DARE.
HE WAS TRYING TO GET WITH EVERY GIRL IN CLASS.
March 6 1999 Well, Matt SUCKS and I HATE boys soooo much. Why'd he have to PLAY
me like that?!
WAIT! Do you think he LIKED me, though?

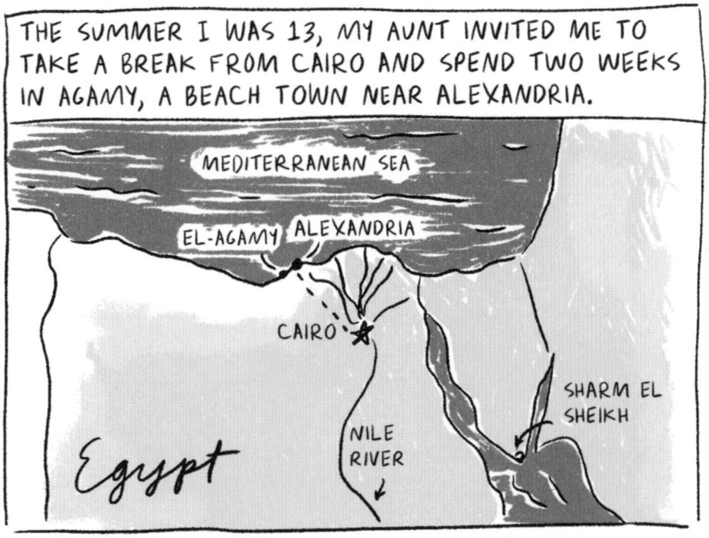
THE SUMMER I WAS 13, MY AUNT INVITED ME TO TAKE A BREAK FROM CAIRO AND SPEND TWO WEEKS IN AGAMY, A BEACH TOWN NEAR ALEXANDRIA.
MEDITERRANEAN SEA
EL-AGAMY
ALEXANDRIA
CAIRO
SHARM EL SHEIKH
NILE RIVER
Egypt

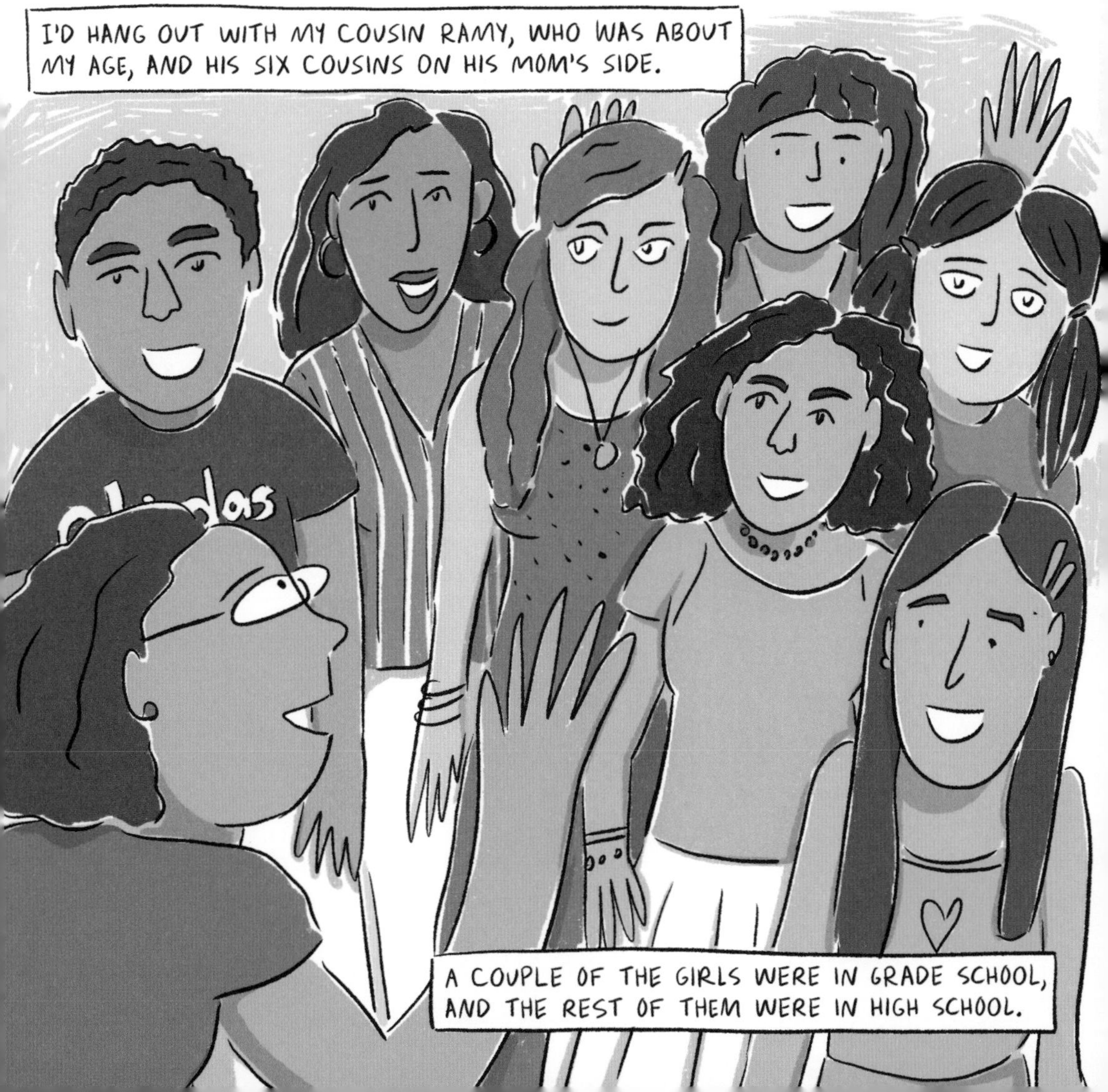
I'D HANG OUT WITH MY COUSIN RAMY, WHO WAS ABOUT MY AGE, AND HIS SIX COUSINS ON HIS MOM'S SIDE.
A COUPLE OF THE GIRLS WERE IN GRADE SCHOOL, AND THE REST OF THEM WERE IN HIGH SCHOOL.

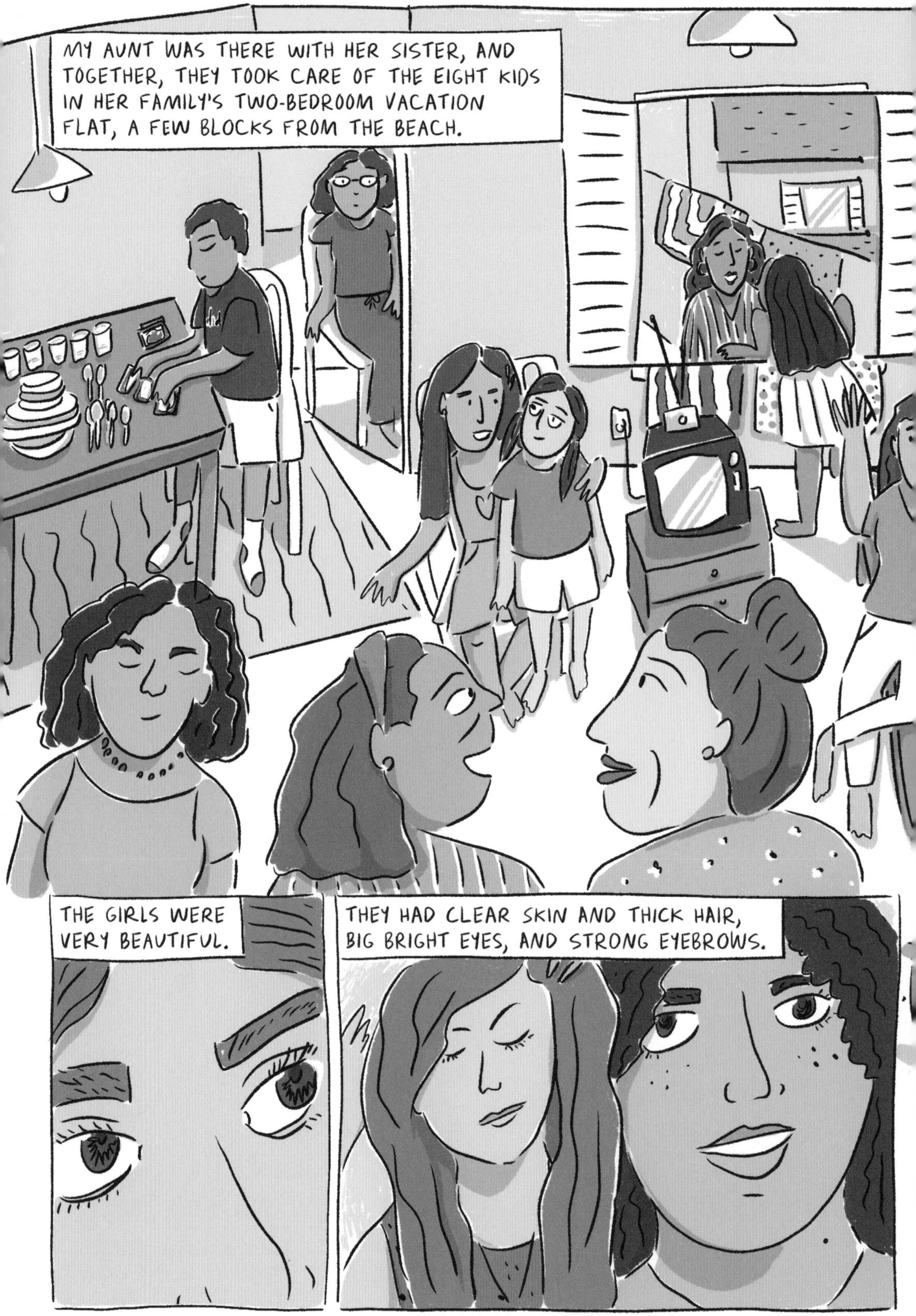
MY AUNT WAS THERE WITH HER SISTER, AND TOGETHER, THEY TOOK CARE OF THE EIGHT KIDS IN HER FAMILY'S TWO-BEDROOM VACATION FLAT, A FEW BLOCKS FROM THE BEACH.
THE GIRLS WERE VERY BEAUTIFUL.
THEY HAD CLEAR SKIN AND THICK HAIR, BIG BRIGHT EYES, AND STRONG EYEBROWS.

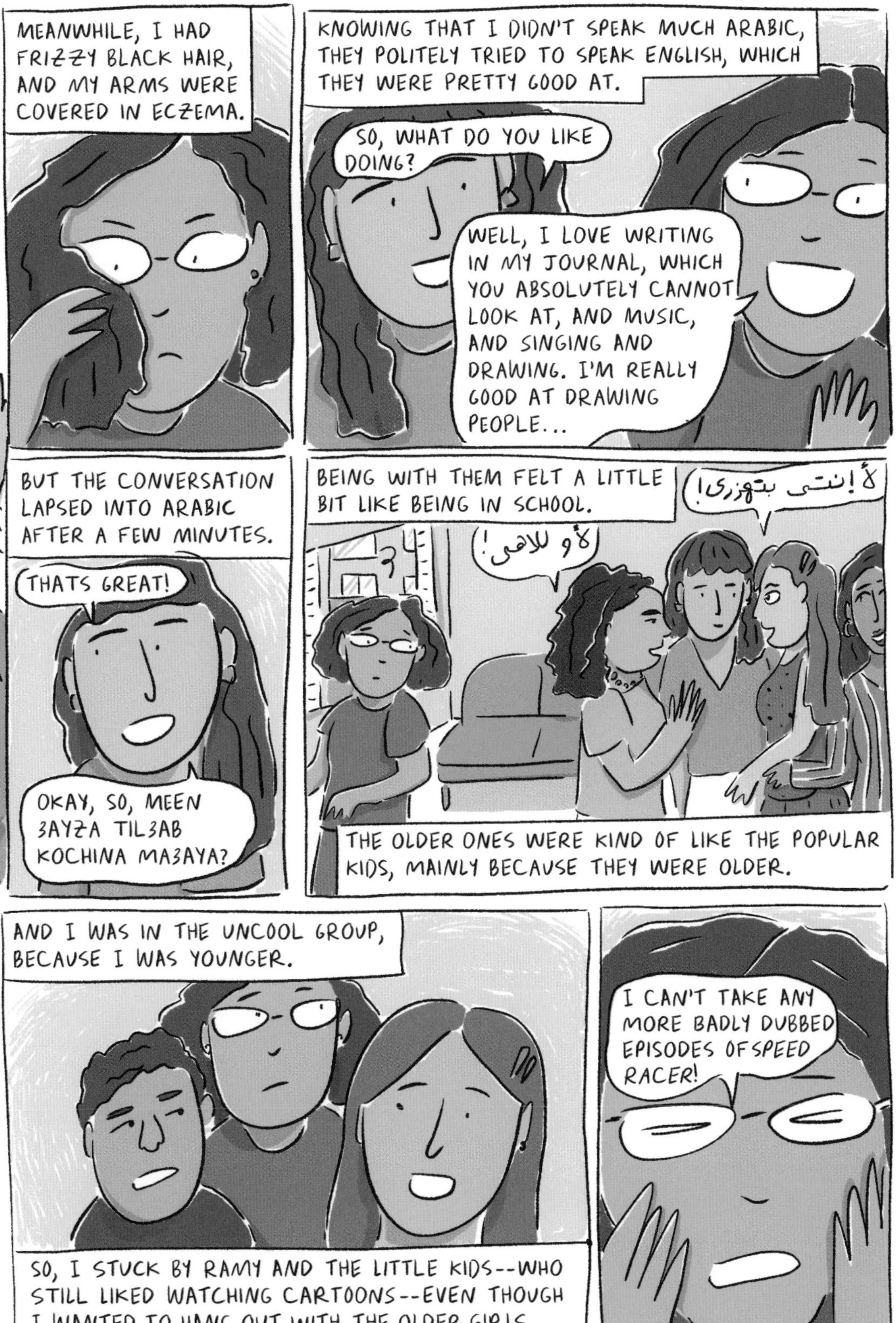
MEANWHILE, I HAD FRIZZY BLACK HAIR, AND MY ARMS WERE COVERED IN ECZEMA.
KNOWING THAT I DIDN'T SPEAK MUCH ARABIC, THEY POLITELY TRIED TO SPEAK ENGLISH, WHICH THEY WERE PRETTY GOOD AT.
SO, WHAT DO YOU LIKE DOING?
WELL, I LOVE WRITING IN MY JOURNAL, WHICH YOU ABSOLUTELY CANNOT LOOK AT, AND MUSIC, AND SINGING AND DRAWING. I'M REALLY GOOD AT DRAWING PEOPLE...
BUT THE CONVERSATION LAPSED INTO ARABIC AFTER A FEW MINUTES.
THATS GREAT!
OKAY, SO, MEEN 3AYZA TIL3AB KOCHINA MA3AYA?
BEING WITH THEM FELT A LITTLE BIT LIKE BEING IN SCHOOL.
لأ! إنتى بتهزرى!
لأ و للاهى!
THE OLDER ONES WERE KIND OF LIKE THE POPULAR KIDS, MAINLY BECAUSE THEY WERE OLDER.
AND I WAS IN THE UNCOOL GROUP, BECAUSE I WAS YOUNGER.
SO, I STUCK BY RAMY AND THE LITTLE KIDS--WHO STILL LIKED WATCHING CARTOONS--EVEN THOUGH I WANTED TO HANG OUT WITH THE OLDER GIRLS.
I CAN'T TAKE ANY MORE BADLY DUBBED EPISODES OF SPEED RACER!

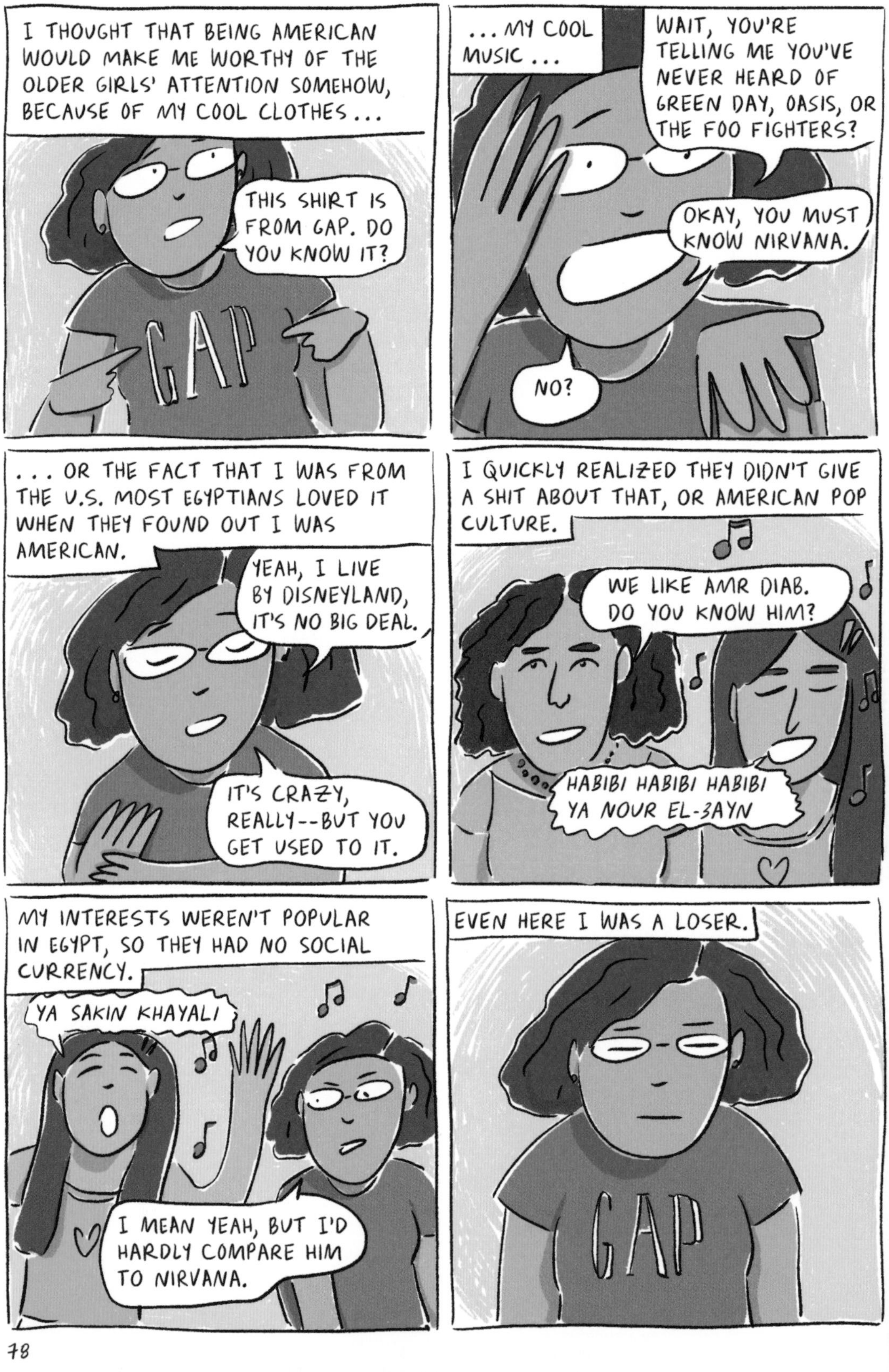
I THOUGHT THAT BEING AMERICAN WOULD MAKE ME WORTHY OF THE OLDER GIRLS' ATTENTION SOMEHOW, BECAUSE OF MY COOL CLOTHES...
THIS SHIRT IS FROM GAP. DO YOU KNOW IT?
GAP
...MY COOL MUSIC...
WAIT, YOU'RE TELLING ME YOU'VE NEVER HEARD OF GREEN DAY, OASIS, OR THE FOO FIGHTERS?
OKAY, YOU MUST KNOW NIRVANA.
NO?
...OR THE FACT THAT I WAS FROM THE U.S. MOST EGYPTIANS LOVED IT WHEN THEY FOUND OUT I WAS AMERICAN.
YEAH, I LIVE BY DISNEYLAND, IT'S NO BIG DEAL.
IT'S CRAZY, REALLY--BUT YOU GET USED TO IT.
I QUICKLY REALIZED THEY DIDN'T GIVE A SHIT ABOUT THAT, OR AMERICAN POP CULTURE.
WE LIKE AMR DIAB. DO YOU KNOW HIM?
HABIBI HABIBI HABIBI YA NOUR EL-3AYN
MY INTERESTS WEREN'T POPULAR IN EGYPT, SO THEY HAD NO SOCIAL CURRENCY.
YA SAKIN KHAYALI
I MEAN YEAH, BUT I'D HARDLY COMPARE HIM TO NIRVANA.
EVEN HERE I WAS A LOSER.
GAP

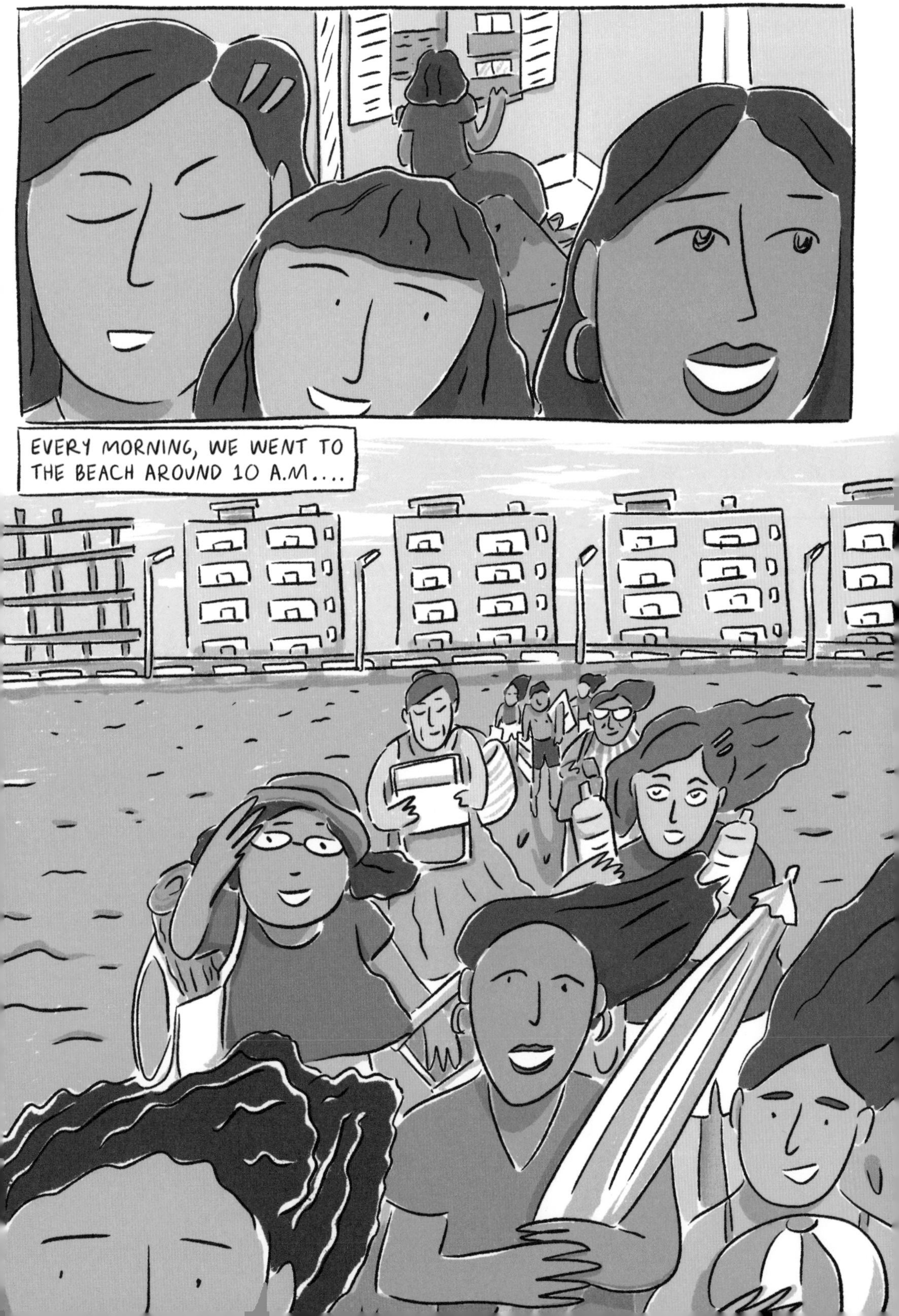
EVERY MORNING, WE WENT TO THE BEACH AROUND 10 A.M....

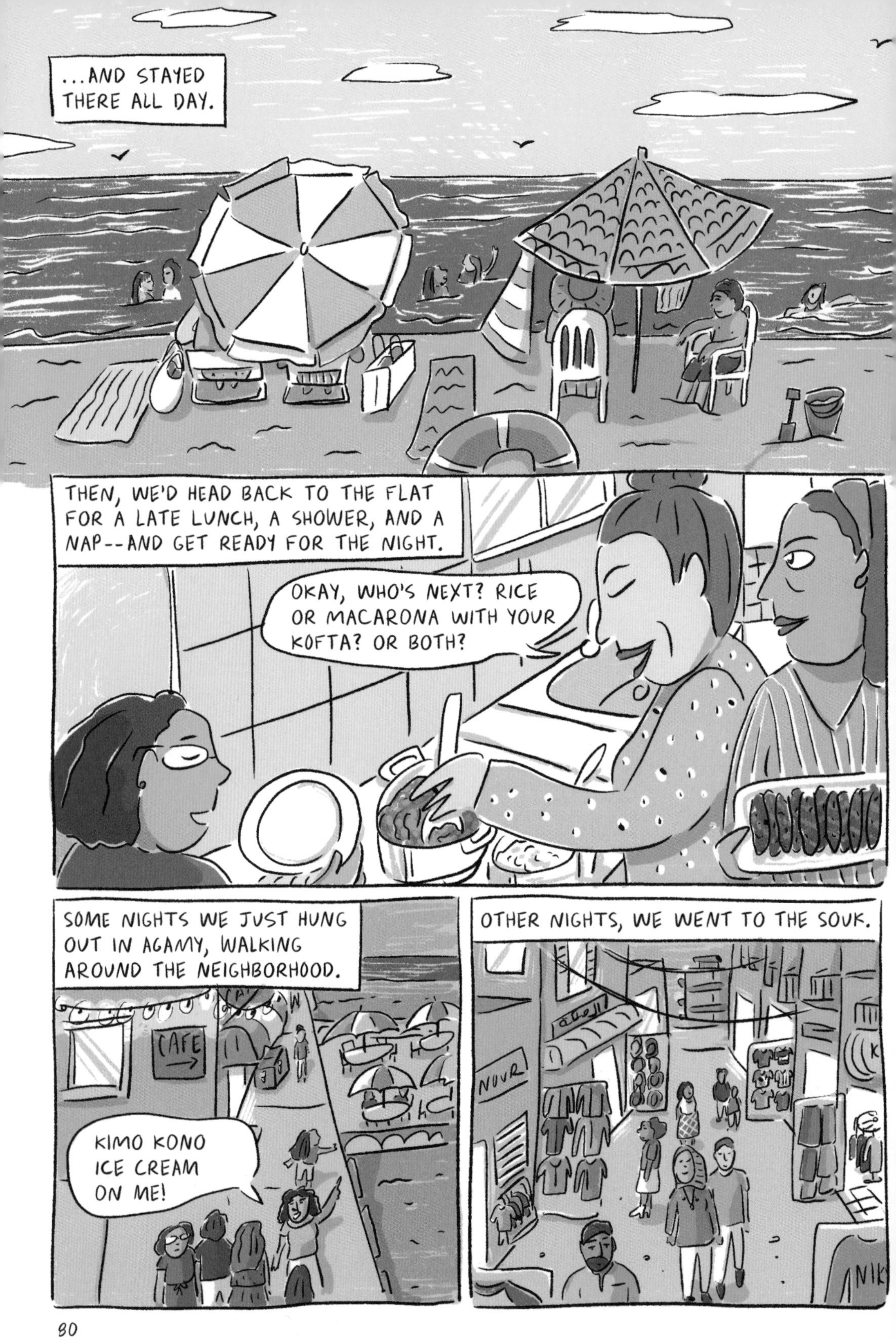
...AND STAYED THERE ALL DAY.
THEN, WE'D HEAD BACK TO THE FLAT FOR A LATE LUNCH, A SHOWER, AND A NAP--AND GET READY FOR THE NIGHT.
OKAY, WHO'S NEXT? RICE OR MACARONA WITH YOUR KOFTA? OR BOTH?
SOME NIGHTS WE JUST HUNG OUT IN AGAMY, WALKING AROUND THE NEIGHBORHOOD.
CAFE
KIMO KONO ICE CREAM ON ME!
OTHER NIGHTS, WE WENT TO THE SOUK.
NUVR

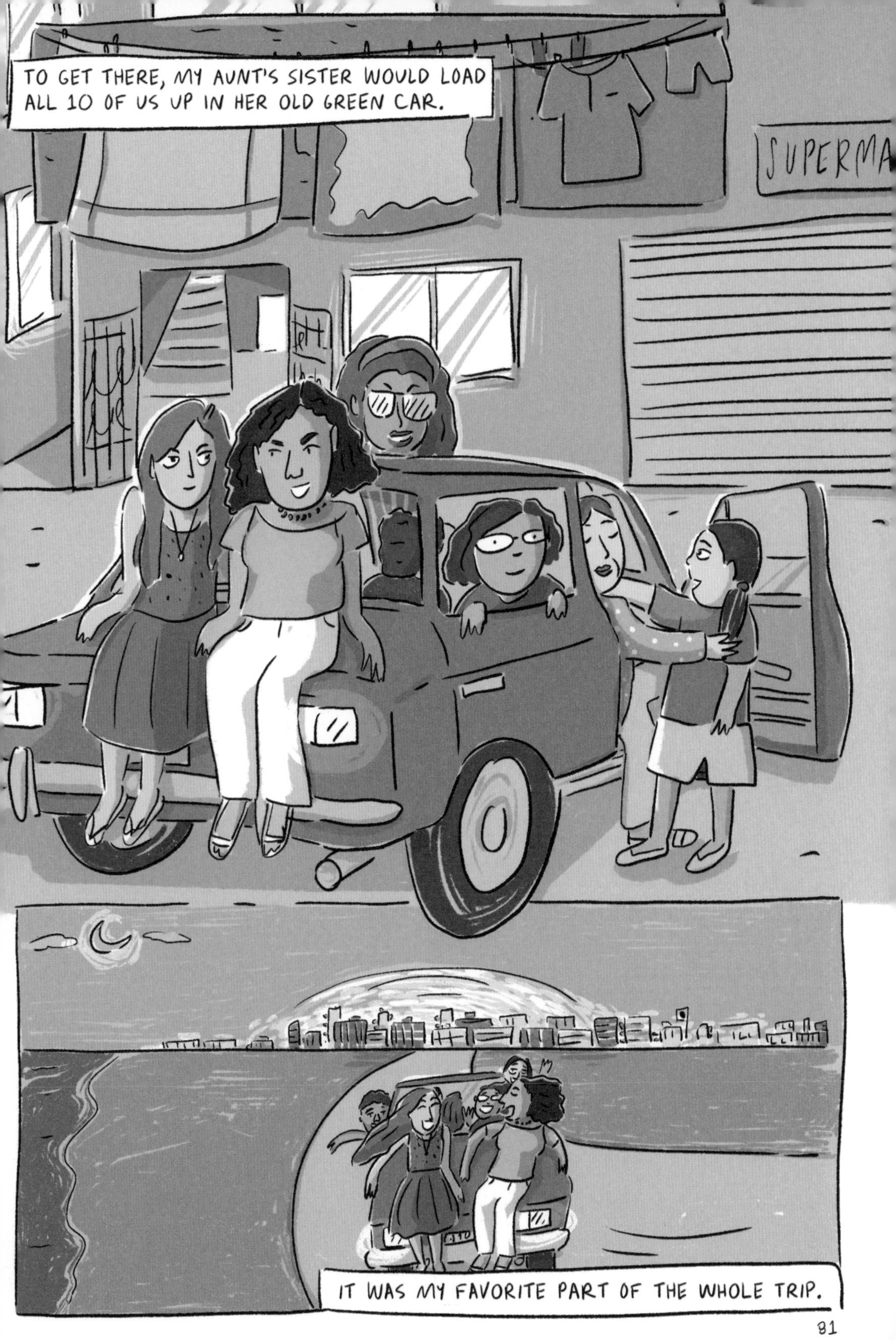
TO GET THERE, MY AUNT'S SISTER WOULD LOAD ALL 10 OF US UP IN HER OLD GREEN CAR.
SUPERMA
IT WAS MY FAVORITE PART OF THE WHOLE TRIP.

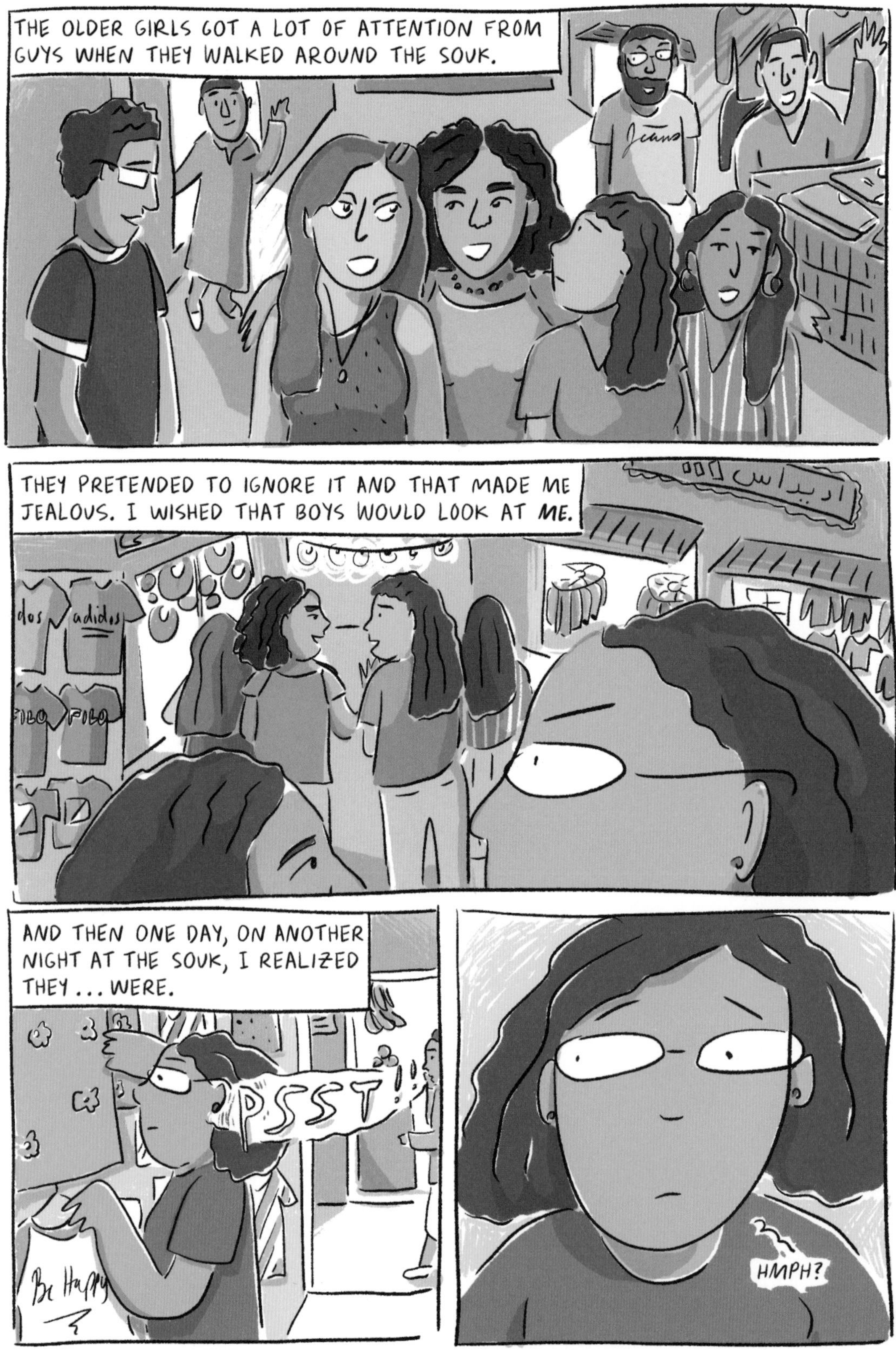
THE OLDER GIRLS GOT A LOT OF ATTENTION FROM GUYS WHEN THEY WALKED AROUND THE SOUK.
Jeans
THEY PRETENDED TO IGNORE IT AND THAT MADE ME JEALOUS. I WISHED THAT BOYS WOULD LOOK AT **ME**.
dos
adidas
FILO
FILO
AND THEN ONE DAY, ON ANOTHER NIGHT AT THE SOUK, I REALIZED THEY . . . WERE.
PSST!
Be Happy
HMPH?

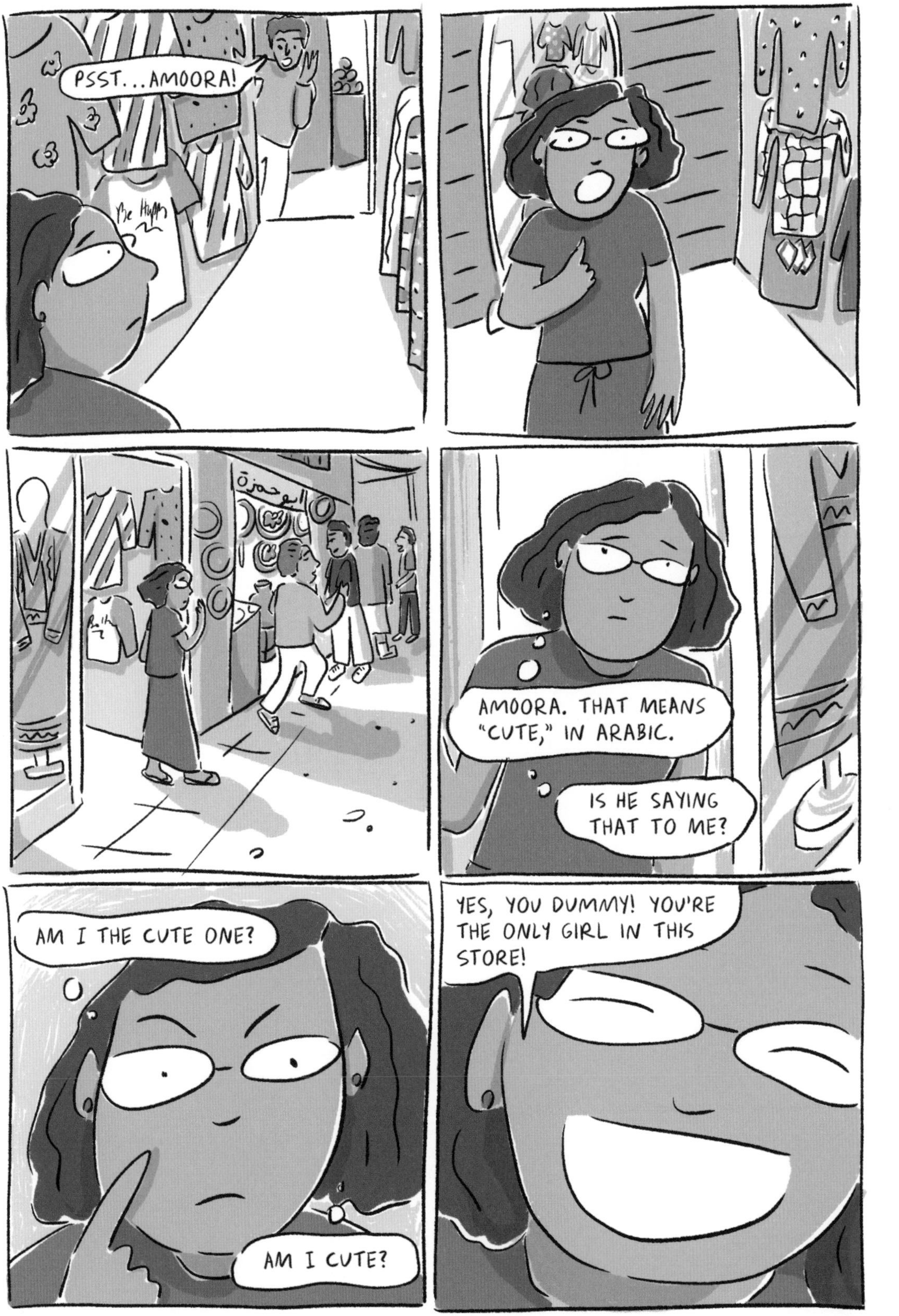
PSST...AMOORA!
AMOORA. THAT MEANS "CUTE," IN ARABIC.
IS HE SAYING THAT TO ME?
AM I THE CUTE ONE?
AM I CUTE?
YES, YOU DUMMY! YOU'RE THE ONLY GIRL IN THIS STORE!

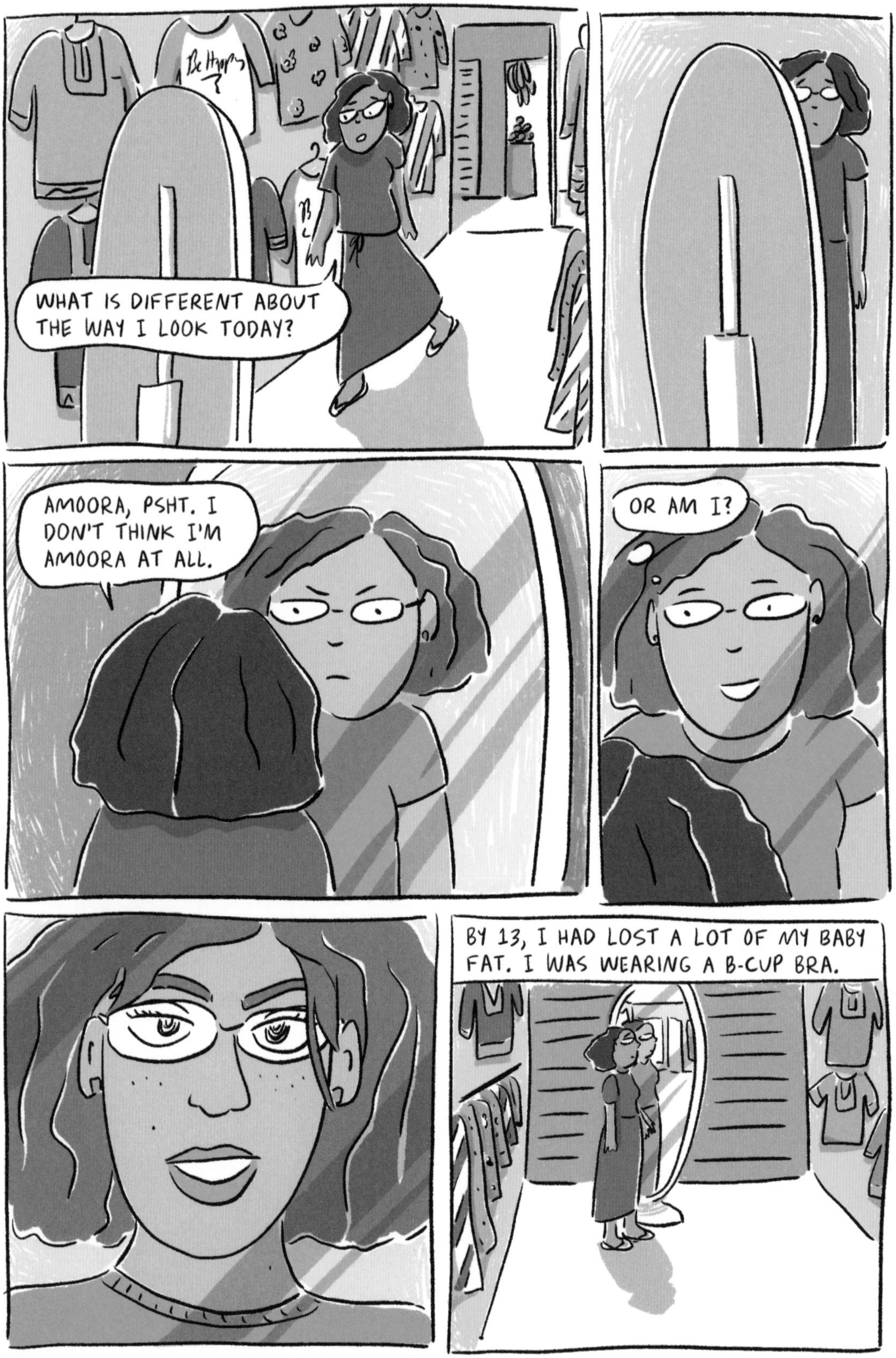

WHAT IS DIFFERENT ABOUT THE WAY I LOOK TODAY?
AMOORA, PSHT. I DON'T THINK I'M AMOORA AT ALL.
OR AM I?
BY 13, I HAD LOST A LOT OF MY BABY FAT. I WAS WEARING A B-CUP BRA.

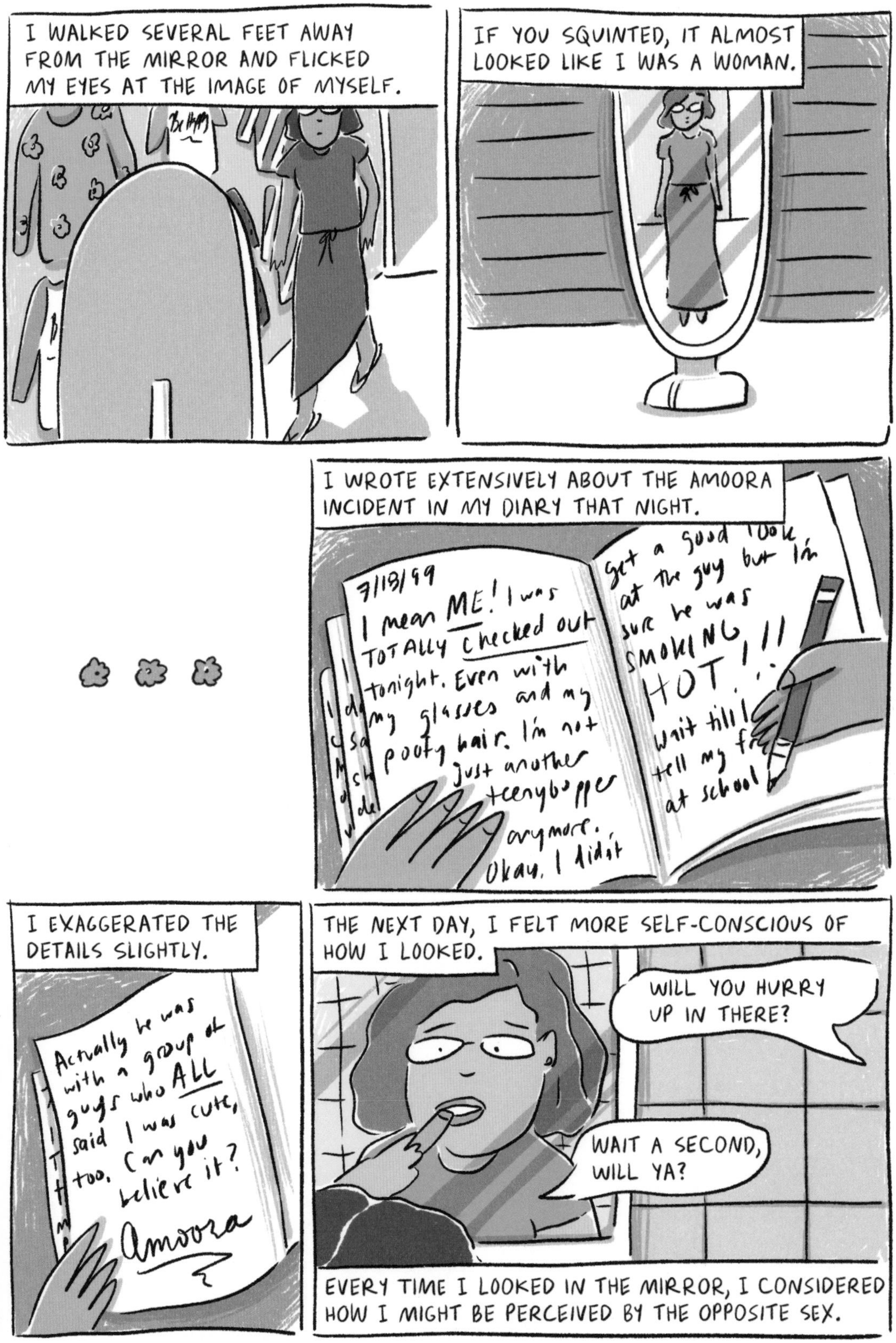

I WALKED SEVERAL FEET AWAY FROM THE MIRROR AND FLICKED MY EYES AT THE IMAGE OF MYSELF.
IF YOU SQUINTED, IT ALMOST LOOKED LIKE I WAS A WOMAN.
I WROTE EXTENSIVELY ABOUT THE AMOORA INCIDENT IN MY DIARY THAT NIGHT.
7/13/99
I mean ME! I was TOTALLY checked out tonight. Even with my glasses and my poofy hair. I'm not just another teenybopper anymore. Okay, I didn't
get a good look at the guy but I'm sure he was SMOKING HOT!!! Wait till I tell my fr at school
I EXAGGERATED THE DETAILS SLIGHTLY.
Actually he was with a group of guys who ALL said I was cute, too. Can you believe it?
Amoora
THE NEXT DAY, I FELT MORE SELF-CONSCIOUS OF HOW I LOOKED.
WILL YOU HURRY UP IN THERE?
WAIT A SECOND, WILL YA?
EVERY TIME I LOOKED IN THE MIRROR, I CONSIDERED HOW I MIGHT BE PERCEIVED BY THE OPPOSITE SEX.

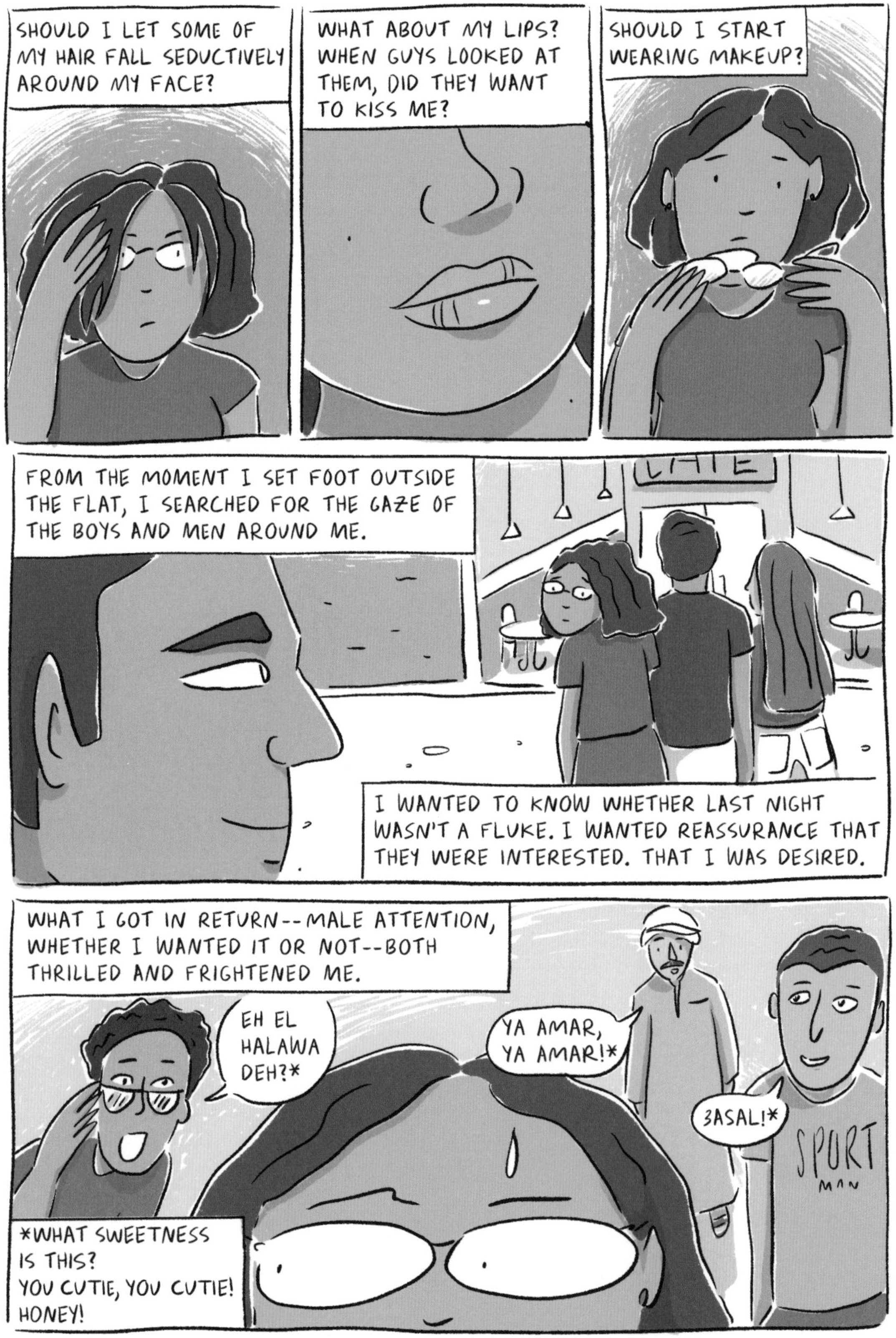
SHOULD I LET SOME OF MY HAIR FALL SEDUCTIVELY AROUND MY FACE?
WHAT ABOUT MY LIPS? WHEN GUYS LOOKED AT THEM, DID THEY WANT TO KISS ME?
SHOULD I START WEARING MAKEUP?
FROM THE MOMENT I SET FOOT OUTSIDE THE FLAT, I SEARCHED FOR THE GAZE OF THE BOYS AND MEN AROUND ME.
I WANTED TO KNOW WHETHER LAST NIGHT WASN'T A FLUKE. I WANTED REASSURANCE THAT THEY WERE INTERESTED. THAT I WAS DESIRED.
WHAT I GOT IN RETURN--MALE ATTENTION, WHETHER I WANTED IT OR NOT--BOTH THRILLED AND FRIGHTENED ME.
EH EL HALAWA DEH?*
YA AMAR, YA AMAR!*
3ASAL!*
SPORT
MAN
*WHAT SWEETNESS IS THIS?
YOU CUTIE, YOU CUTIE!
HONEY!

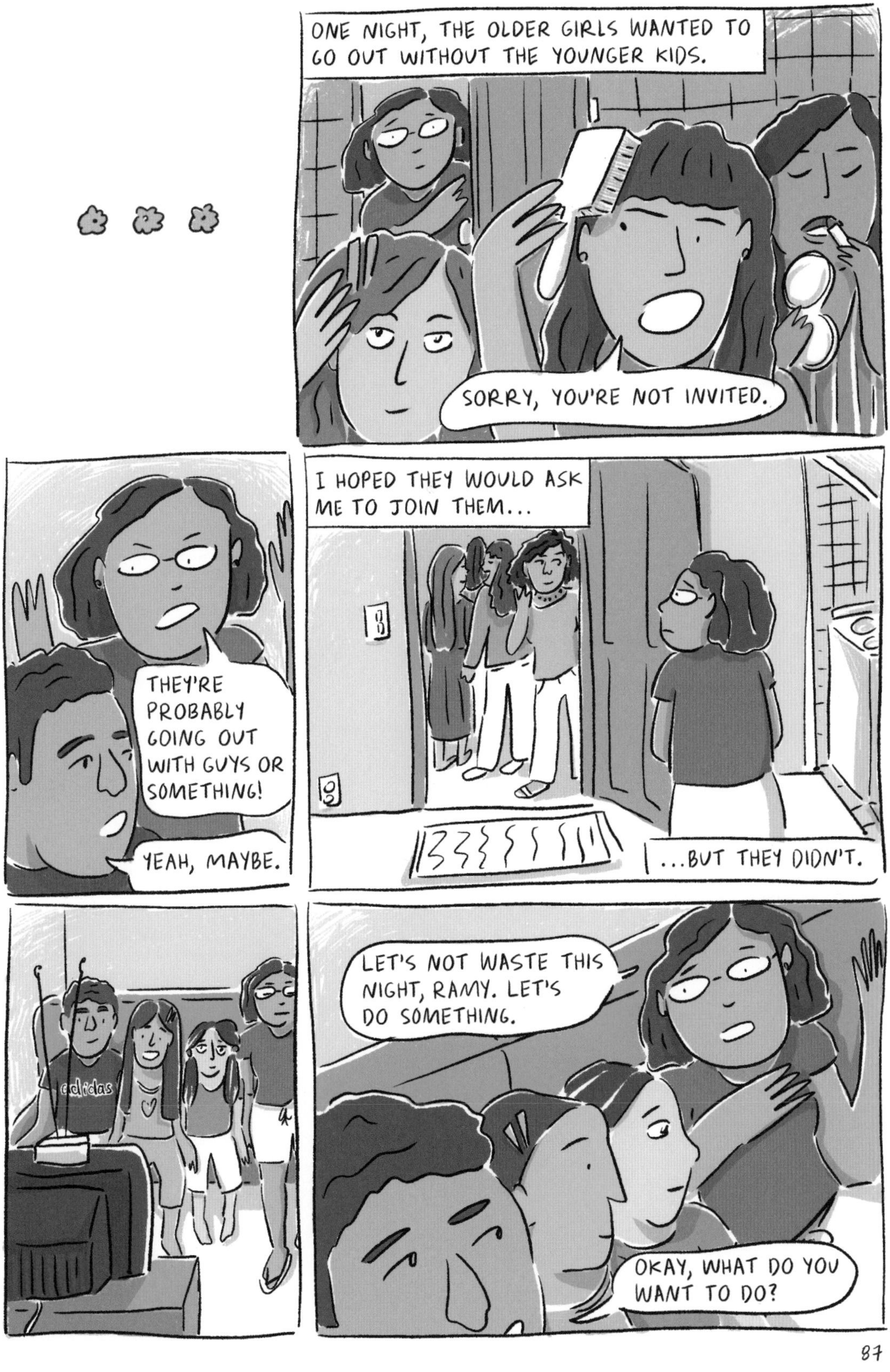

ONE NIGHT, THE OLDER GIRLS WANTED TO GO OUT WITHOUT THE YOUNGER KIDS.
SORRY, YOU'RE NOT INVITED.
THEY'RE PROBABLY GOING OUT WITH GUYS OR SOMETHING!
YEAH, MAYBE.
I HOPED THEY WOULD ASK ME TO JOIN THEM...
...BUT THEY DIDN'T.
adidas
LET'S NOT WASTE THIS NIGHT, RAMY. LET'S DO SOMETHING.
OKAY, WHAT DO YOU WANT TO DO?

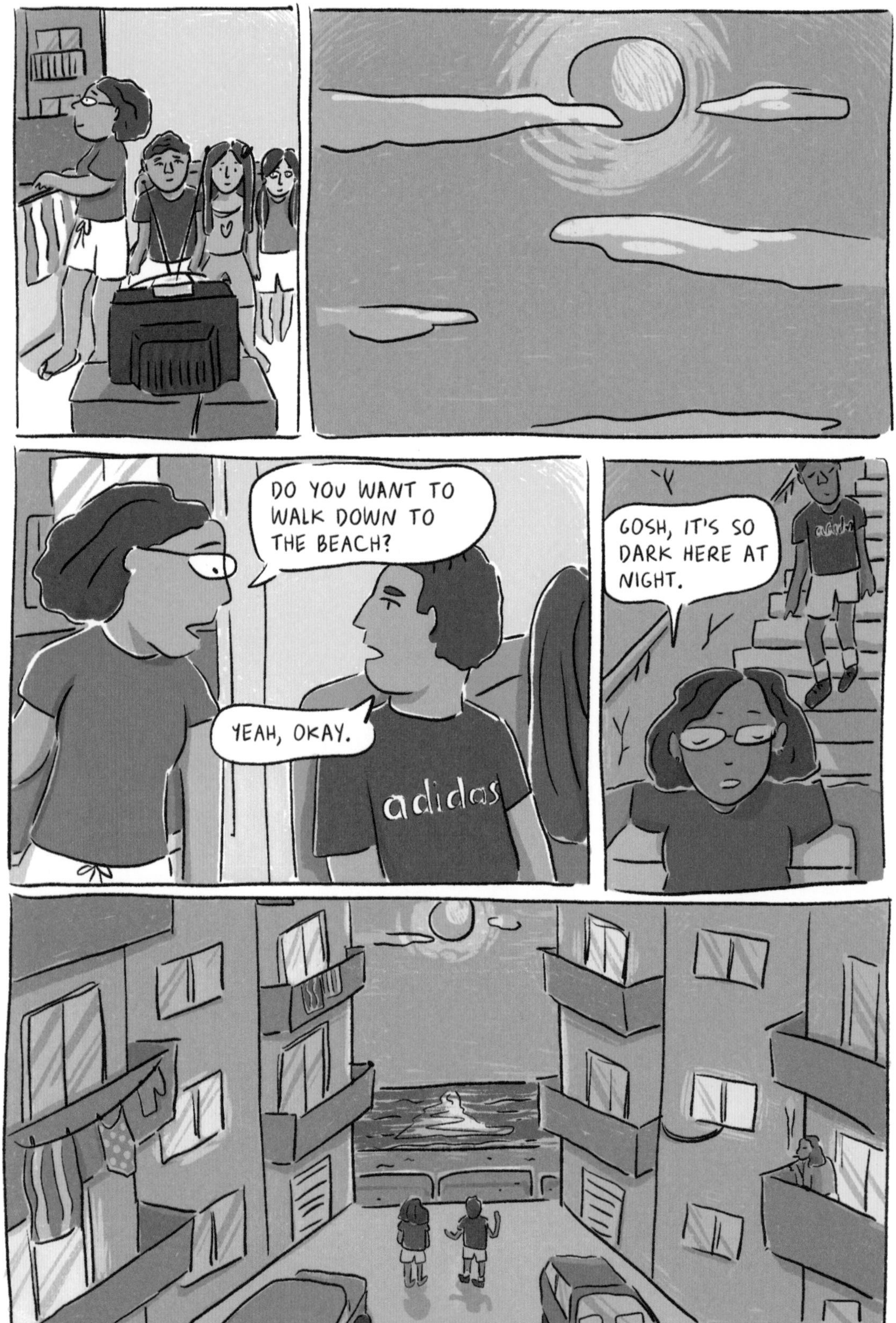
DO YOU WANT TO WALK DOWN TO THE BEACH?
YEAH, OKAY.
adidas
GOSH, IT'S SO DARK HERE AT NIGHT.

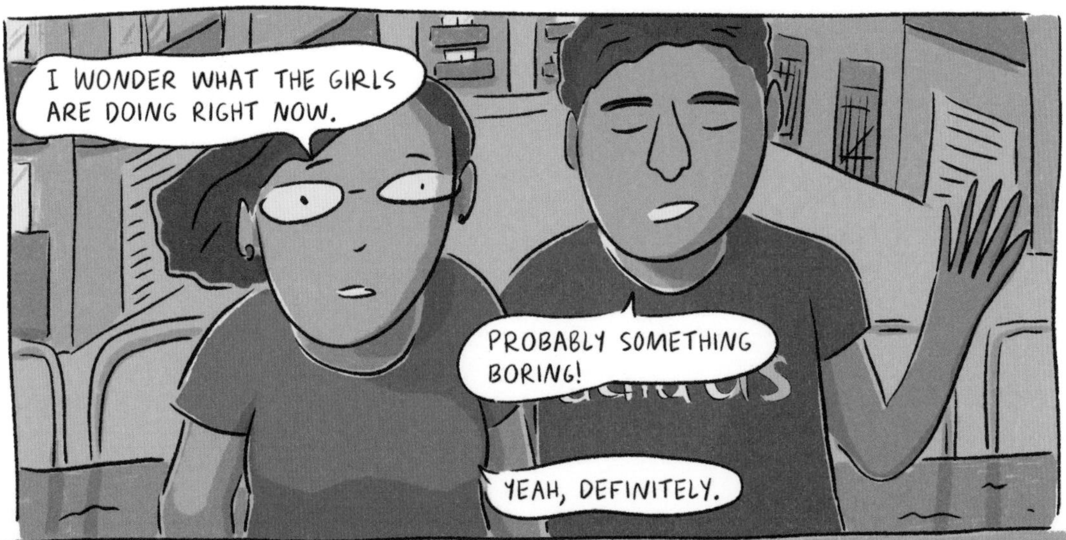
I WONDER WHAT THE GIRLS ARE DOING RIGHT NOW.
PROBABLY SOMETHING BORING!
YEAH, DEFINITELY.

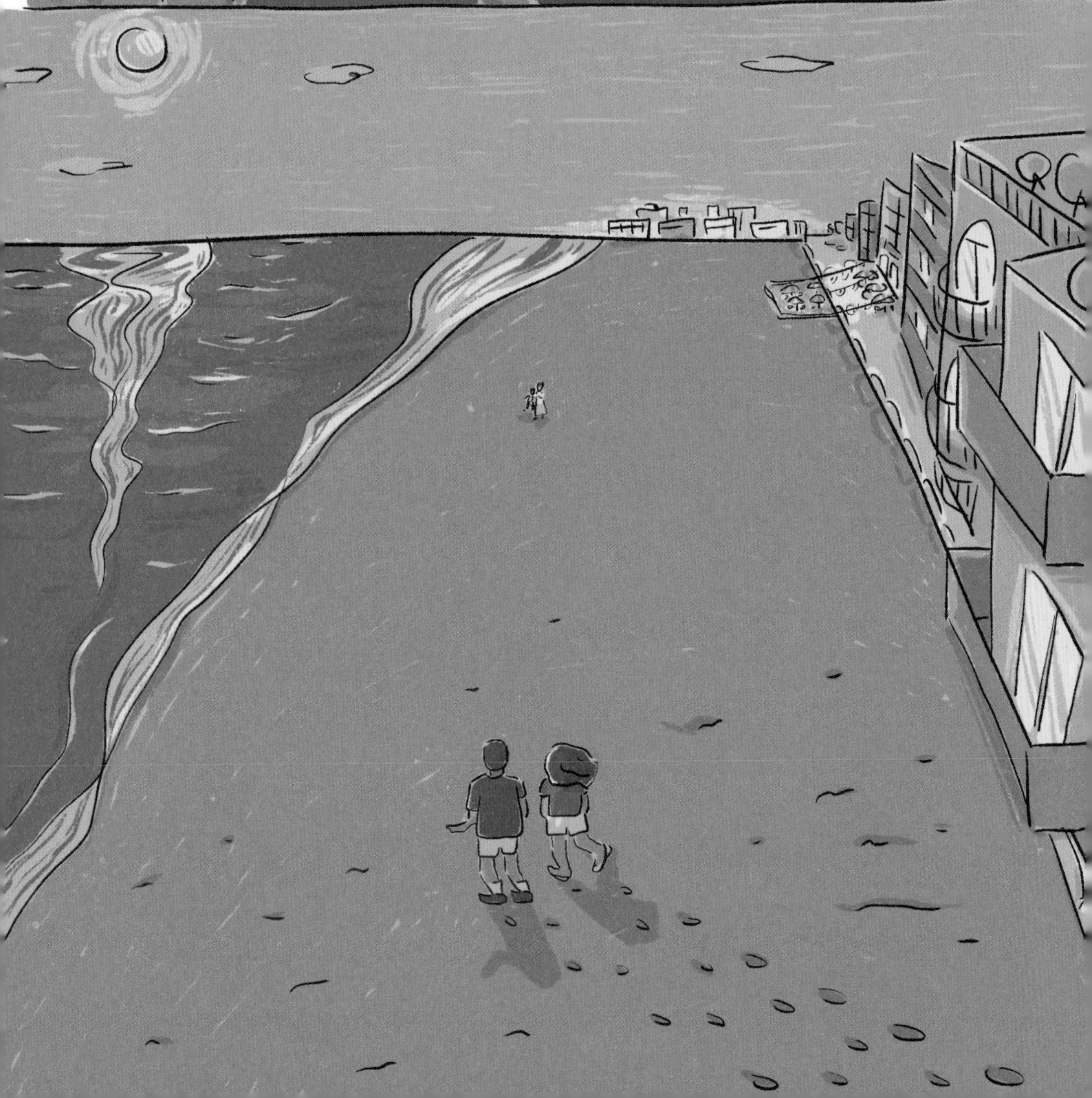

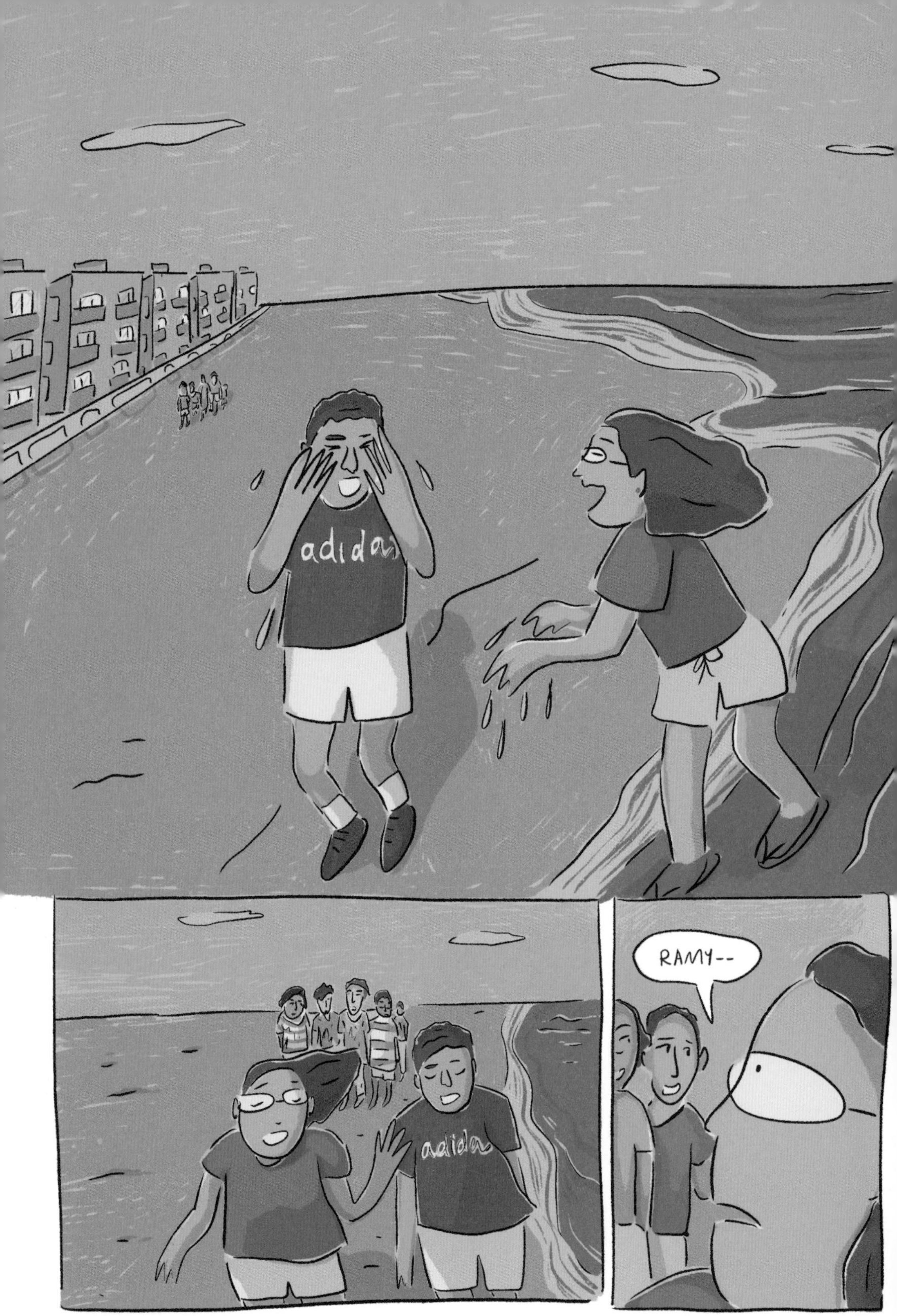
RAMY--

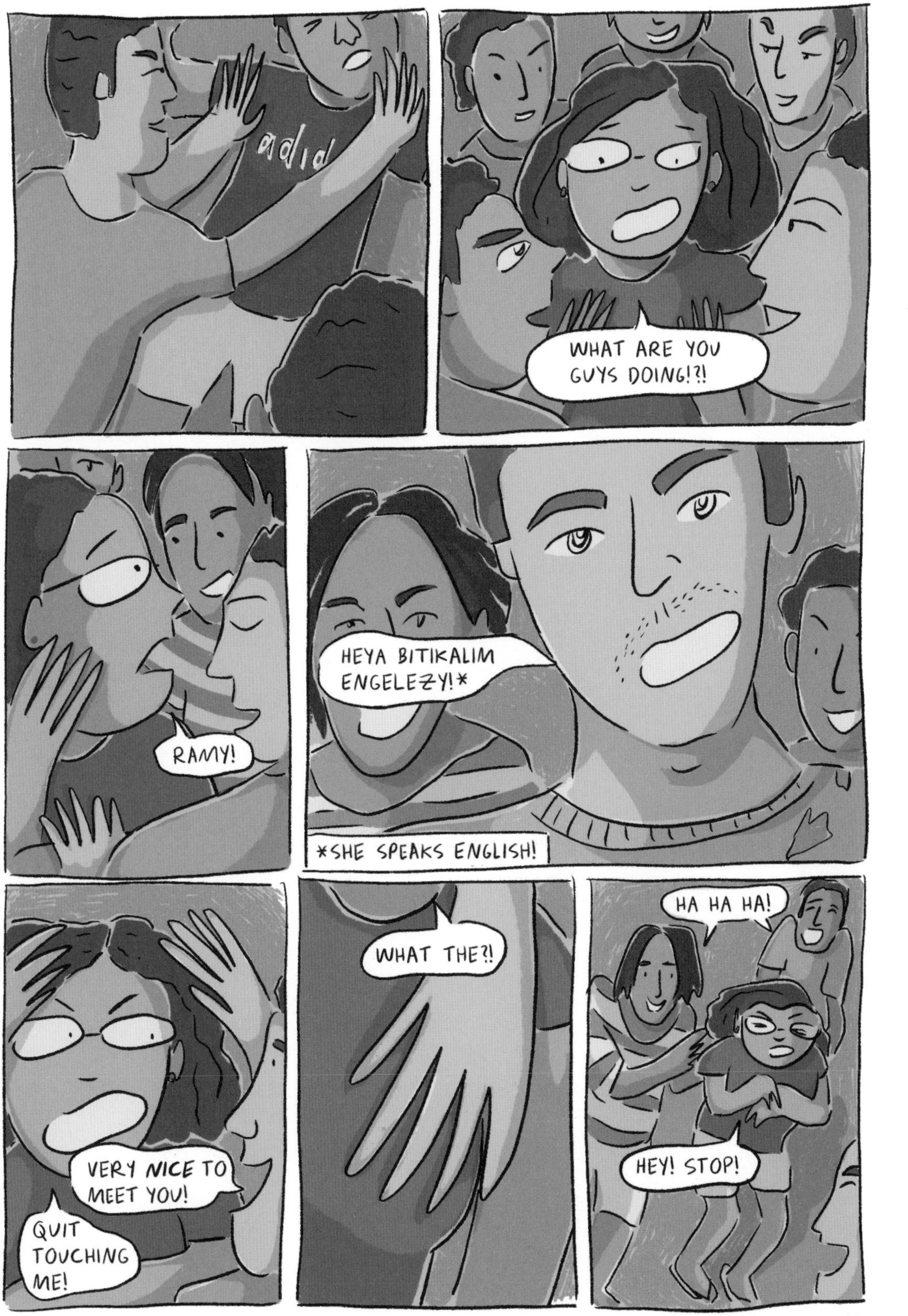
WHAT ARE YOU GUYS DOING!?!
RAMY!
HEYA BITIKALIM ENGELEZY!*
*SHE SPEAKS ENGLISH!
VERY NICE TO MEET YOU!
QUIT TOUCHING ME!
WHAT THE?!
HA HA HA!
HEY! STOP!

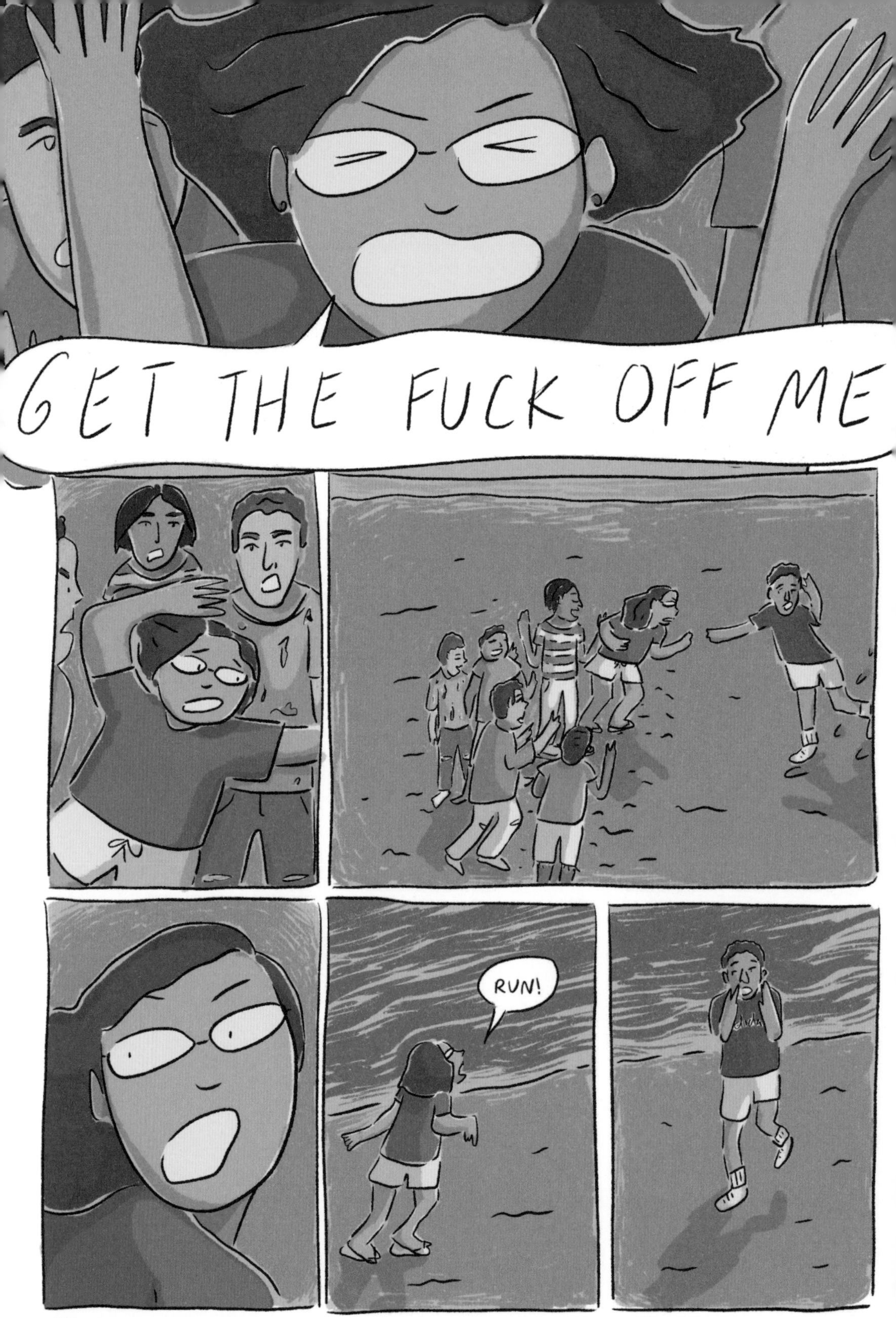

GET THE FUCK OFF ME
RUN!

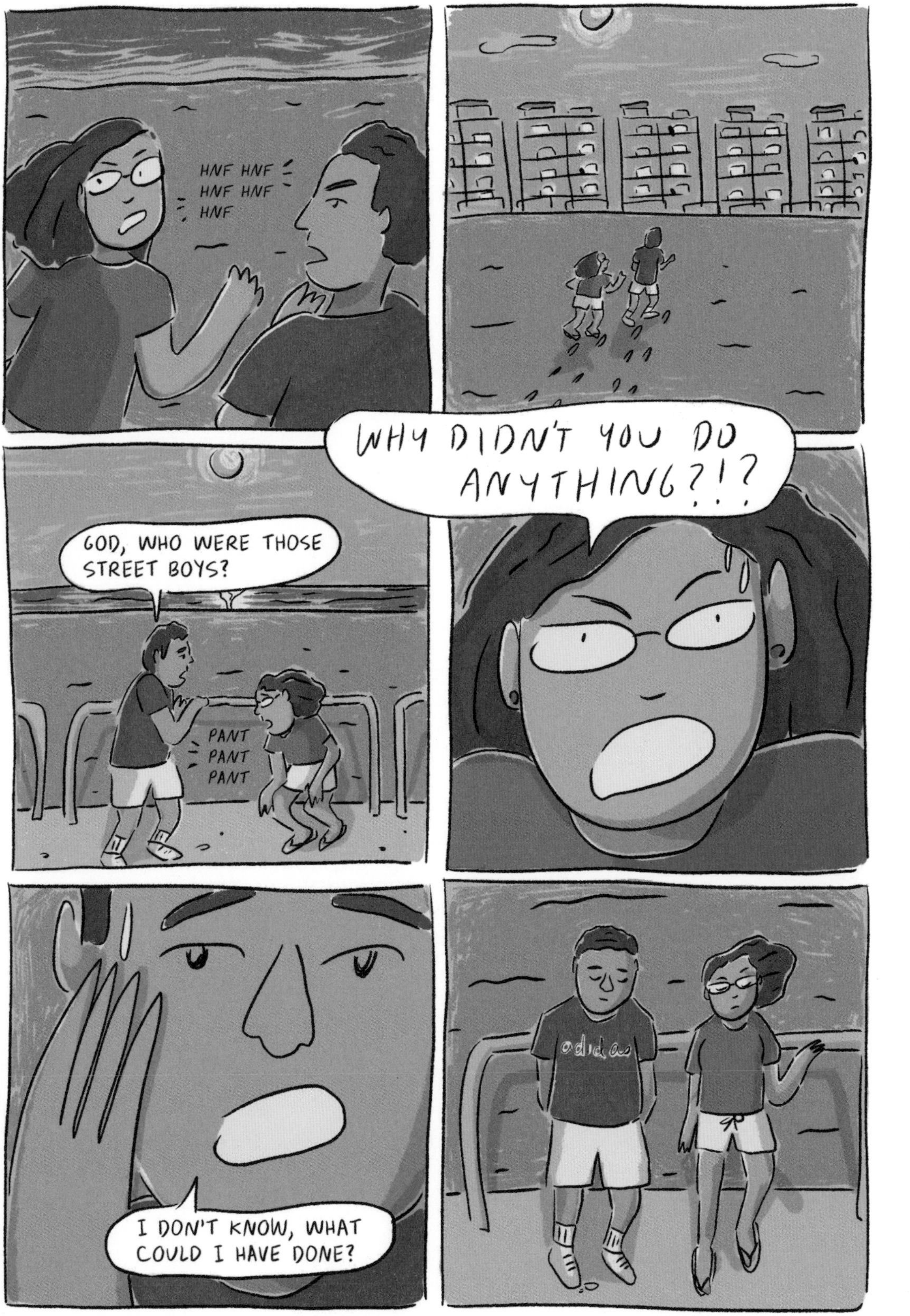
HNF HNF
HNF HNF
HNF
GOD, WHO WERE THOSE STREET BOYS?
PANT
PANT
PANT
WHY DIDN'T YOU DO ANYTHING?!?
I DON'T KNOW, WHAT COULD I HAVE DONE?
adidas

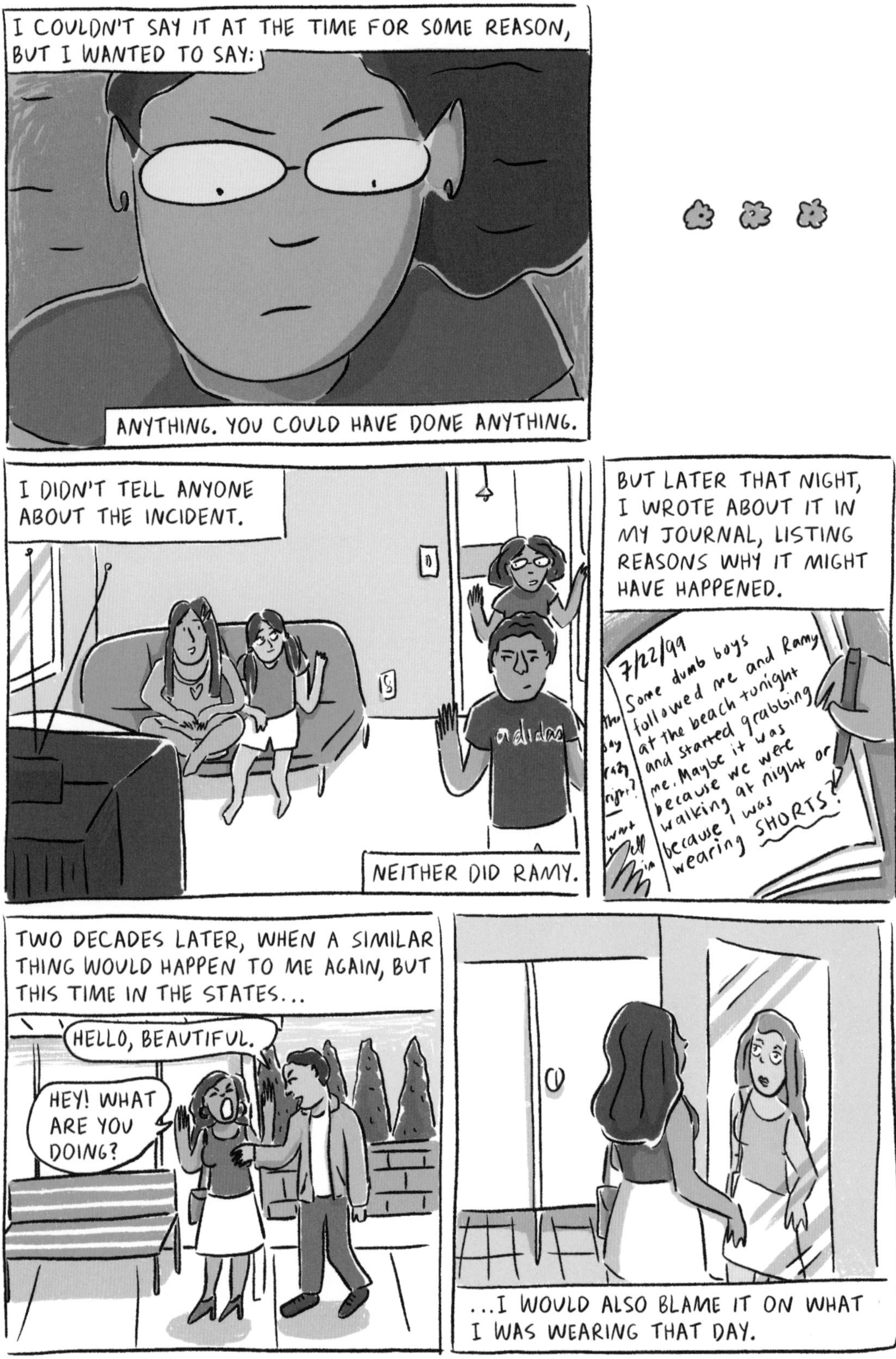
I COULDN'T SAY IT AT THE TIME FOR SOME REASON, BUT I WANTED TO SAY:
ANYTHING. YOU COULD HAVE DONE ANYTHING.
I DIDN'T TELL ANYONE ABOUT THE INCIDENT.
adidas
NEITHER DID RAMY.
BUT LATER THAT NIGHT, I WROTE ABOUT IT IN MY JOURNAL, LISTING REASONS WHY IT MIGHT HAVE HAPPENED.
7/22/99
Some dumb boys followed me and Ramy at the beach tonight and started grabbing me. Maybe it was because we were walking at night or because I was wearing SHORTS?
TWO DECADES LATER, WHEN A SIMILAR THING WOULD HAPPEN TO ME AGAIN, BUT THIS TIME IN THE STATES...
HELLO, BEAUTIFUL.
HEY! WHAT ARE YOU DOING?
...I WOULD ALSO BLAME IT ON WHAT I WAS WEARING THAT DAY.

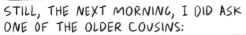
STILL, THE NEXT MORNING, I DID ASK ONE OF THE OLDER COUSINS:

HOW DO YOU SAY "GET THE FUCK AWAY FROM ME" IN ARABIC?

I MEAN, LIKE, WHAT'S THE CONTEXT.

I DUNNO, LIKE...

...IF YOU WANT A GUY TO GO AWAY.

GHOUR.

SHE MUST HAVE NOTICED SOMETHING IN MY FACIAL EXPRESSION...

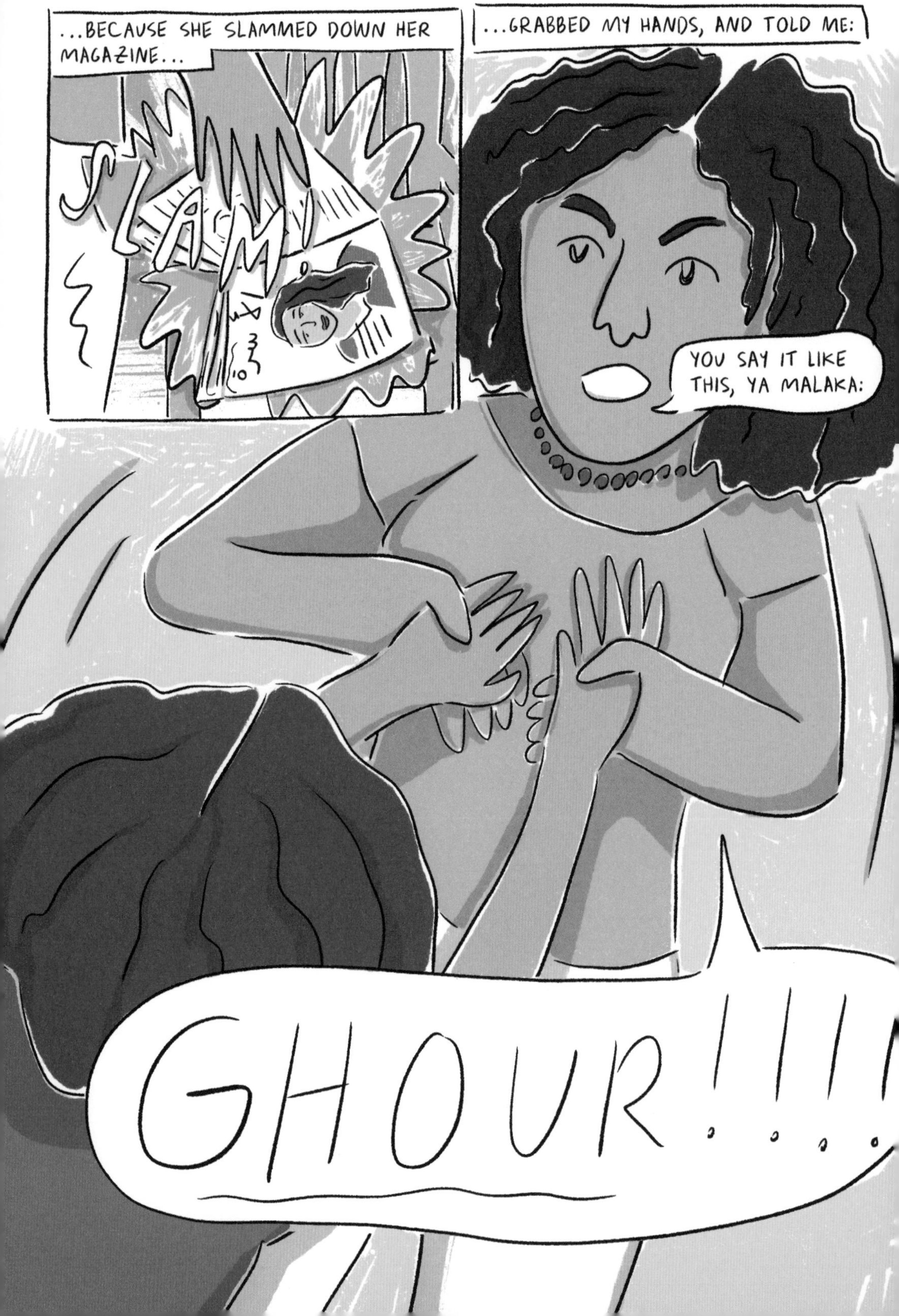
...BECAUSE SHE SLAMMED DOWN HER MAGAZINE...
SLAM!
...GRABBED MY HANDS, AND TOLD ME:
YOU SAY IT LIKE THIS, YA MALAKA:
GHOUR!!!!

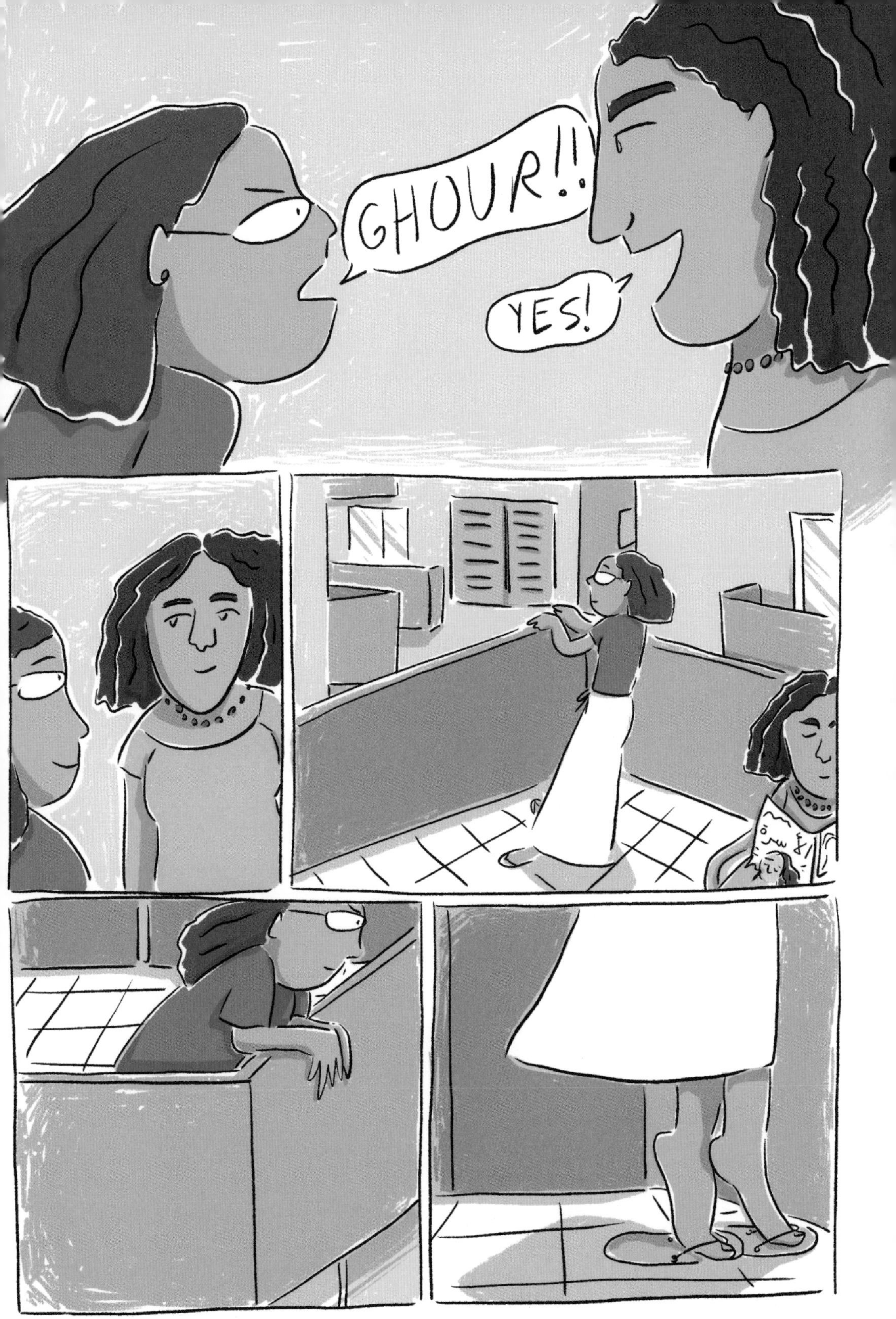
GHOUR!!
YES!

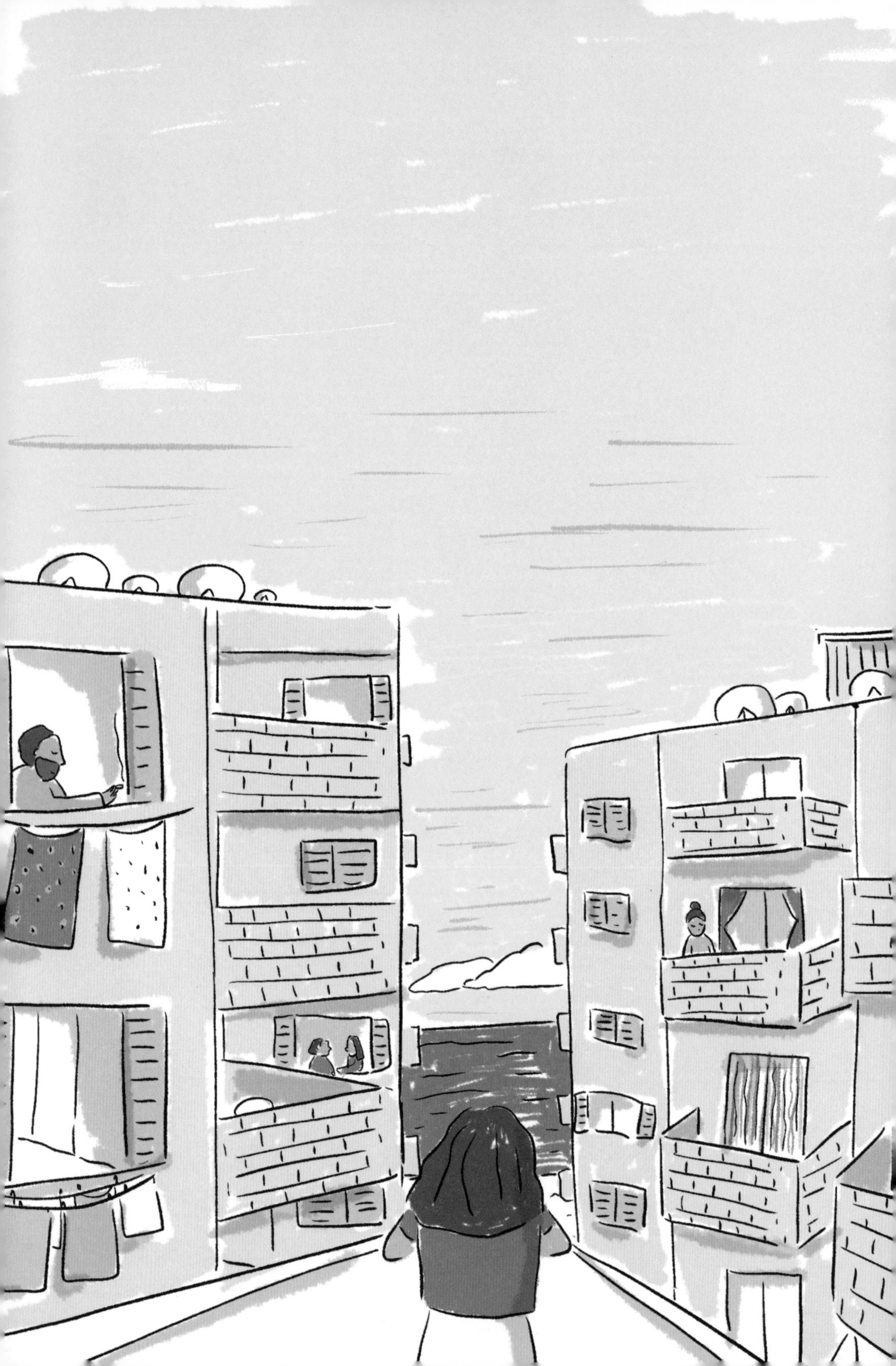

CHAPTER 5

The Photo

Buddy List
Online
Budd
soCAL
girL3
Aman
cerea
coffe
Mike
Buddy Info: Malaka86
Personal Profile
OK
Close
15/f/sOCaL
all i want to be is washed out by the sea // <3 <3<3
IM
Add Buddy
Info
Instant Message
sucks here and
come home
miss you...
time is it?
amn.
Info
Send

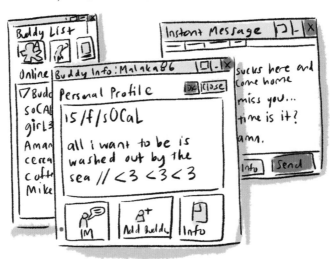

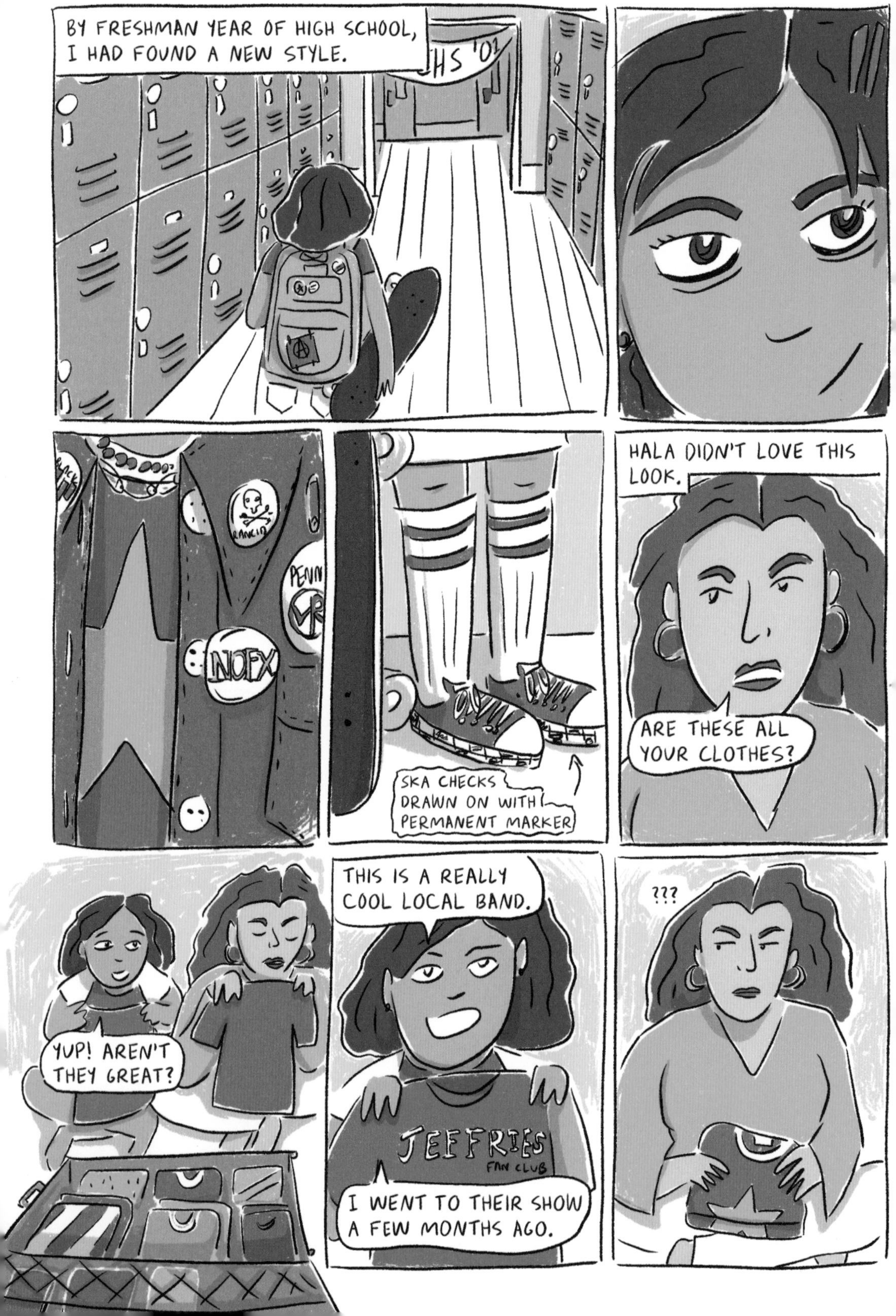
BY FRESHMAN YEAR OF HIGH SCHOOL, I HAD FOUND A NEW STYLE.
HS '01
NOFX
SKA CHECKS DRAWN ON WITH PERMANENT MARKER
HALA DIDN'T LOVE THIS LOOK.
ARE THESE ALL YOUR CLOTHES?
YUP! AREN'T THEY GREAT?
THIS IS A REALLY COOL LOCAL BAND.
JEFFRIES FAN CLUB
I WENT TO THEIR SHOW A FEW MONTHS AGO.
???

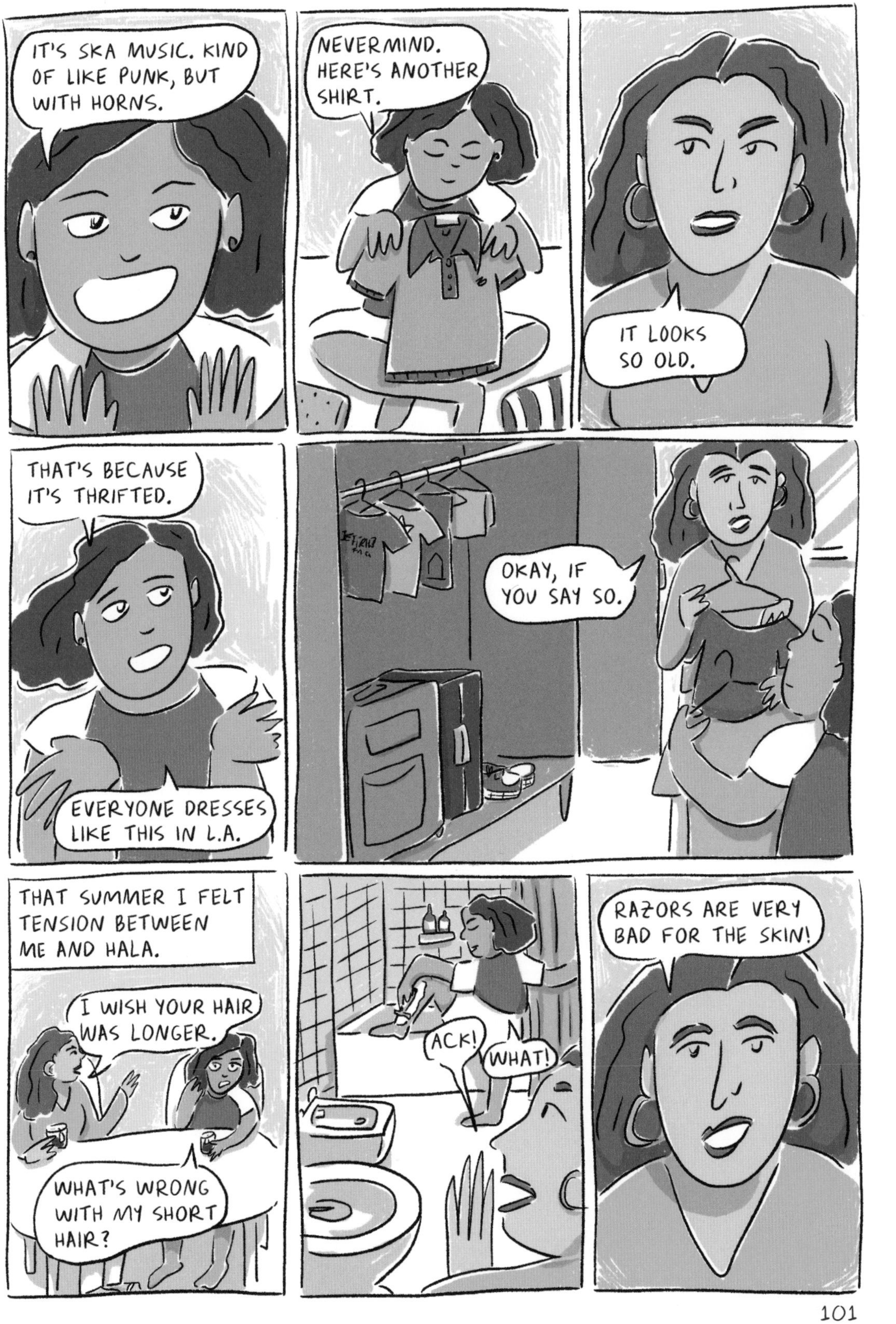
IT'S SKA MUSIC. KIND OF LIKE PUNK, BUT WITH HORNS.
NEVERMIND. HERE'S ANOTHER SHIRT.
IT LOOKS SO OLD.
THAT'S BECAUSE IT'S THRIFTED.
EVERYONE DRESSES LIKE THIS IN L.A.
OKAY, IF YOU SAY SO.
THAT SUMMER I FELT TENSION BETWEEN ME AND HALA.
I WISH YOUR HAIR WAS LONGER.
WHAT'S WRONG WITH MY SHORT HAIR?
ACK!
WHAT!
RAZORS ARE VERY BAD FOR THE SKIN!

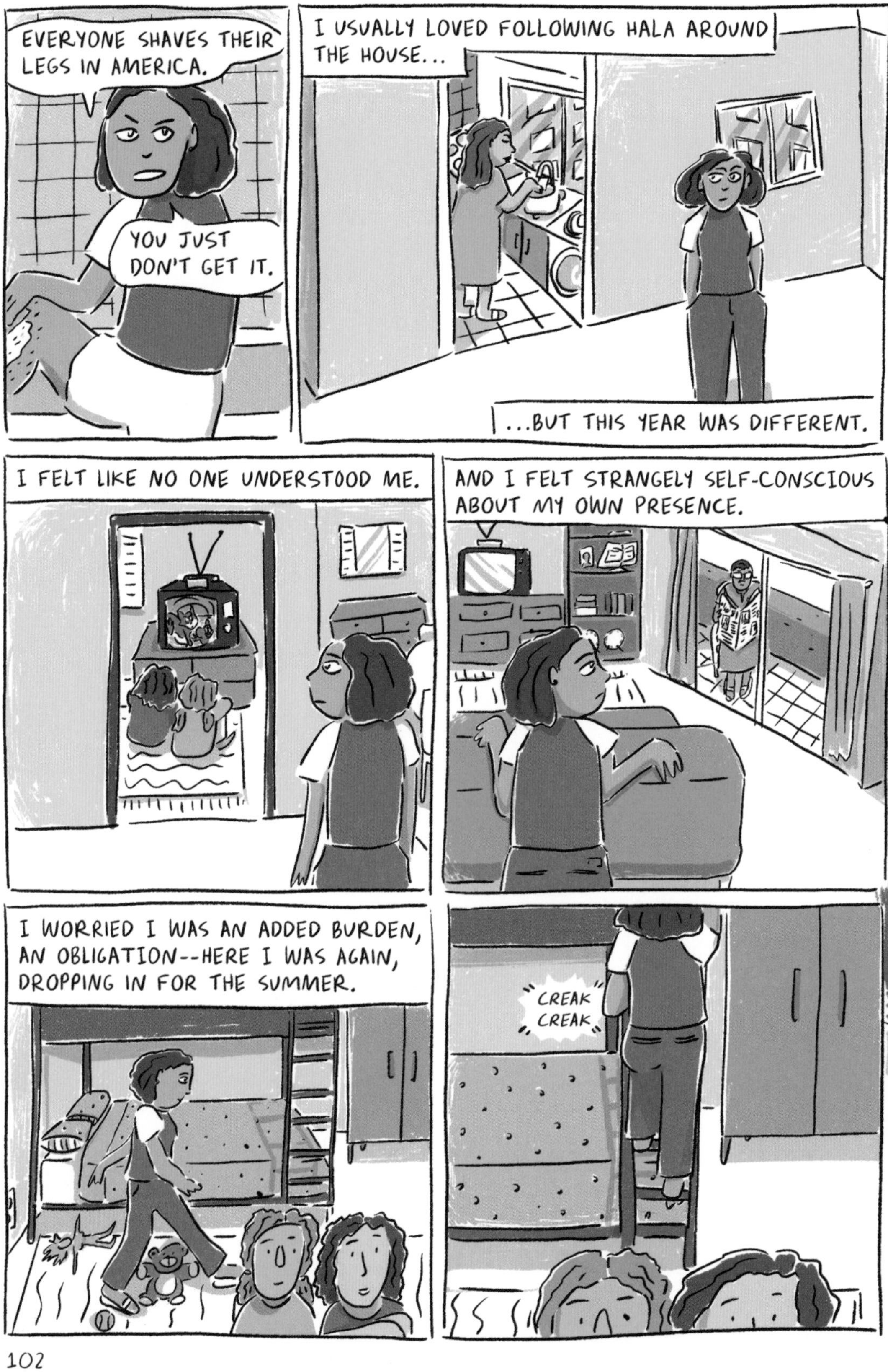
EVERYONE SHAVES THEIR LEGS IN AMERICA.
YOU JUST DON'T GET IT.
I USUALLY LOVED FOLLOWING HALA AROUND THE HOUSE...
...BUT THIS YEAR WAS DIFFERENT.
I FELT LIKE NO ONE UNDERSTOOD ME.
AND I FELT STRANGELY SELF-CONSCIOUS ABOUT MY OWN PRESENCE.
I WORRIED I WAS AN ADDED BURDEN, AN OBLIGATION--HERE I WAS AGAIN, DROPPING IN FOR THE SUMMER.
CREAK CREAK

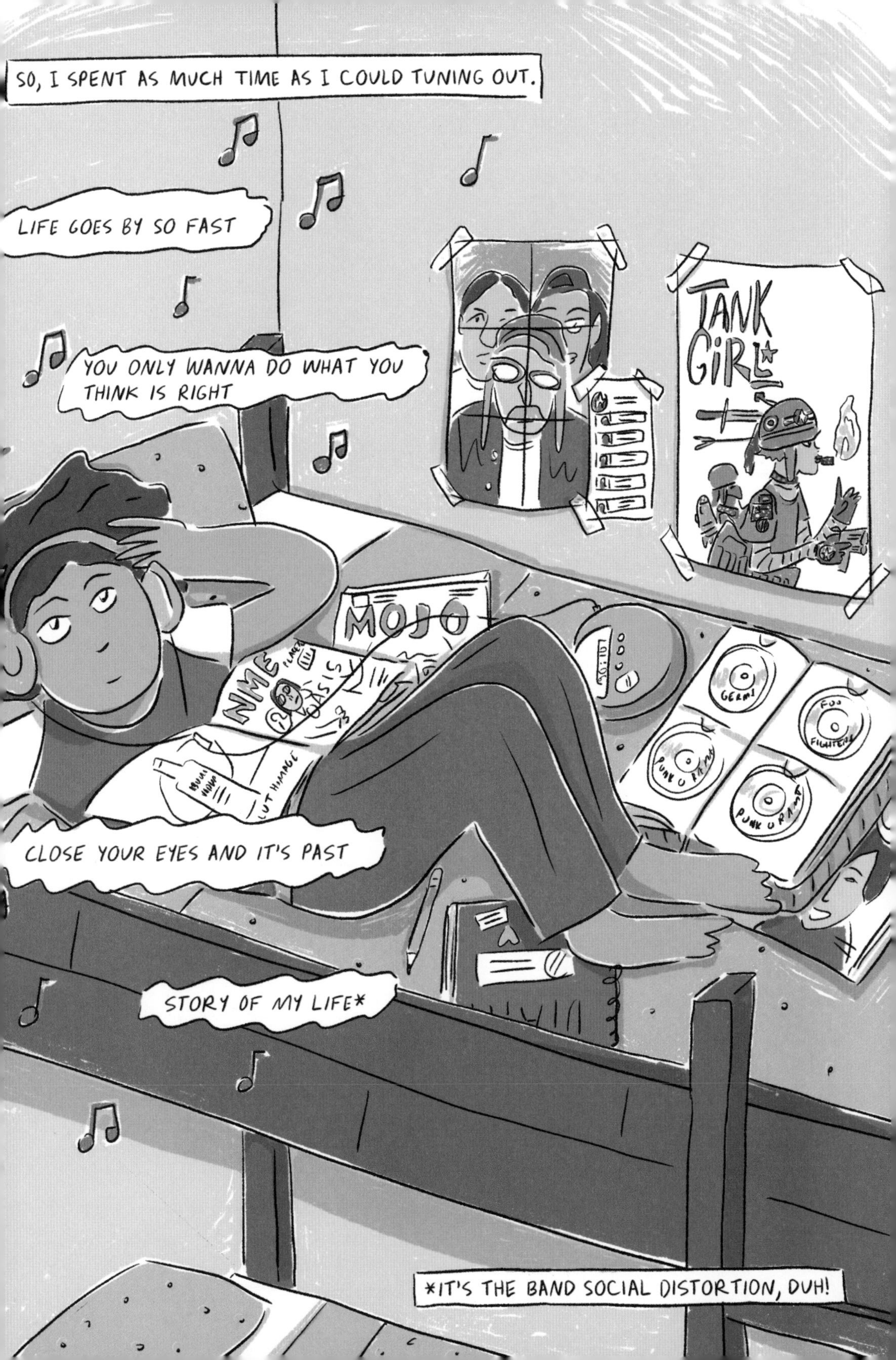
SO, I SPENT AS MUCH TIME AS I COULD TUNING OUT.
LIFE GOES BY SO FAST
YOU ONLY WANNA DO WHAT YOU THINK IS RIGHT
CLOSE YOUR EYES AND IT'S PAST
STORY OF MY LIFE*
*IT'S THE BAND SOCIAL DISTORTION, DUH!
TANK GIRL
MOJO
NME
OASIS
GERMS
FOO FIGHTERS
PUNK O RAMA
PUNK O RAMA

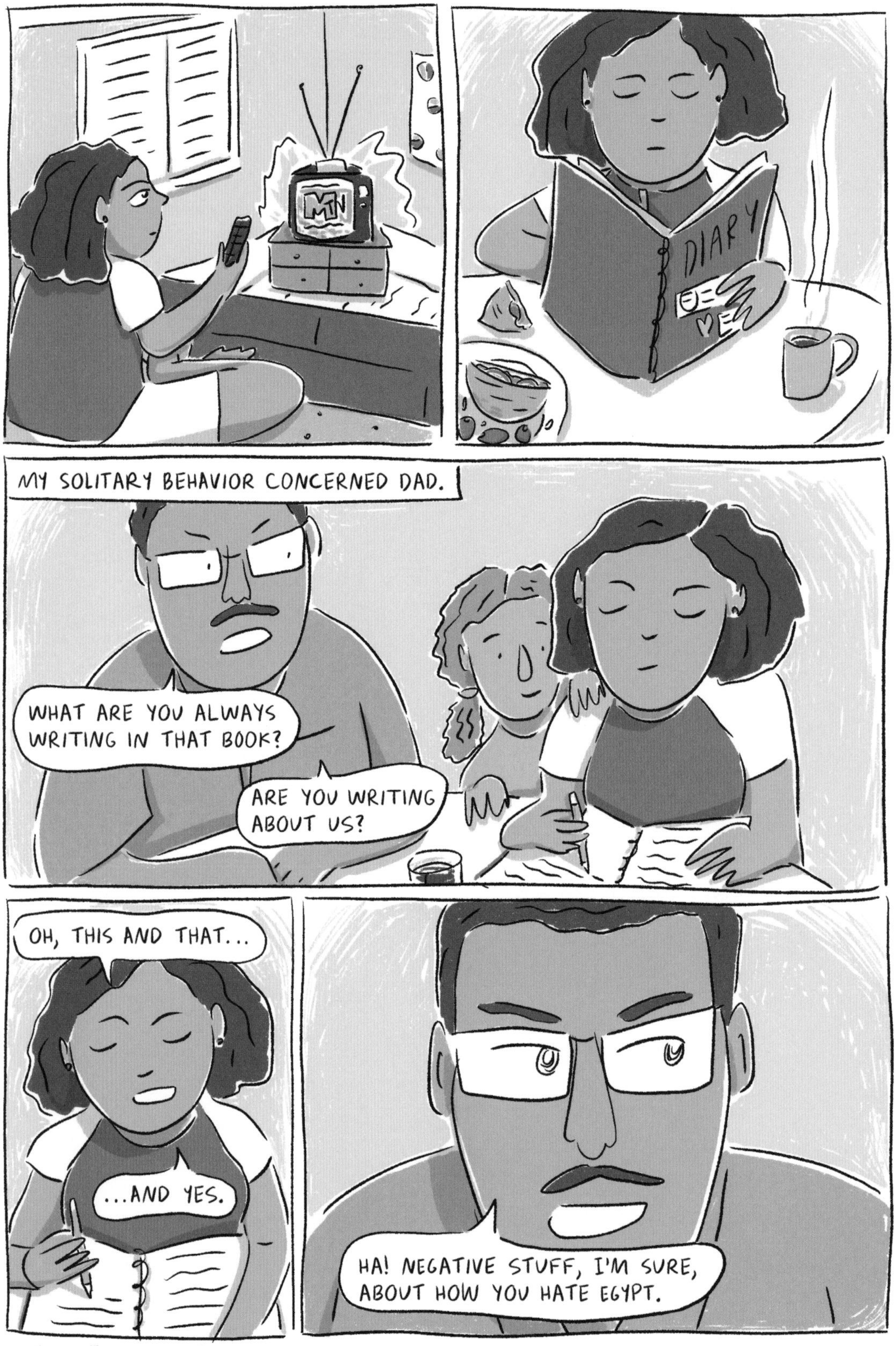
DIARY
MY SOLITARY BEHAVIOR CONCERNED DAD.
WHAT ARE YOU ALWAYS WRITING IN THAT BOOK?
ARE YOU WRITING ABOUT US?
OH, THIS AND THAT...
...AND YES.
HA! NEGATIVE STUFF, I'M SURE, ABOUT HOW YOU HATE EGYPT.

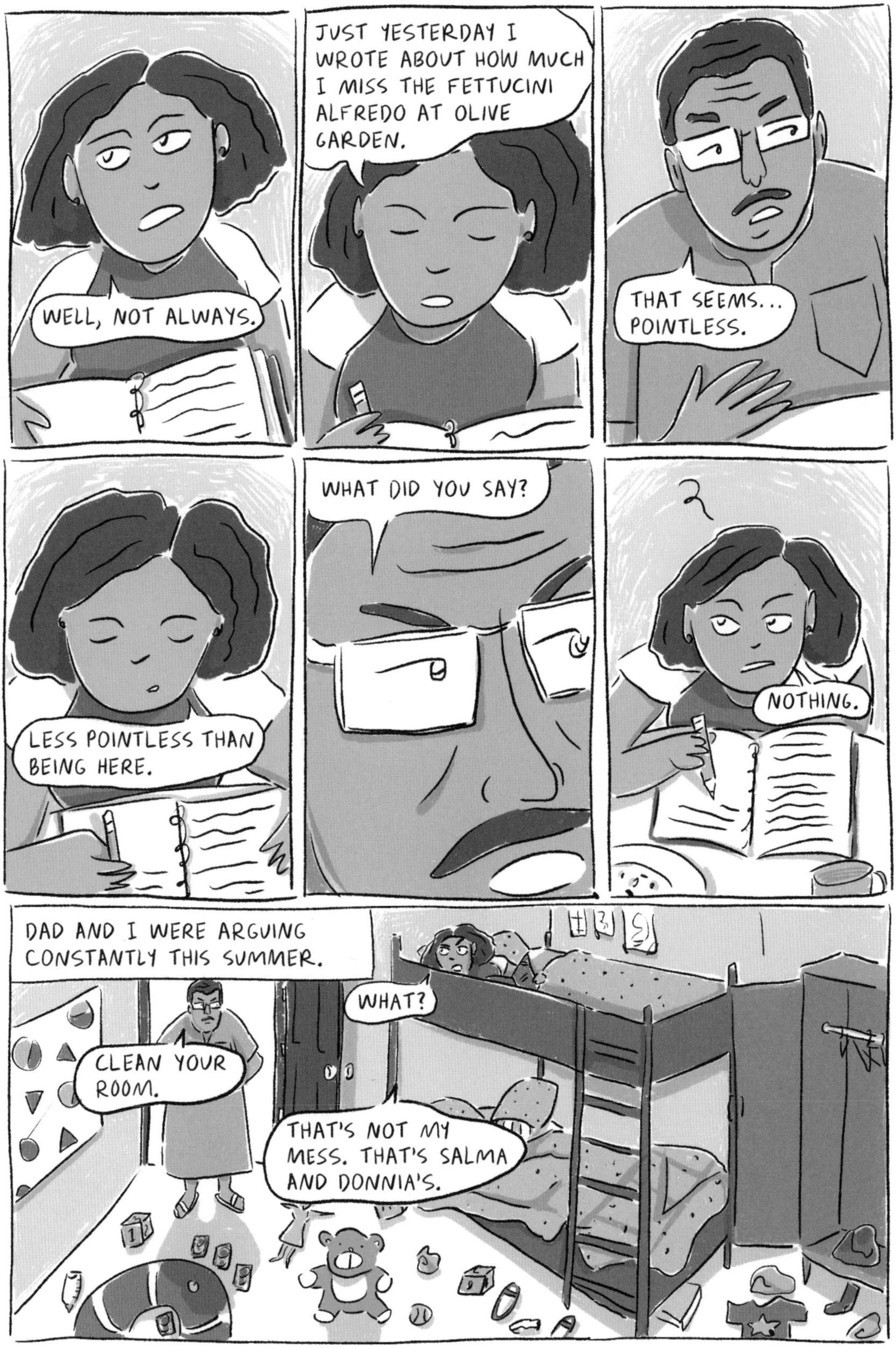
WELL, NOT ALWAYS.
JUST YESTERDAY I WROTE ABOUT HOW MUCH I MISS THE FETTUCINI ALFREDO AT OLIVE GARDEN.
THAT SEEMS... POINTLESS.
LESS POINTLESS THAN BEING HERE.
WHAT DID YOU SAY?
NOTHING.
DAD AND I WERE ARGUING CONSTANTLY THIS SUMMER.
CLEAN YOUR ROOM.
WHAT?
THAT'S NOT MY MESS. THAT'S SALMA AND DONNIA'S.

(TO BE FAIR, I WASN'T EASY ON MOM BACK IN L.A., EITHER.)

MALAKA!

I **TOLD YOU** TO MAKE RICE BEFORE I GOT HOME FROM WORK.

I WAS DOING MY HOMEWORK!* GOD, YOU EXPECT ME TO DO EVERYTHING AROUND HERE!!!

*I WAS ON THE PHONE :D

BUT DAD HARPED ON A DIFFERENT KIND OF THING.

CHANGE YOUR SHIRT.

SOMETHING THAT COVERS YOUR BUTT.

DAD, HOW CAN I WEAR A LONG SHIRT OVER A DENIM SKIRT?

DOES THAT MAKE SENSE TO YOU, FASHION-WISE?

DO YOU SEE ANYONE ELSE WEARING TIGHT CLOTHES HERE?

LOOK AT WHAT HALA'S WEARING.

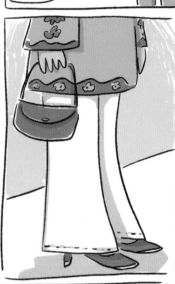

UGH.

NO OFFENSE, HALA.

THE THING THAT BOTHERED ME MOST, THOUGH, WAS HOW DAD ACTED WHEN AHMAD, MY SECOND COUSIN, WAS AROUND.

DAD WOULDN'T LET US HANG OUT TOGETHER IN A ROOM WITH THE DOOR CLOSED.

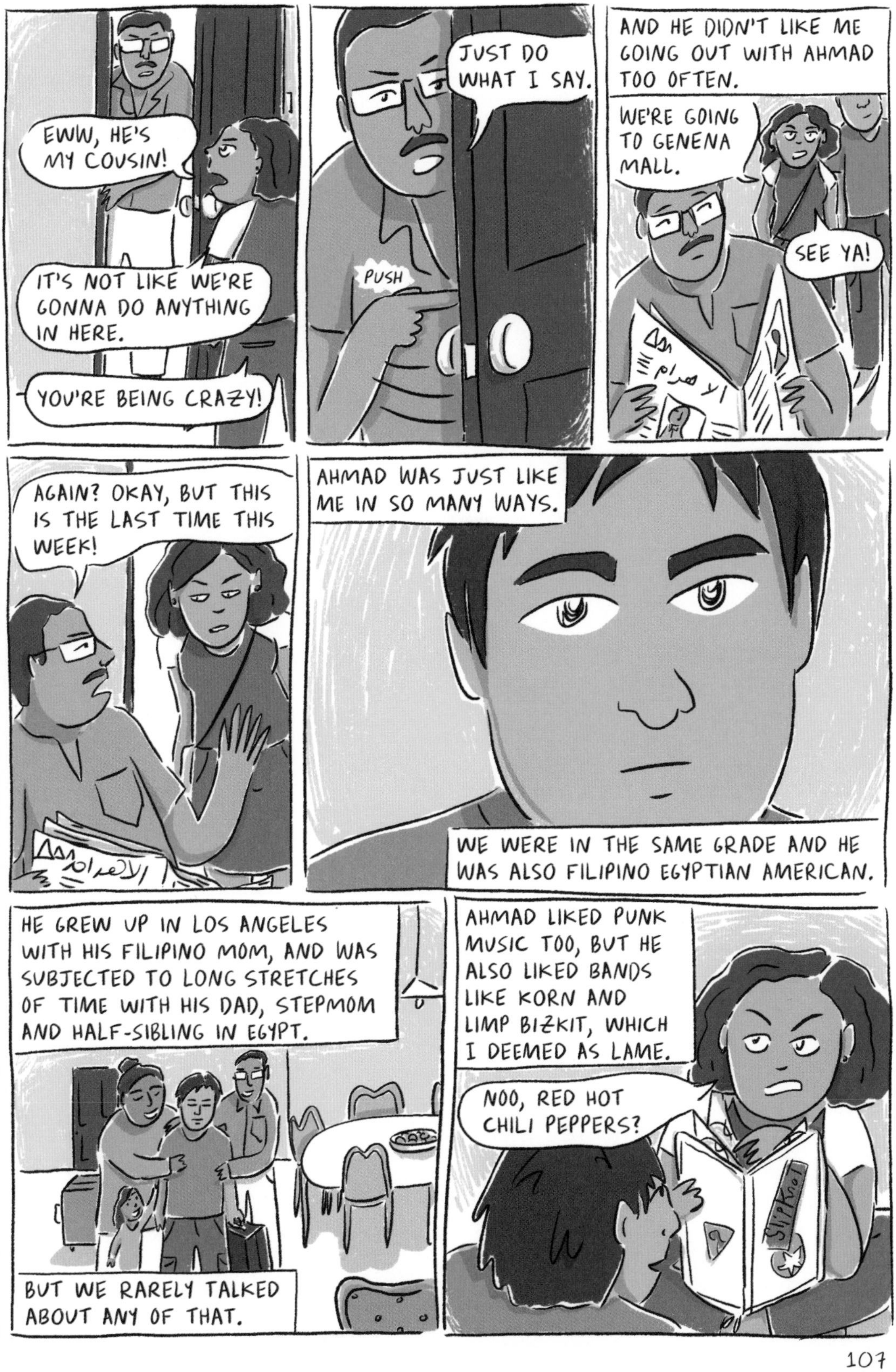
EWW, HE'S MY COUSIN!
IT'S NOT LIKE WE'RE GONNA DO ANYTHING IN HERE.
YOU'RE BEING CRAZY!
JUST DO WHAT I SAY.
PUSH
AND HE DIDN'T LIKE ME GOING OUT WITH AHMAD TOO OFTEN.
WE'RE GOING TO GENENA MALL.
SEE YA!
الاهرام
AGAIN? OKAY, BUT THIS IS THE LAST TIME THIS WEEK!
AHMAD WAS JUST LIKE ME IN SO MANY WAYS.
WE WERE IN THE SAME GRADE AND HE WAS ALSO FILIPINO EGYPTIAN AMERICAN.
HE GREW UP IN LOS ANGELES WITH HIS FILIPINO MOM, AND WAS SUBJECTED TO LONG STRETCHES OF TIME WITH HIS DAD, STEPMOM AND HALF-SIBLING IN EGYPT.
BUT WE RARELY TALKED ABOUT ANY OF THAT.
AHMAD LIKED PUNK MUSIC TOO, BUT HE ALSO LIKED BANDS LIKE KORN AND LIMP BIZKIT, WHICH I DEEMED AS LAME.
NOO, RED HOT CHILI PEPPERS?
SlipKnot

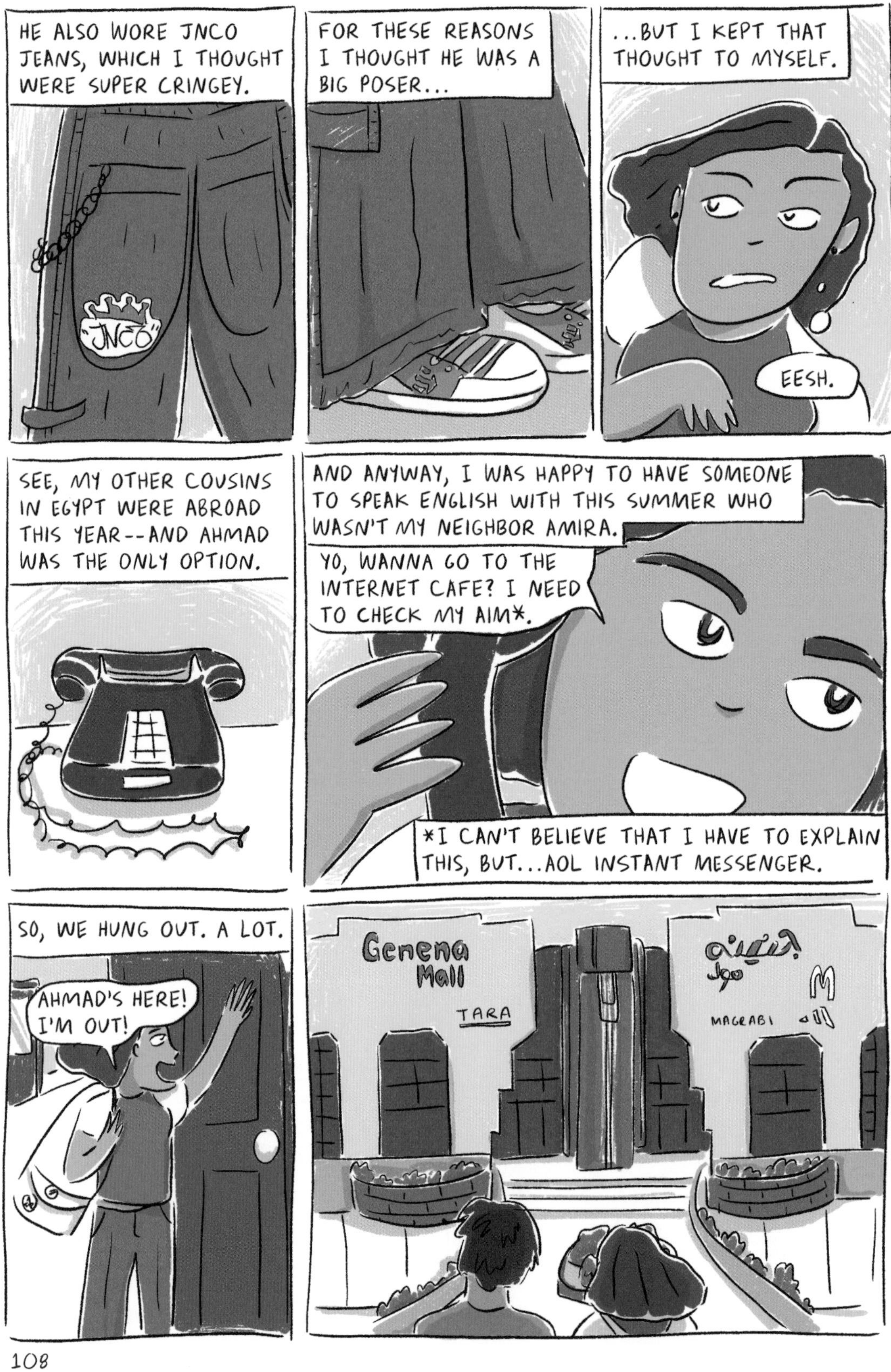

HE ALSO WORE JNCO JEANS, WHICH I THOUGHT WERE SUPER CRINGEY.
"JNCO"
FOR THESE REASONS I THOUGHT HE WAS A BIG POSER...
...BUT I KEPT THAT THOUGHT TO MYSELF.
EESH.
SEE, MY OTHER COUSINS IN EGYPT WERE ABROAD THIS YEAR--AND AHMAD WAS THE ONLY OPTION.
AND ANYWAY, I WAS HAPPY TO HAVE SOMEONE TO SPEAK ENGLISH WITH THIS SUMMER WHO WASN'T MY NEIGHBOR AMIRA.
YO, WANNA GO TO THE INTERNET CAFE? I NEED TO CHECK MY AIM*.
*I CAN'T BELIEVE THAT I HAVE TO EXPLAIN THIS, BUT...AOL INSTANT MESSENGER.
SO, WE HUNG OUT. A LOT.
AHMAD'S HERE! I'M OUT!
Genena Mall
TARA
MAGRABI

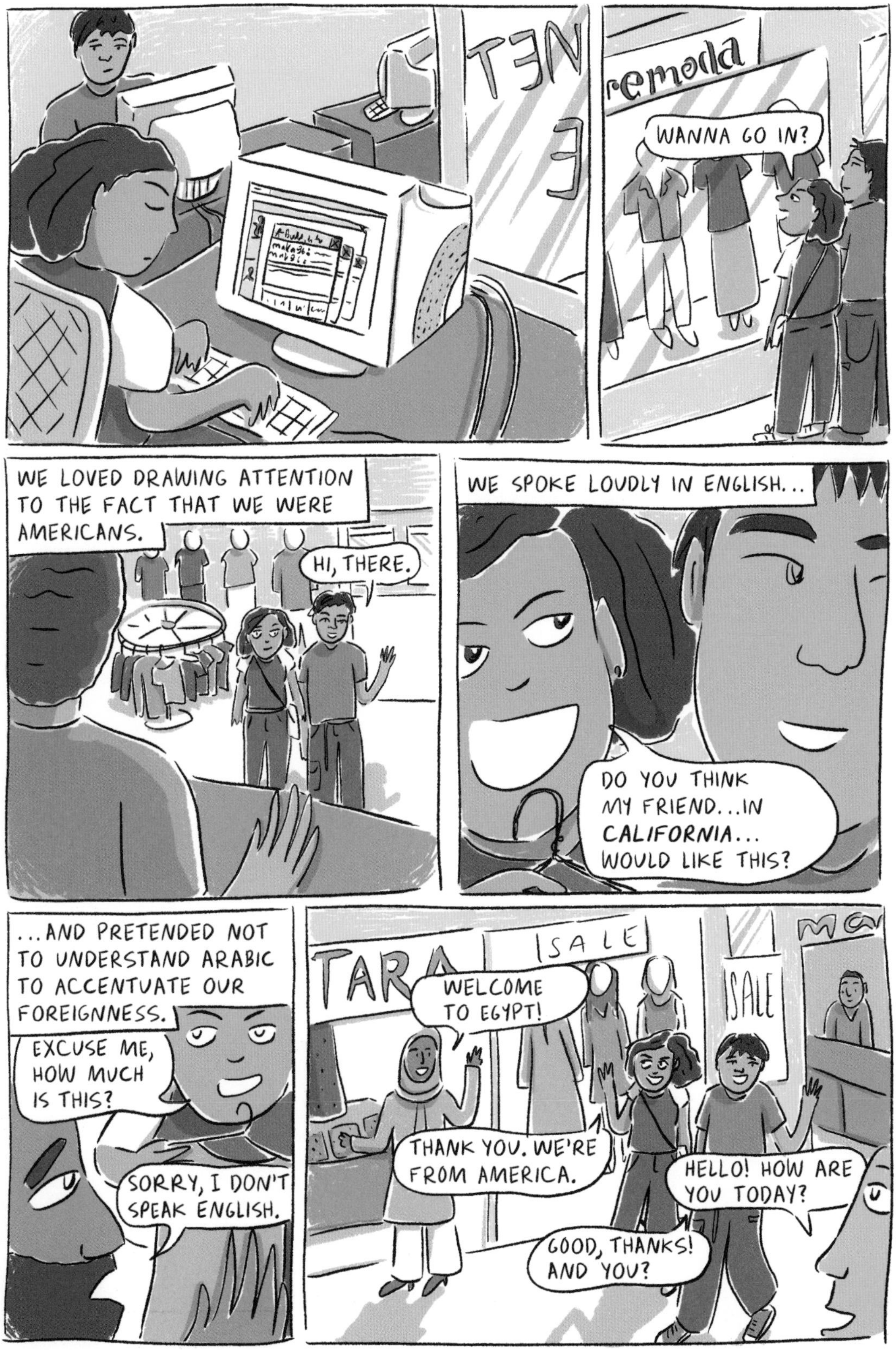
NET
remoda
WANNA GO IN?
WE LOVED DRAWING ATTENTION TO THE FACT THAT WE WERE AMERICANS.
HI, THERE.
WE SPOKE LOUDLY IN ENGLISH...
DO YOU THINK MY FRIEND...IN **CALIFORNIA**... WOULD LIKE THIS?
...AND PRETENDED NOT TO UNDERSTAND ARABIC TO ACCENTUATE OUR FOREIGNNESS.
EXCUSE ME, HOW MUCH IS THIS?
SORRY, I DON'T SPEAK ENGLISH.
TARA
SALE
SALE
WELCOME TO EGYPT!
THANK YOU. WE'RE FROM AMERICA.
HELLO! HOW ARE YOU TODAY?
GOOD, THANKS! AND YOU?

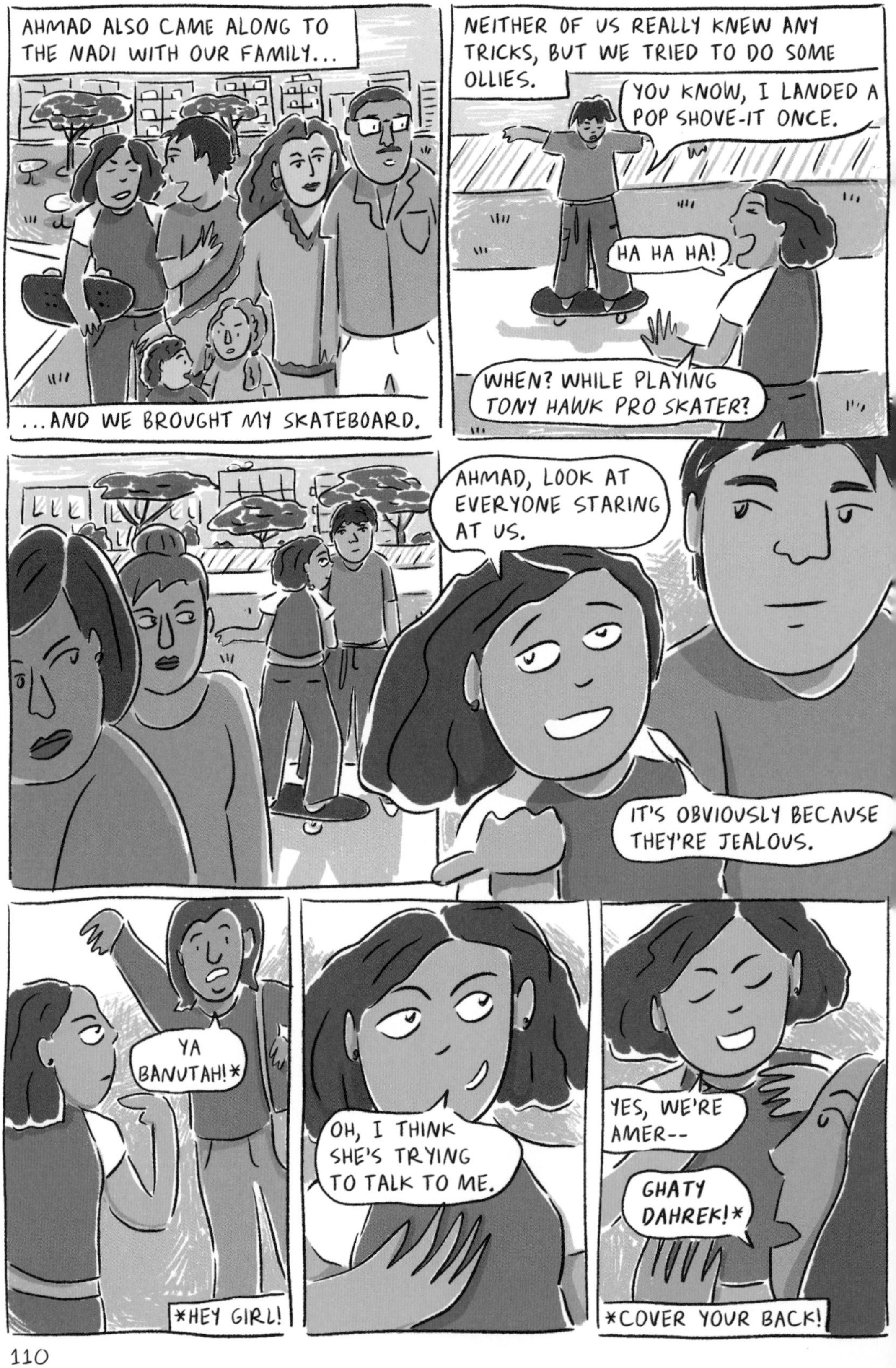
AHMAD ALSO CAME ALONG TO THE NADI WITH OUR FAMILY...
...AND WE BROUGHT MY SKATEBOARD.
NEITHER OF US REALLY KNEW ANY TRICKS, BUT WE TRIED TO DO SOME OLLIES.
YOU KNOW, I LANDED A POP SHOVE-IT ONCE.
HA HA HA!
WHEN? WHILE PLAYING TONY HAWK PRO SKATER?
AHMAD, LOOK AT EVERYONE STARING AT US.
IT'S OBVIOUSLY BECAUSE THEY'RE JEALOUS.
YA BANUTAH!*
*HEY GIRL!
OH, I THINK SHE'S TRYING TO TALK TO ME.
YES, WE'RE AMER--
GHATY DAHREK!*
*COVER YOUR BACK!

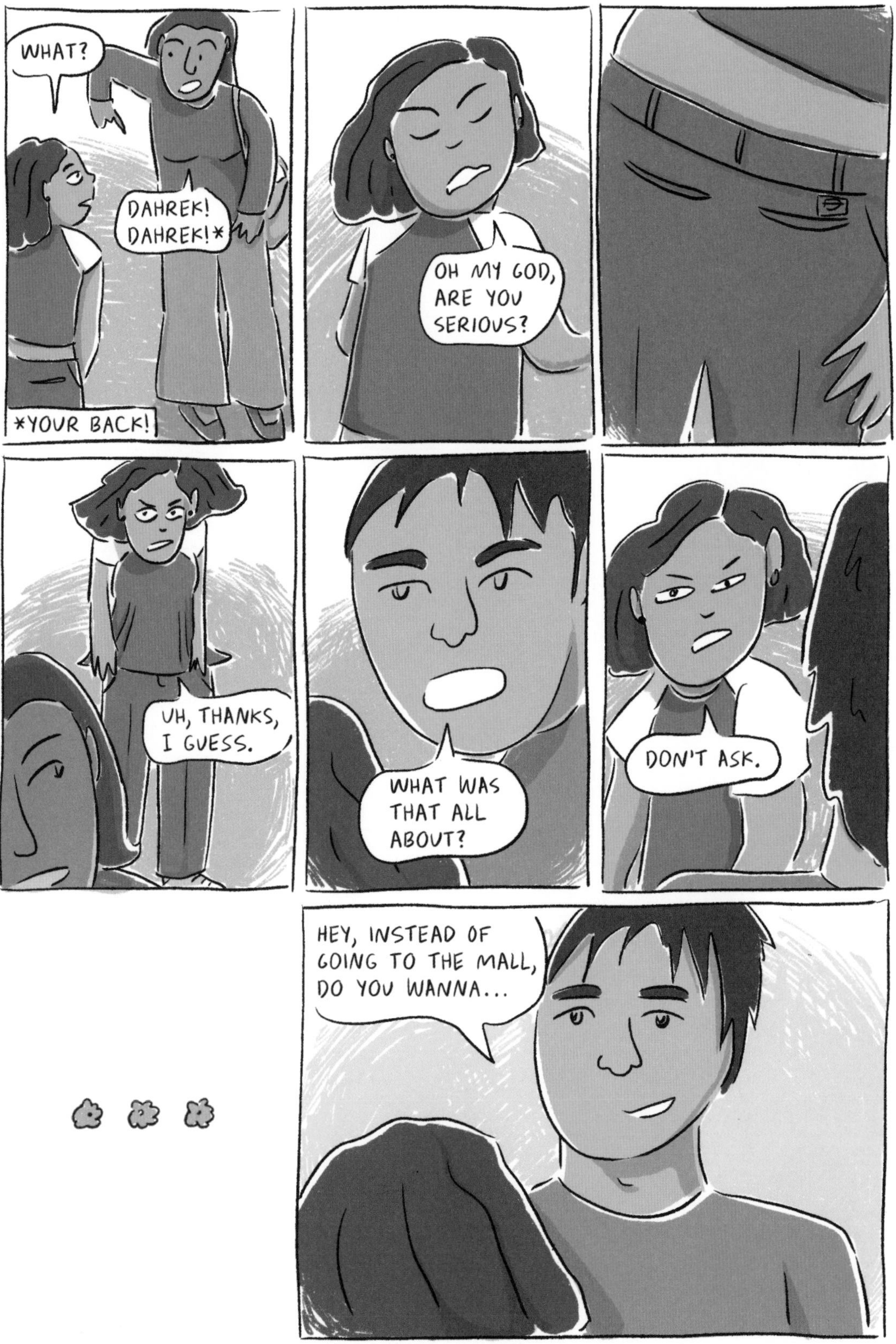
WHAT?
DAHREK! DAHREK!*
*YOUR BACK!
OH MY GOD, ARE YOU SERIOUS?
UH, THANKS, I GUESS.
WHAT WAS THAT ALL ABOUT?
DON'T ASK.
HEY, INSTEAD OF GOING TO THE MALL, DO YOU WANNA...

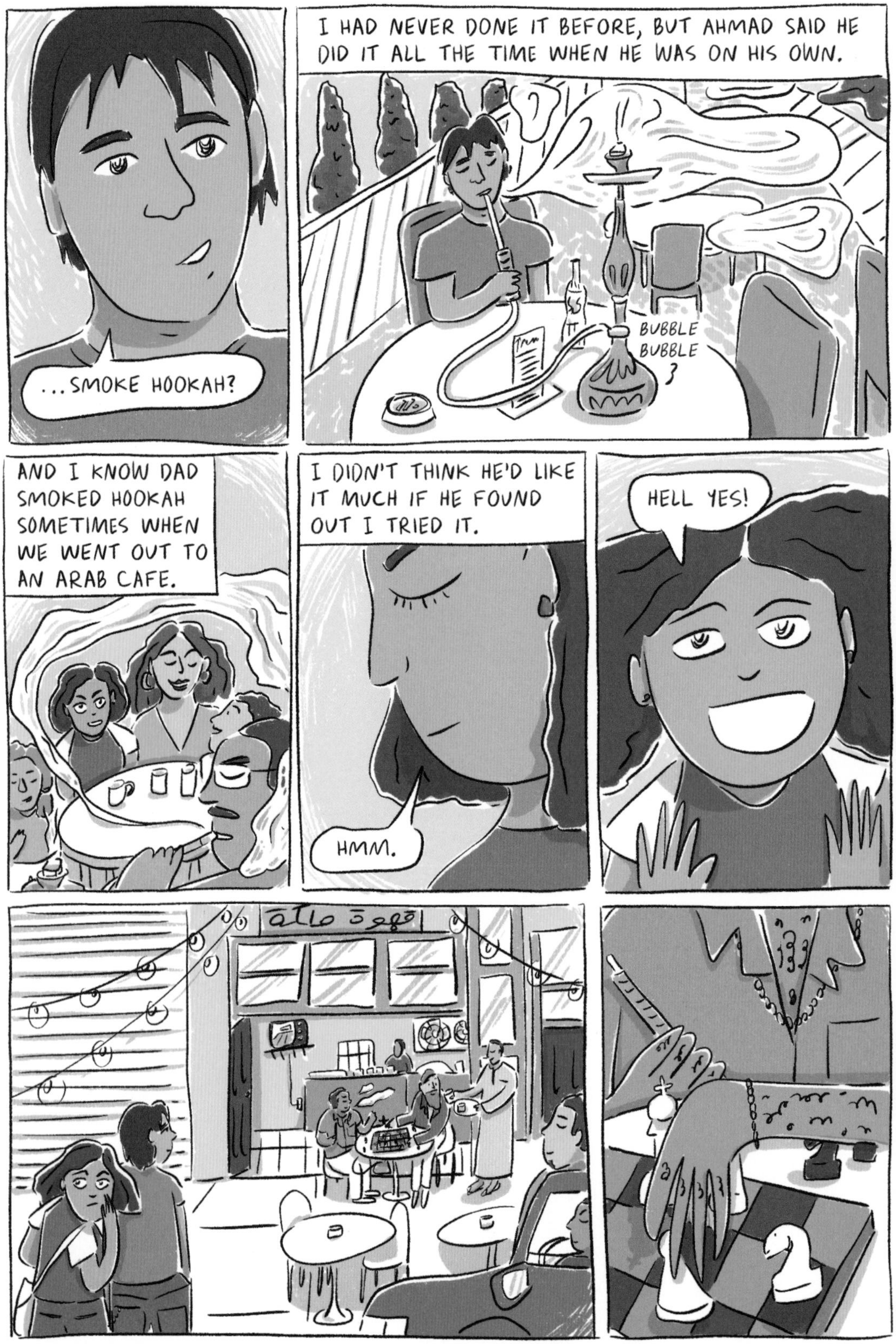

...SMOKE HOOKAH?
I HAD NEVER DONE IT BEFORE, BUT AHMAD SAID HE DID IT ALL THE TIME WHEN HE WAS ON HIS OWN.
BUBBLE
BUBBLE
AND I KNOW DAD SMOKED HOOKAH SOMETIMES WHEN WE WENT OUT TO AN ARAB CAFE.
I DIDN'T THINK HE'D LIKE IT MUCH IF HE FOUND OUT I TRIED IT.
HMM.
HELL YES!

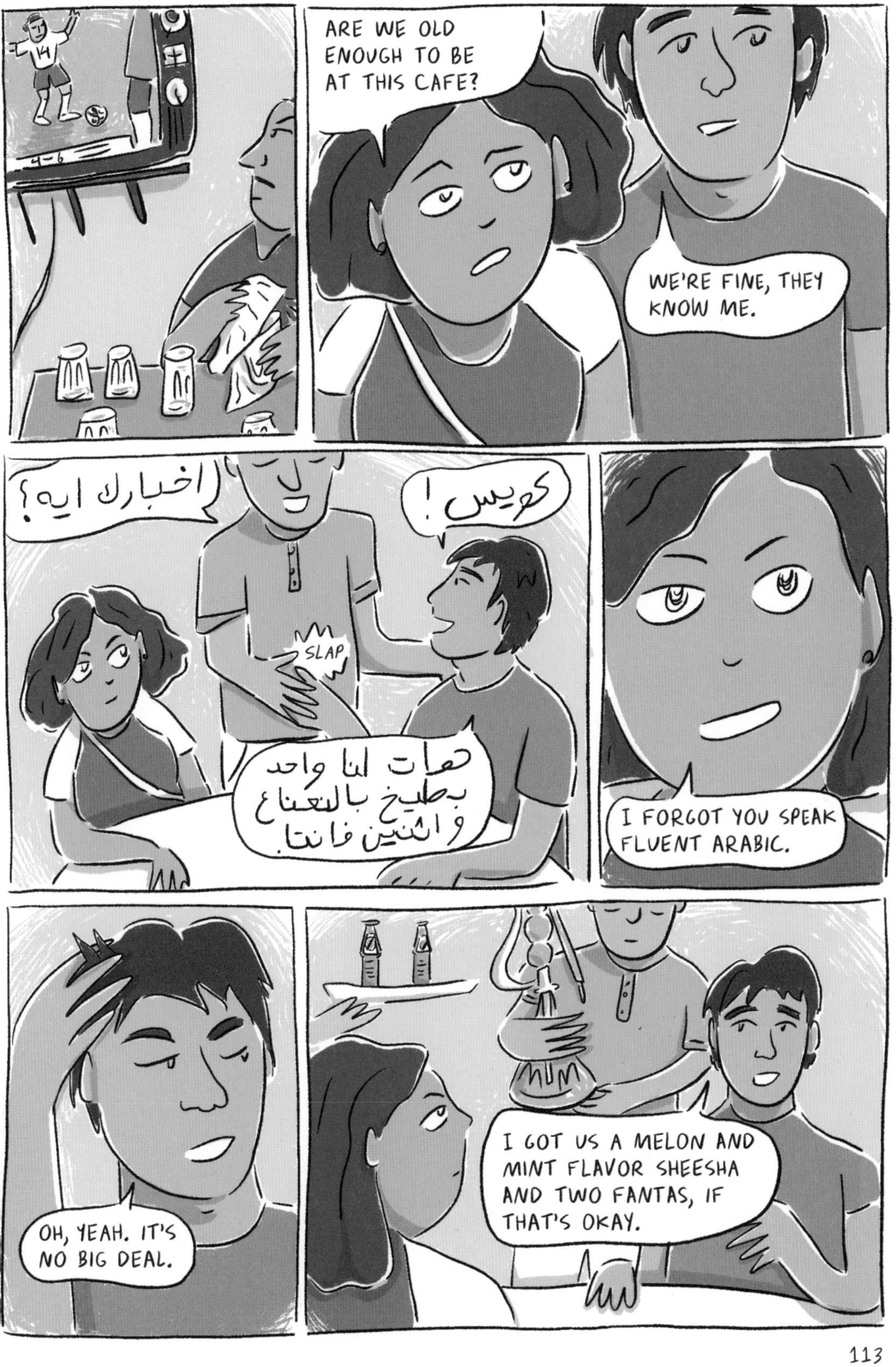
ARE WE OLD ENOUGH TO BE AT THIS CAFE?
WE'RE FINE, THEY KNOW ME.
اخبارك ايه؟
كريس!
SLAP
هات لنا واحد بطيخ بالنعناع واتنين فانتا.
I FORGOT YOU SPEAK FLUENT ARABIC.
OH, YEAH. IT'S NO BIG DEAL.
I GOT US A MELON AND MINT FLAVOR SHEESHA AND TWO FANTAS, IF THAT'S OKAY.

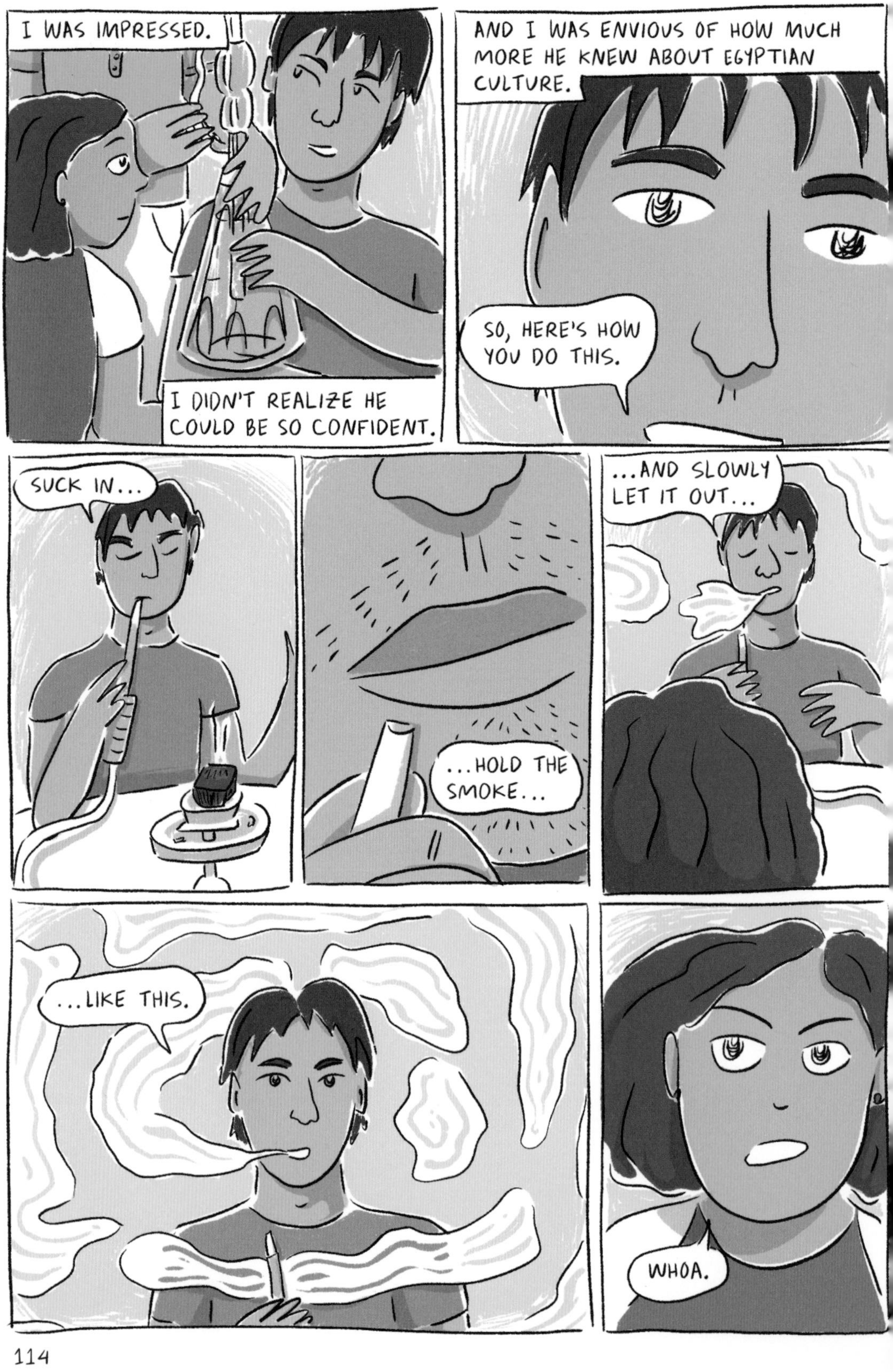
I WAS IMPRESSED.
I DIDN'T REALIZE HE COULD BE SO CONFIDENT.
AND I WAS ENVIOUS OF HOW MUCH MORE HE KNEW ABOUT EGYPTIAN CULTURE.
SO, HERE'S HOW YOU DO THIS.
SUCK IN...
...HOLD THE SMOKE...
...AND SLOWLY LET IT OUT...
...LIKE THIS.
WHOA.

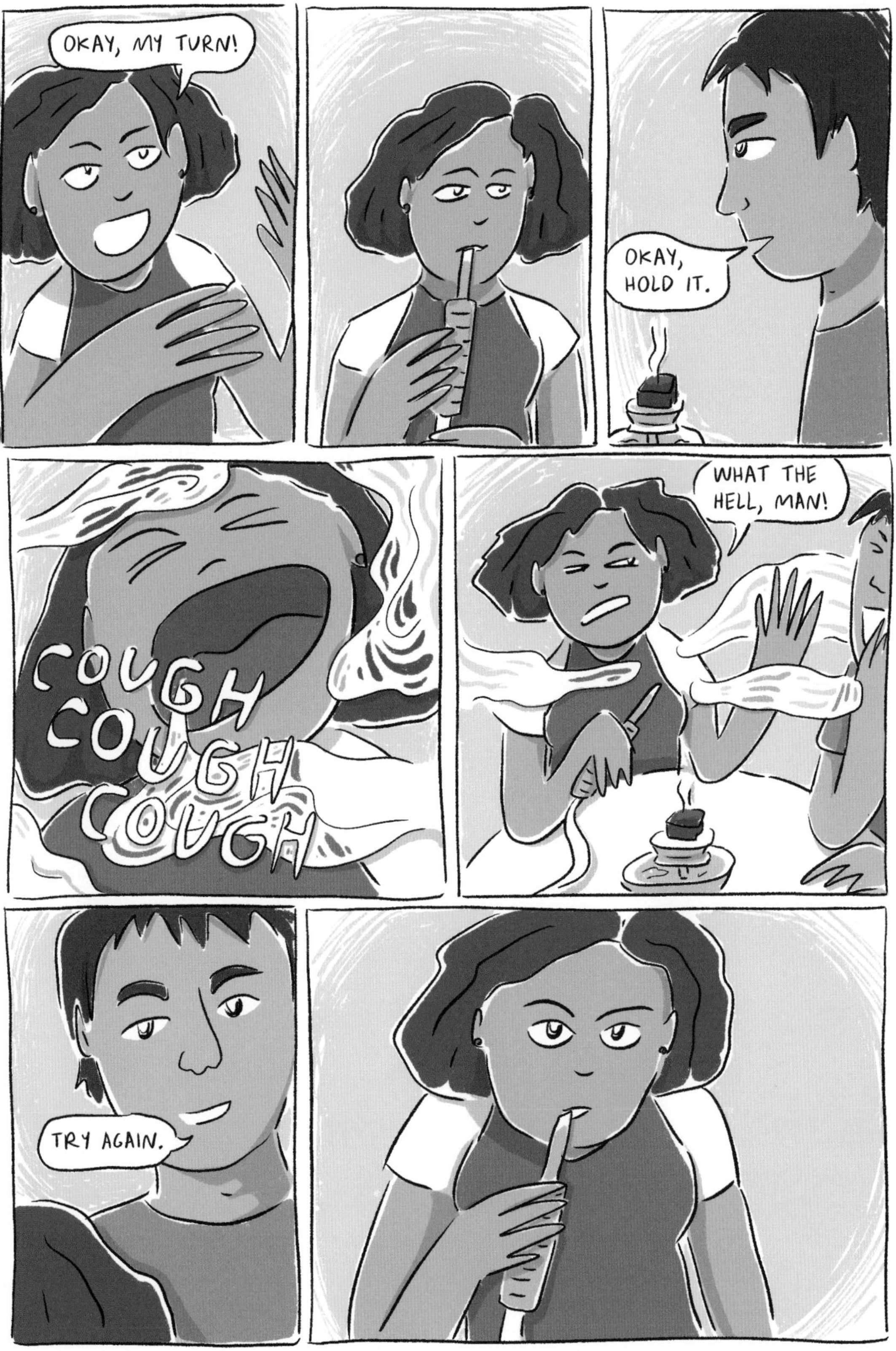
OKAY, MY TURN!
OKAY, HOLD IT.
COUGH COUGH COUGH
WHAT THE HELL, MAN!
TRY AGAIN.

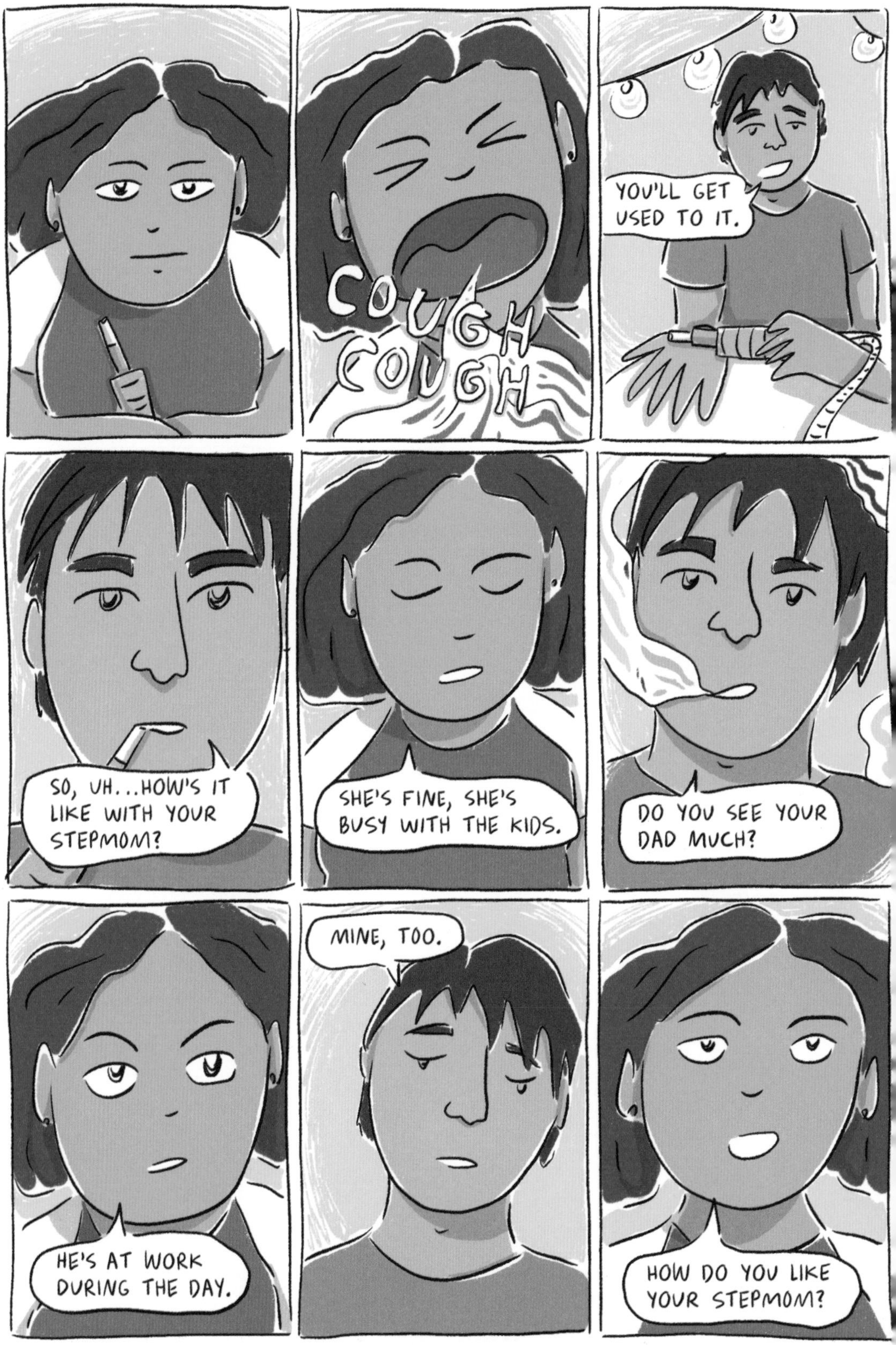

COUGH
COUGH
YOU'LL GET USED TO IT.
SO, UH...HOW'S IT LIKE WITH YOUR STEPMOM?
SHE'S FINE, SHE'S BUSY WITH THE KIDS.
DO YOU SEE YOUR DAD MUCH?
HE'S AT WORK DURING THE DAY.
MINE, TOO.
HOW DO YOU LIKE YOUR STEPMOM?

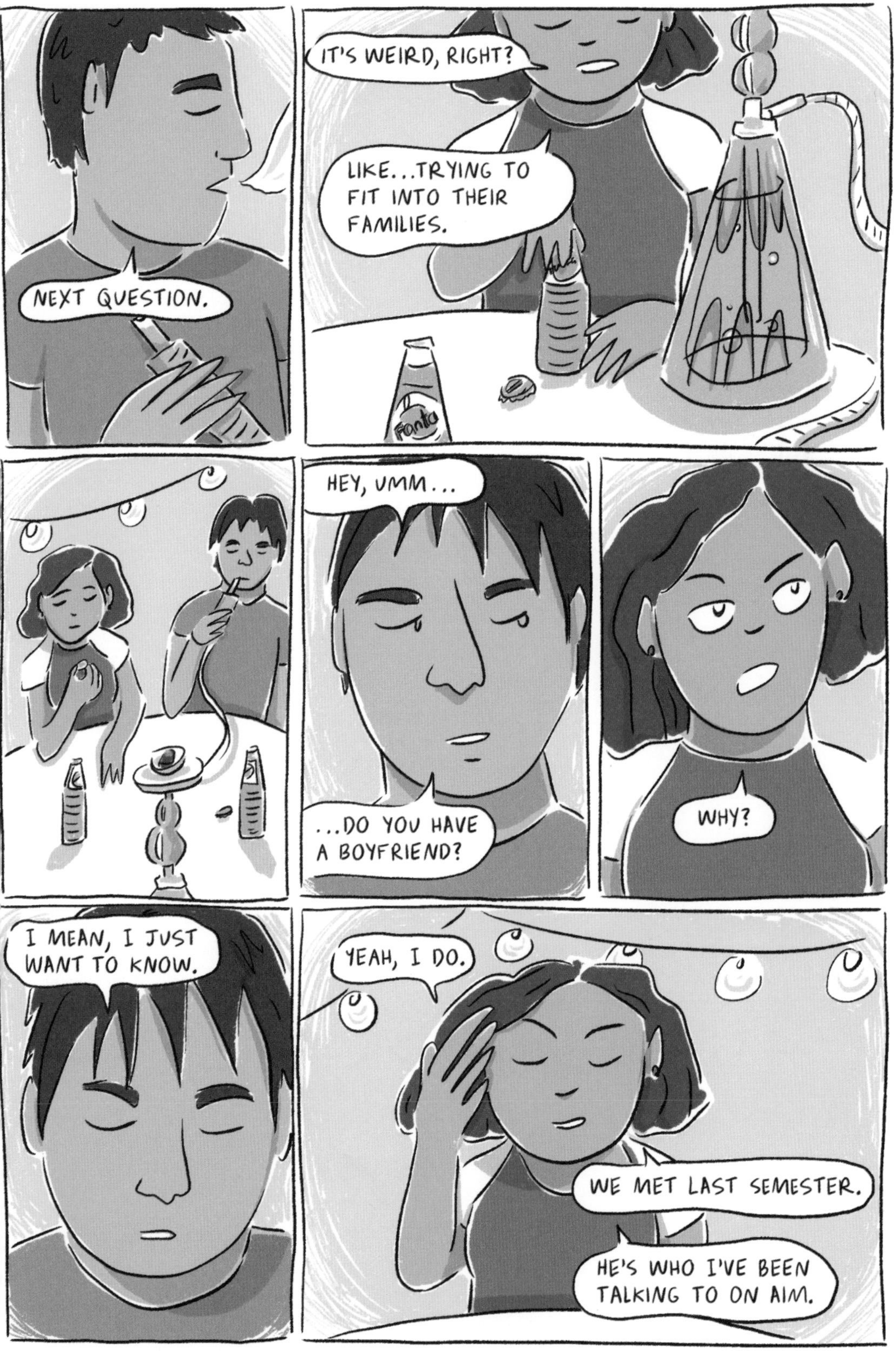
NEXT QUESTION.
IT'S WEIRD, RIGHT?
LIKE...TRYING TO FIT INTO THEIR FAMILIES.
Fanta
HEY, UMM...
...DO YOU HAVE A BOYFRIEND?
WHY?
I MEAN, I JUST WANT TO KNOW.
YEAH, I DO.
WE MET LAST SEMESTER.
HE'S WHO I'VE BEEN TALKING TO ON AIM.

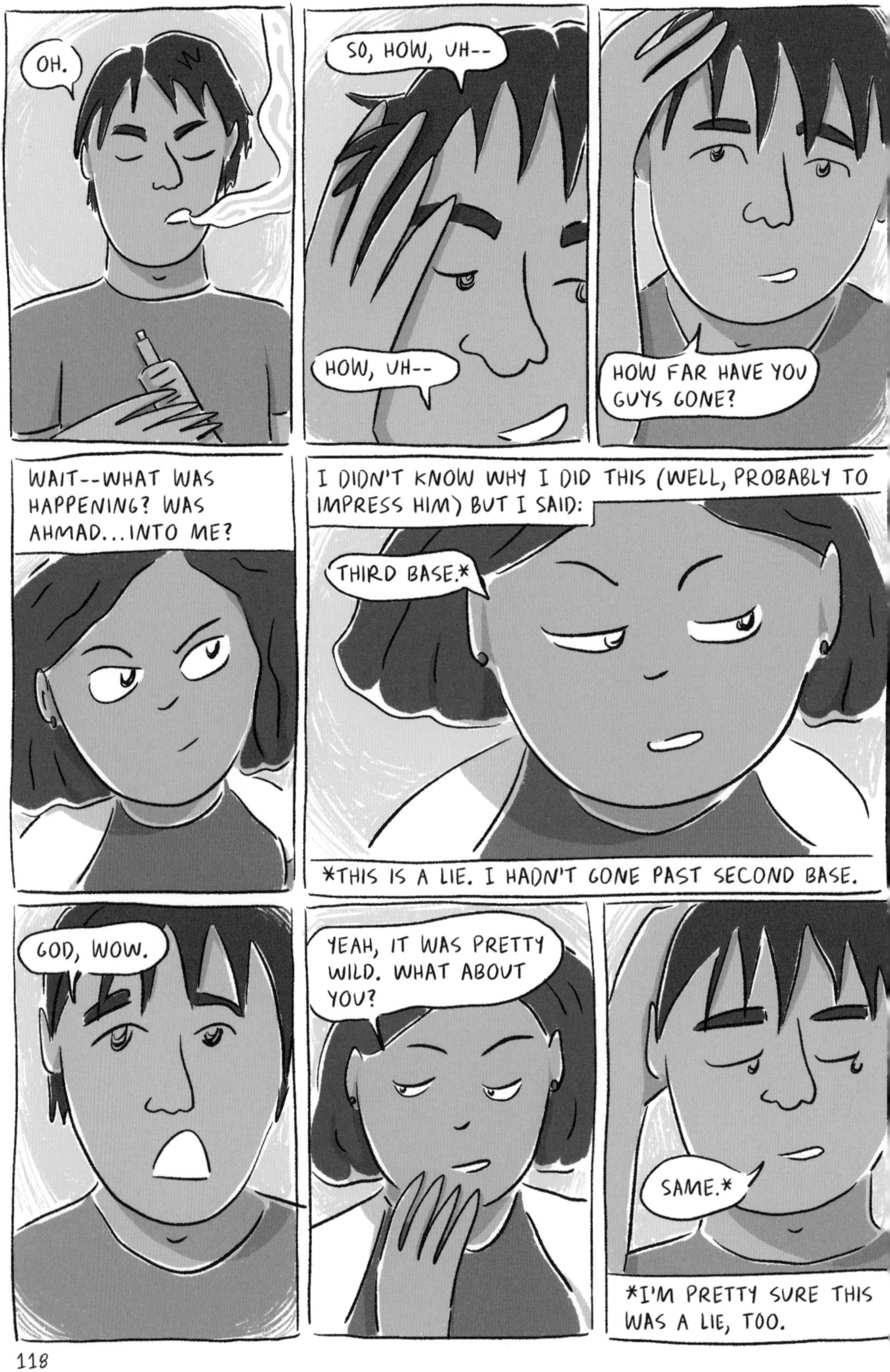
OH.
SO, HOW, UH--
HOW, UH--
HOW FAR HAVE YOU GUYS GONE?
WAIT--WHAT WAS HAPPENING? WAS AHMAD...INTO ME?
I DIDN'T KNOW WHY I DID THIS (WELL, PROBABLY TO IMPRESS HIM) BUT I SAID:
THIRD BASE.*
*THIS IS A LIE. I HADN'T GONE PAST SECOND BASE.
GOD, WOW.
YEAH, IT WAS PRETTY WILD. WHAT ABOUT YOU?
SAME.*
*I'M PRETTY SURE THIS WAS A LIE, TOO.

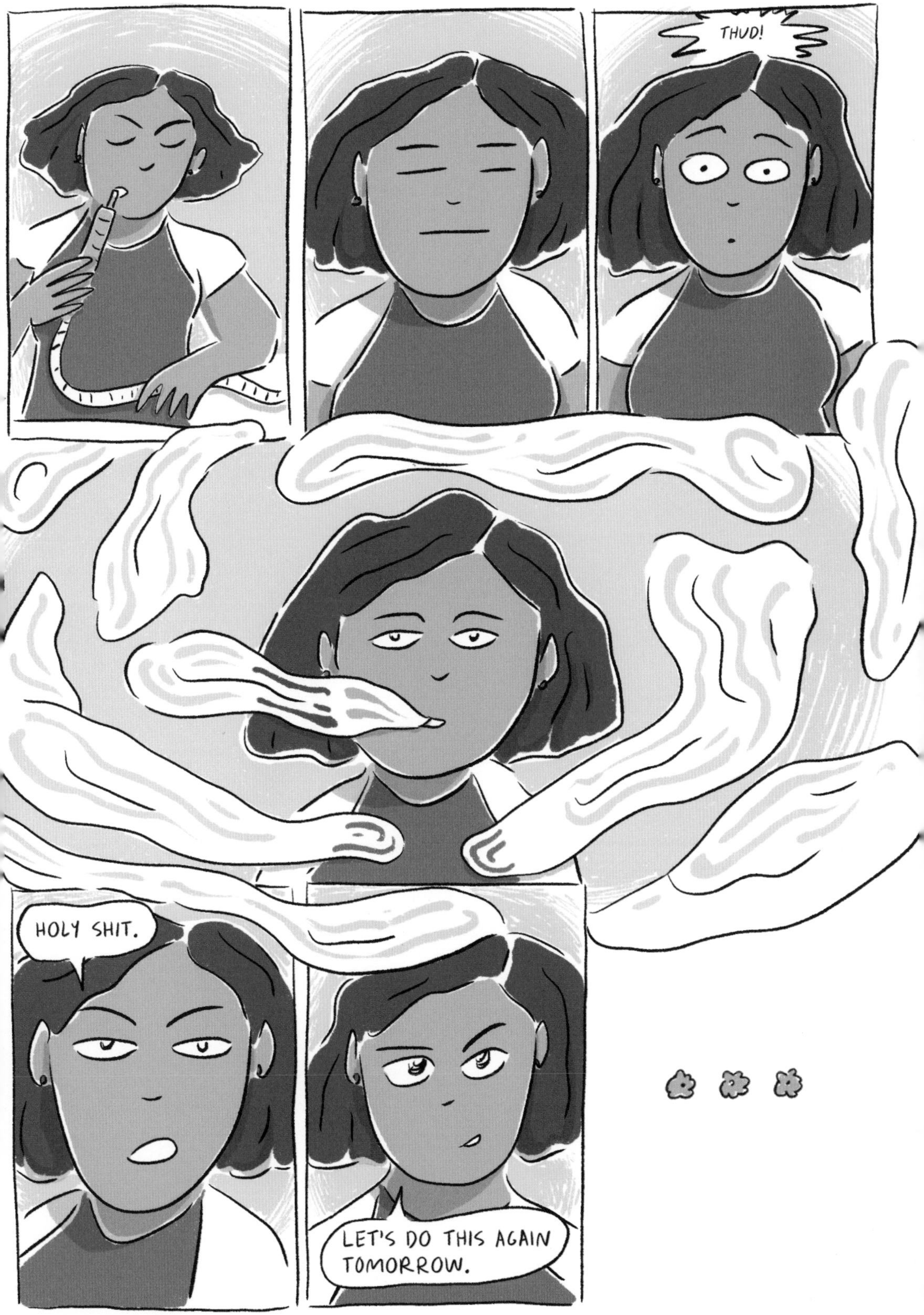
THUD!
HOLY SHIT.
LET'S DO THIS AGAIN TOMORROW.

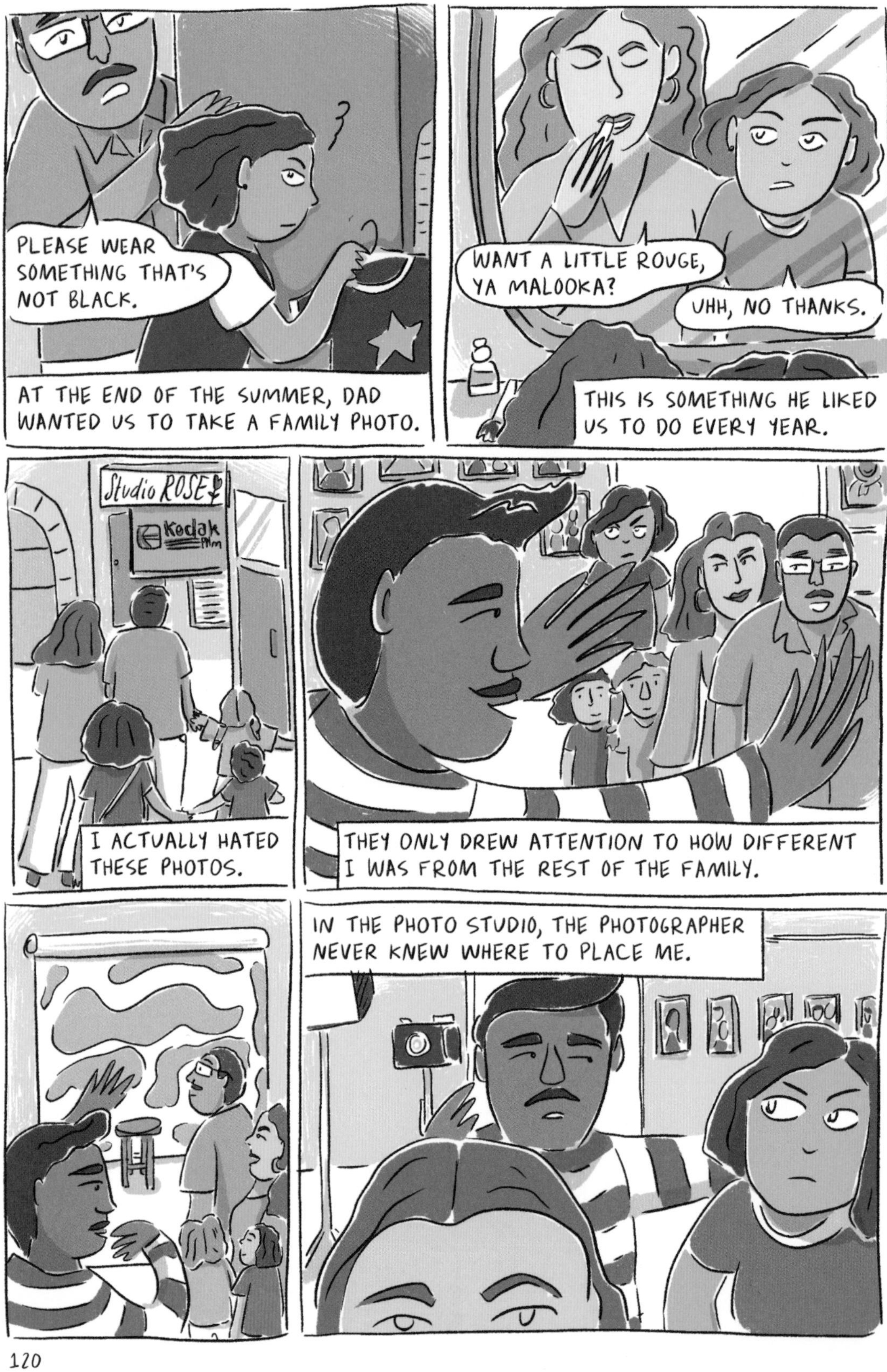
PLEASE WEAR SOMETHING THAT'S NOT BLACK.
AT THE END OF THE SUMMER, DAD WANTED US TO TAKE A FAMILY PHOTO.
WANT A LITTLE ROUGE, YA MALOOKA?
UHH, NO THANKS.
THIS IS SOMETHING HE LIKED US TO DO EVERY YEAR.
Studio ROSE
Kodak film
I ACTUALLY HATED THESE PHOTOS.
THEY ONLY DREW ATTENTION TO HOW DIFFERENT I WAS FROM THE REST OF THE FAMILY.
IN THE PHOTO STUDIO, THE PHOTOGRAPHER NEVER KNEW WHERE TO PLACE ME.

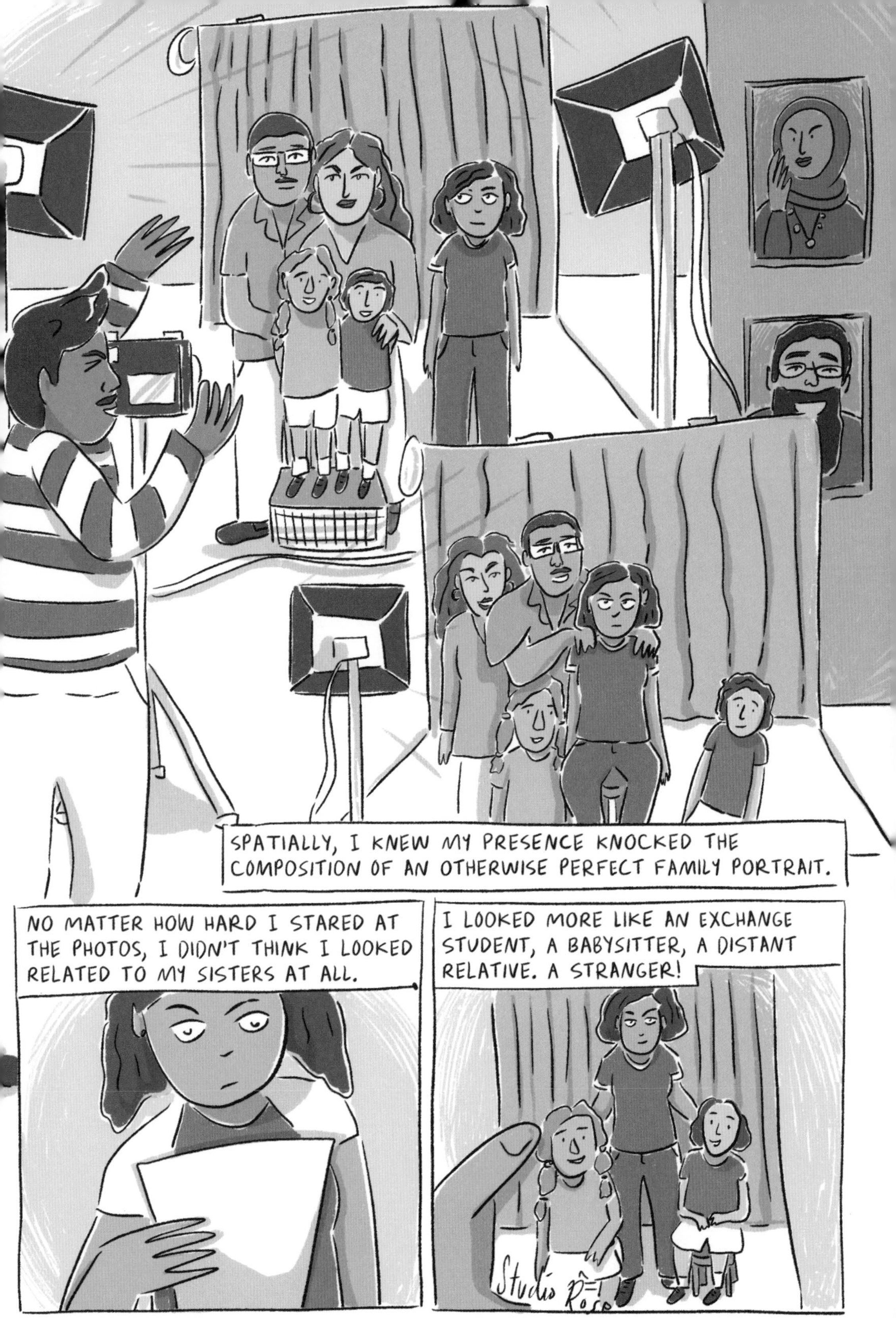
SPATIALLY, I KNEW MY PRESENCE KNOCKED THE COMPOSITION OF AN OTHERWISE PERFECT FAMILY PORTRAIT.
NO MATTER HOW HARD I STARED AT THE PHOTOS, I DIDN'T THINK I LOOKED RELATED TO MY SISTERS AT ALL.
I LOOKED MORE LIKE AN EXCHANGE STUDENT, A BABYSITTER, A DISTANT RELATIVE. A STRANGER!

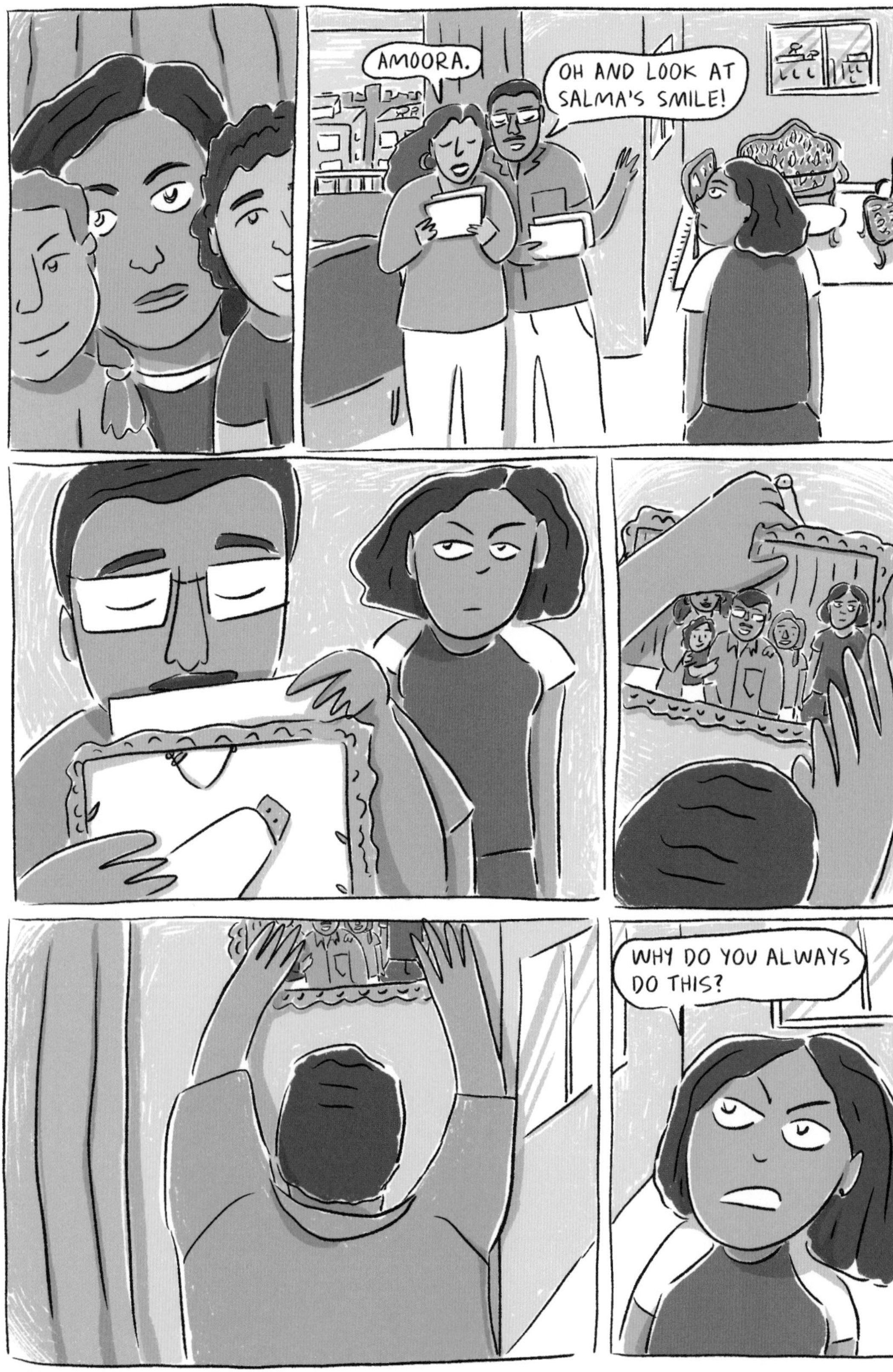
AMOORA.
OH AND LOOK AT SALMA'S SMILE!
WHY DO YOU ALWAYS DO THIS?

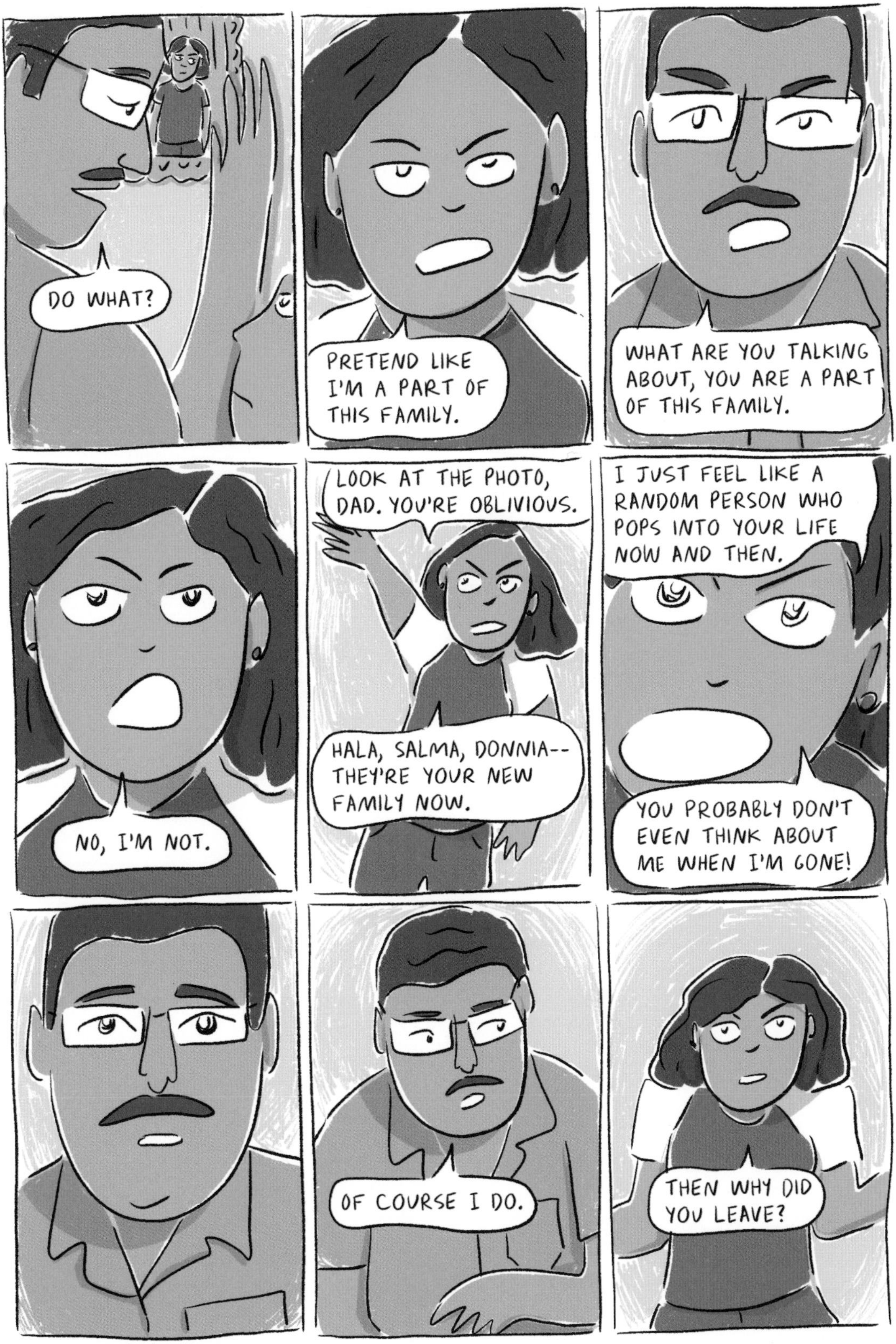
DO WHAT?
PRETEND LIKE I'M A PART OF THIS FAMILY.
WHAT ARE YOU TALKING ABOUT, YOU ARE A PART OF THIS FAMILY.
NO, I'M NOT.
LOOK AT THE PHOTO, DAD. YOU'RE OBLIVIOUS.
HALA, SALMA, DONNIA-- THEY'RE YOUR NEW FAMILY NOW.
I JUST FEEL LIKE A RANDOM PERSON WHO POPS INTO YOUR LIFE NOW AND THEN.
YOU PROBABLY DON'T EVEN THINK ABOUT ME WHEN I'M GONE!
OF COURSE I DO.
THEN WHY DID YOU LEAVE?

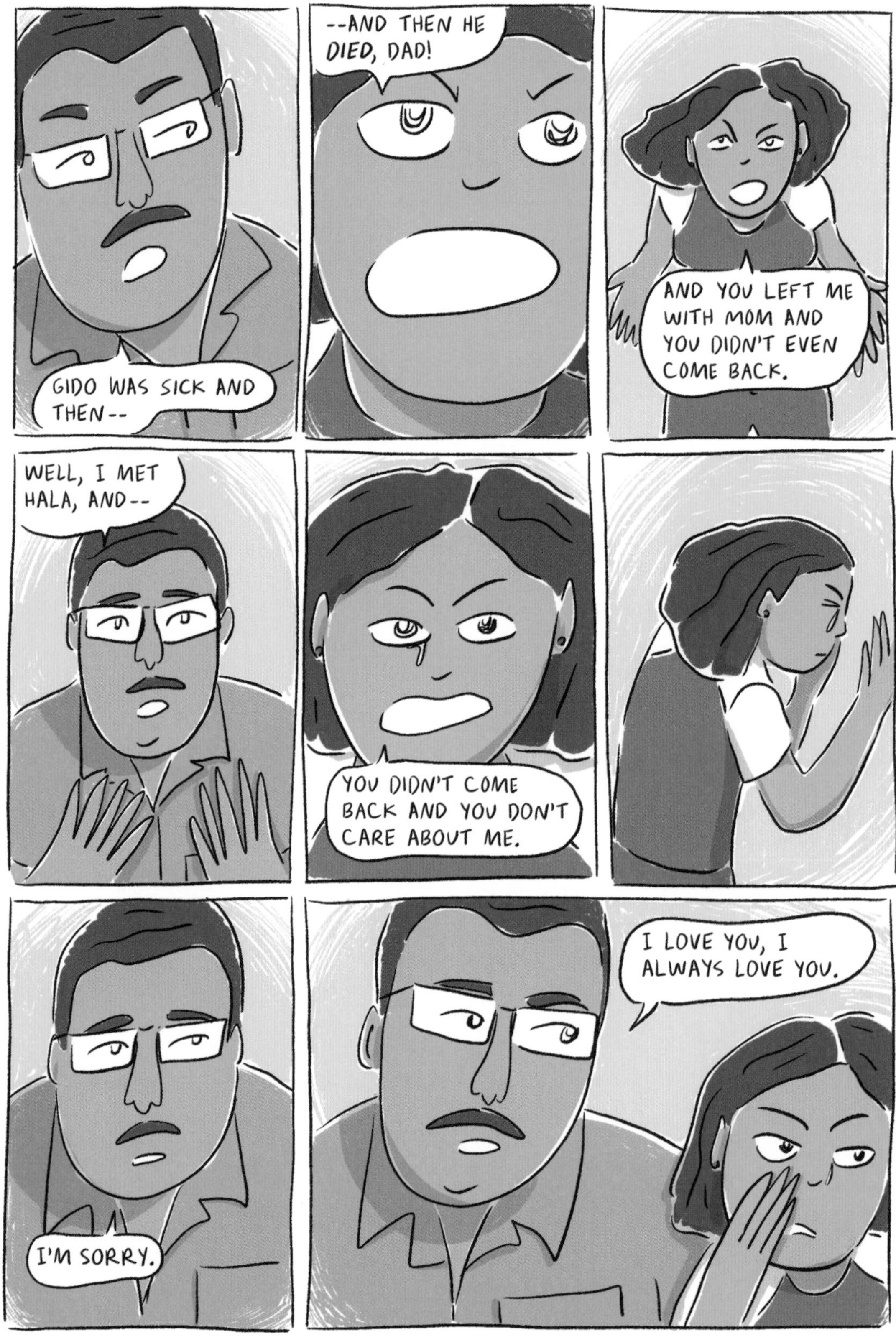
GIDO WAS SICK AND THEN--
--AND THEN HE DIED, DAD!
AND YOU LEFT ME WITH MOM AND YOU DIDN'T EVEN COME BACK.
WELL, I MET HALA, AND--
YOU DIDN'T COME BACK AND YOU DON'T CARE ABOUT ME.
I'M SORRY.
I LOVE YOU, I ALWAYS LOVE YOU.

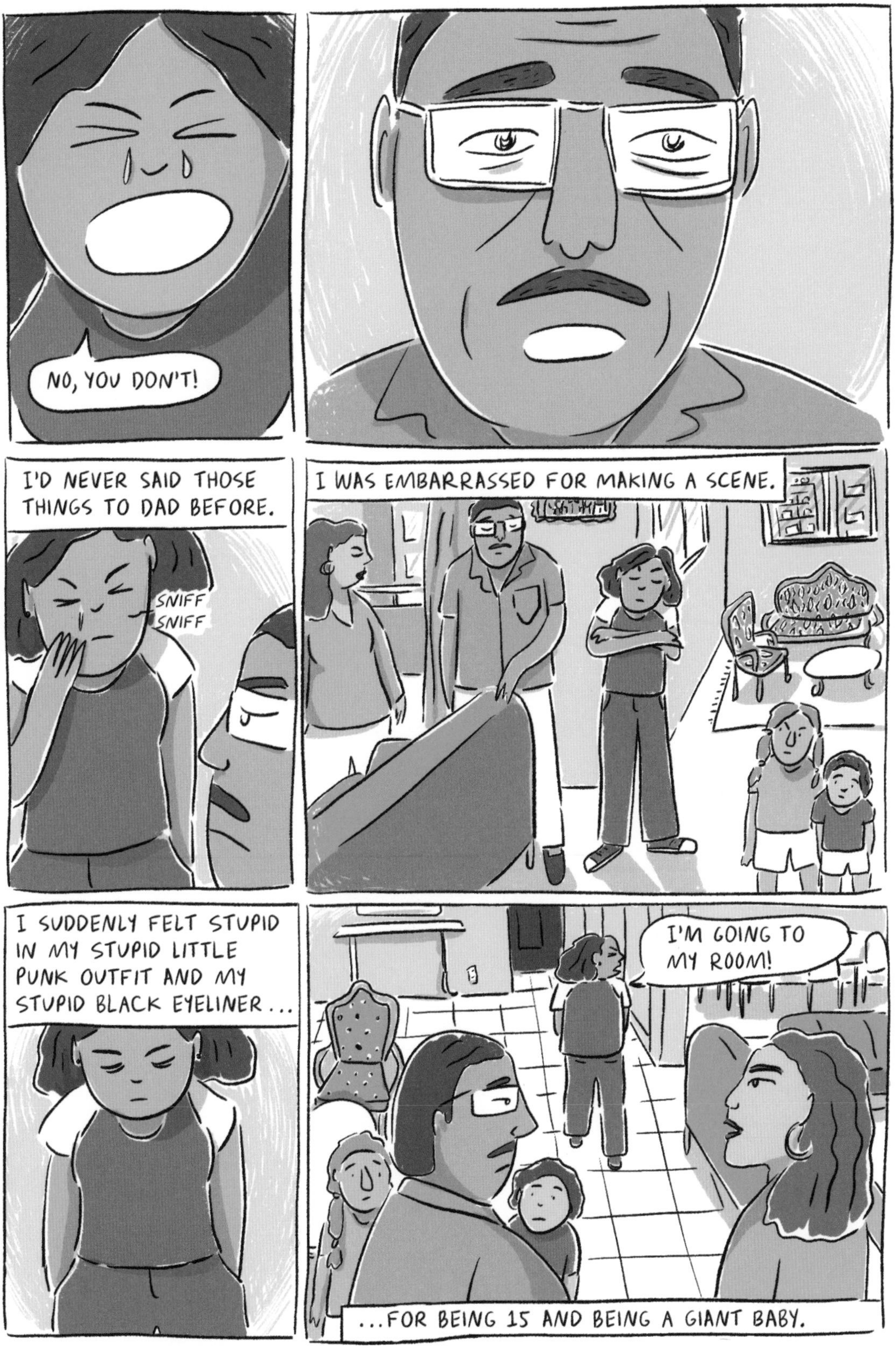

NO, YOU DON'T!
I'D NEVER SAID THOSE THINGS TO DAD BEFORE.
SNIFF
SNIFF
I WAS EMBARRASSED FOR MAKING A SCENE.
I SUDDENLY FELT STUPID IN MY STUPID LITTLE PUNK OUTFIT AND MY STUPID BLACK EYELINER...
I'M GOING TO MY ROOM!
...FOR BEING 15 AND BEING A GIANT BABY.

CHAPTER 6

The Egg

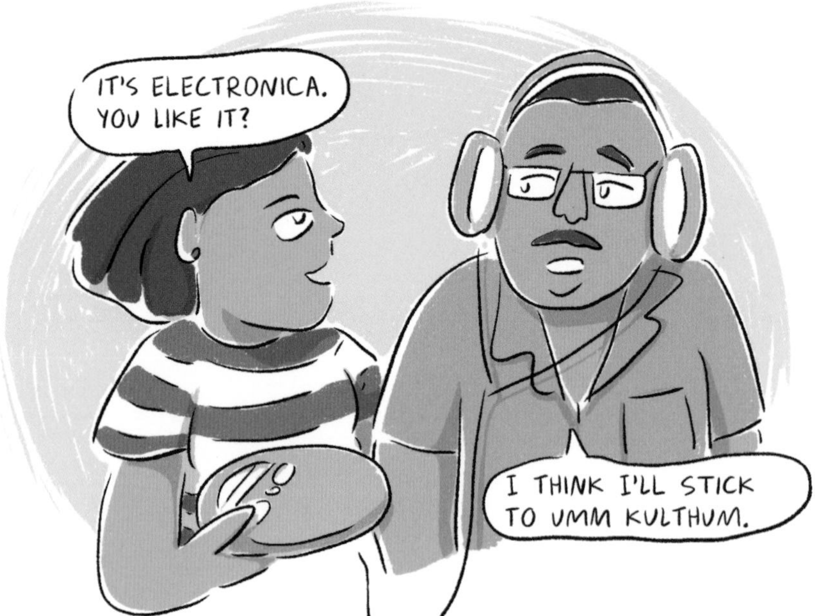

IT'S ELECTRONICA. YOU LIKE IT?
I THINK I'LL STICK TO UMM KULTHUM.

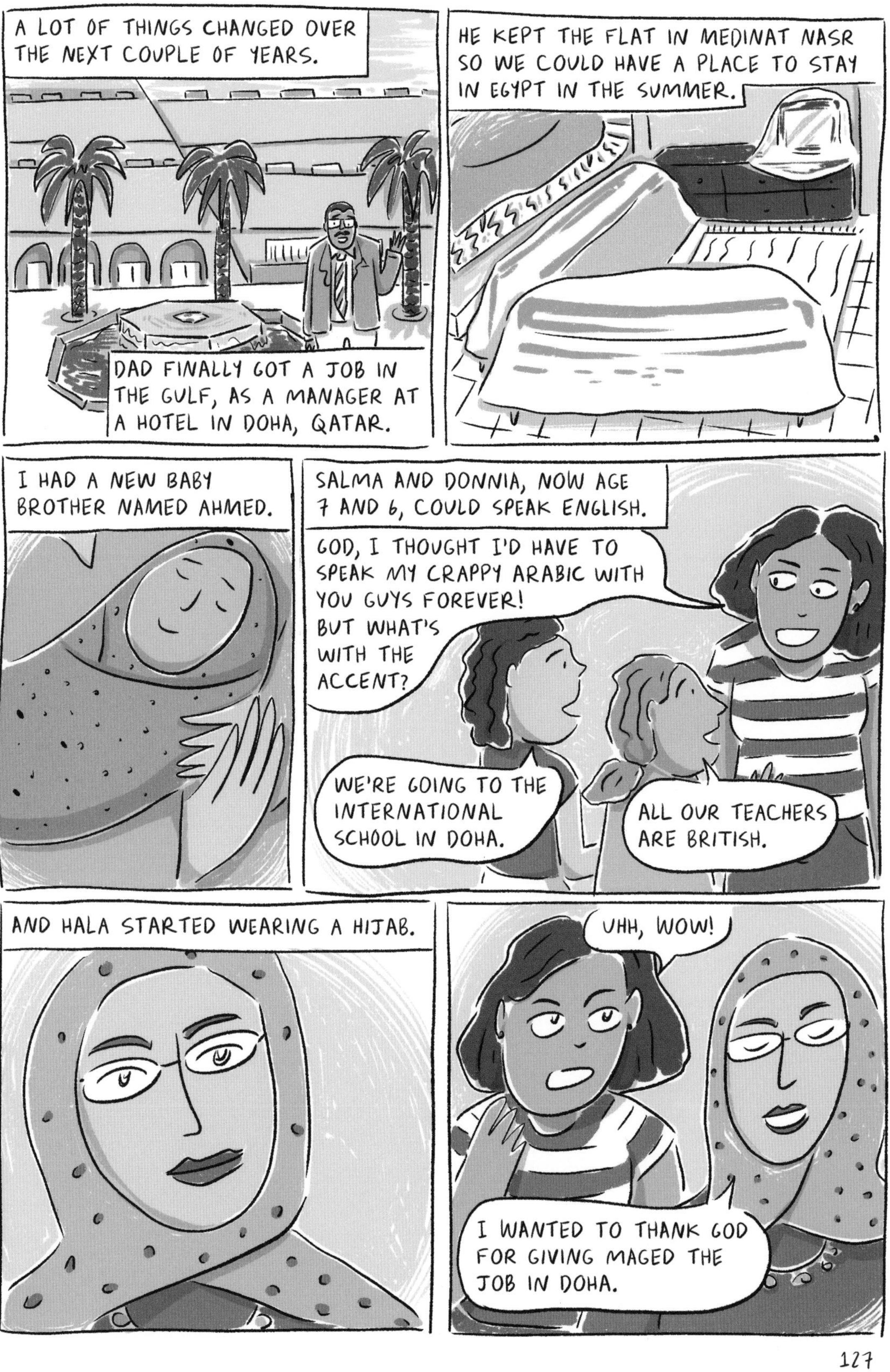
A LOT OF THINGS CHANGED OVER THE NEXT COUPLE OF YEARS.
DAD FINALLY GOT A JOB IN THE GULF, AS A MANAGER AT A HOTEL IN DOHA, QATAR.
HE KEPT THE FLAT IN MEDINAT NASR SO WE COULD HAVE A PLACE TO STAY IN EGYPT IN THE SUMMER.
I HAD A NEW BABY BROTHER NAMED AHMED.
SALMA AND DONNIA, NOW AGE 7 AND 6, COULD SPEAK ENGLISH.
GOD, I THOUGHT I'D HAVE TO SPEAK MY CRAPPY ARABIC WITH YOU GUYS FOREVER! BUT WHAT'S WITH THE ACCENT?
WE'RE GOING TO THE INTERNATIONAL SCHOOL IN DOHA.
ALL OUR TEACHERS ARE BRITISH.
AND HALA STARTED WEARING A HIJAB.
UHH, WOW!
I WANTED TO THANK GOD FOR GIVING MAGED THE JOB IN DOHA.

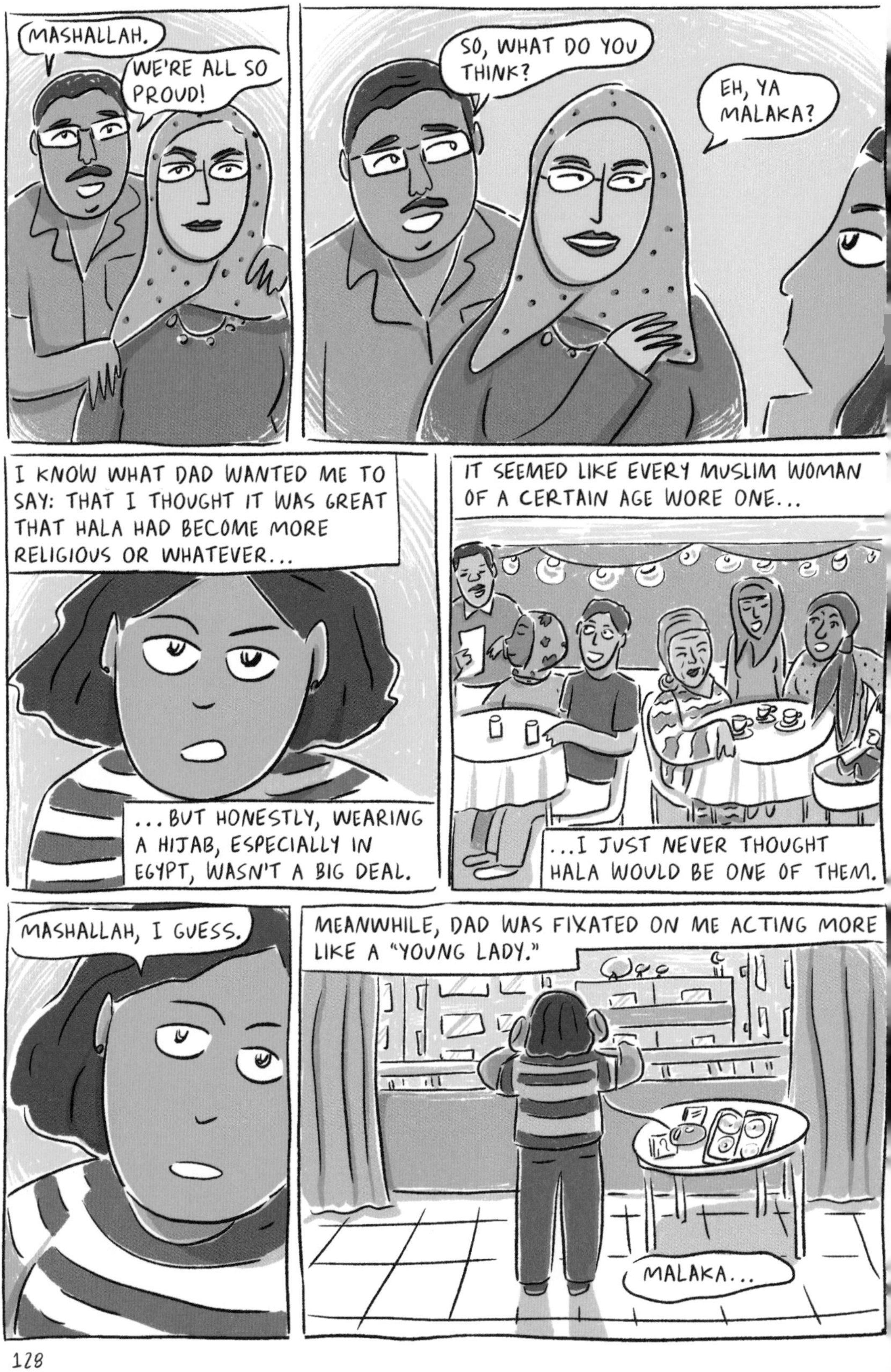

MASHALLAH.
WE'RE ALL SO PROUD!
SO, WHAT DO YOU THINK?
EH, YA MALAKA?
I KNOW WHAT DAD WANTED ME TO SAY: THAT I THOUGHT IT WAS GREAT THAT HALA HAD BECOME MORE RELIGIOUS OR WHATEVER...
...BUT HONESTLY, WEARING A HIJAB, ESPECIALLY IN EGYPT, WASN'T A BIG DEAL.
IT SEEMED LIKE EVERY MUSLIM WOMAN OF A CERTAIN AGE WORE ONE...
...I JUST NEVER THOUGHT HALA WOULD BE ONE OF THEM.
MASHALLAH, I GUESS.
MEANWHILE, DAD WAS FIXATED ON ME ACTING MORE LIKE A "YOUNG LADY."
MALAKA...

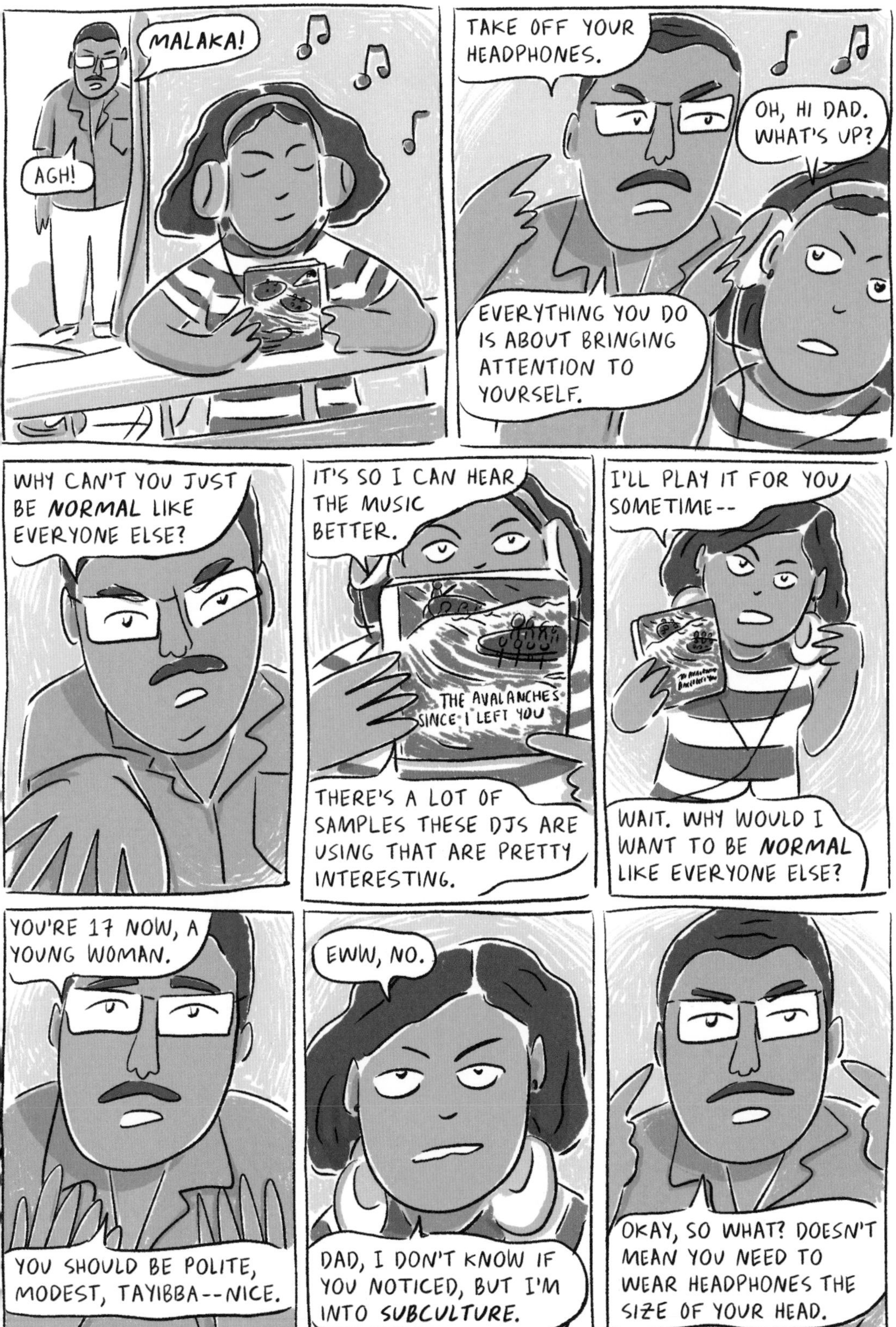
MALAKA!
AGH!
TAKE OFF YOUR HEADPHONES.
OH, HI DAD. WHAT'S UP?
EVERYTHING YOU DO IS ABOUT BRINGING ATTENTION TO YOURSELF.
WHY CAN'T YOU JUST BE **NORMAL** LIKE EVERYONE ELSE?
IT'S SO I CAN HEAR THE MUSIC BETTER.
THE AVALANCHES SINCE I LEFT YOU
THERE'S A LOT OF SAMPLES THESE DJS ARE USING THAT ARE PRETTY INTERESTING.
I'LL PLAY IT FOR YOU SOMETIME--
WAIT. WHY WOULD I WANT TO BE **NORMAL** LIKE EVERYONE ELSE?
YOU'RE 17 NOW, A YOUNG WOMAN.
YOU SHOULD BE POLITE, MODEST, TAYIBBA--NICE.
EWW, NO.
DAD, I DON'T KNOW IF YOU NOTICED, BUT I'M INTO **SUBCULTURE**.
OKAY, SO WHAT? DOESN'T MEAN YOU NEED TO WEAR HEADPHONES THE SIZE OF YOUR HEAD.

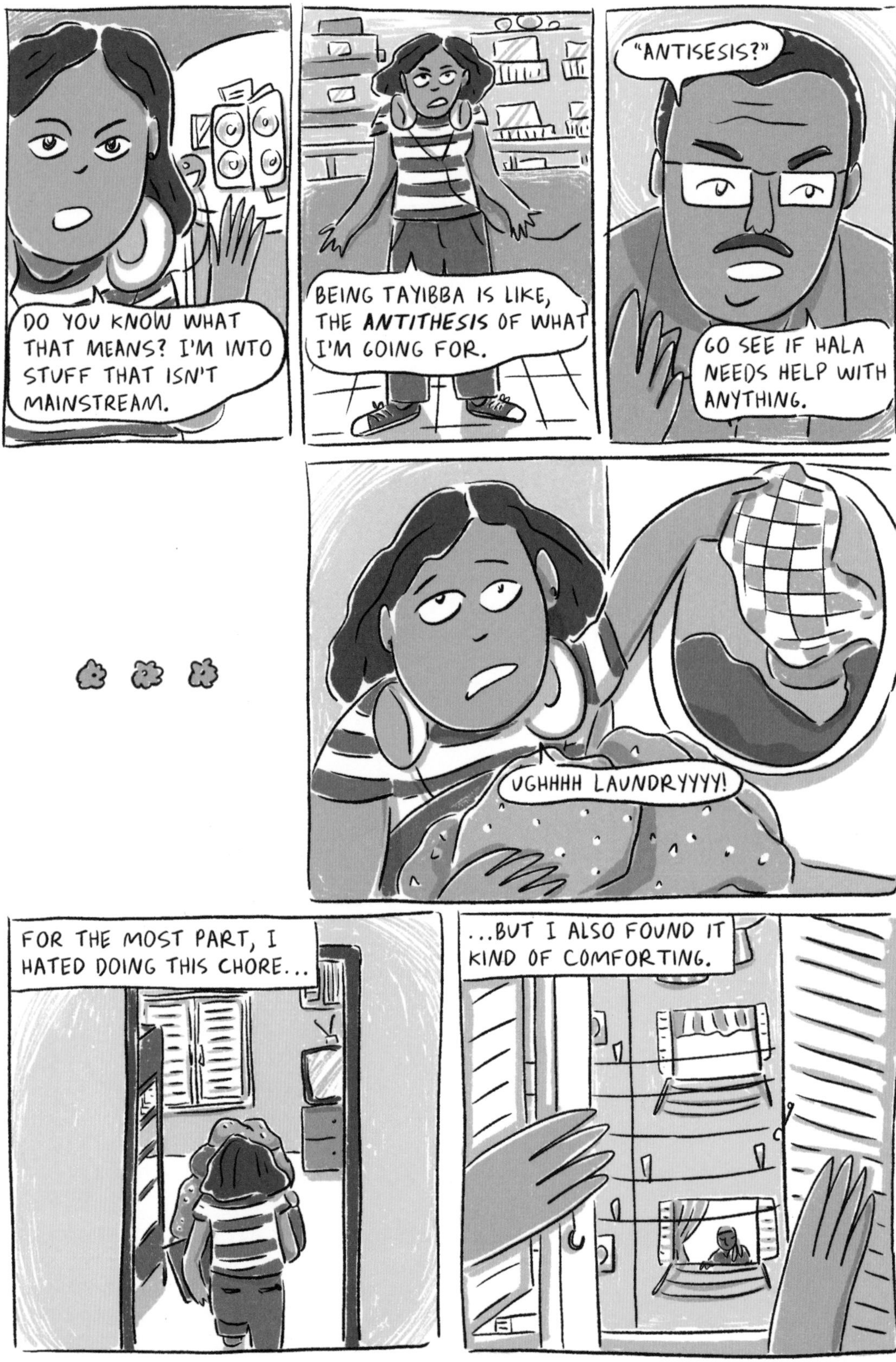

DO YOU KNOW WHAT THAT MEANS? I'M INTO STUFF THAT ISN'T MAINSTREAM.
BEING TAYIBBA IS LIKE, THE **ANTITHESIS** OF WHAT I'M GOING FOR.
"ANTISESIS?"
GO SEE IF HALA NEEDS HELP WITH ANYTHING.
UGHHHH LAUNDRYYYY!
FOR THE MOST PART, I HATED DOING THIS CHORE...
...BUT I ALSO FOUND IT KIND OF COMFORTING.

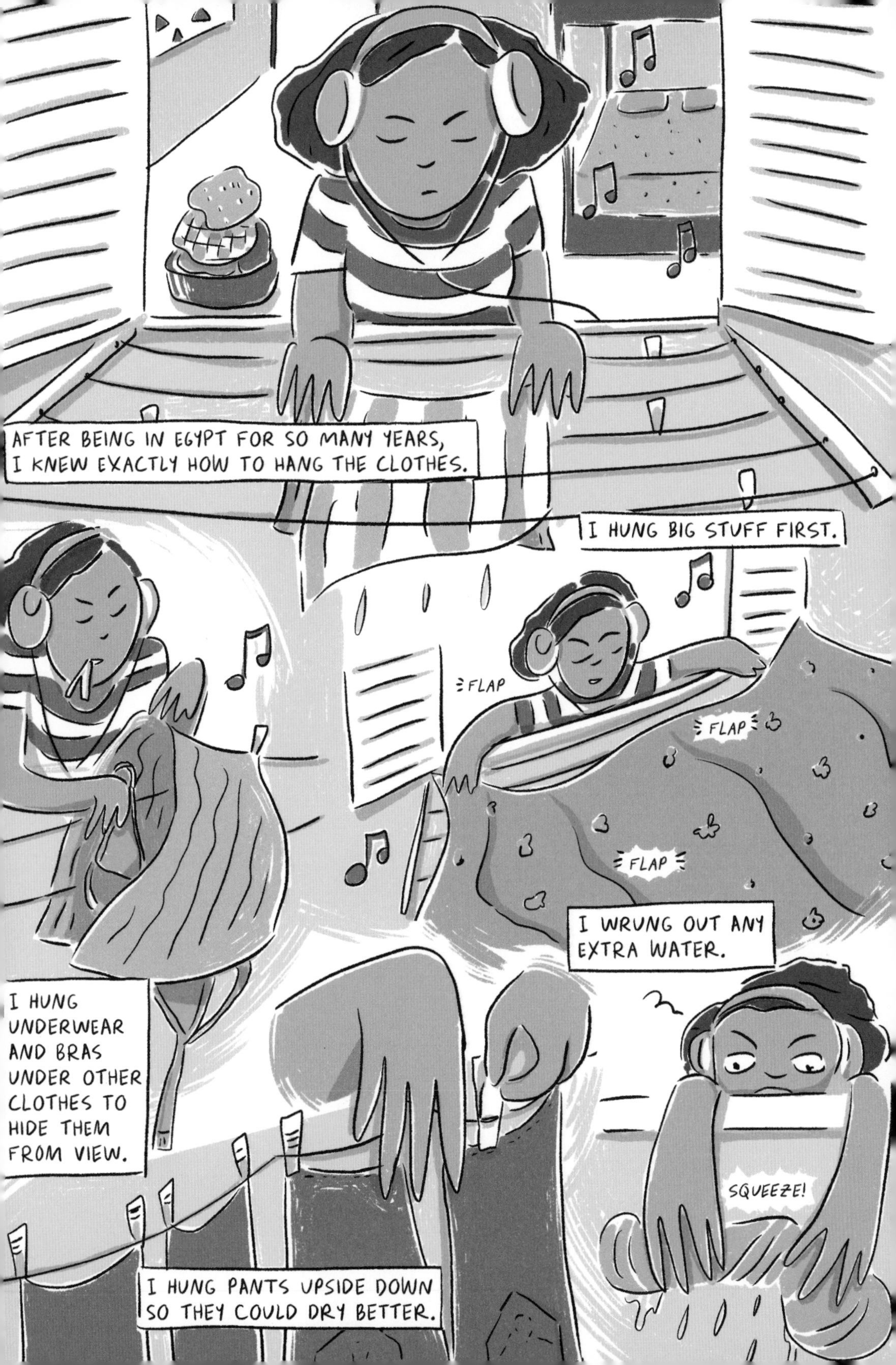
AFTER BEING IN EGYPT FOR SO MANY YEARS, I KNEW EXACTLY HOW TO HANG THE CLOTHES.
I HUNG BIG STUFF FIRST.
FLAP
FLAP
FLAP
I WRUNG OUT ANY EXTRA WATER.
I HUNG UNDERWEAR AND BRAS UNDER OTHER CLOTHES TO HIDE THEM FROM VIEW.
SQUEEZE!
I HUNG PANTS UPSIDE DOWN SO THEY COULD DRY BETTER.

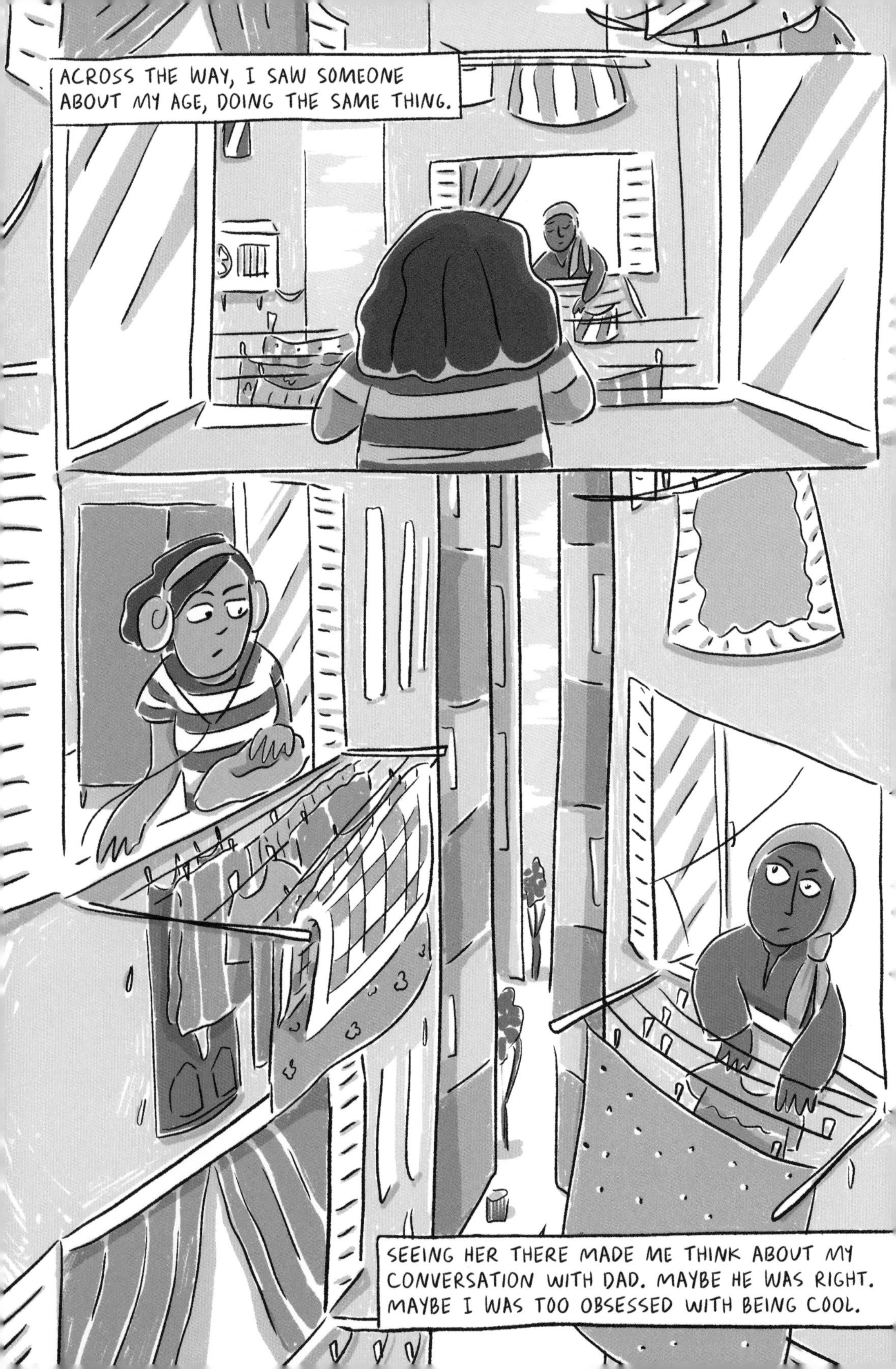
ACROSS THE WAY, I SAW SOMEONE ABOUT MY AGE, DOING THE SAME THING.
SEEING HER THERE MADE ME THINK ABOUT MY CONVERSATION WITH DAD. MAYBE HE WAS RIGHT. MAYBE I WAS TOO OBSESSED WITH BEING COOL.

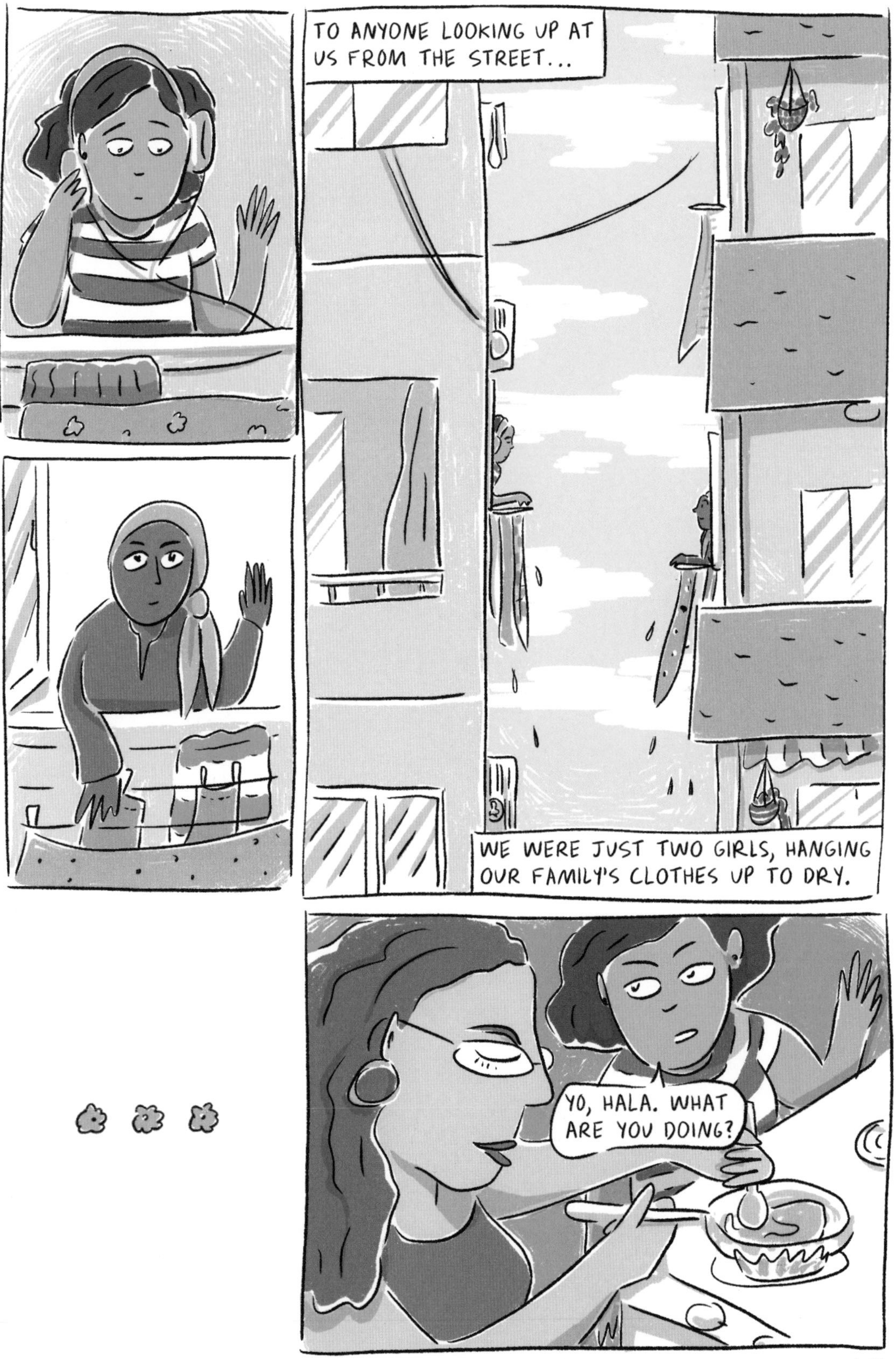
TO ANYONE LOOKING UP AT US FROM THE STREET...
WE WERE JUST TWO GIRLS, HANGING OUR FAMILY'S CLOTHES UP TO DRY.
YO, HALA. WHAT ARE YOU DOING?

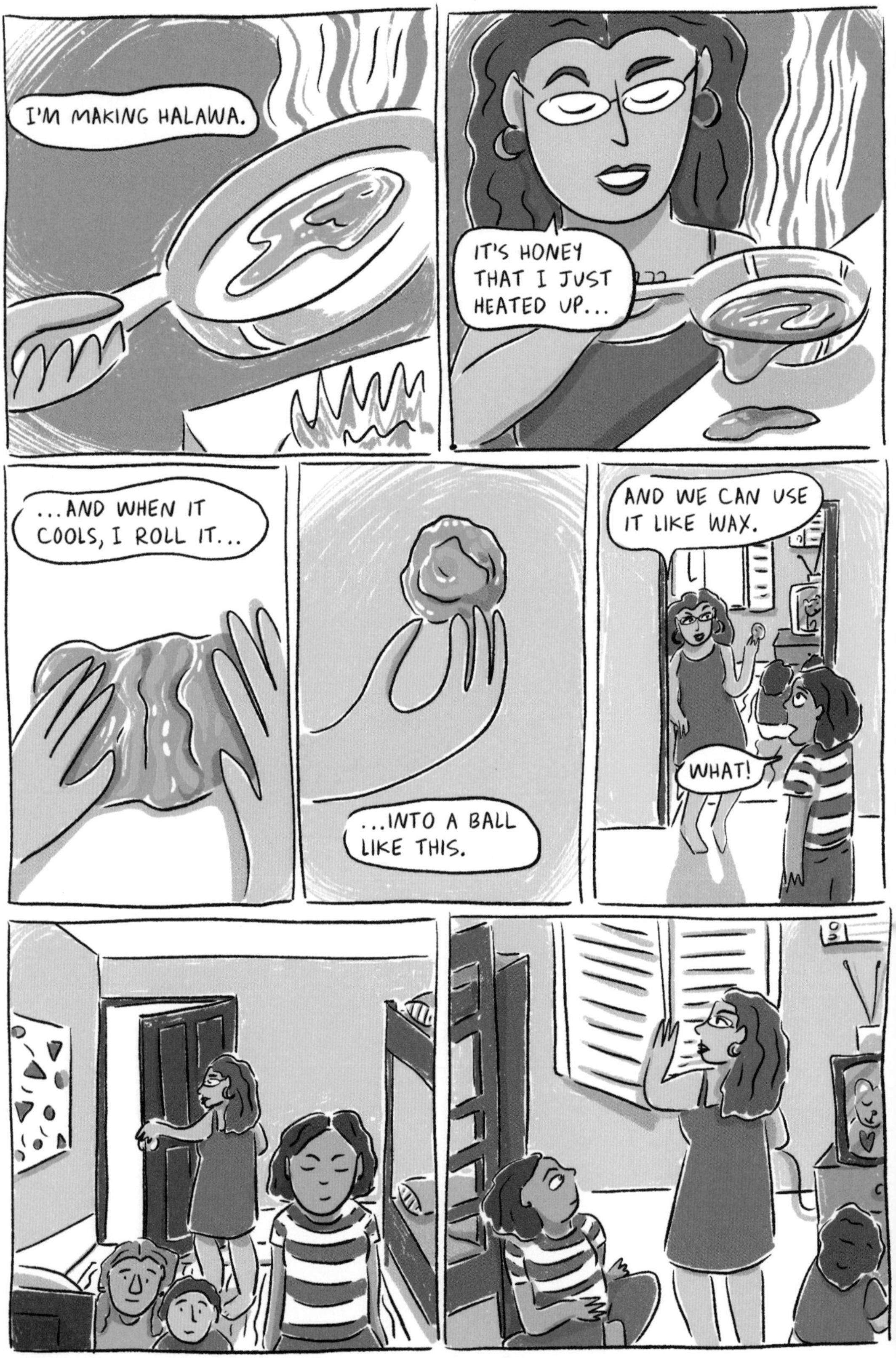
I'M MAKING HALAWA.
IT'S HONEY THAT I JUST HEATED UP...
...AND WHEN IT COOLS, I ROLL IT...
...INTO A BALL LIKE THIS.
AND WE CAN USE IT LIKE WAX.
WHAT!

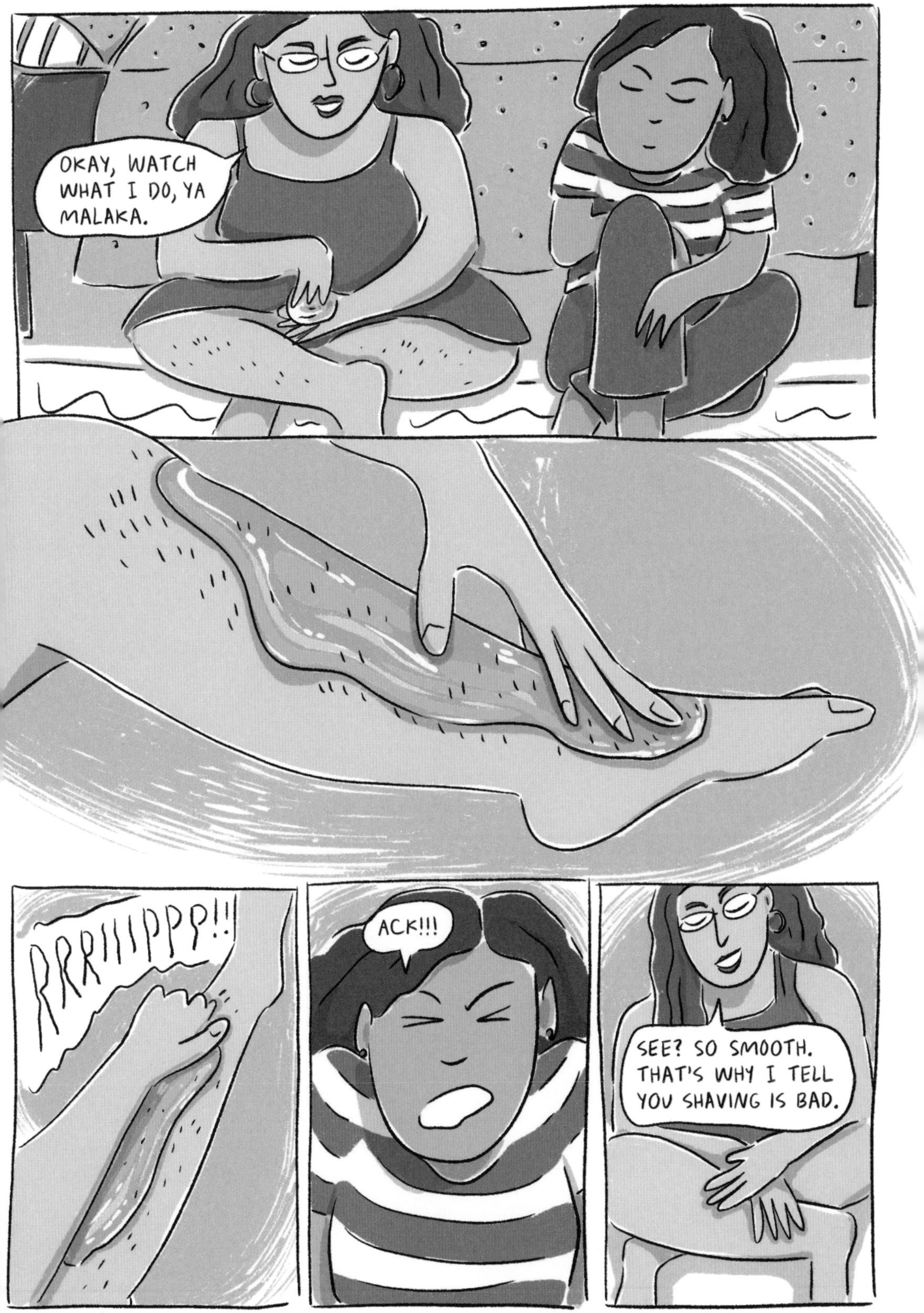
OKAY, WATCH WHAT I DO, YA MALAKA.
RRRIIIPPP!!!
ACK!!!
SEE? SO SMOOTH. THAT'S WHY I TELL YOU SHAVING IS BAD.

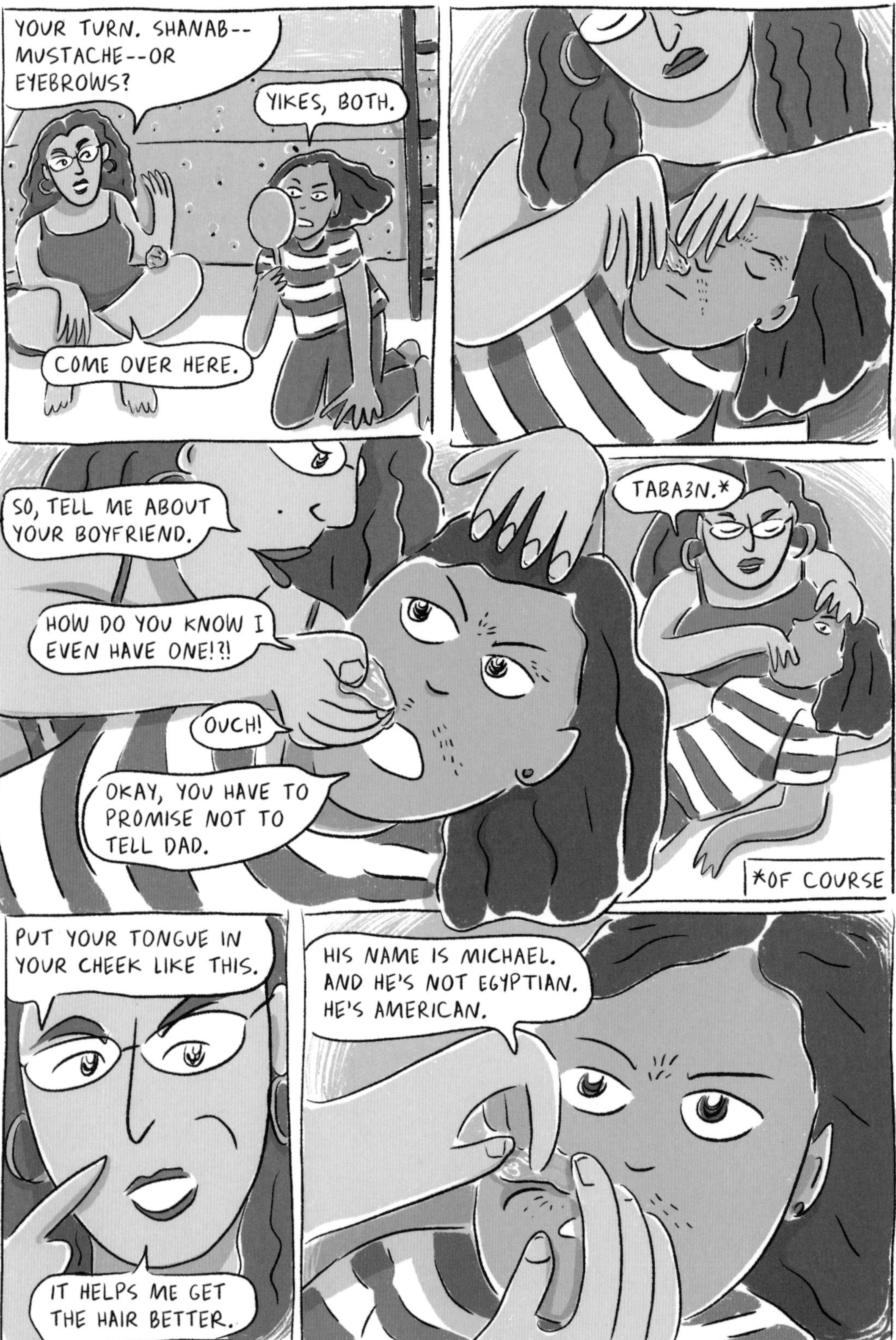
YOUR TURN. SHANAB--MUSTACHE--OR EYEBROWS?
YIKES, BOTH.
COME OVER HERE.
SO, TELL ME ABOUT YOUR BOYFRIEND.
HOW DO YOU KNOW I EVEN HAVE ONE!?!
OUCH!
OKAY, YOU HAVE TO PROMISE NOT TO TELL DAD.
TABA3N.*
*OF COURSE
PUT YOUR TONGUE IN YOUR CHEEK LIKE THIS.
IT HELPS ME GET THE HAIR BETTER.
HIS NAME IS MICHAEL. AND HE'S NOT EGYPTIAN. HE'S AMERICAN.

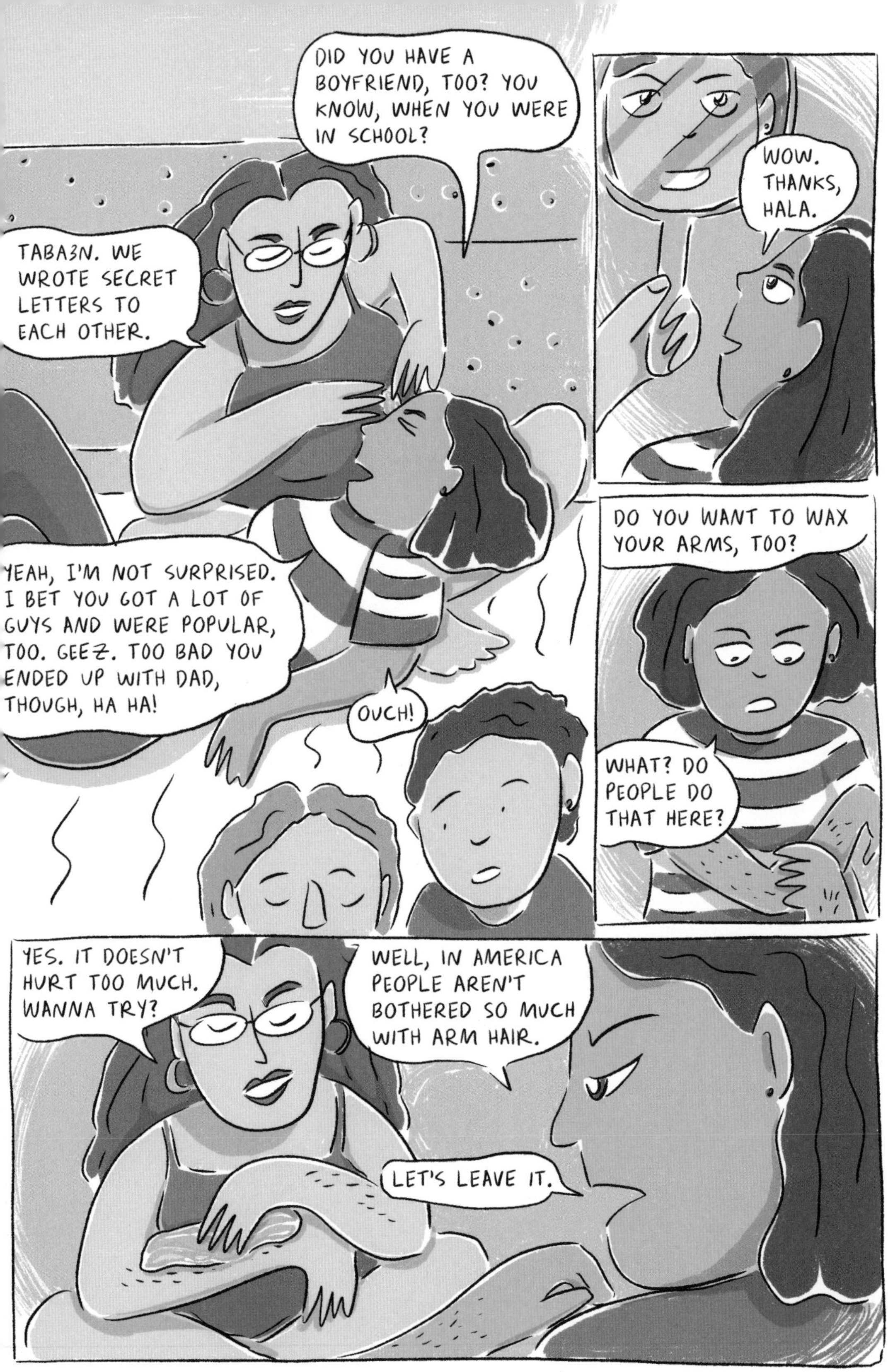
DID YOU HAVE A BOYFRIEND, TOO? YOU KNOW, WHEN YOU WERE IN SCHOOL?
TABA3N. WE WROTE SECRET LETTERS TO EACH OTHER.
WOW. THANKS, HALA.
YEAH, I'M NOT SURPRISED. I BET YOU GOT A LOT OF GUYS AND WERE POPULAR, TOO. GEEZ. TOO BAD YOU ENDED UP WITH DAD, THOUGH, HA HA!
OUCH!
DO YOU WANT TO WAX YOUR ARMS, TOO?
WHAT? DO PEOPLE DO THAT HERE?
YES. IT DOESN'T HURT TOO MUCH. WANNA TRY?
WELL, IN AMERICA PEOPLE AREN'T BOTHERED SO MUCH WITH ARM HAIR.
LET'S LEAVE IT.

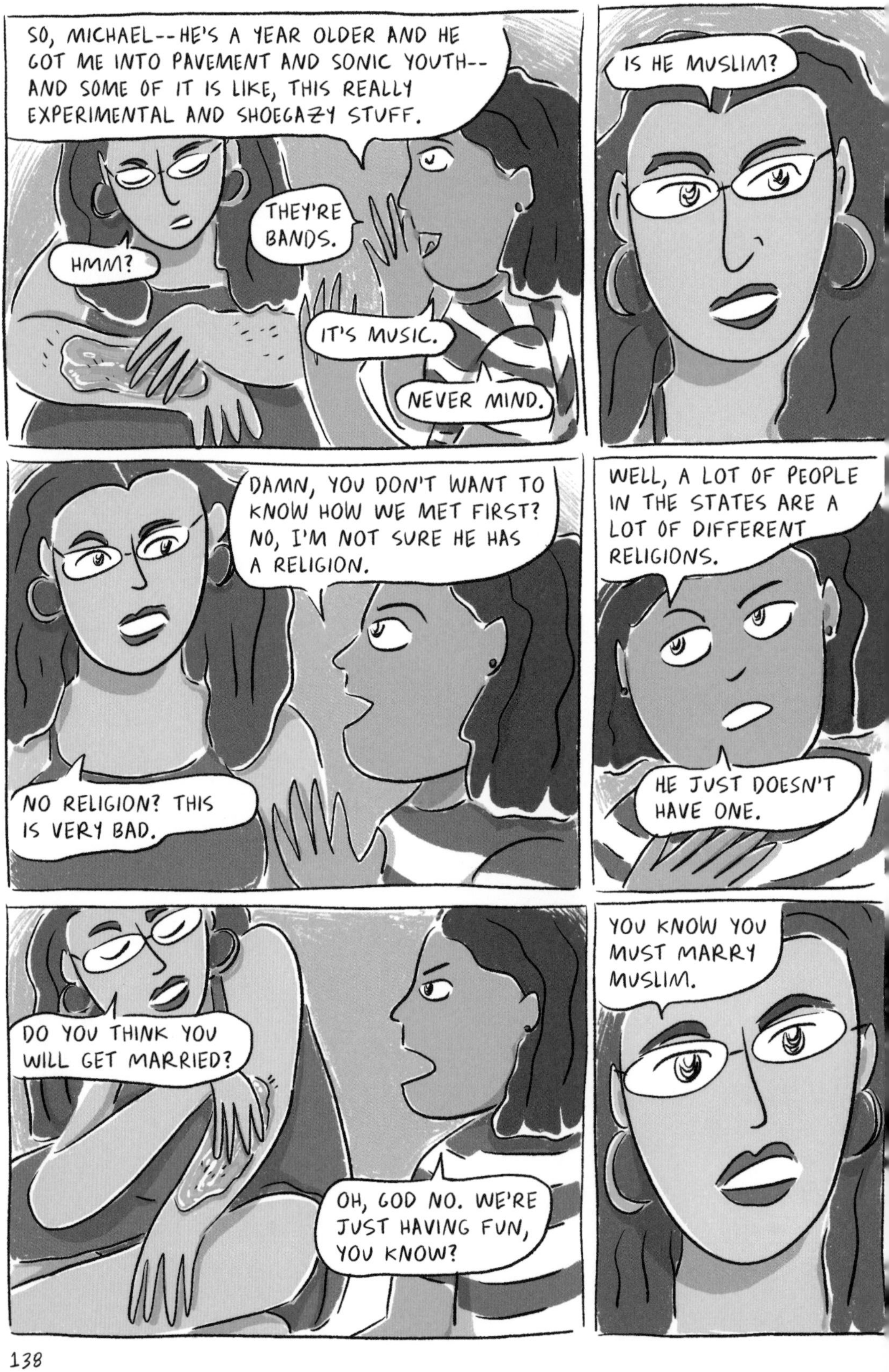
SO, MICHAEL--HE'S A YEAR OLDER AND HE GOT ME INTO PAVEMENT AND SONIC YOUTH--AND SOME OF IT IS LIKE, THIS REALLY EXPERIMENTAL AND SHOEGAZY STUFF.
HMM?
THEY'RE BANDS.
IT'S MUSIC.
NEVER MIND.
IS HE MUSLIM?
DAMN, YOU DON'T WANT TO KNOW HOW WE MET FIRST? NO, I'M NOT SURE HE HAS A RELIGION.
NO RELIGION? THIS IS VERY BAD.
WELL, A LOT OF PEOPLE IN THE STATES ARE A LOT OF DIFFERENT RELIGIONS.
HE JUST DOESN'T HAVE ONE.
DO YOU THINK YOU WILL GET MARRIED?
OH, GOD NO. WE'RE JUST HAVING FUN, YOU KNOW?
YOU KNOW YOU MUST MARRY MUSLIM.

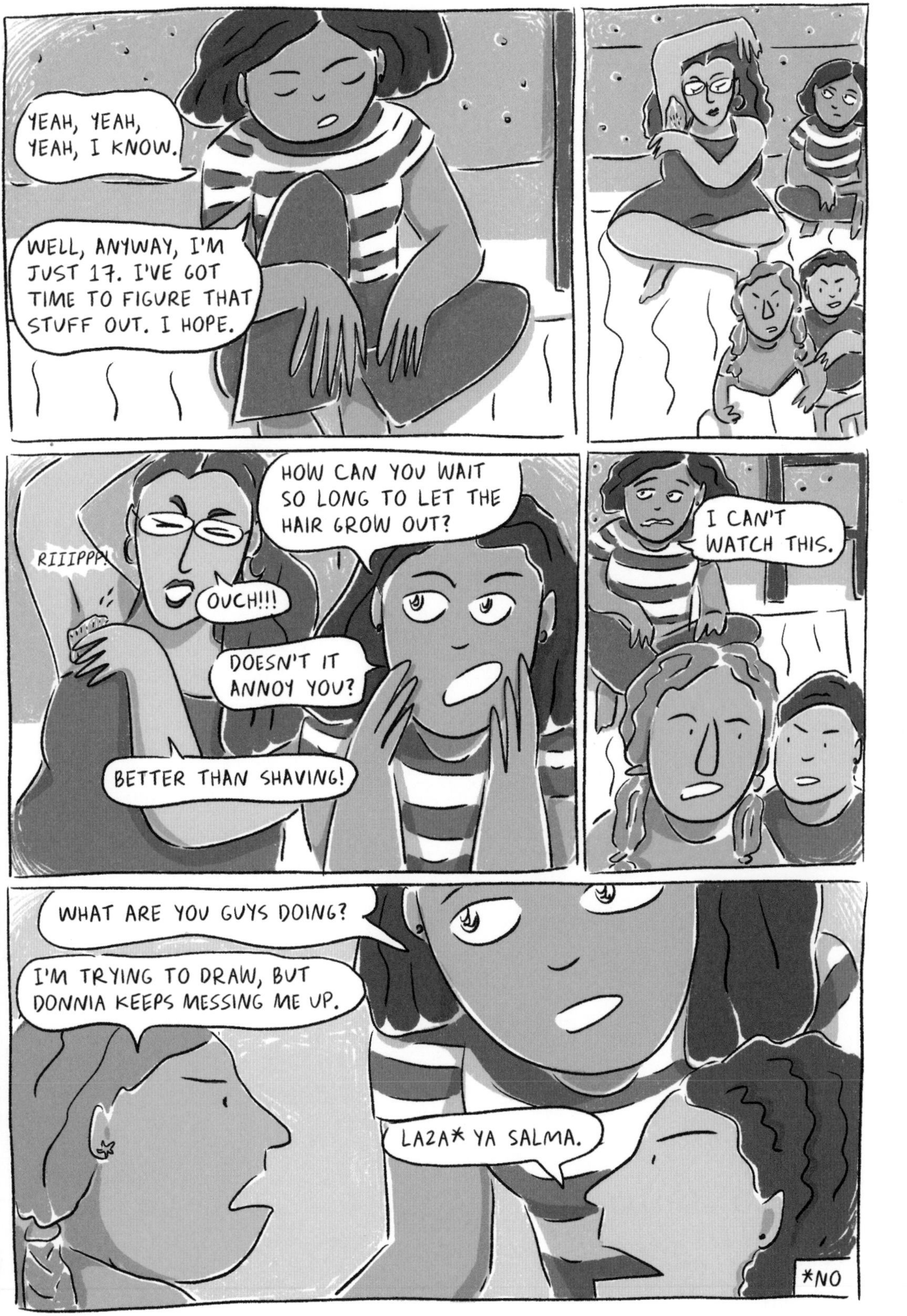
YEAH, YEAH, YEAH, I KNOW.
WELL, ANYWAY, I'M JUST 17. I'VE GOT TIME TO FIGURE THAT STUFF OUT. I HOPE.
HOW CAN YOU WAIT SO LONG TO LET THE HAIR GROW OUT?
RIIIPPP!
OUCH!!!
DOESN'T IT ANNOY YOU?
BETTER THAN SHAVING!
I CAN'T WATCH THIS.
WHAT ARE YOU GUYS DOING?
I'M TRYING TO DRAW, BUT DONNIA KEEPS MESSING ME UP.
LAZA* YA SALMA.
*NO

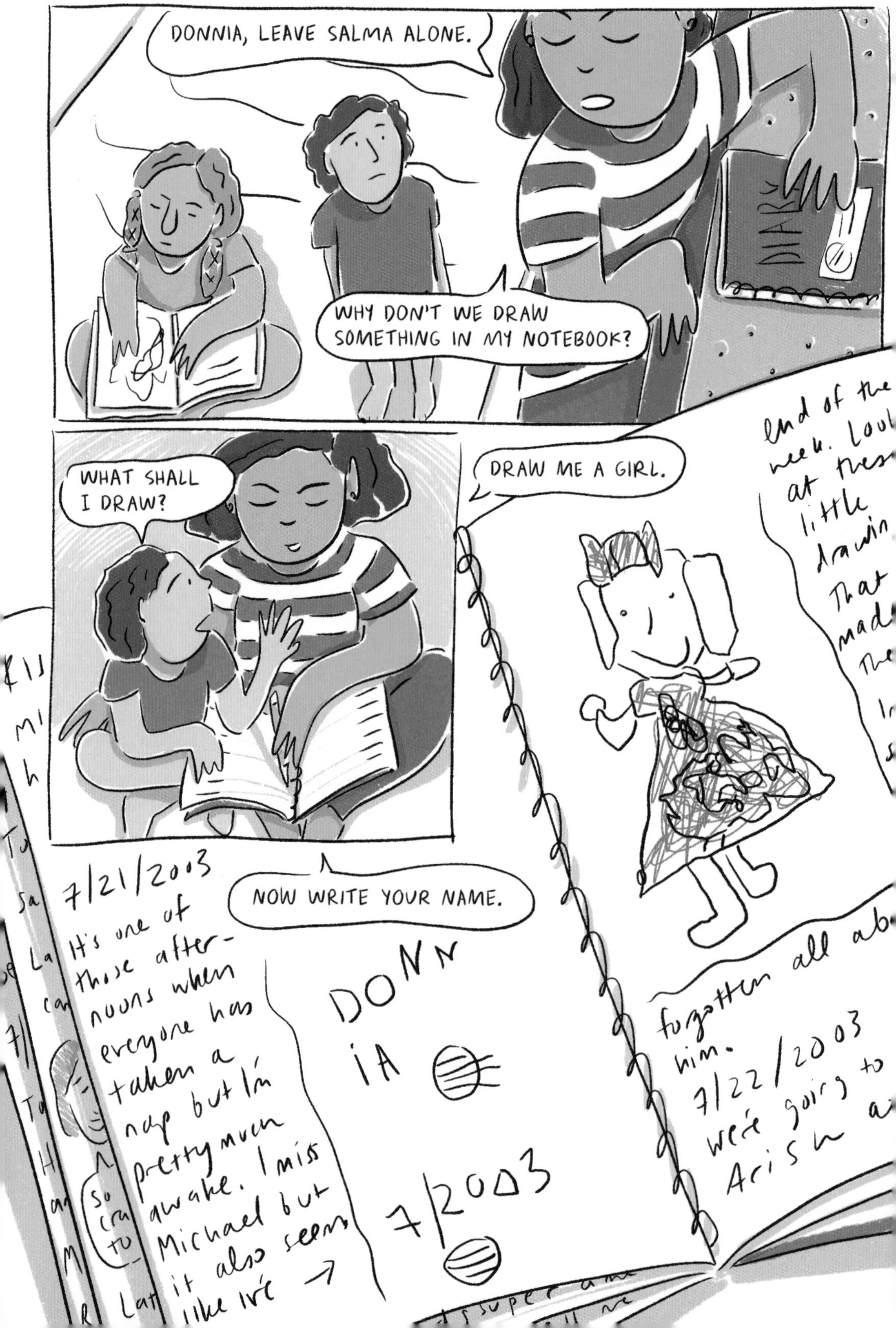
DONNIA, LEAVE SALMA ALONE.
WHY DON'T WE DRAW SOMETHING IN MY NOTEBOOK?
DIARY
WHAT SHALL I DRAW?
DRAW ME A GIRL.
NOW WRITE YOUR NAME.
7/21/2003
It's one of those after-noons when everyone has taken a nap but I'm pretty much awake. I miss Michael but it also seems like I've →
DONN iA
7/2003
end of the week. Look at these little drawin
forgotten all ab
him.
7/22/2003
we're going to Arish

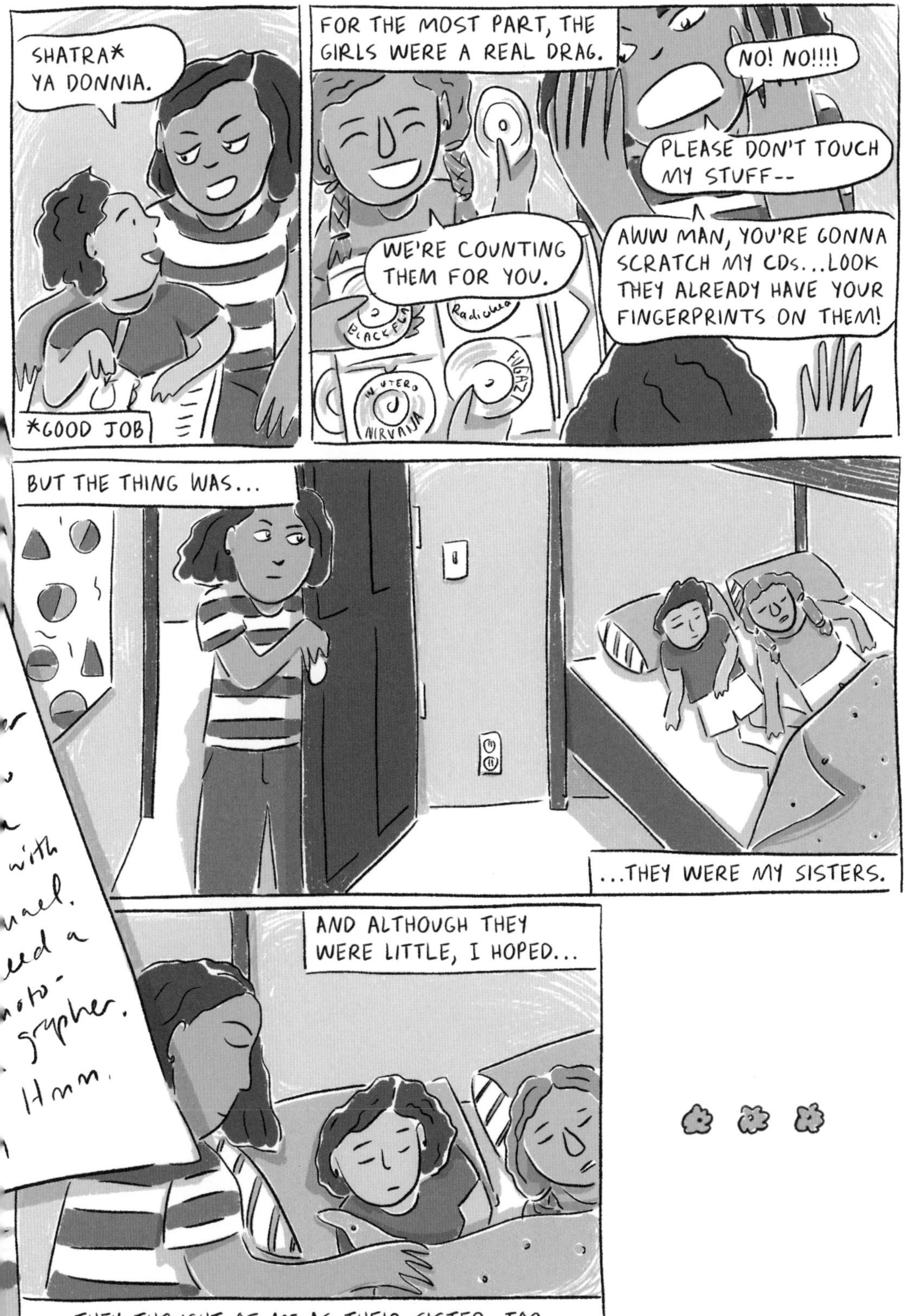
SHATRA* YA DONNIA.
*GOOD JOB
FOR THE MOST PART, THE GIRLS WERE A REAL DRAG.
WE'RE COUNTING THEM FOR YOU.
NO! NO!!!!
PLEASE DON'T TOUCH MY STUFF--
AWW MAN, YOU'RE GONNA SCRATCH MY CDs...LOOK THEY ALREADY HAVE YOUR FINGERPRINTS ON THEM!
BLACK FLAG
Radiohead
IN UTERO
NIRVANA
FUGAZI
BUT THE THING WAS...
...THEY WERE MY SISTERS.
AND ALTHOUGH THEY WERE LITTLE, I HOPED...
...THEY THOUGHT OF ME AS THEIR SISTER, TOO.

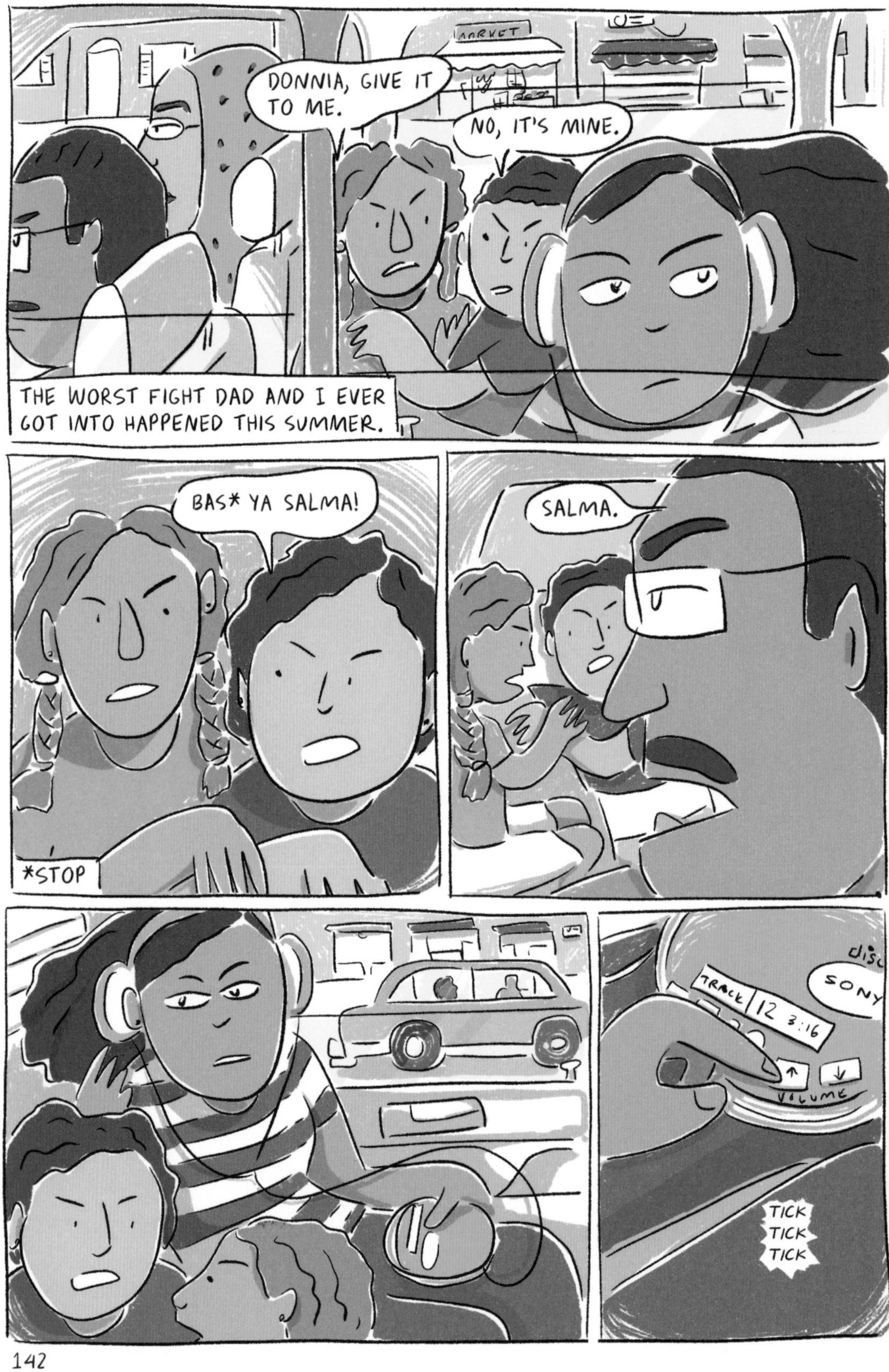
DONNIA, GIVE IT TO ME.
NO, IT'S MINE.
THE WORST FIGHT DAD AND I EVER GOT INTO HAPPENED THIS SUMMER.
BAS* YA SALMA!
*STOP
SALMA.
SONY
TRACK
12 3:16
VOLUME
TICK
TICK
TICK

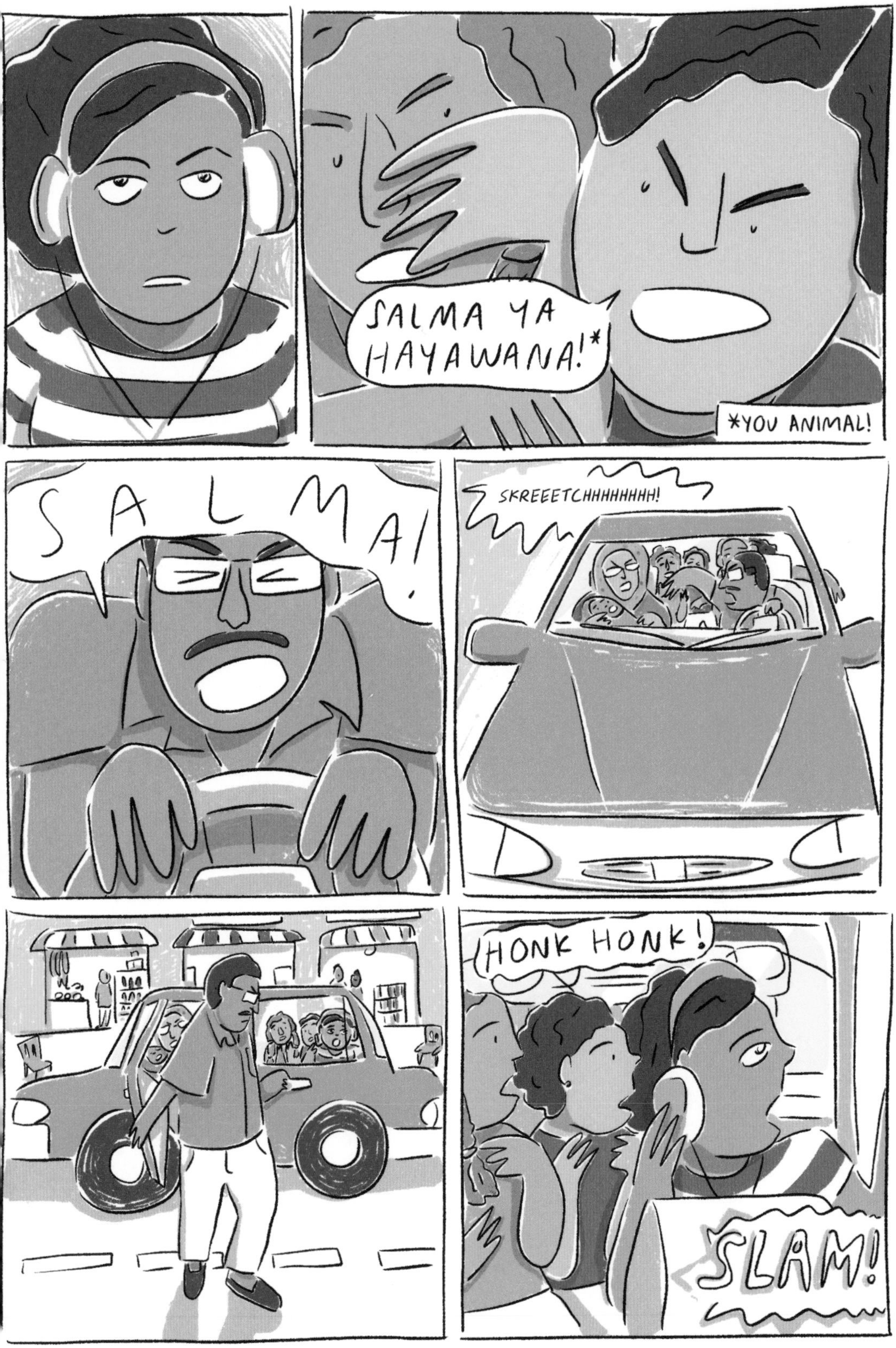
SALMA YA HAYAWANA!*
*YOU ANIMAL!
SALMA!
SKREEETCHHHHHHHH!
HONK HONK!
SLAM!

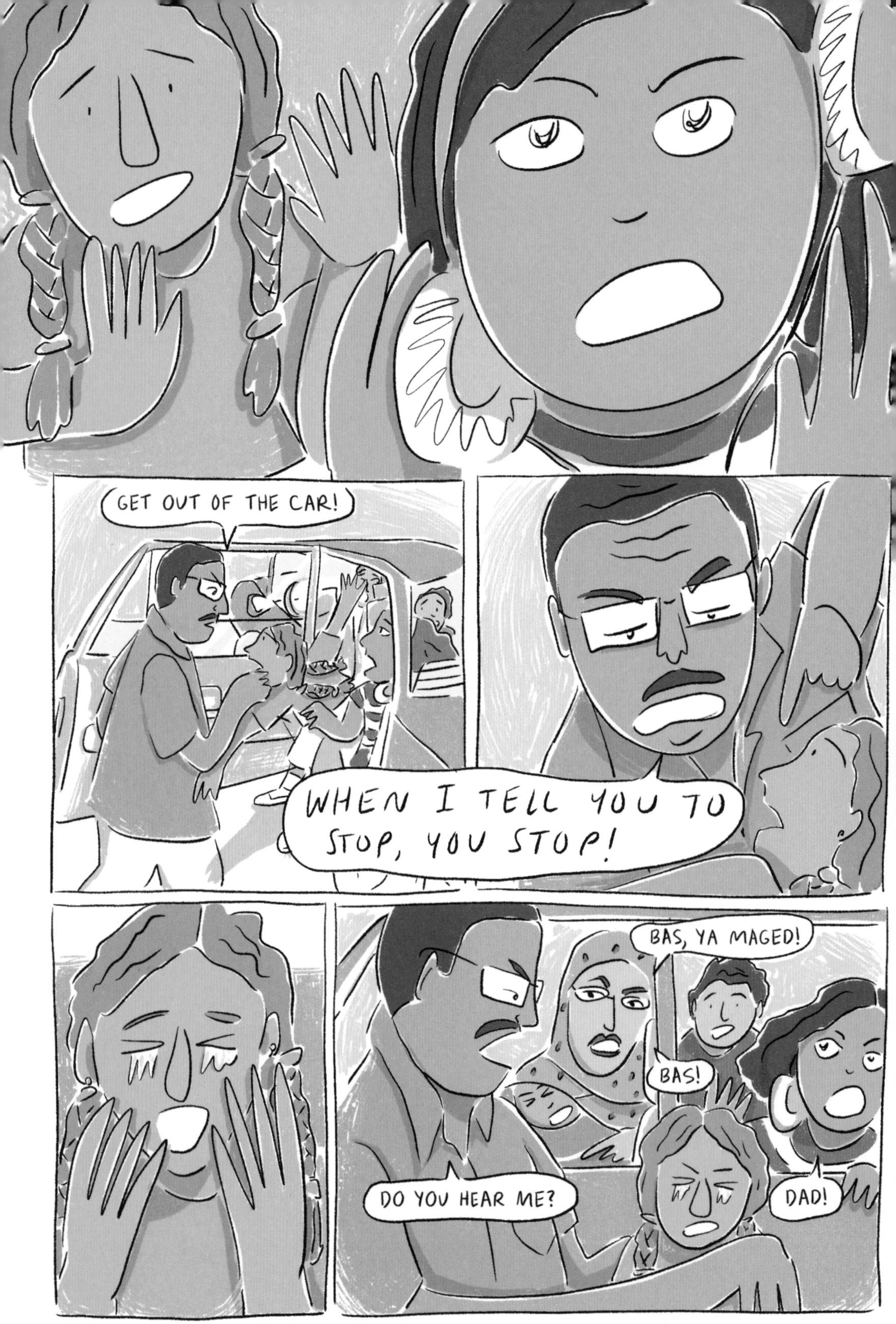
GET OUT OF THE CAR!
WHEN I TELL YOU TO STOP, YOU STOP!
BAS, YA MAGED!
BAS!
DO YOU HEAR ME?
DAD!

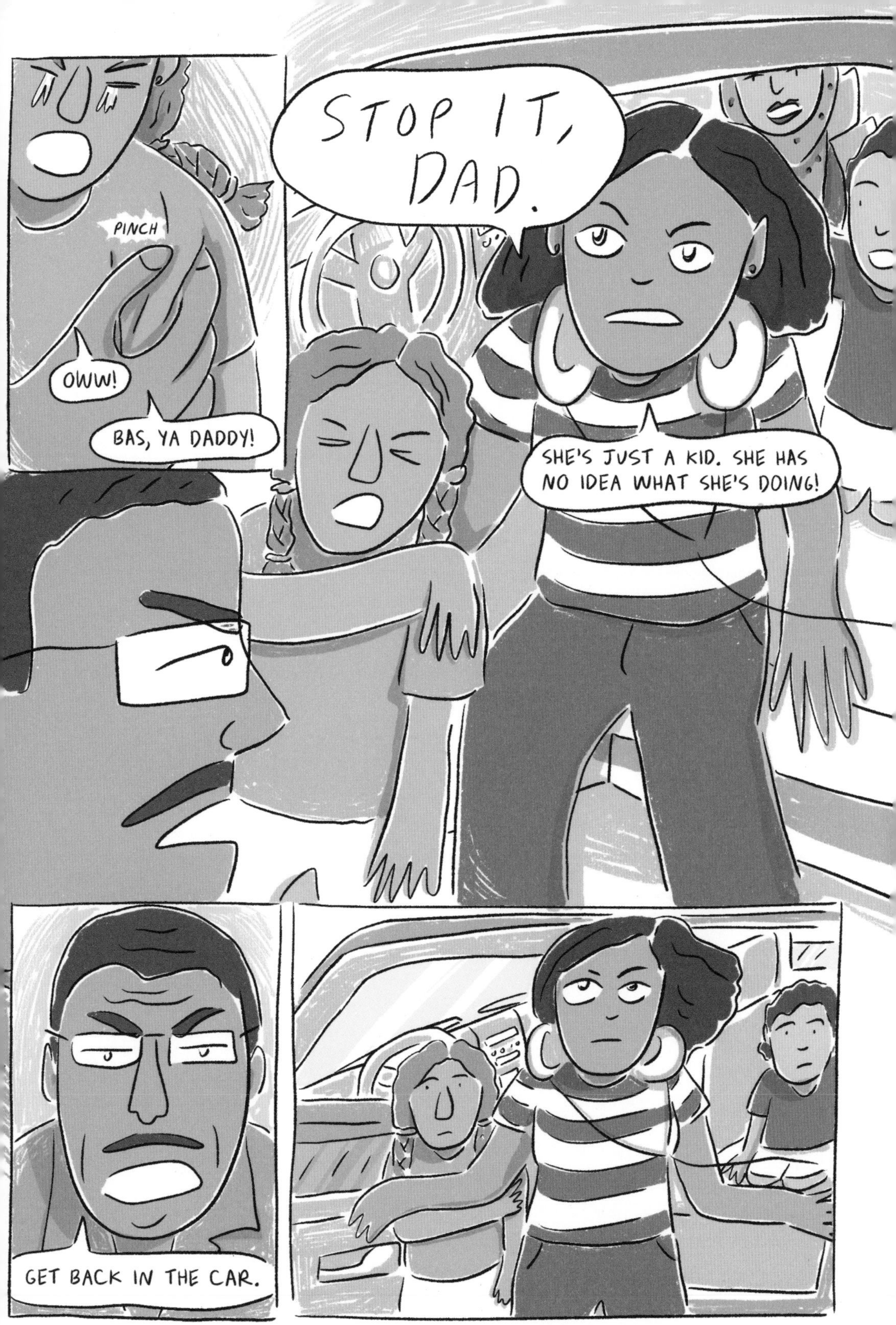
PINCH
OWW!
BAS, YA DADDY!
STOP IT, DAD.
SHE'S JUST A KID. SHE HAS NO IDEA WHAT SHE'S DOING!
GET BACK IN THE CAR.

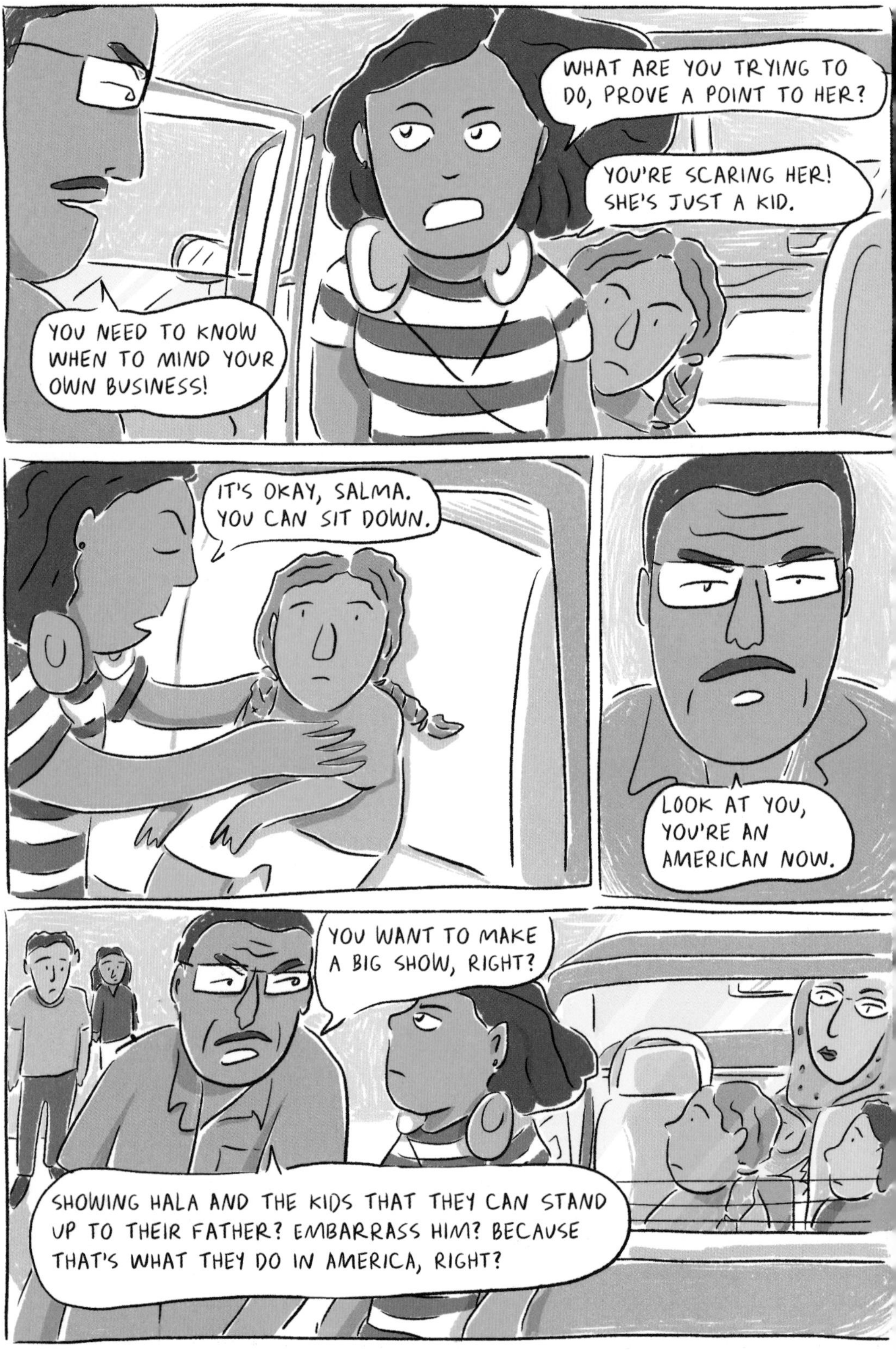
WHAT ARE YOU TRYING TO DO, PROVE A POINT TO HER?
YOU'RE SCARING HER! SHE'S JUST A KID.
YOU NEED TO KNOW WHEN TO MIND YOUR OWN BUSINESS!
IT'S OKAY, SALMA. YOU CAN SIT DOWN.
LOOK AT YOU, YOU'RE AN AMERICAN NOW.
YOU WANT TO MAKE A BIG SHOW, RIGHT?
SHOWING HALA AND THE KIDS THAT THEY CAN STAND UP TO THEIR FATHER? EMBARRASS HIM? BECAUSE THAT'S WHAT THEY DO IN AMERICA, RIGHT?

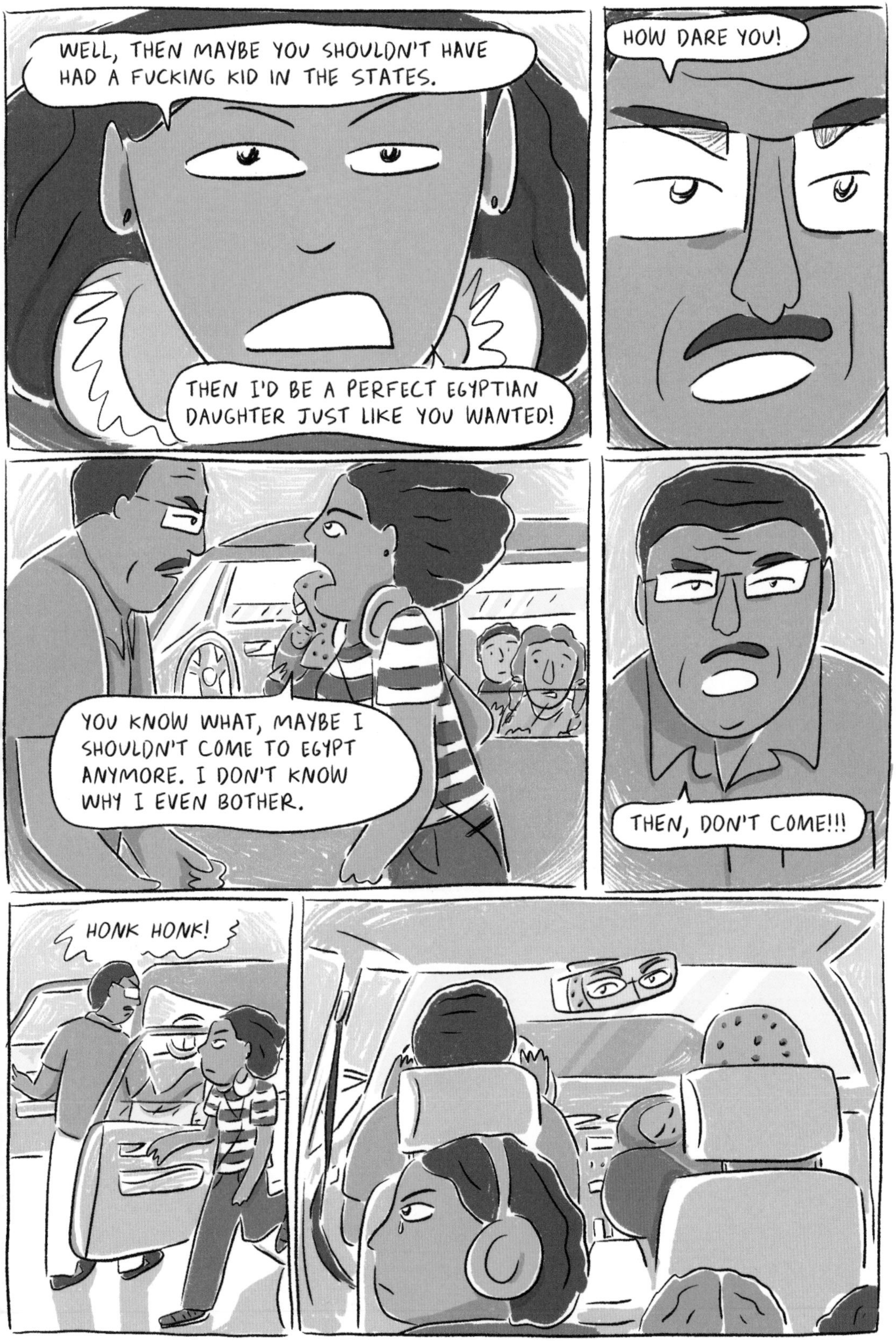
WELL, THEN MAYBE YOU SHOULDN'T HAVE HAD A FUCKING KID IN THE STATES.
THEN I'D BE A PERFECT EGYPTIAN DAUGHTER JUST LIKE YOU WANTED!
HOW DARE YOU!
YOU KNOW WHAT, MAYBE I SHOULDN'T COME TO EGYPT ANYMORE. I DON'T KNOW WHY I EVEN BOTHER.
THEN, DON'T COME!!!
HONK HONK!

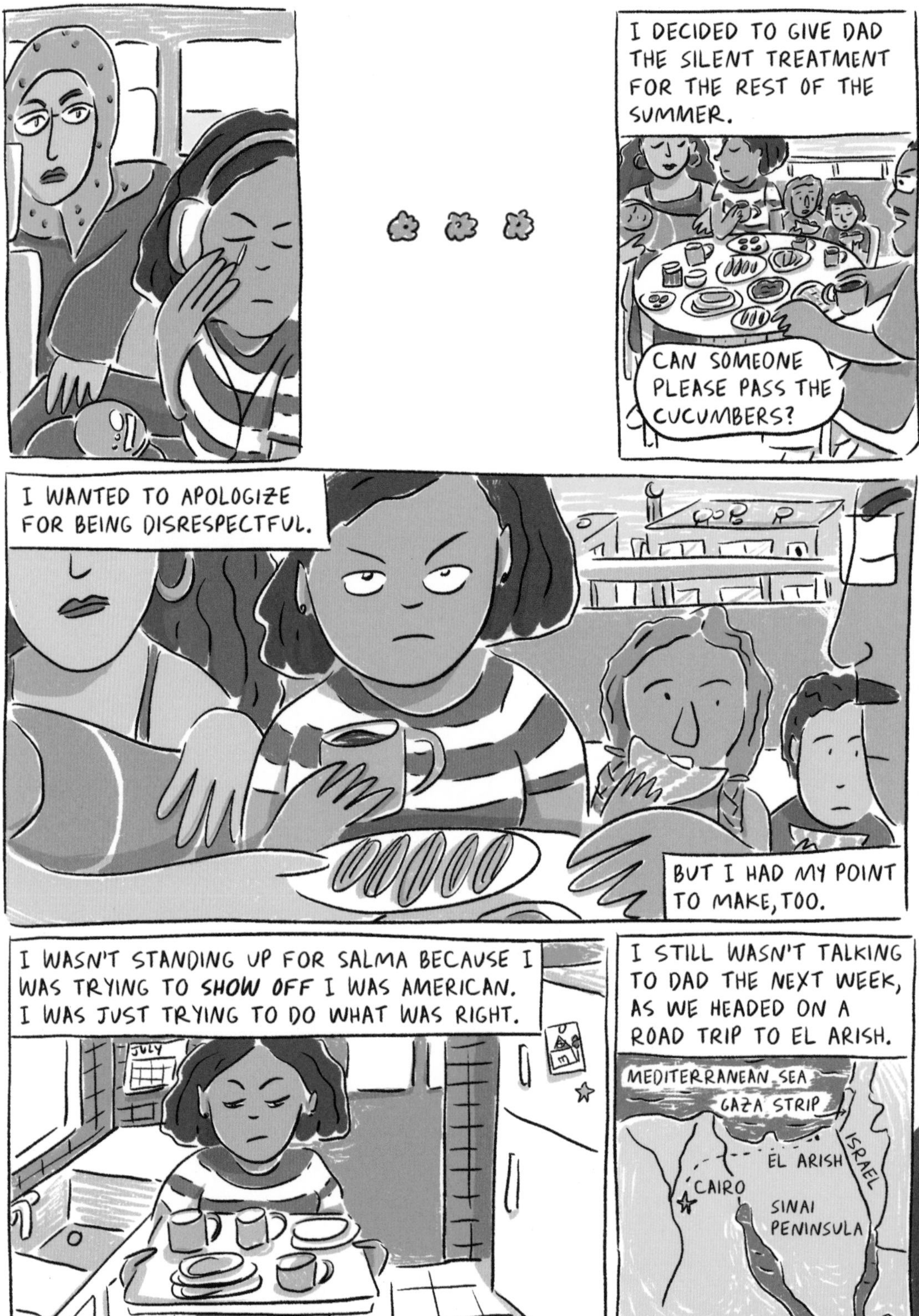
I DECIDED TO GIVE DAD THE SILENT TREATMENT FOR THE REST OF THE SUMMER.
CAN SOMEONE PLEASE PASS THE CUCUMBERS?
I WANTED TO APOLOGIZE FOR BEING DISRESPECTFUL.
BUT I HAD MY POINT TO MAKE, TOO.
I WASN'T STANDING UP FOR SALMA BECAUSE I WAS TRYING TO SHOW OFF I WAS AMERICAN. I WAS JUST TRYING TO DO WHAT WAS RIGHT.
JULY
I STILL WASN'T TALKING TO DAD THE NEXT WEEK, AS WE HEADED ON A ROAD TRIP TO EL ARISH.
MEDITERRANEAN SEA
GAZA STRIP
EL ARISH
ISRAEL
CAIRO
SINAI PENINSULA
Egypt
SHARM EL SHEIKH

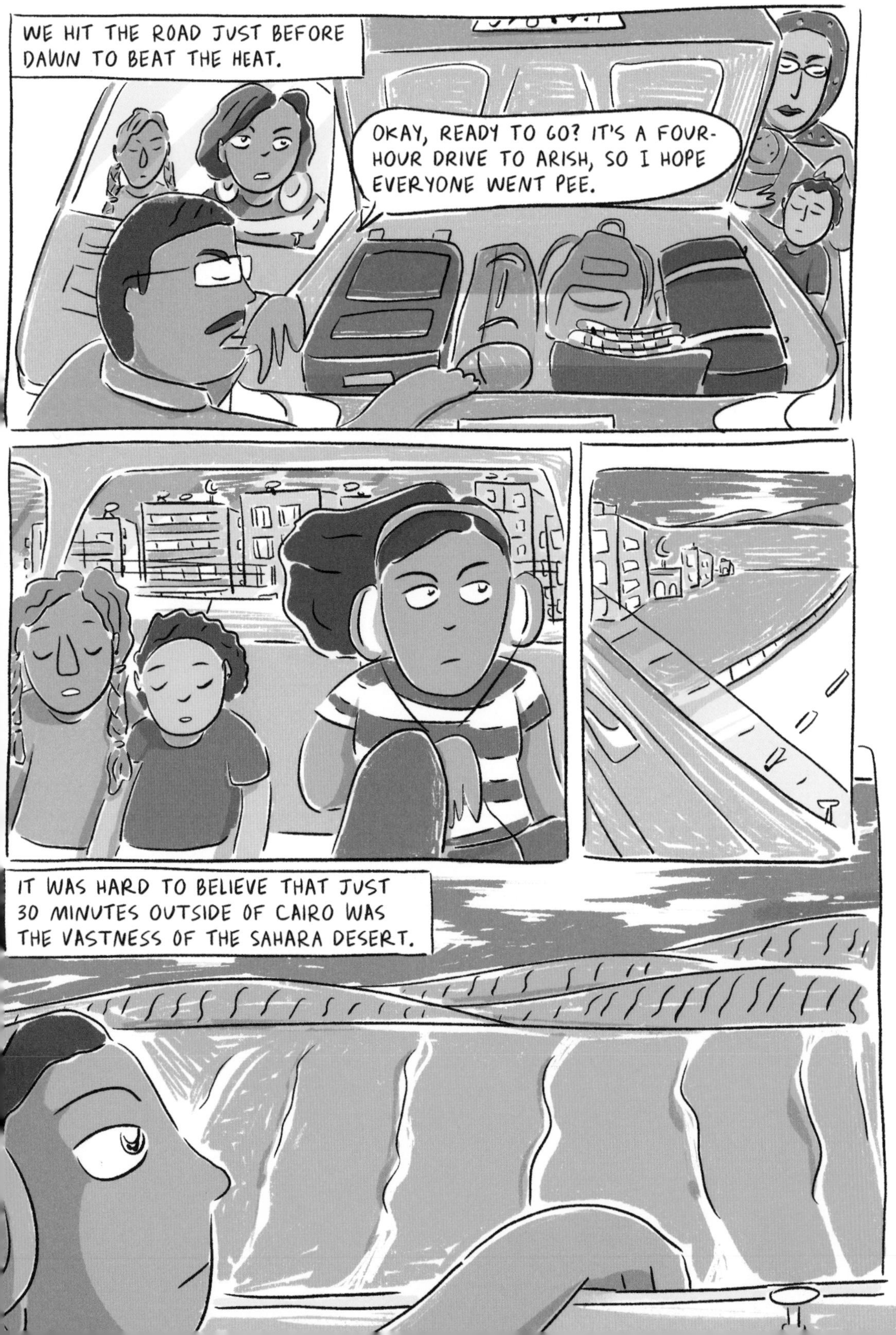
WE HIT THE ROAD JUST BEFORE DAWN TO BEAT THE HEAT.
OKAY, READY TO GO? IT'S A FOUR-HOUR DRIVE TO ARISH, SO I HOPE EVERYONE WENT PEE.
IT WAS HARD TO BELIEVE THAT JUST 30 MINUTES OUTSIDE OF CAIRO WAS THE VASTNESS OF THE SAHARA DESERT.

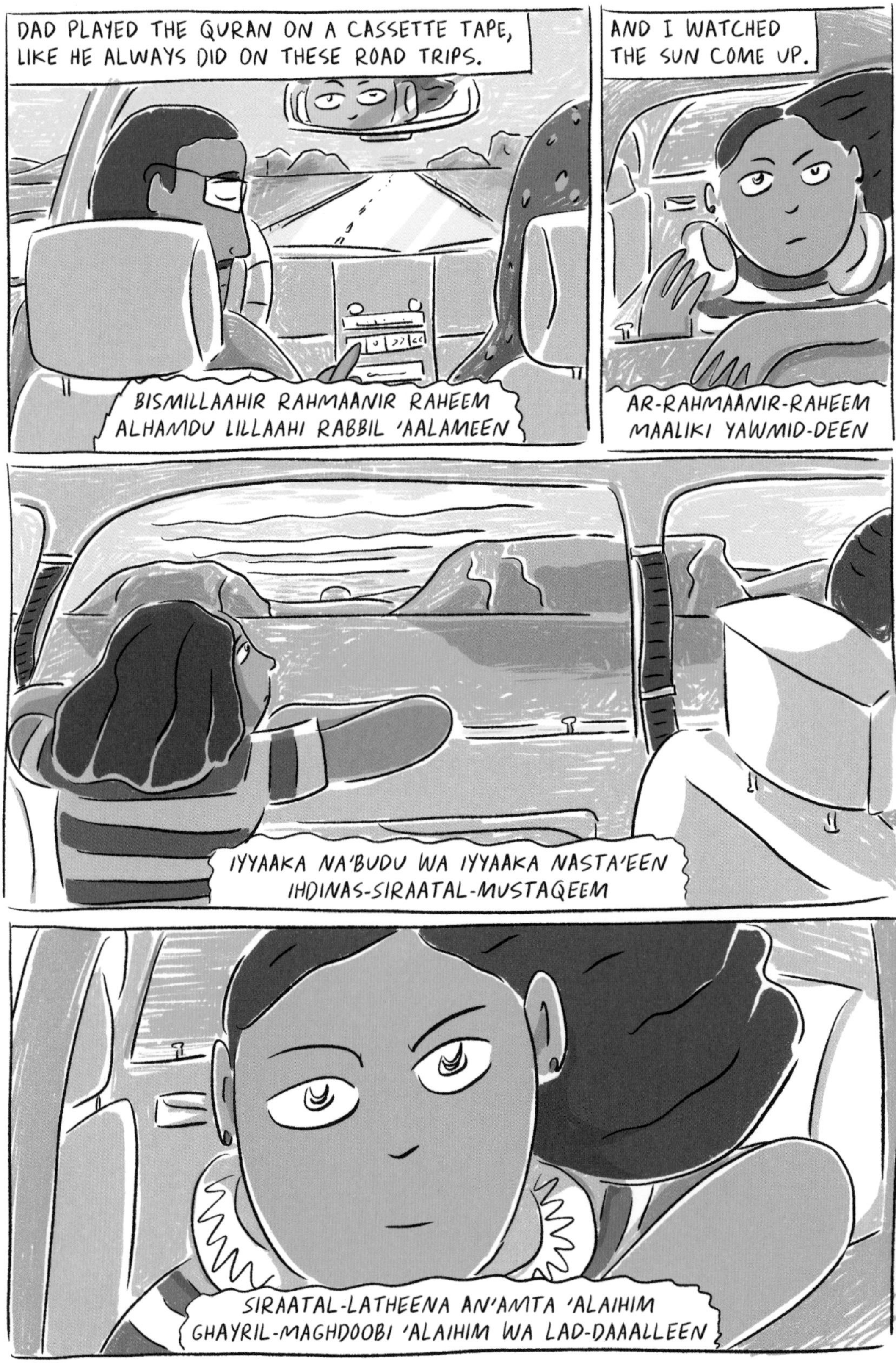
DAD PLAYED THE QURAN ON A CASSETTE TAPE, LIKE HE ALWAYS DID ON THESE ROAD TRIPS.
BISMILLAAHIR RAHMAANIR RAHEEM ALHAMDU LILLAAHI RABBIL 'AALAMEEN
AND I WATCHED THE SUN COME UP.
AR-RAHMAANIR-RAHEEM MAALIKI YAWMID-DEEN
IYYAAKA NA'BUDU WA IYYAAKA NASTA'EEN IHDINAS-SIRAATAL-MUSTAQEEM
SIRAATAL-LATHEENA AN'AMTA 'ALAIHIM GHAYRIL-MAGHDOOBI 'ALAIHIM WA LAD-DAAALLEEN

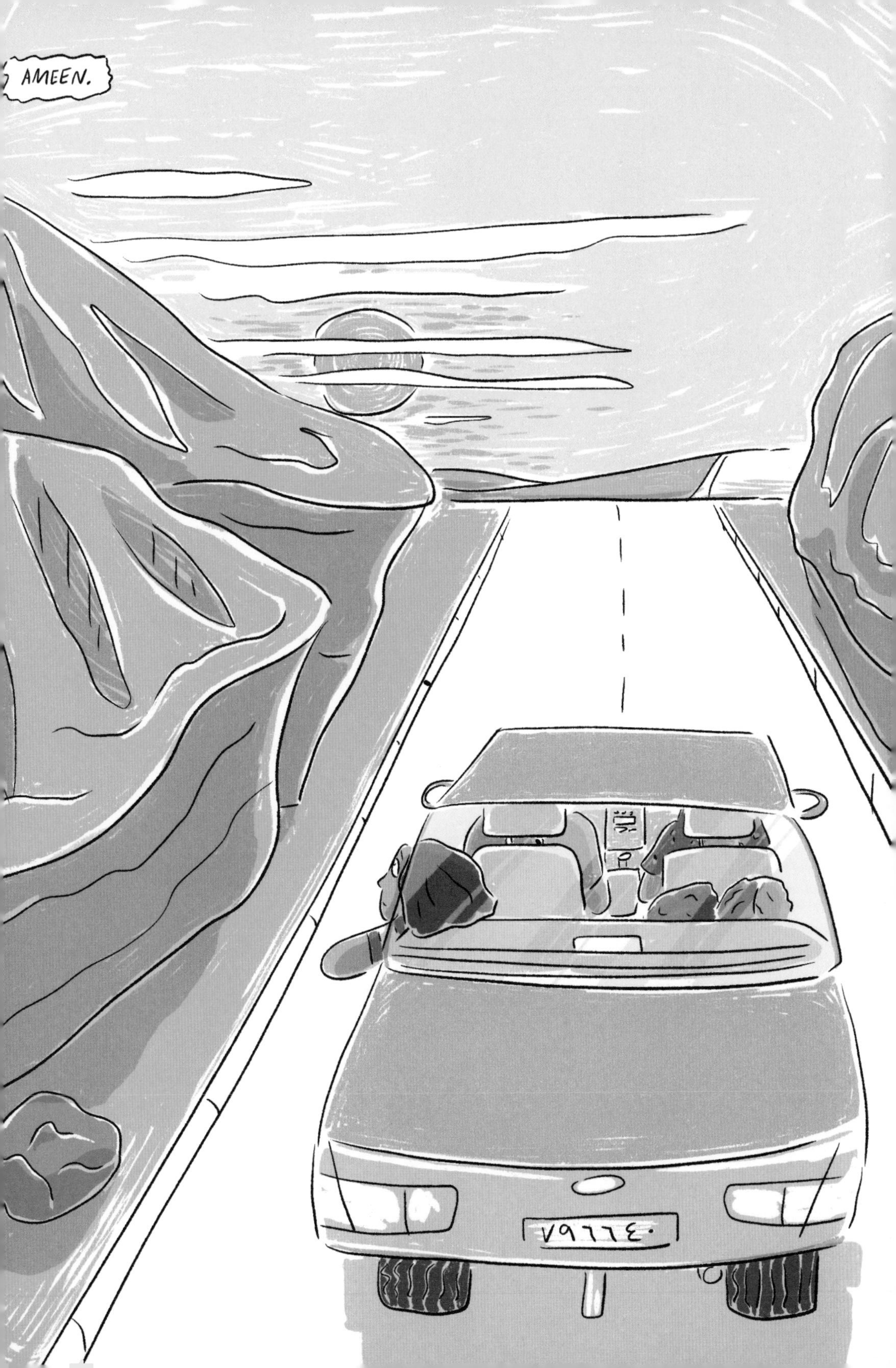
AMEEN.

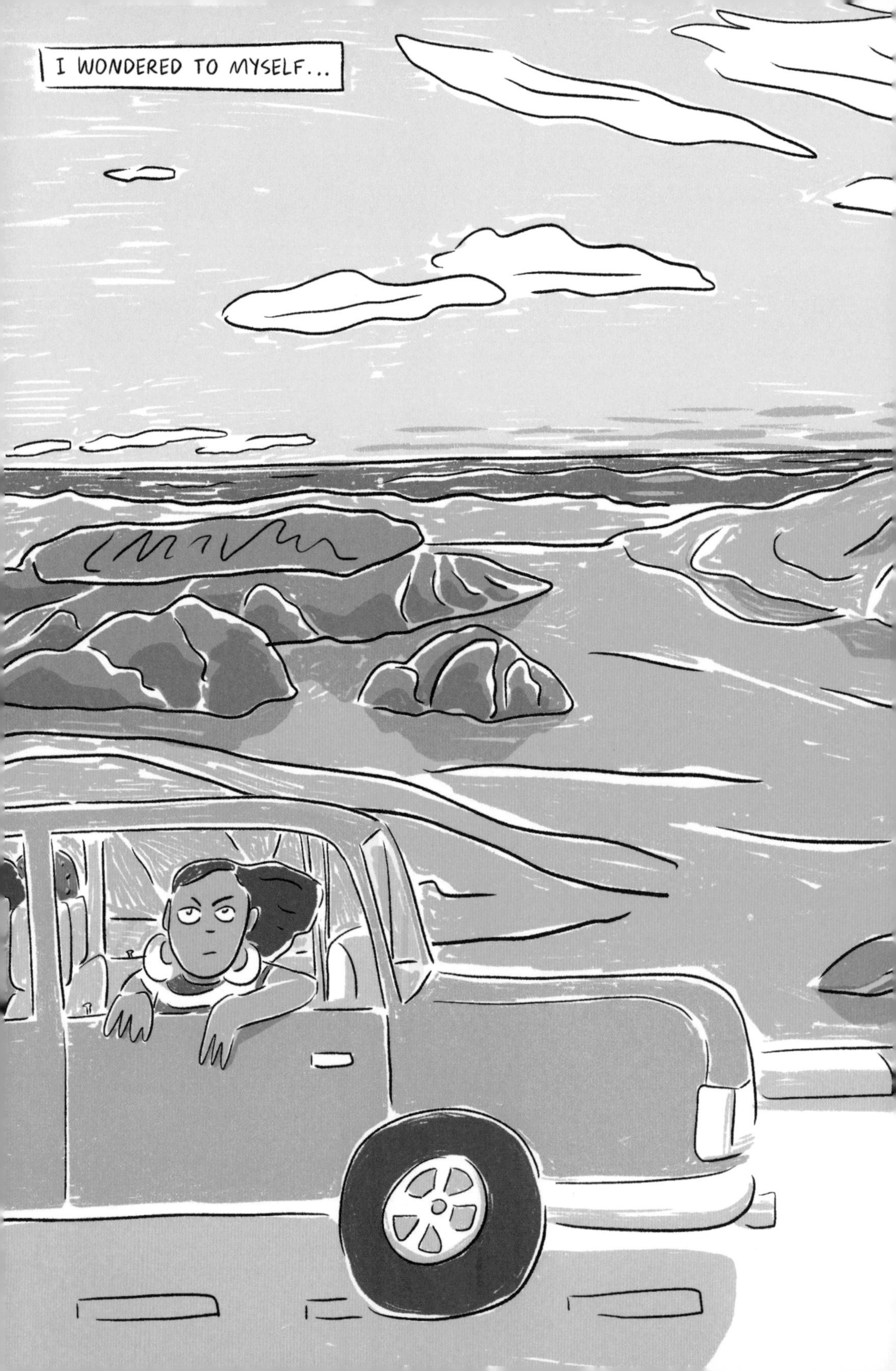
I WONDERED TO MYSELF...

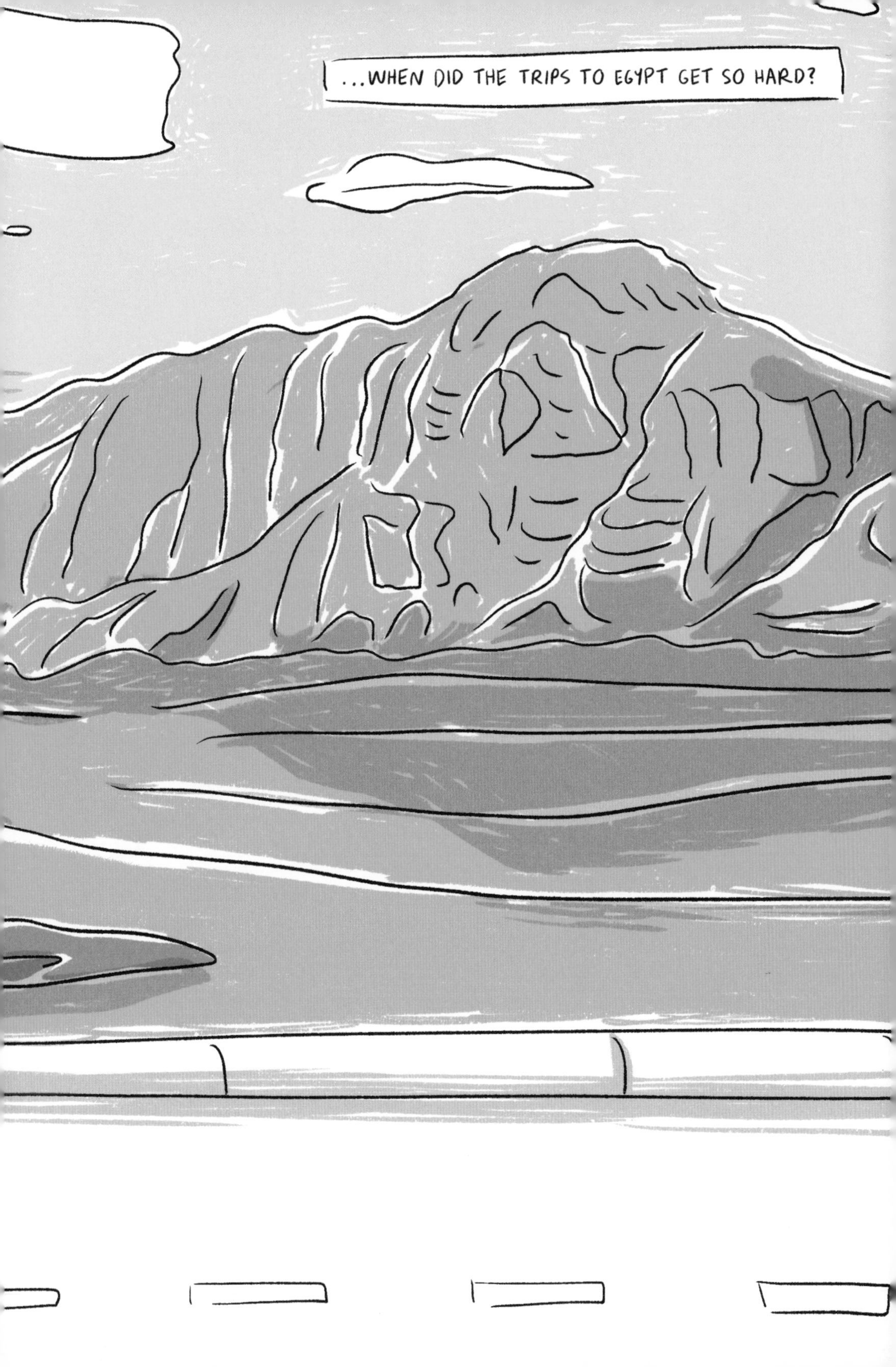
...WHEN DID THE TRIPS TO EGYPT GET SO HARD?

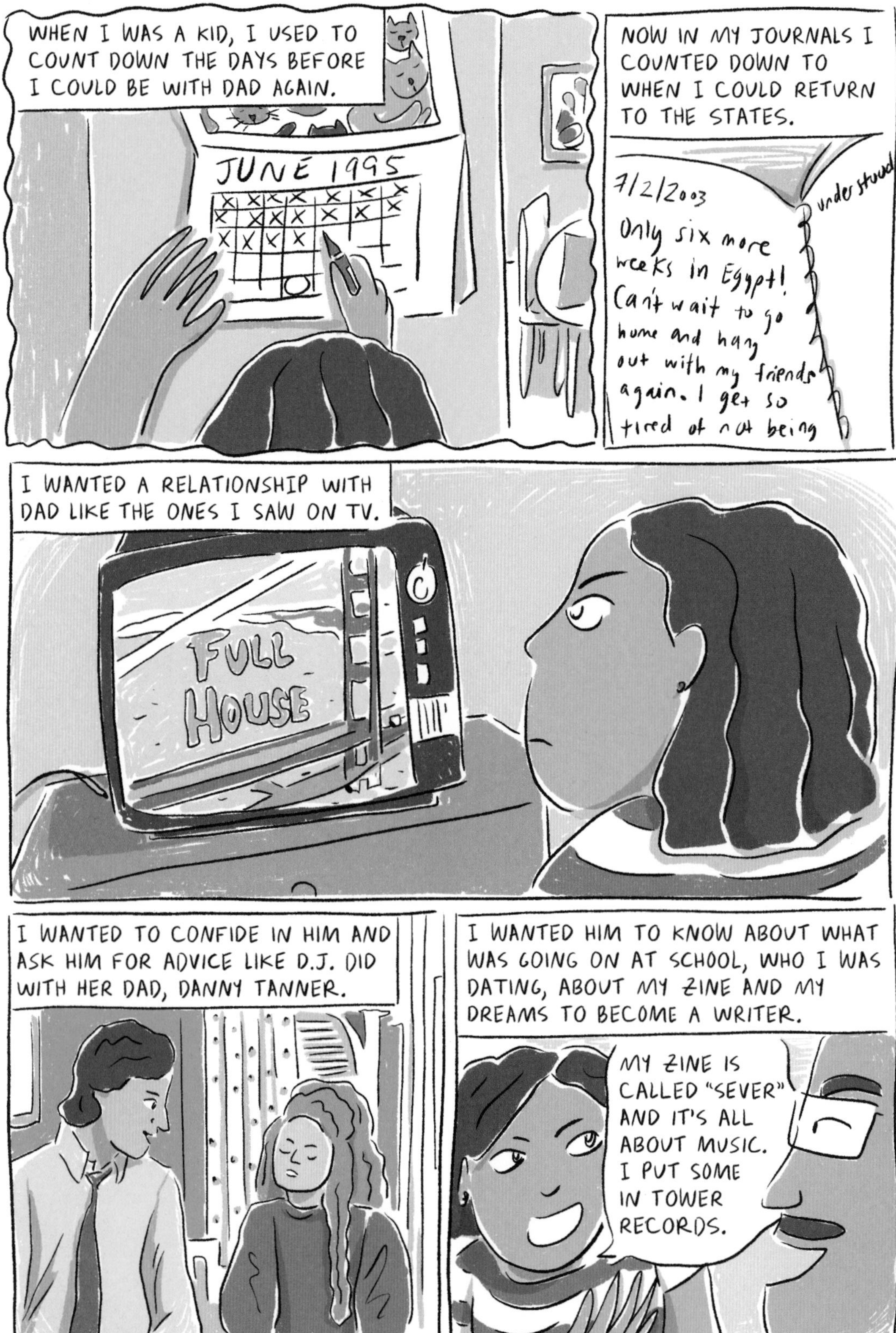
WHEN I WAS A KID, I USED TO COUNT DOWN THE DAYS BEFORE I COULD BE WITH DAD AGAIN.
JUNE 1995
NOW IN MY JOURNALS I COUNTED DOWN TO WHEN I COULD RETURN TO THE STATES.
7/2/2003
Only six more weeks in Egypt! Can't wait to go home and hang out with my friends again. I get so tired of not being understood
I WANTED A RELATIONSHIP WITH DAD LIKE THE ONES I SAW ON TV.
FULL HOUSE
I WANTED TO CONFIDE IN HIM AND ASK HIM FOR ADVICE LIKE D.J. DID WITH HER DAD, DANNY TANNER.
I WANTED HIM TO KNOW ABOUT WHAT WAS GOING ON AT SCHOOL, WHO I WAS DATING, ABOUT MY ZINE AND MY DREAMS TO BECOME A WRITER.
MY ZINE IS CALLED "SEVER" AND IT'S ALL ABOUT MUSIC. I PUT SOME IN TOWER RECORDS.

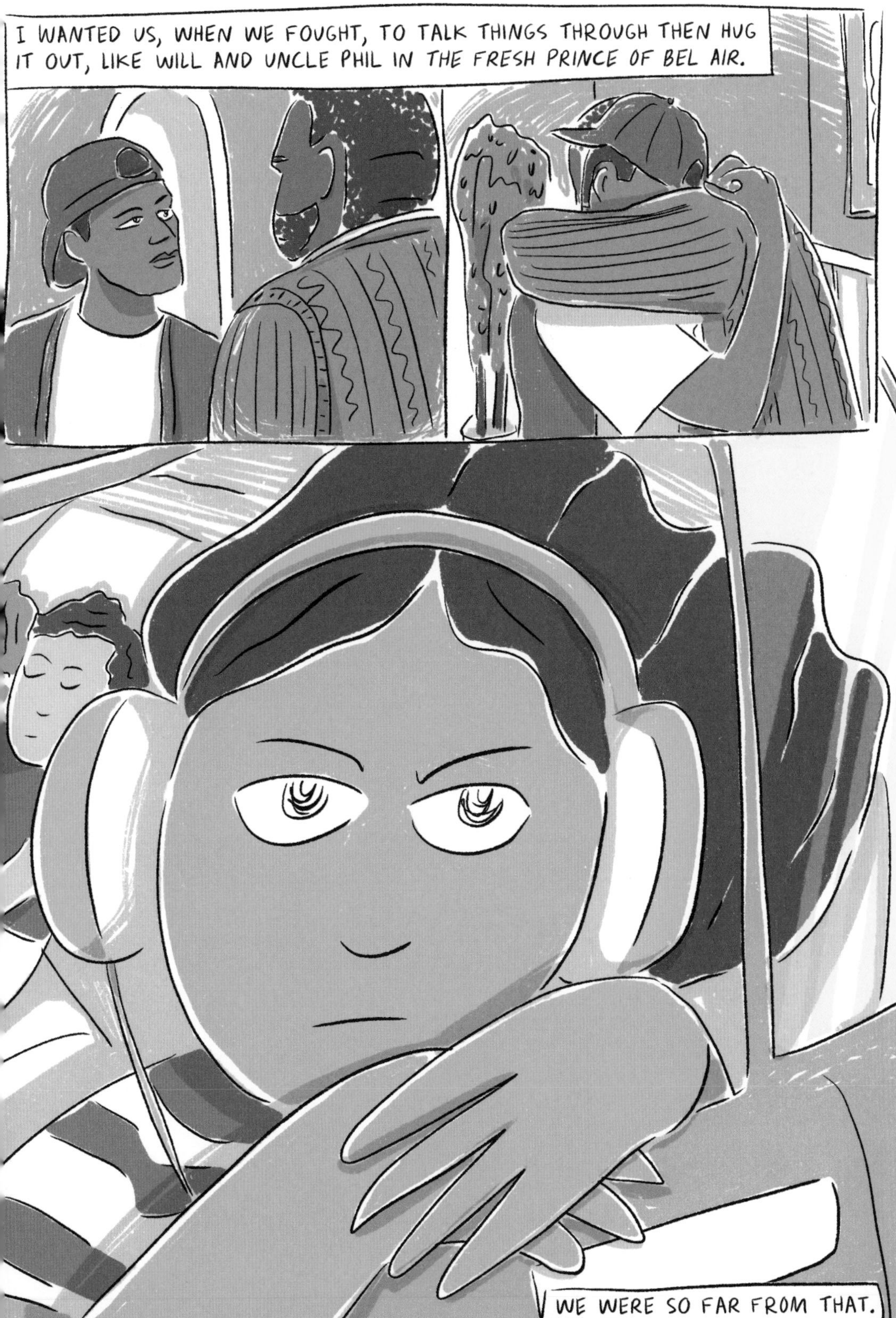
I WANTED US, WHEN WE FOUGHT, TO TALK THINGS THROUGH THEN HUG IT OUT, LIKE WILL AND UNCLE PHIL IN THE FRESH PRINCE OF BEL AIR.
WE WERE SO FAR FROM THAT.

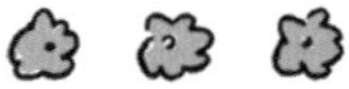

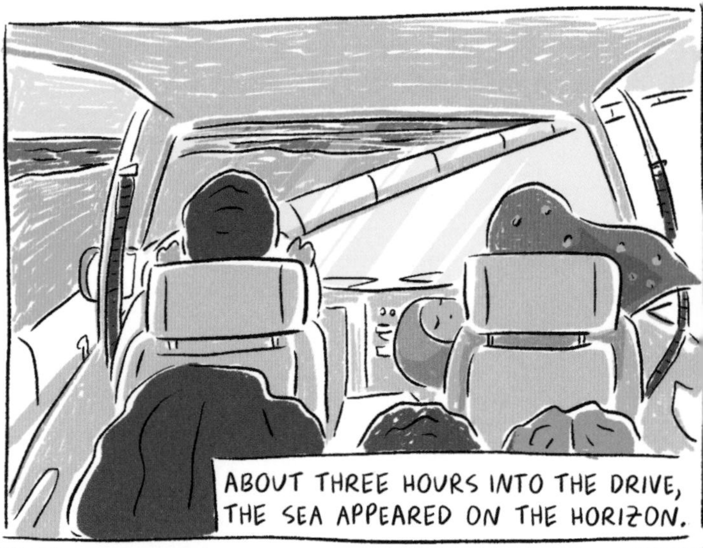
ABOUT THREE HOURS INTO THE DRIVE, THE SEA APPEARED ON THE HORIZON.

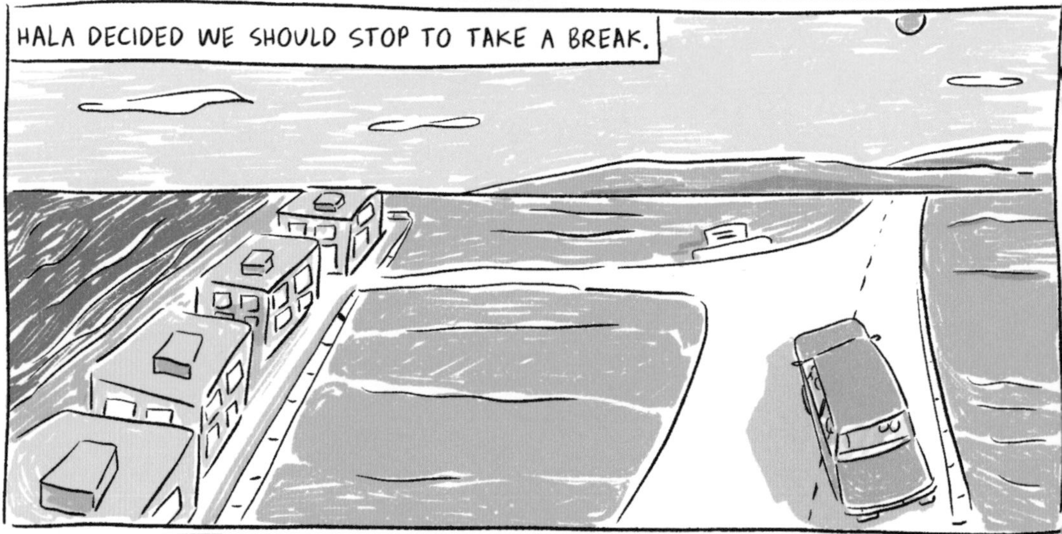
HALA DECIDED WE SHOULD STOP TO TAKE A BREAK.

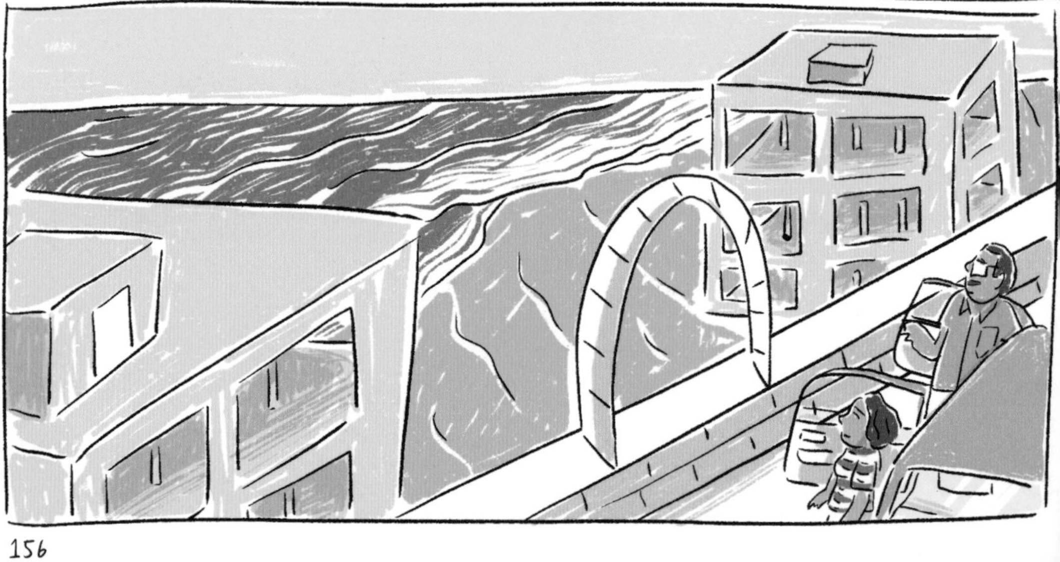

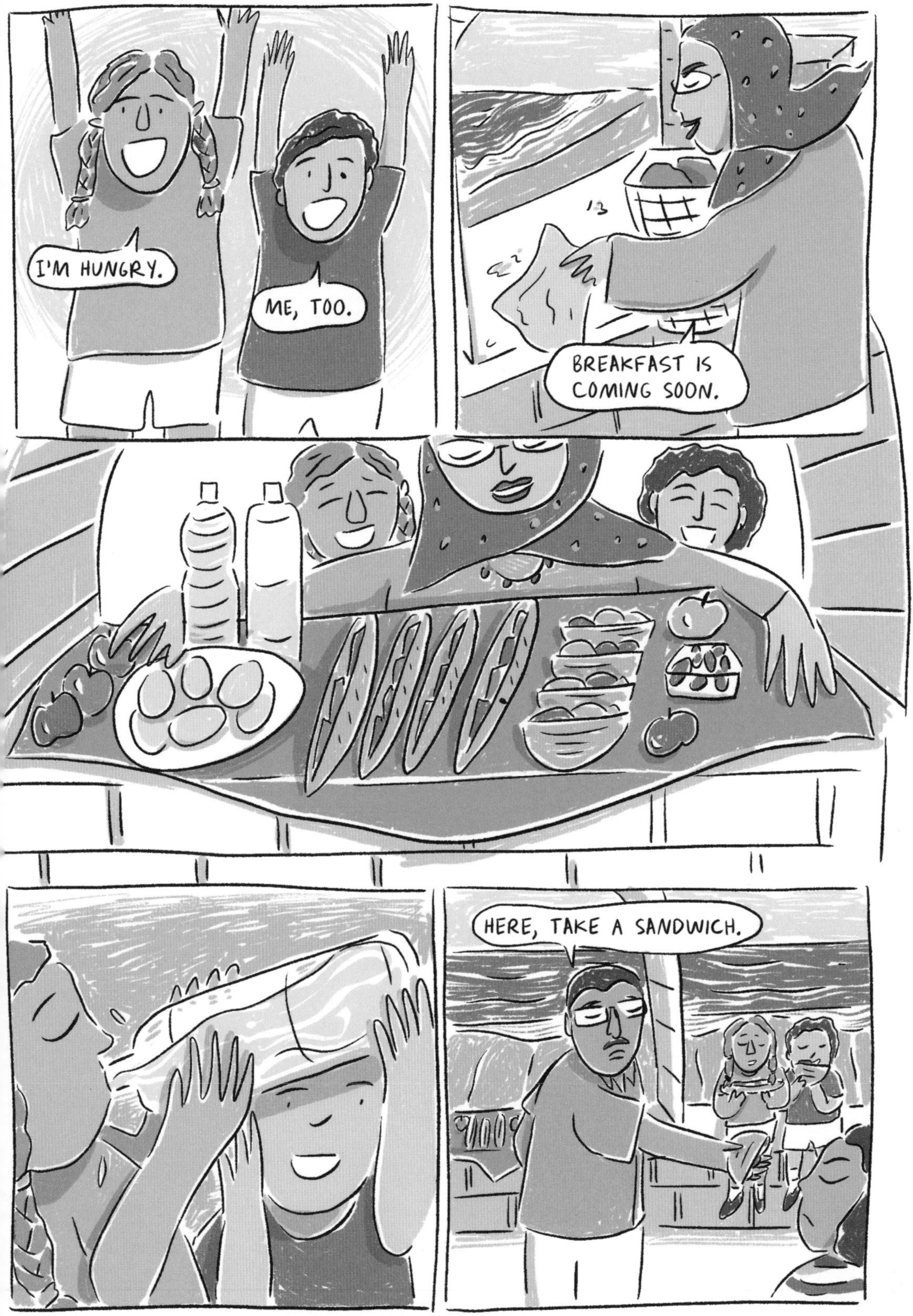
I'M HUNGRY.
ME, TOO.
BREAKFAST IS COMING SOON.
HERE, TAKE A SANDWICH.

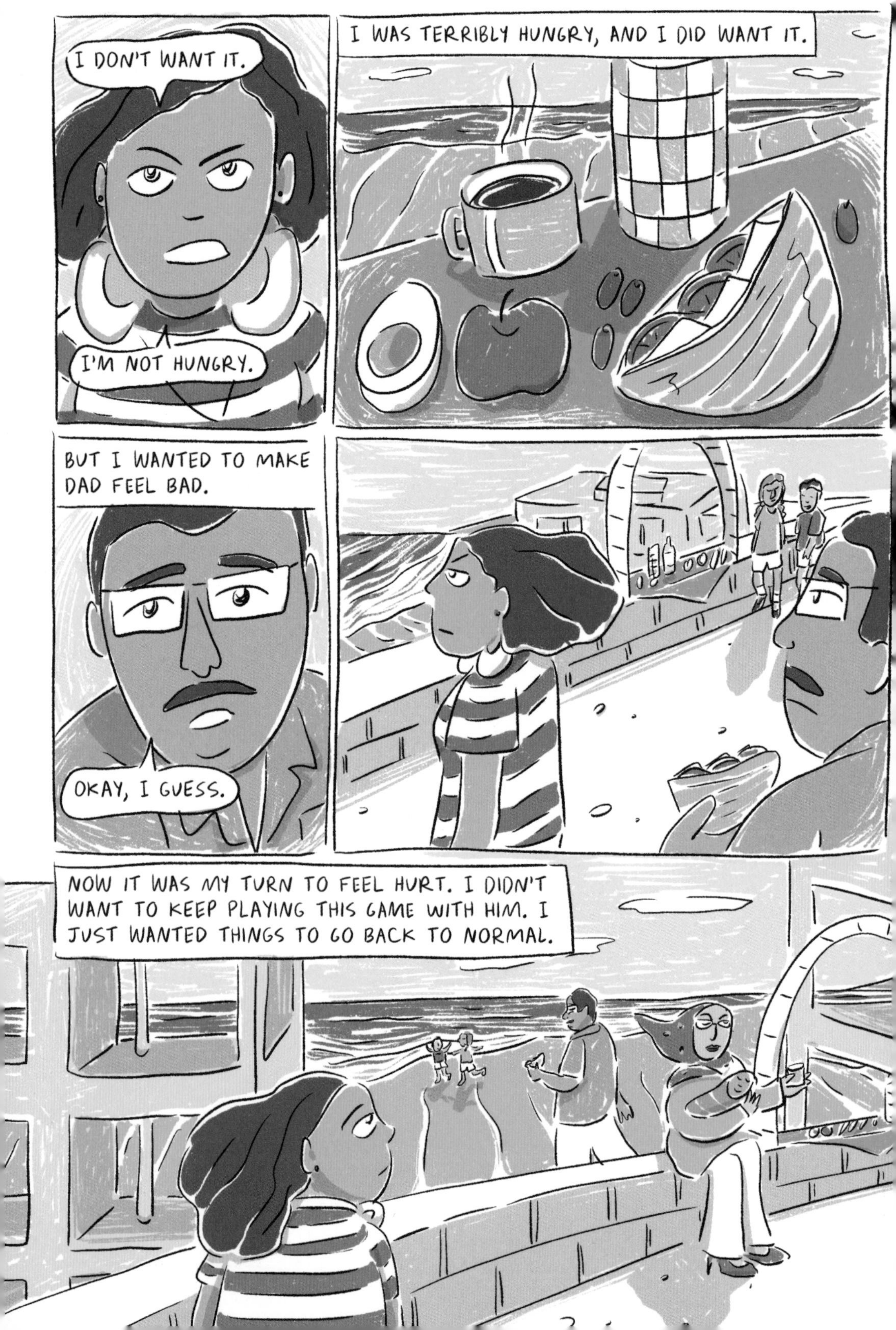
I DON'T WANT IT.
I'M NOT HUNGRY.
I WAS TERRIBLY HUNGRY, AND I DID WANT IT.
BUT I WANTED TO MAKE DAD FEEL BAD.
OKAY, I GUESS.
NOW IT WAS MY TURN TO FEEL HURT. I DIDN'T WANT TO KEEP PLAYING THIS GAME WITH HIM. I JUST WANTED THINGS TO GO BACK TO NORMAL.

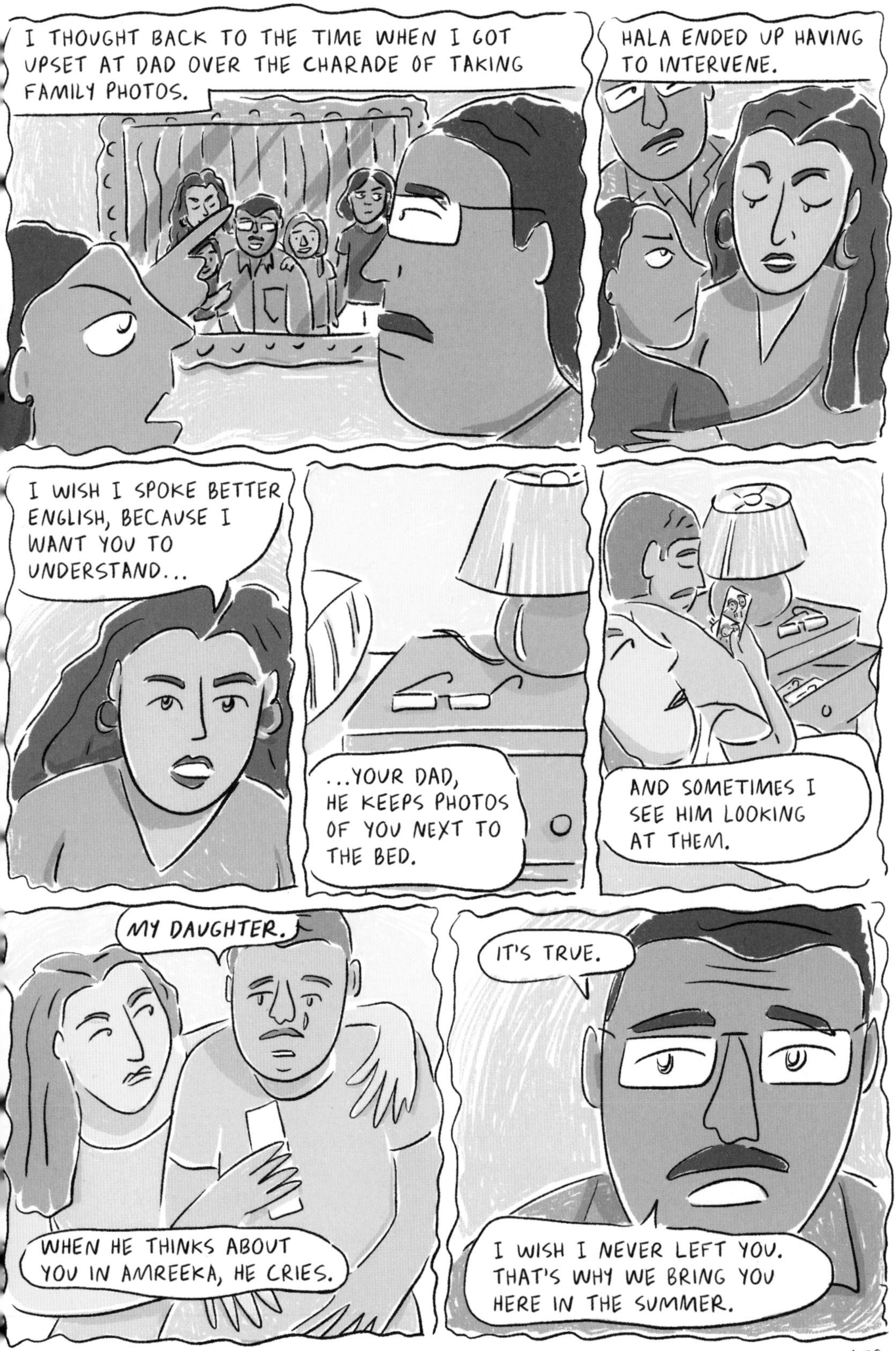
I THOUGHT BACK TO THE TIME WHEN I GOT UPSET AT DAD OVER THE CHARADE OF TAKING FAMILY PHOTOS.
HALA ENDED UP HAVING TO INTERVENE.
I WISH I SPOKE BETTER ENGLISH, BECAUSE I WANT YOU TO UNDERSTAND...
...YOUR DAD, HE KEEPS PHOTOS OF YOU NEXT TO THE BED.
AND SOMETIMES I SEE HIM LOOKING AT THEM.
MY DAUGHTER.
WHEN HE THINKS ABOUT YOU IN AMREEKA, HE CRIES.
IT'S TRUE.
I WISH I NEVER LEFT YOU. THAT'S WHY WE BRING YOU HERE IN THE SUMMER.

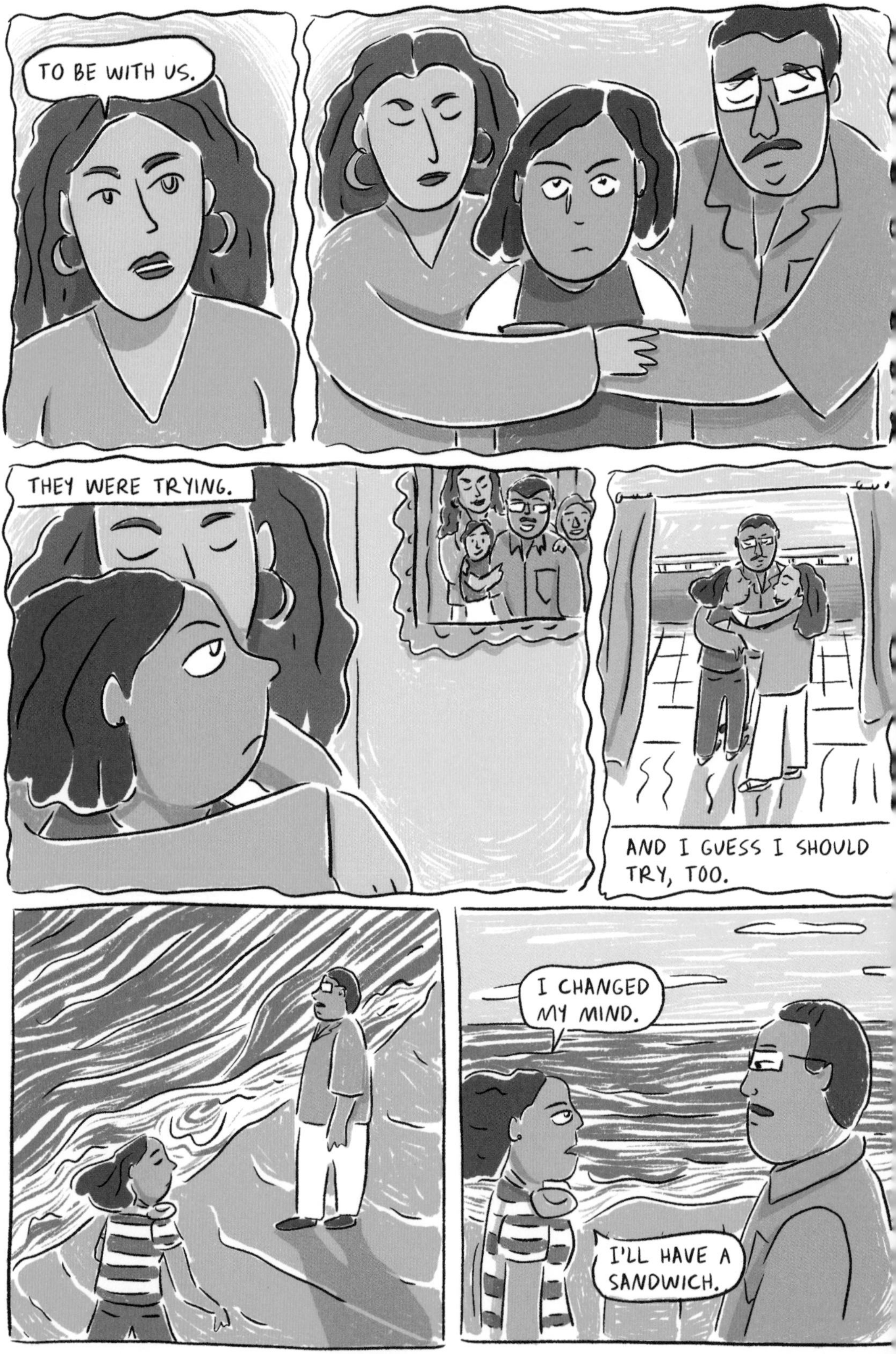
TO BE WITH US.
THEY WERE TRYING.
AND I GUESS I SHOULD TRY, TOO.
I CHANGED MY MIND.
I'LL HAVE A SANDWICH.

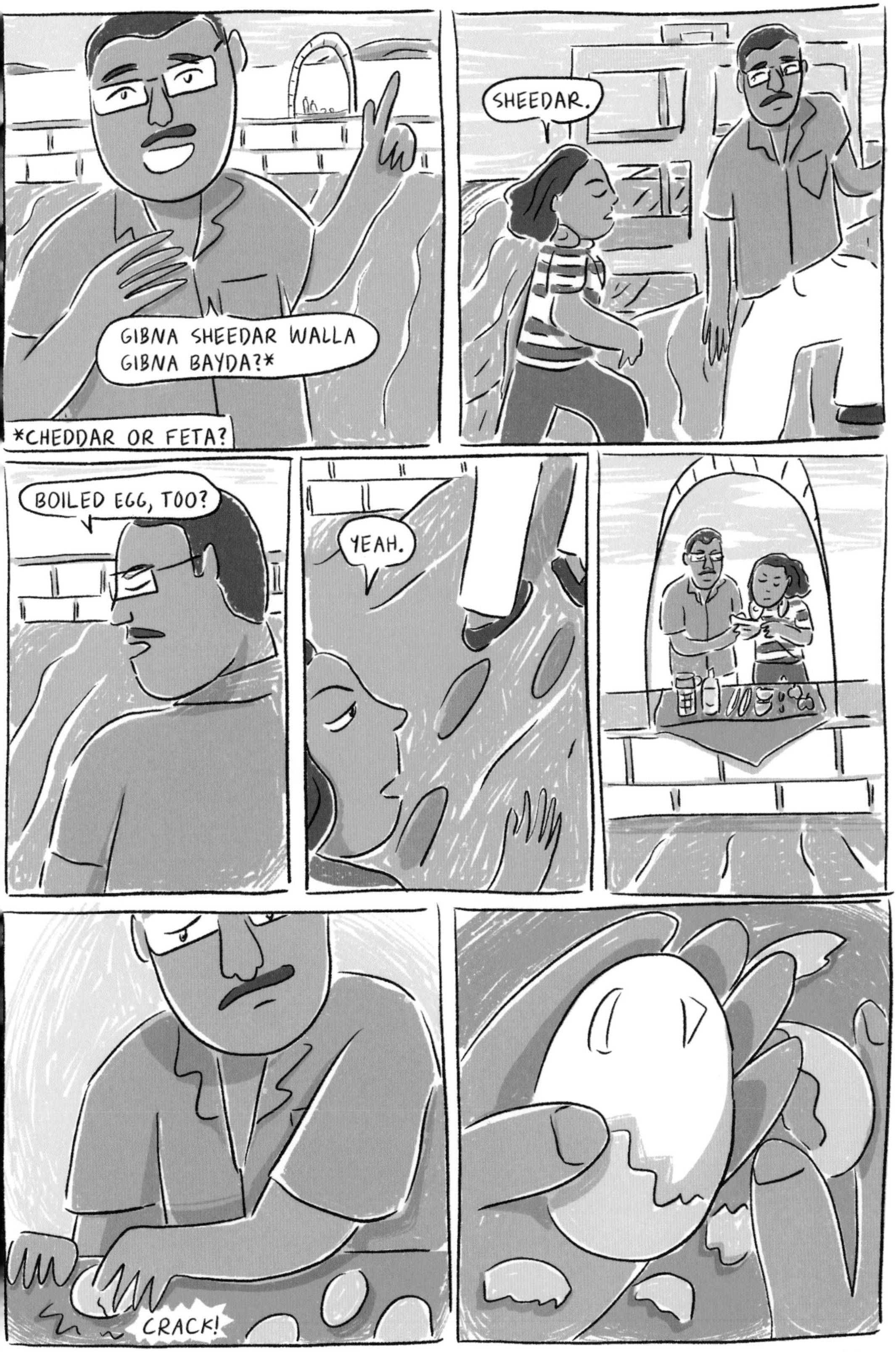
GIBNA SHEEDAR WALLA GIBNA BAYDA?*
*CHEDDAR OR FETA?
SHEEDAR.
BOILED EGG, TOO?
YEAH.
CRACK!

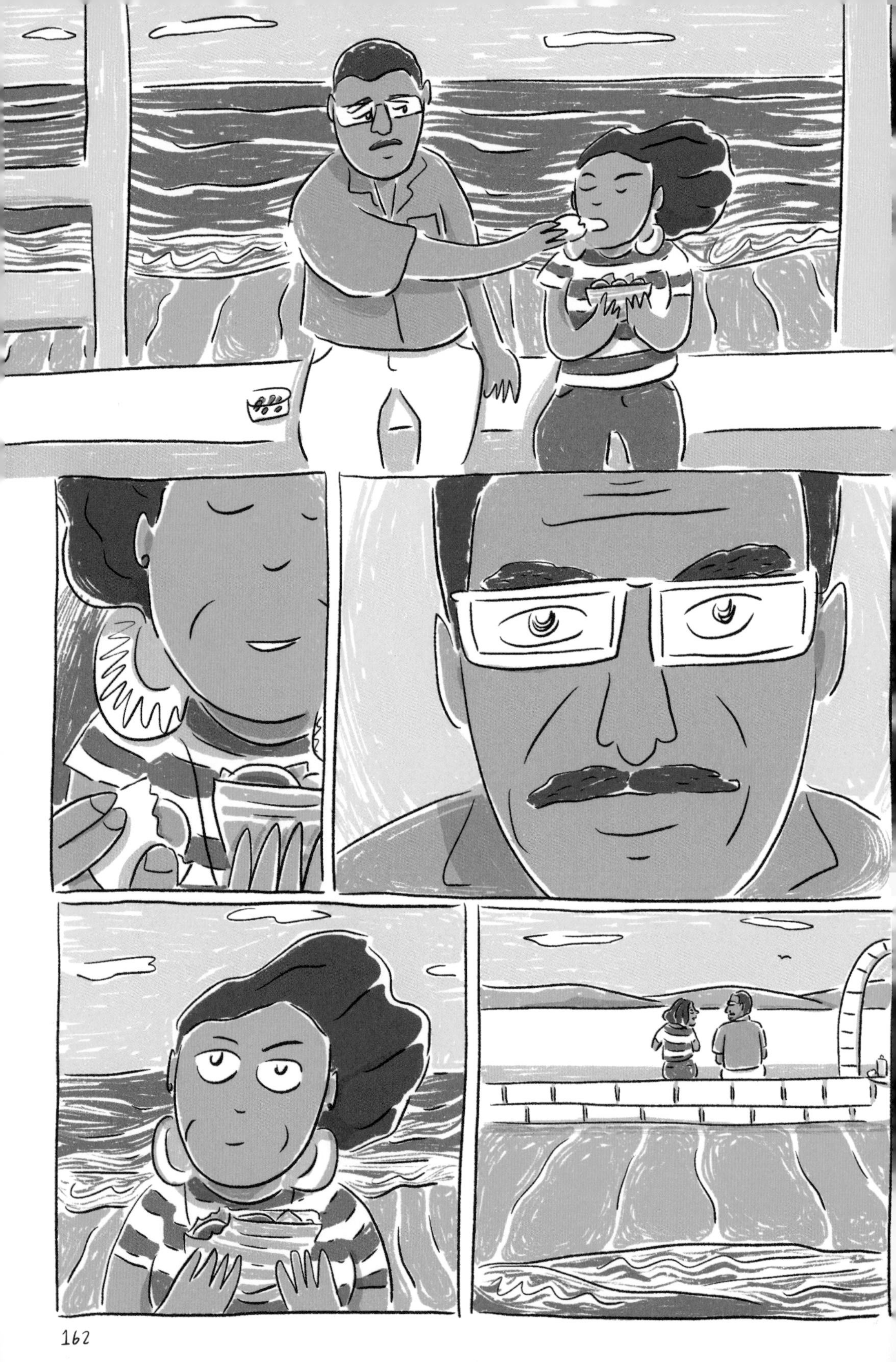

CHAPTER 7

Sushi Party

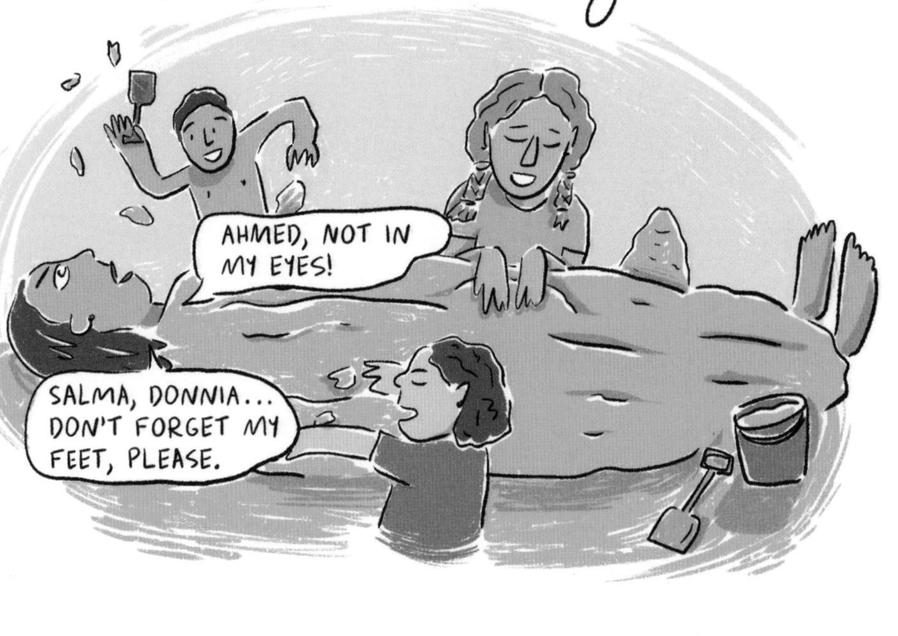
AHMED, NOT IN MY EYES!
SALMA, DONNIA... DON'T FORGET MY FEET, PLEASE.

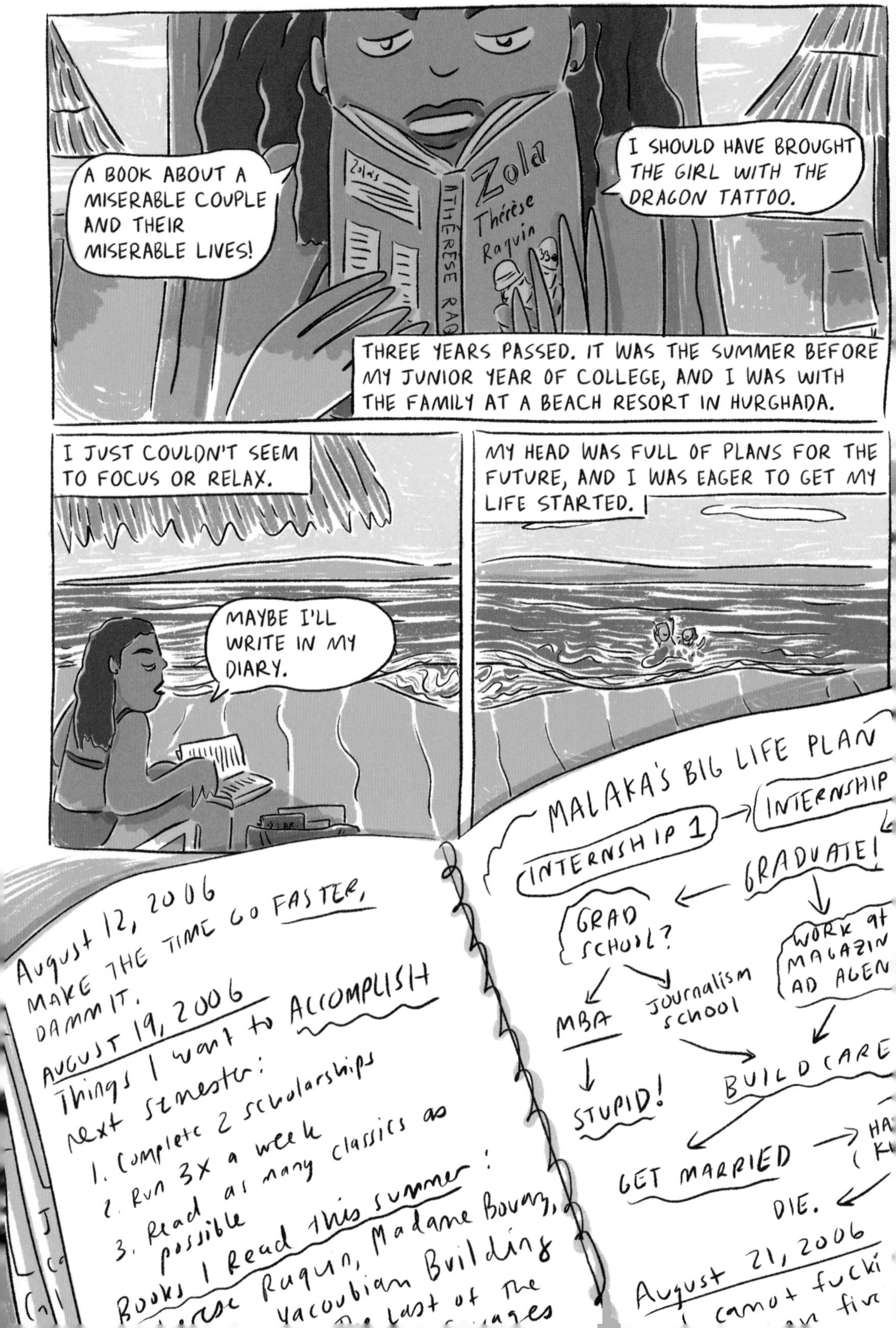

A BOOK ABOUT A MISERABLE COUPLE AND THEIR MISERABLE LIVES!
Zola's
Zola
Thérèse Raquin
THÉRÈSE RAQ
I SHOULD HAVE BROUGHT THE GIRL WITH THE DRAGON TATTOO.
THREE YEARS PASSED. IT WAS THE SUMMER BEFORE MY JUNIOR YEAR OF COLLEGE, AND I WAS WITH THE FAMILY AT A BEACH RESORT IN HURGHADA.
I JUST COULDN'T SEEM TO FOCUS OR RELAX.
MAYBE I'LL WRITE IN MY DIARY.
MY HEAD WAS FULL OF PLANS FOR THE FUTURE, AND I WAS EAGER TO GET MY LIFE STARTED.
August 12, 2006
MAKE THE TIME GO FASTER, DAMMIT.
AUGUST 19, 2006
Things I want to ACCOMPLISH next semester:
1. Complete 2 scholarships
2. Run 3X a week
3. Read as many classics as possible
Books I Read this summer:
Raquin, Madame Bovary,
Yacoubian Building
Last of the
MALAKA'S BIG LIFE PLAN
INTERNSHIP 1
INTERNSHIP
GRADUATE!
GRAD SCHOOL?
MBA
Journalism school
STUPID!
GET MARRIED
DIE.
August 21, 2006

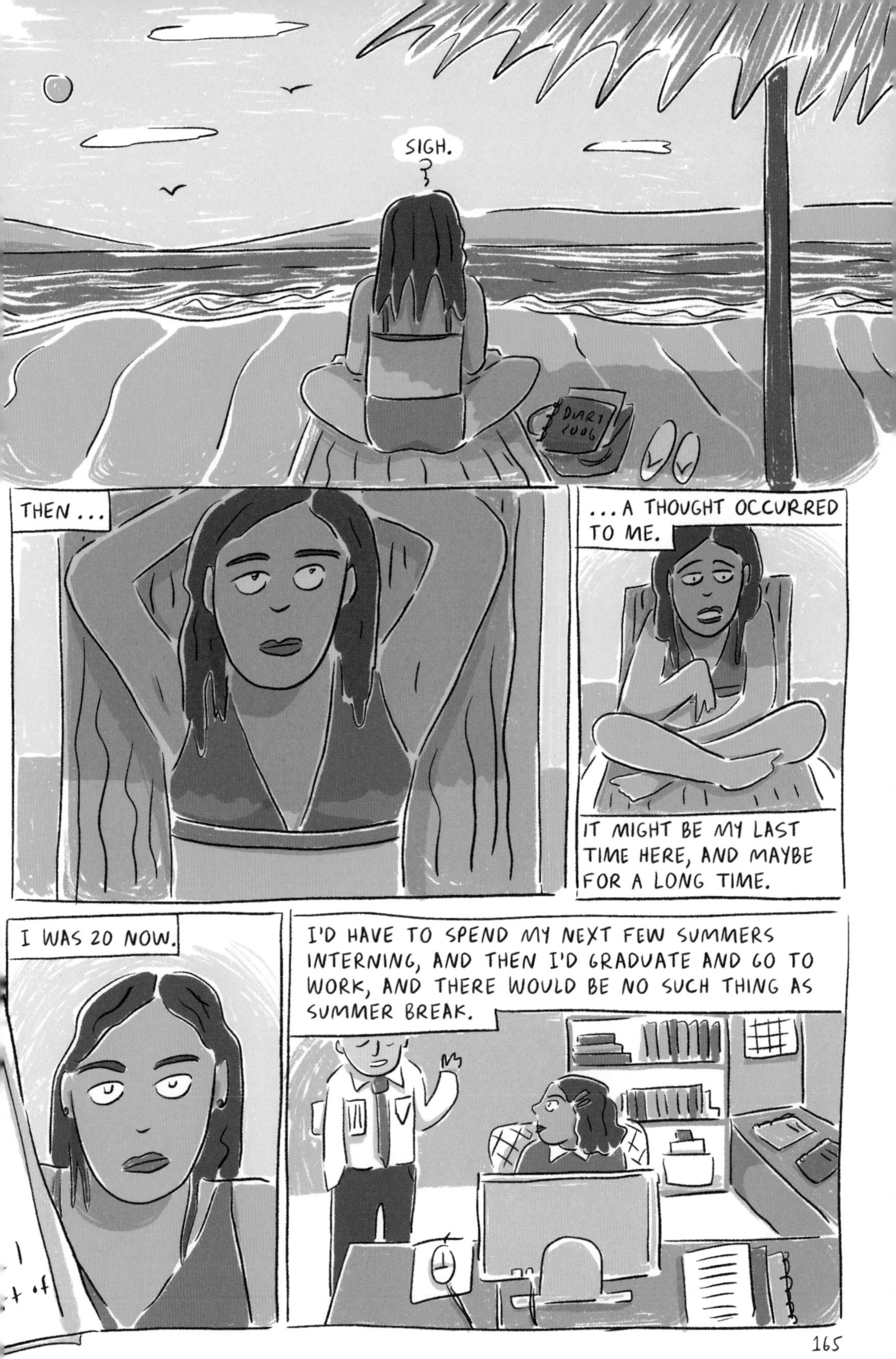

SIGH.
DIARY 2006
THEN . . .
. . . A THOUGHT OCCURRED TO ME.
IT MIGHT BE MY LAST TIME HERE, AND MAYBE FOR A LONG TIME.
I WAS 20 NOW.
I'D HAVE TO SPEND MY NEXT FEW SUMMERS INTERNING, AND THEN I'D GRADUATE AND GO TO WORK, AND THERE WOULD BE NO SUCH THING AS SUMMER BREAK.

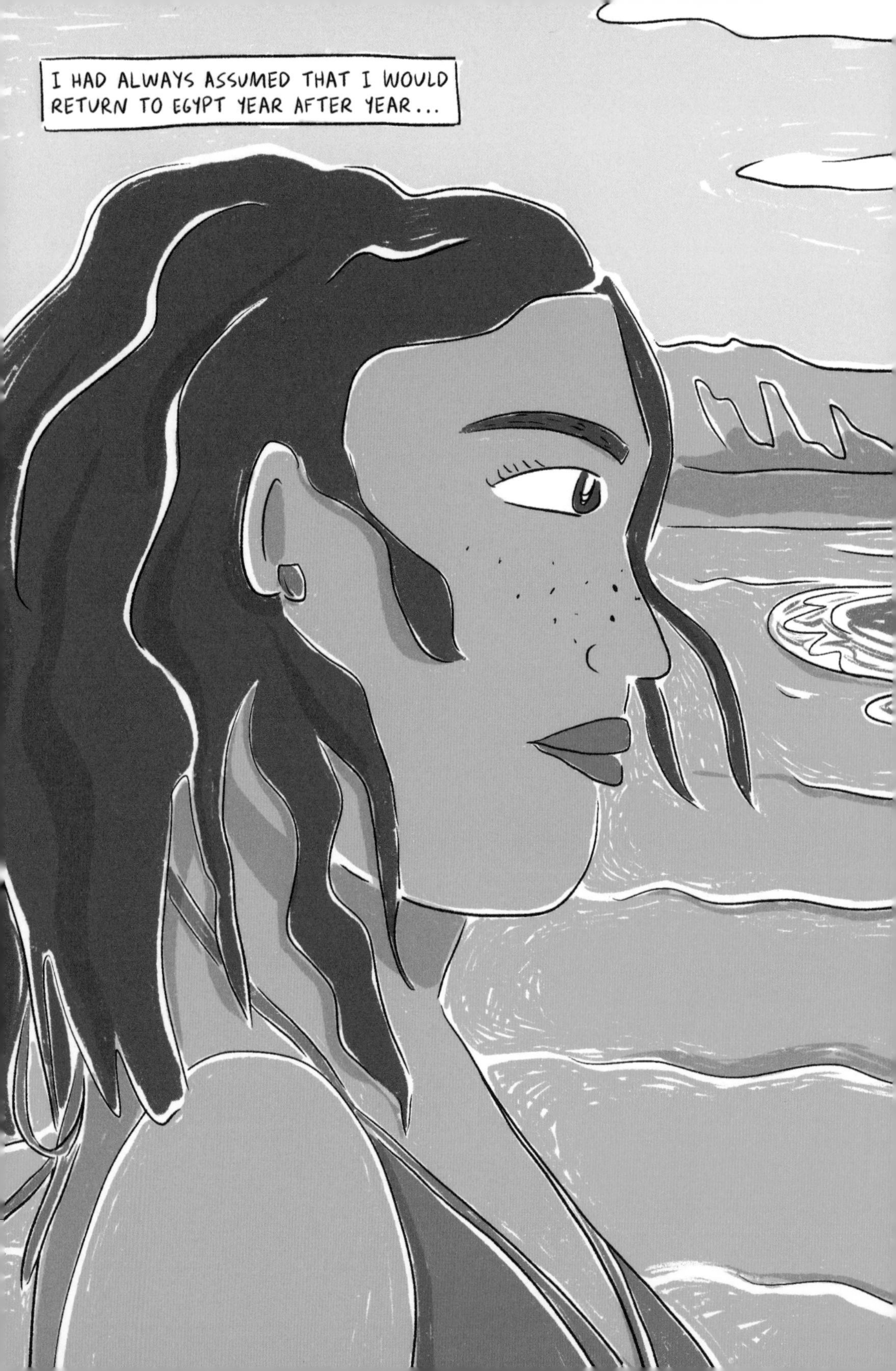
I HAD ALWAYS ASSUMED THAT I WOULD RETURN TO EGYPT YEAR AFTER YEAR...

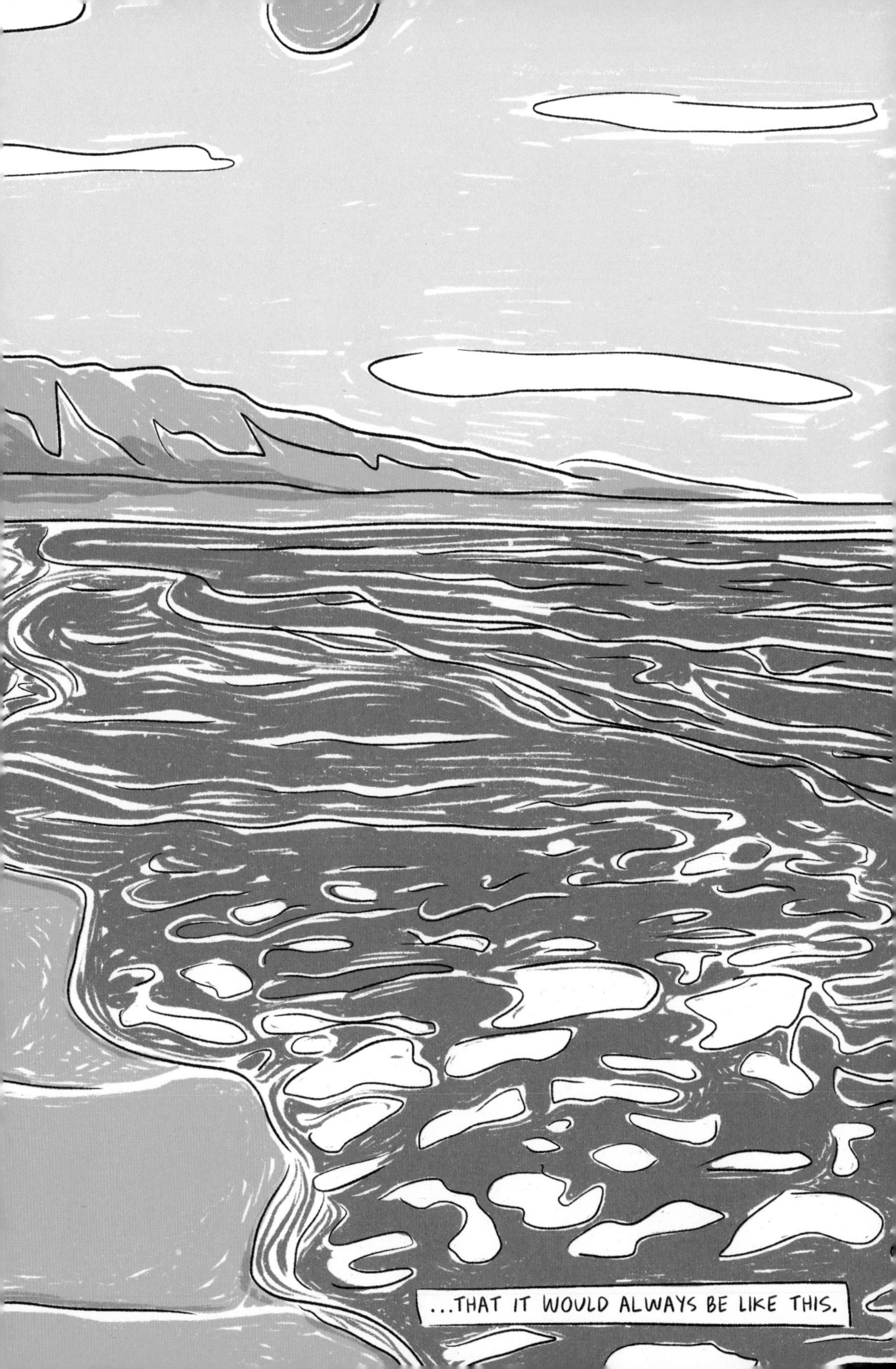
...THAT IT WOULD ALWAYS BE LIKE THIS.

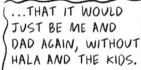
ISN'T THIS PERFECT?

I THOUGHT ABOUT THIS WISH I USED TO MAKE ON MY BIRTHDAYS AS A KID...

...THAT IT WOULD JUST BE ME AND DAD AGAIN, WITHOUT HALA AND THE KIDS.

BUT I DIDN'T WANT THAT ANYMORE.

I WAS GRATEFUL FOR OUR FAMILY, THAT THEY TOOK CARE OF HIM...

...THAT HE WASN'T ON HIS OWN.

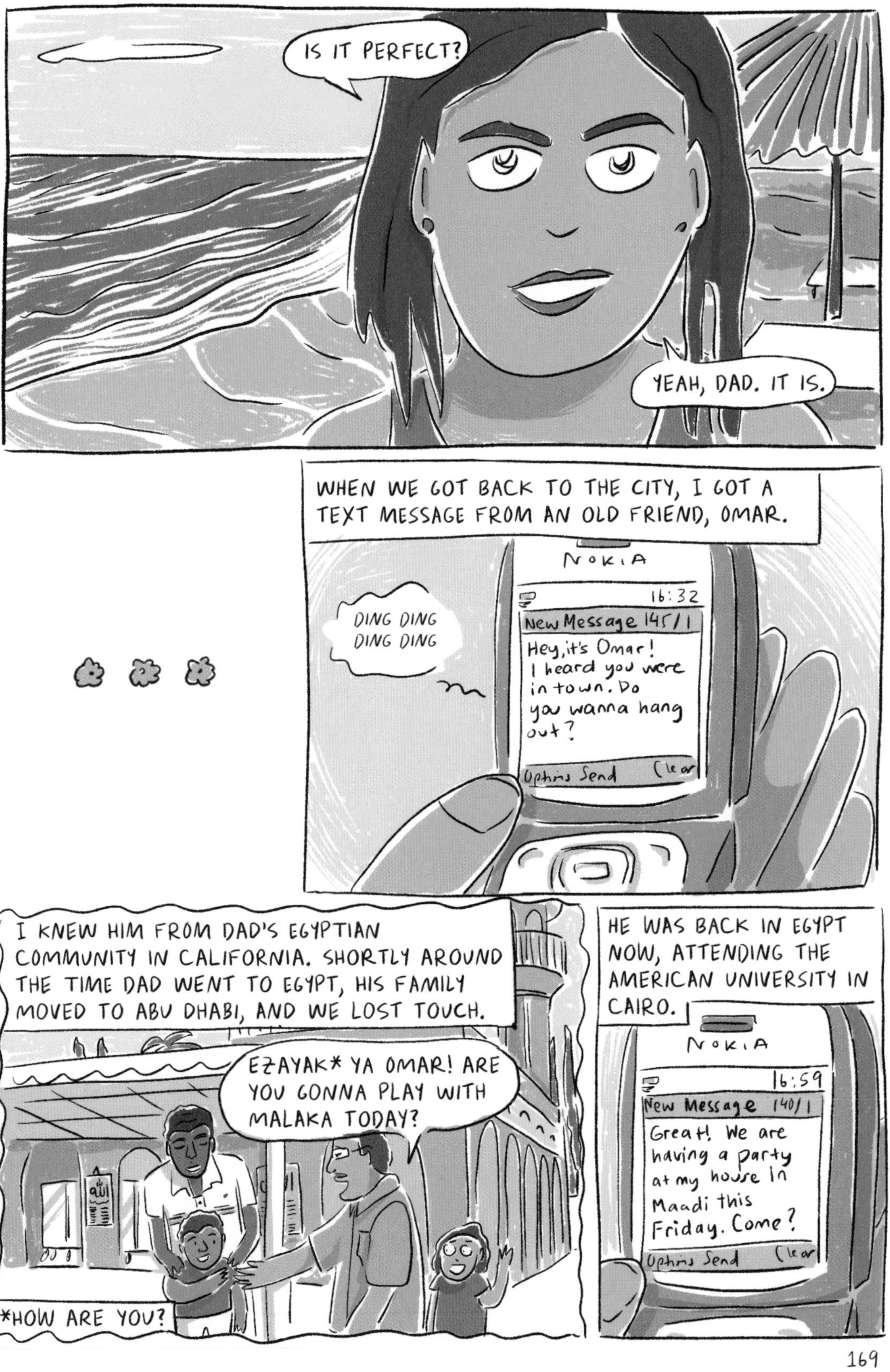
IS IT PERFECT?
YEAH, DAD. IT IS.
WHEN WE GOT BACK TO THE CITY, I GOT A TEXT MESSAGE FROM AN OLD FRIEND, OMAR.
NOKIA
16:32
New Message 145/1
Hey, it's Omar! I heard you were in town. Do you wanna hang out?
Options Send Clear
DING DING DING DING
I KNEW HIM FROM DAD'S EGYPTIAN COMMUNITY IN CALIFORNIA. SHORTLY AROUND THE TIME DAD WENT TO EGYPT, HIS FAMILY MOVED TO ABU DHABI, AND WE LOST TOUCH.
EZAYAK* YA OMAR! ARE YOU GONNA PLAY WITH MALAKA TODAY?
*HOW ARE YOU?
HE WAS BACK IN EGYPT NOW, ATTENDING THE AMERICAN UNIVERSITY IN CAIRO.
NOKIA
16:59
New Message 140/1
Great! We are having a party at my house in Maadi this Friday. Come?
Options Send Clear

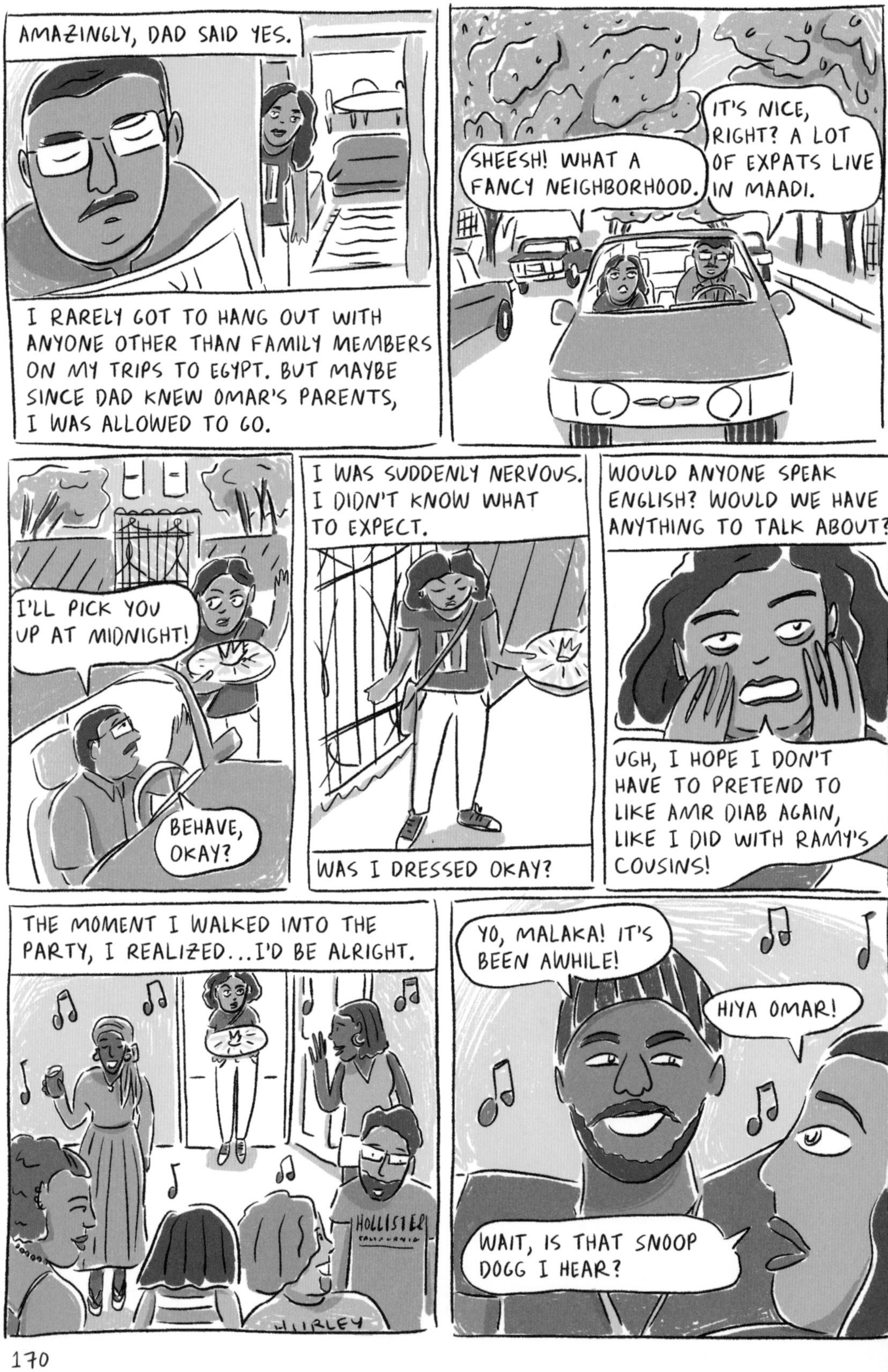
AMAZINGLY, DAD SAID YES.
I RARELY GOT TO HANG OUT WITH ANYONE OTHER THAN FAMILY MEMBERS ON MY TRIPS TO EGYPT. BUT MAYBE SINCE DAD KNEW OMAR'S PARENTS, I WAS ALLOWED TO GO.
SHEESH! WHAT A FANCY NEIGHBORHOOD.
IT'S NICE, RIGHT? A LOT OF EXPATS LIVE IN MAADI.
I'LL PICK YOU UP AT MIDNIGHT!
BEHAVE, OKAY?
I WAS SUDDENLY NERVOUS. I DIDN'T KNOW WHAT TO EXPECT.
WAS I DRESSED OKAY?
WOULD ANYONE SPEAK ENGLISH? WOULD WE HAVE ANYTHING TO TALK ABOUT?
UGH, I HOPE I DON'T HAVE TO PRETEND TO LIKE AMR DIAB AGAIN, LIKE I DID WITH RAMY'S COUSINS!
THE MOMENT I WALKED INTO THE PARTY, I REALIZED...I'D BE ALRIGHT.
HOLLISTER
HURLEY
YO, MALAKA! IT'S BEEN AWHILE!
HIYA OMAR!
WAIT, IS THAT SNOOP DOGG I HEAR?

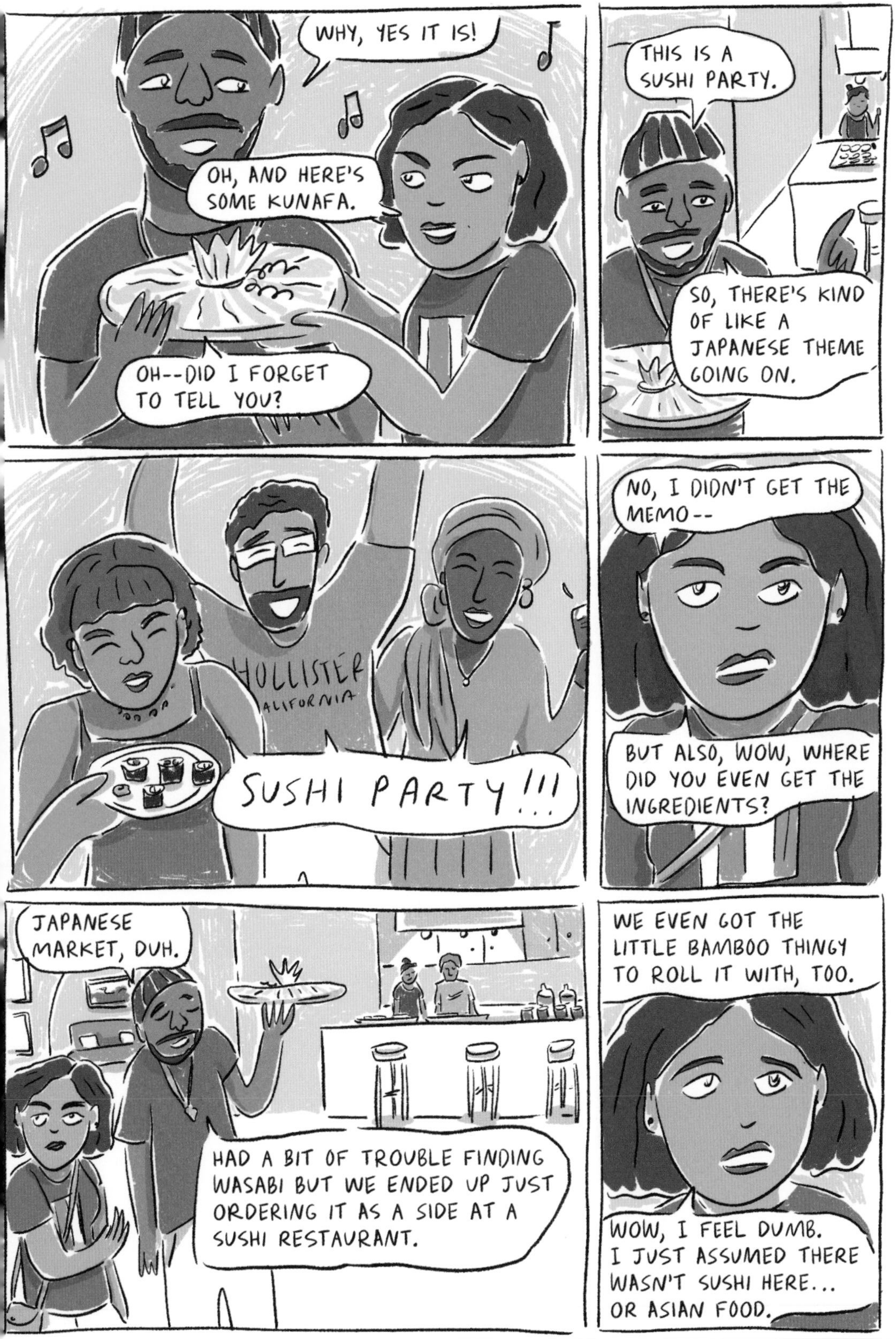
WHY, YES IT IS!
OH, AND HERE'S SOME KUNAFA.
OH--DID I FORGET TO TELL YOU?
THIS IS A SUSHI PARTY.
SO, THERE'S KIND OF LIKE A JAPANESE THEME GOING ON.
HOLLISTER CALIFORNIA
SUSHI PARTY!!!
NO, I DIDN'T GET THE MEMO--
BUT ALSO, WOW, WHERE DID YOU EVEN GET THE INGREDIENTS?
JAPANESE MARKET, DUH.
HAD A BIT OF TROUBLE FINDING WASABI BUT WE ENDED UP JUST ORDERING IT AS A SIDE AT A SUSHI RESTAURANT.
WE EVEN GOT THE LITTLE BAMBOO THINGY TO ROLL IT WITH, TOO.
WOW, I FEEL DUMB. I JUST ASSUMED THERE WASN'T SUSHI HERE... OR ASIAN FOOD.

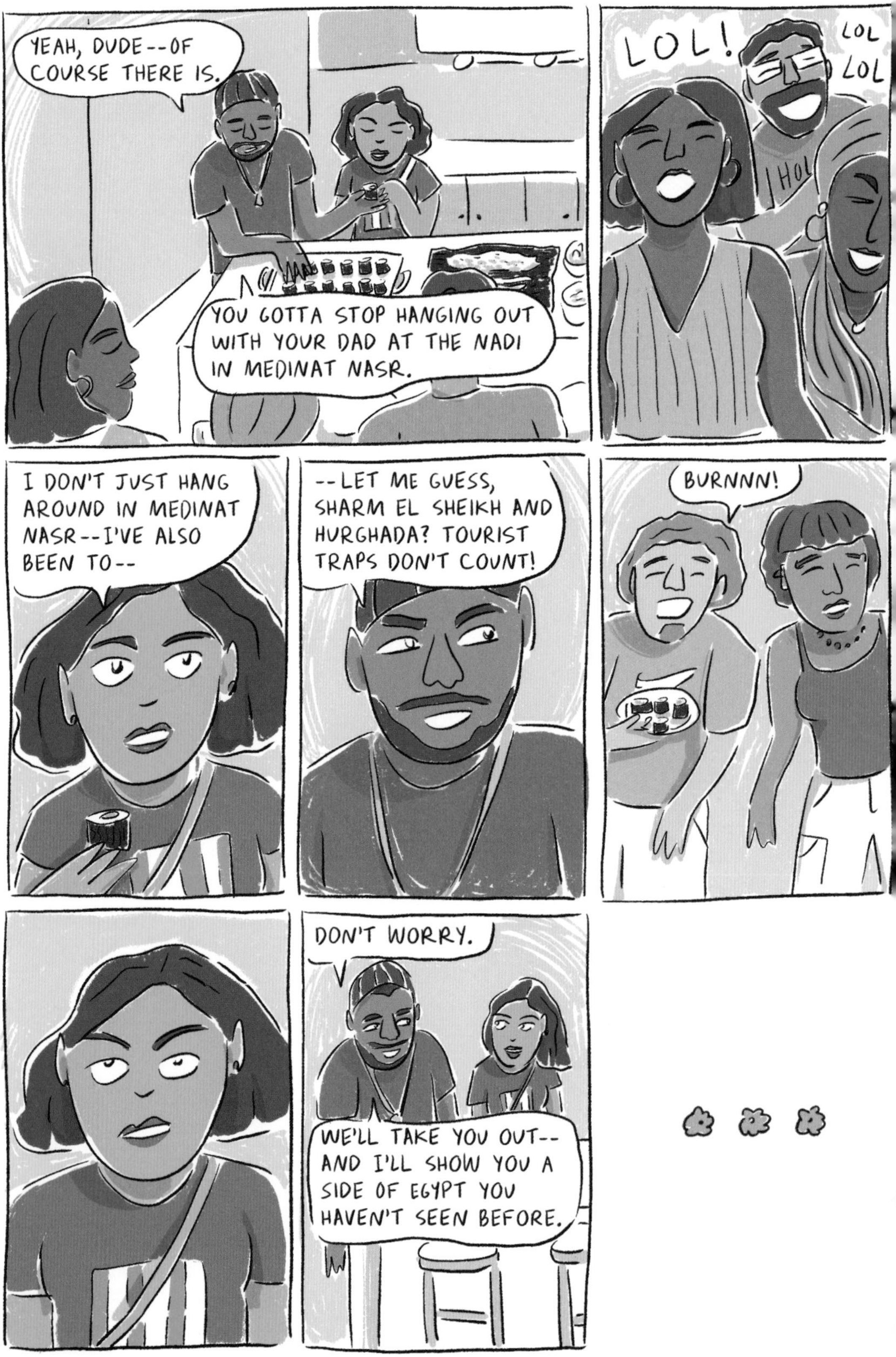
YEAH, DUDE--OF COURSE THERE IS.
YOU GOTTA STOP HANGING OUT WITH YOUR DAD AT THE NADI IN MEDINAT NASR.
LOL!
LOL
LOL
I DON'T JUST HANG AROUND IN MEDINAT NASR--I'VE ALSO BEEN TO--
--LET ME GUESS, SHARM EL SHEIKH AND HURGHADA? TOURIST TRAPS DON'T COUNT!
BURNNN!
DON'T WORRY.
WE'LL TAKE YOU OUT--AND I'LL SHOW YOU A SIDE OF EGYPT YOU HAVEN'T SEEN BEFORE.

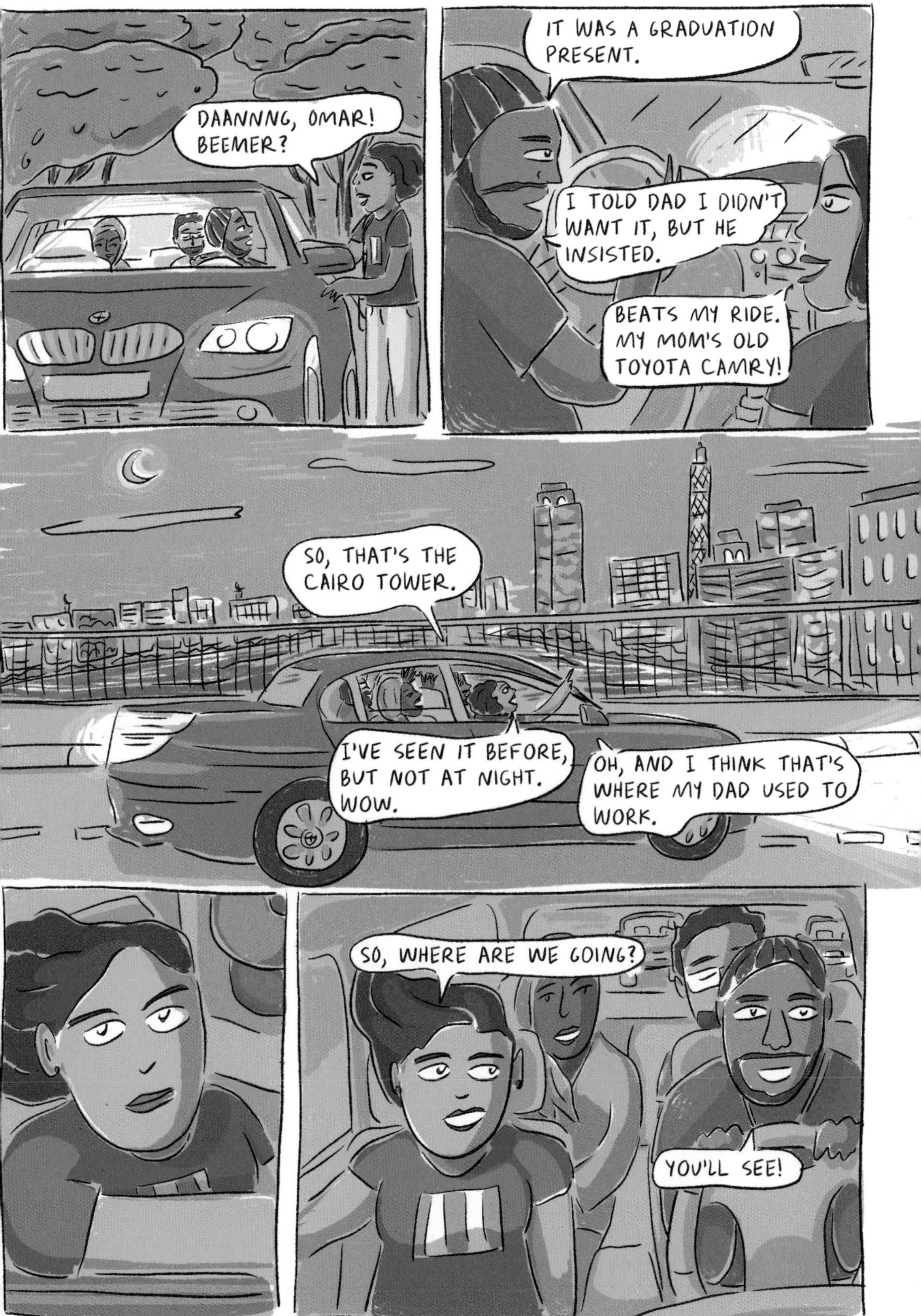
DAANNNG, OMAR! BEEMER?
IT WAS A GRADUATION PRESENT.
I TOLD DAD I DIDN'T WANT IT, BUT HE INSISTED.
BEATS MY RIDE. MY MOM'S OLD TOYOTA CAMRY!
SO, THAT'S THE CAIRO TOWER.
I'VE SEEN IT BEFORE, BUT NOT AT NIGHT. WOW.
OH, AND I THINK THAT'S WHERE MY DAD USED TO WORK.
SO, WHERE ARE WE GOING?
YOU'LL SEE!

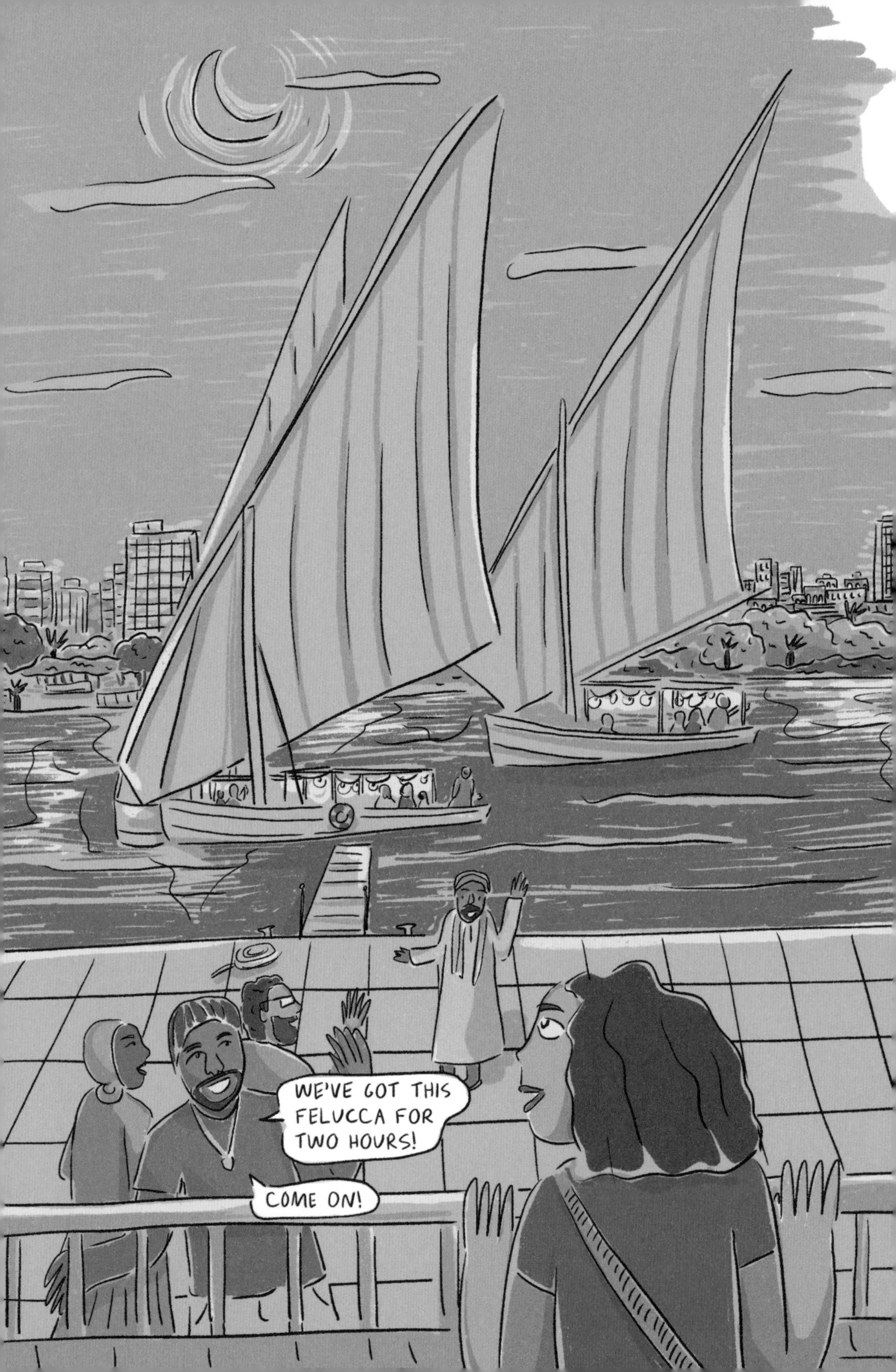
WE'VE GOT THIS FELUCCA FOR TWO HOURS!
COME ON!

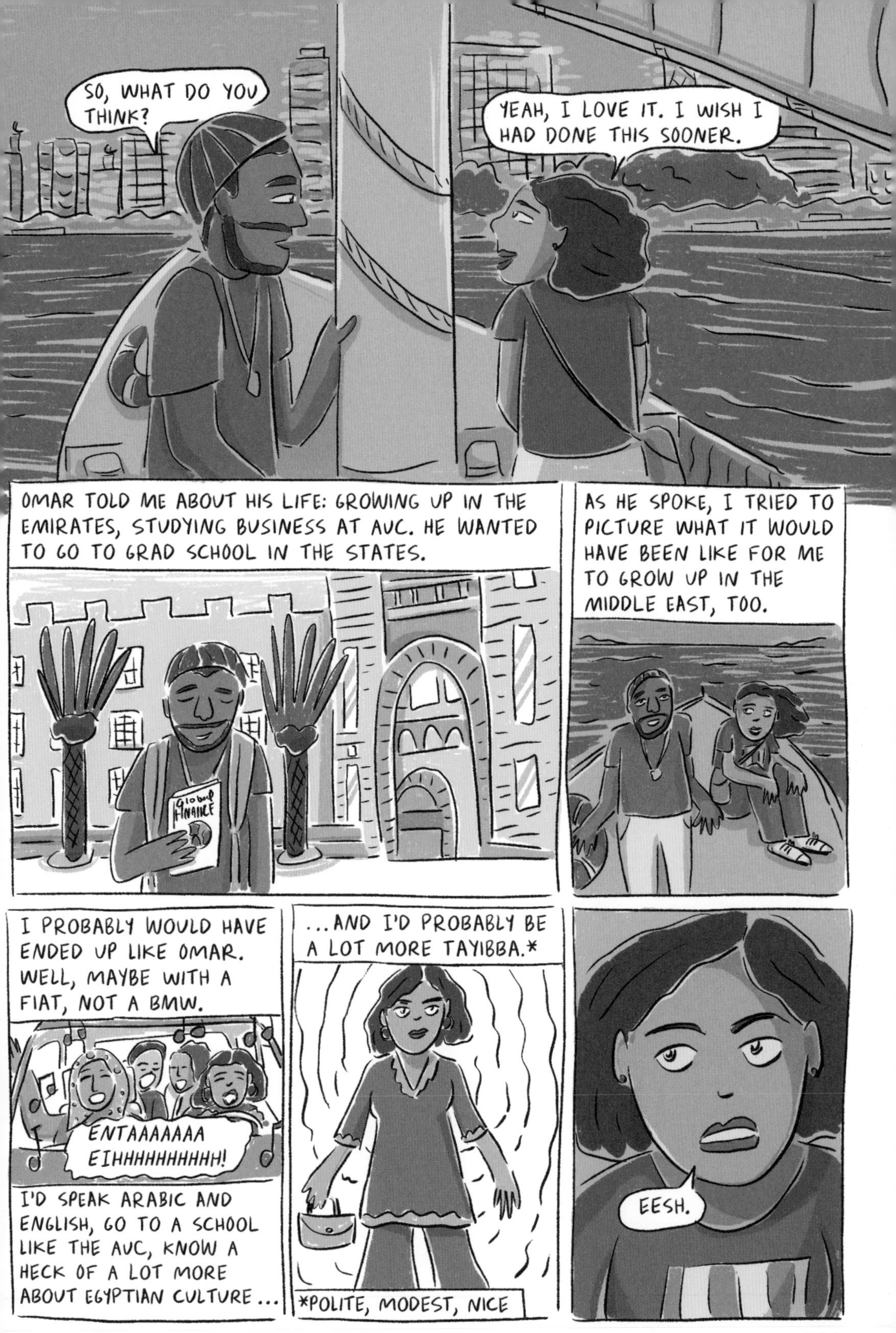

SO, WHAT DO YOU THINK?
YEAH, I LOVE IT. I WISH I HAD DONE THIS SOONER.
OMAR TOLD ME ABOUT HIS LIFE: GROWING UP IN THE EMIRATES, STUDYING BUSINESS AT AUC. HE WANTED TO GO TO GRAD SCHOOL IN THE STATES.
Global FINANCE
AS HE SPOKE, I TRIED TO PICTURE WHAT IT WOULD HAVE BEEN LIKE FOR ME TO GROW UP IN THE MIDDLE EAST, TOO.
I PROBABLY WOULD HAVE ENDED UP LIKE OMAR. WELL, MAYBE WITH A FIAT, NOT A BMW.
ENTAAAAAAA EIHHHHHHHHH!
I'D SPEAK ARABIC AND ENGLISH, GO TO A SCHOOL LIKE THE AUC, KNOW A HECK OF A LOT MORE ABOUT EGYPTIAN CULTURE...
...AND I'D PROBABLY BE A LOT MORE TAYIBBA.*
*POLITE, MODEST, NICE
EESH.

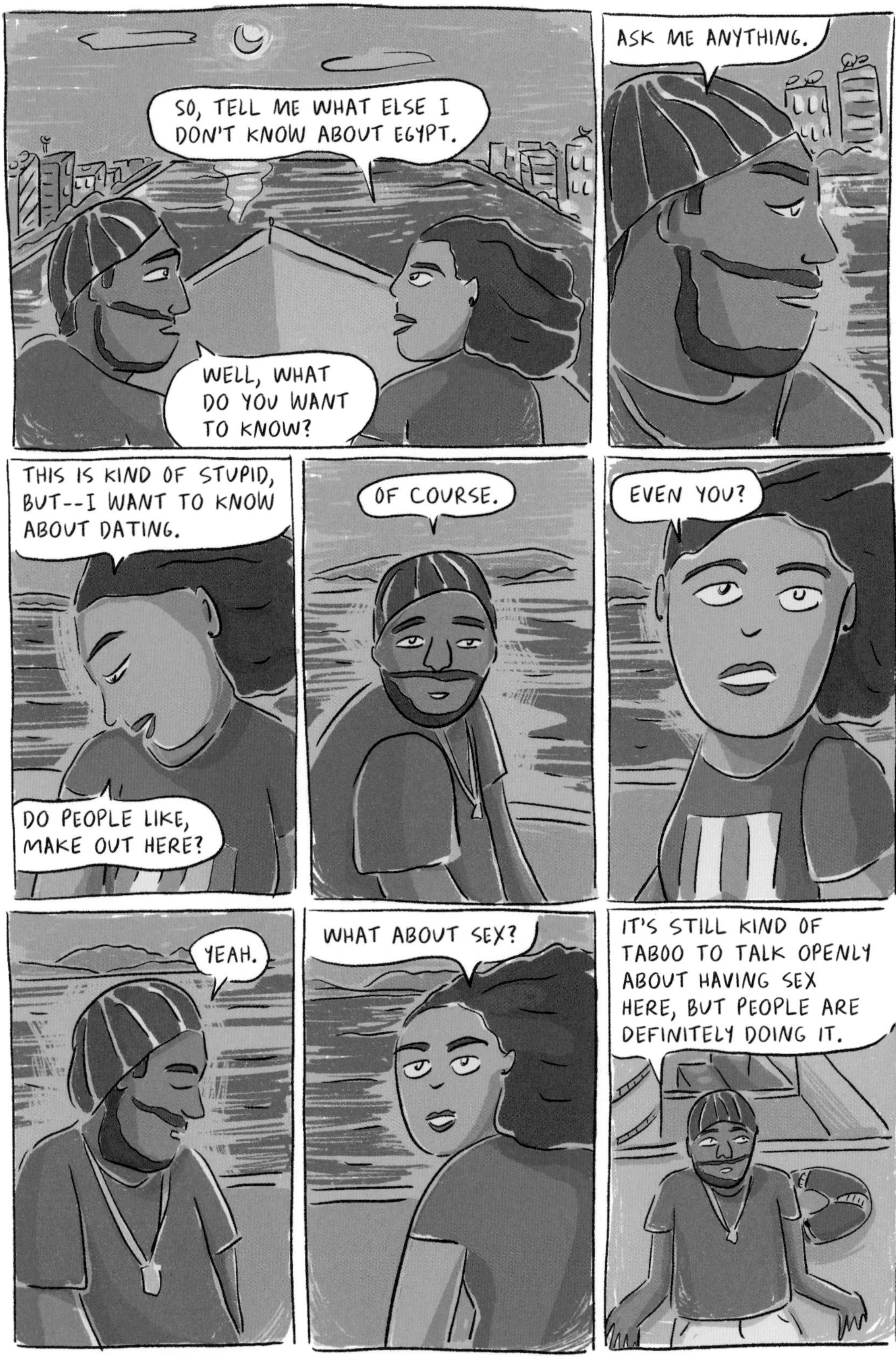
SO, TELL ME WHAT ELSE I DON'T KNOW ABOUT EGYPT.
WELL, WHAT DO YOU WANT TO KNOW?
ASK ME ANYTHING.
THIS IS KIND OF STUPID, BUT--I WANT TO KNOW ABOUT DATING.
DO PEOPLE LIKE, MAKE OUT HERE?
OF COURSE.
EVEN YOU?
YEAH.
WHAT ABOUT SEX?
IT'S STILL KIND OF TABOO TO TALK OPENLY ABOUT HAVING SEX HERE, BUT PEOPLE ARE DEFINITELY DOING IT.

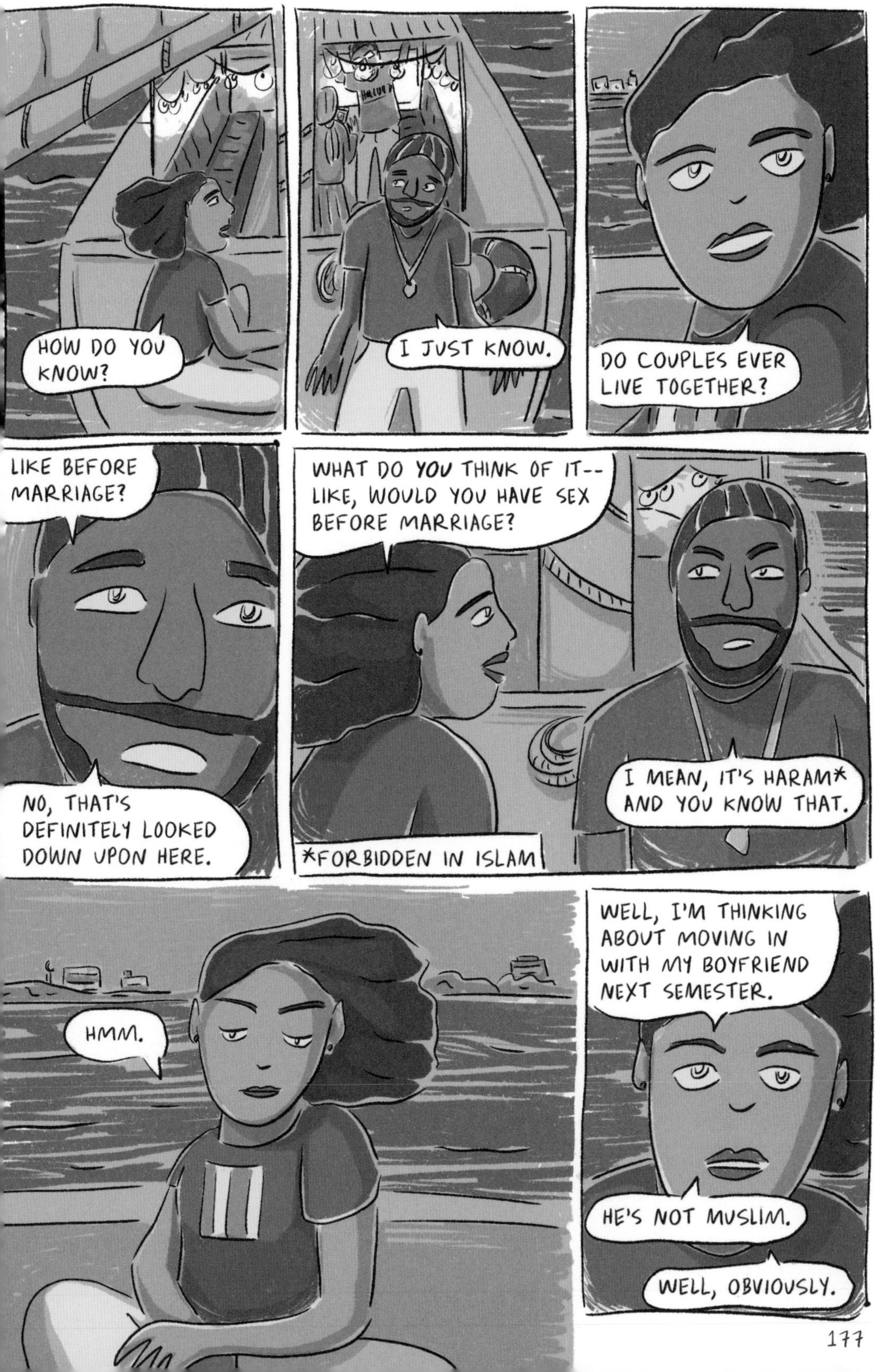
HOW DO YOU KNOW?
I JUST KNOW.
DO COUPLES EVER LIVE TOGETHER?
LIKE BEFORE MARRIAGE?
NO, THAT'S DEFINITELY LOOKED DOWN UPON HERE.
WHAT DO YOU THINK OF IT-- LIKE, WOULD YOU HAVE SEX BEFORE MARRIAGE?
I MEAN, IT'S HARAM* AND YOU KNOW THAT.
*FORBIDDEN IN ISLAM
HMM.
WELL, I'M THINKING ABOUT MOVING IN WITH MY BOYFRIEND NEXT SEMESTER.
HE'S NOT MUSLIM.
WELL, OBVIOUSLY.

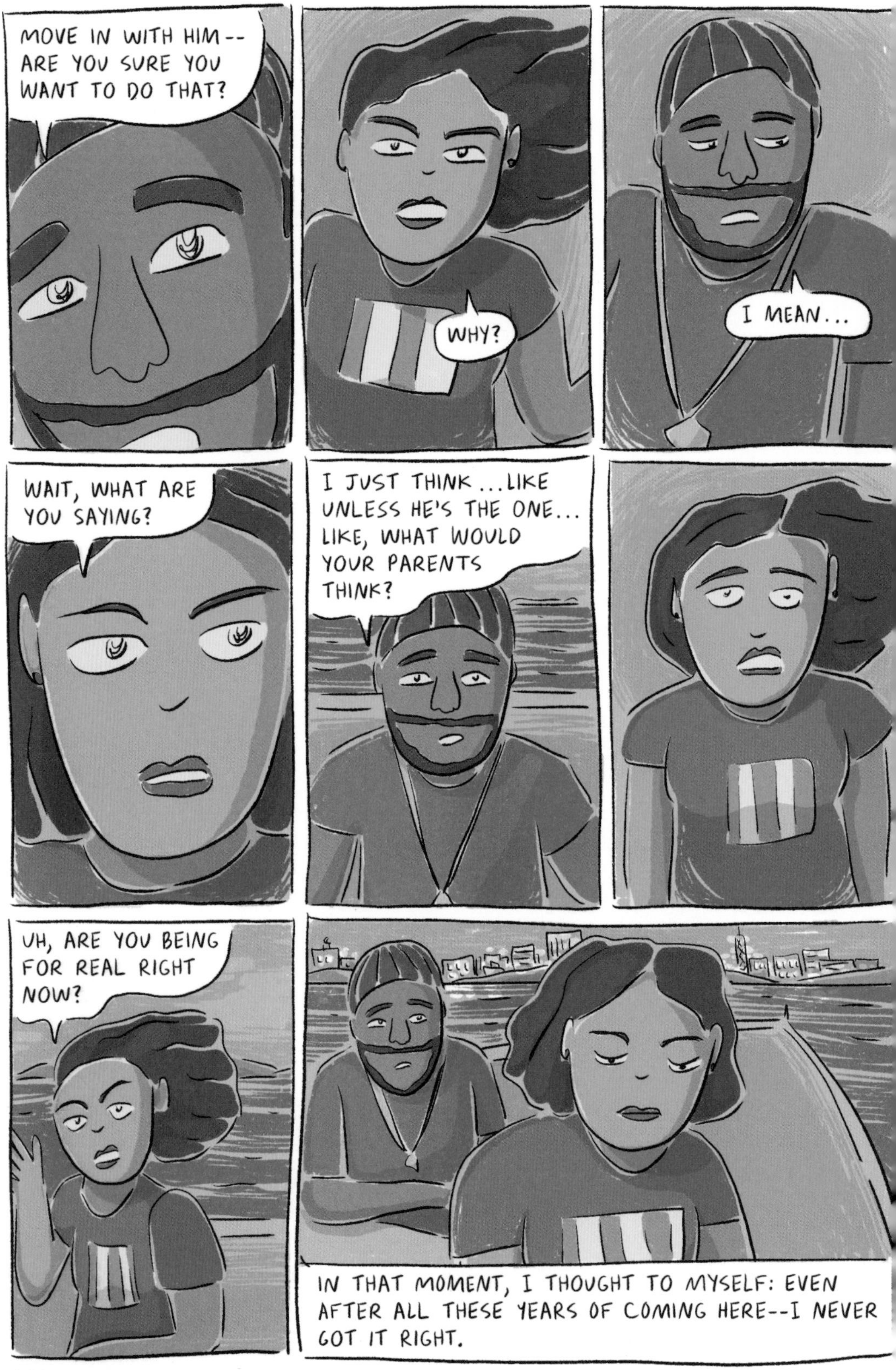

MOVE IN WITH HIM-- ARE YOU SURE YOU WANT TO DO THAT?
WHY?
I MEAN...
WAIT, WHAT ARE YOU SAYING?
I JUST THINK...LIKE UNLESS HE'S THE ONE... LIKE, WHAT WOULD YOUR PARENTS THINK?
UH, ARE YOU BEING FOR REAL RIGHT NOW?
IN THAT MOMENT, I THOUGHT TO MYSELF: EVEN AFTER ALL THESE YEARS OF COMING HERE--I NEVER GOT IT RIGHT.

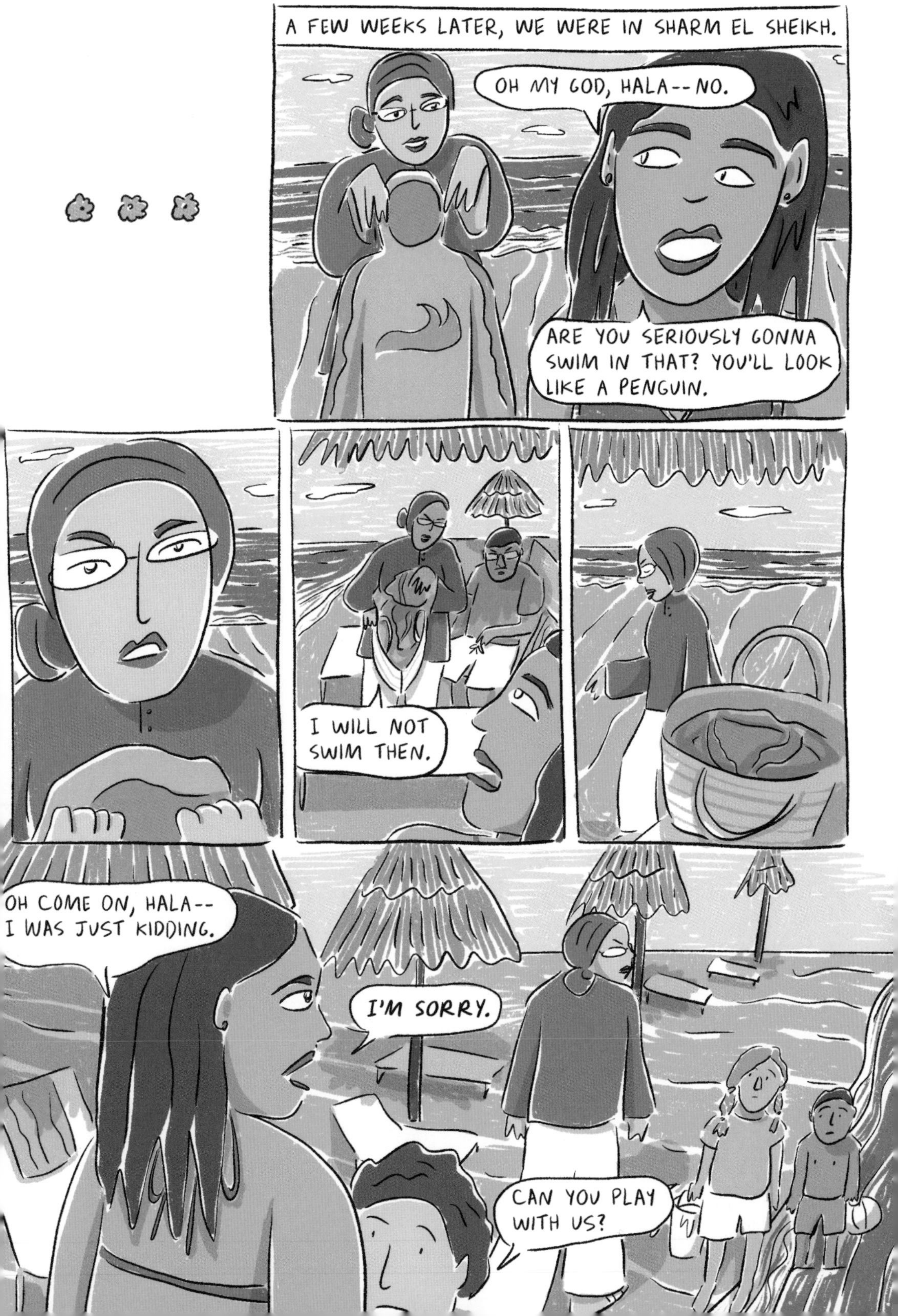
A FEW WEEKS LATER, WE WERE IN SHARM EL SHEIKH.
OH MY GOD, HALA--NO.
ARE YOU SERIOUSLY GONNA SWIM IN THAT? YOU'LL LOOK LIKE A PENGUIN.
I WILL NOT SWIM THEN.
OH COME ON, HALA-- I WAS JUST KIDDING.
I'M SORRY.
CAN YOU PLAY WITH US?

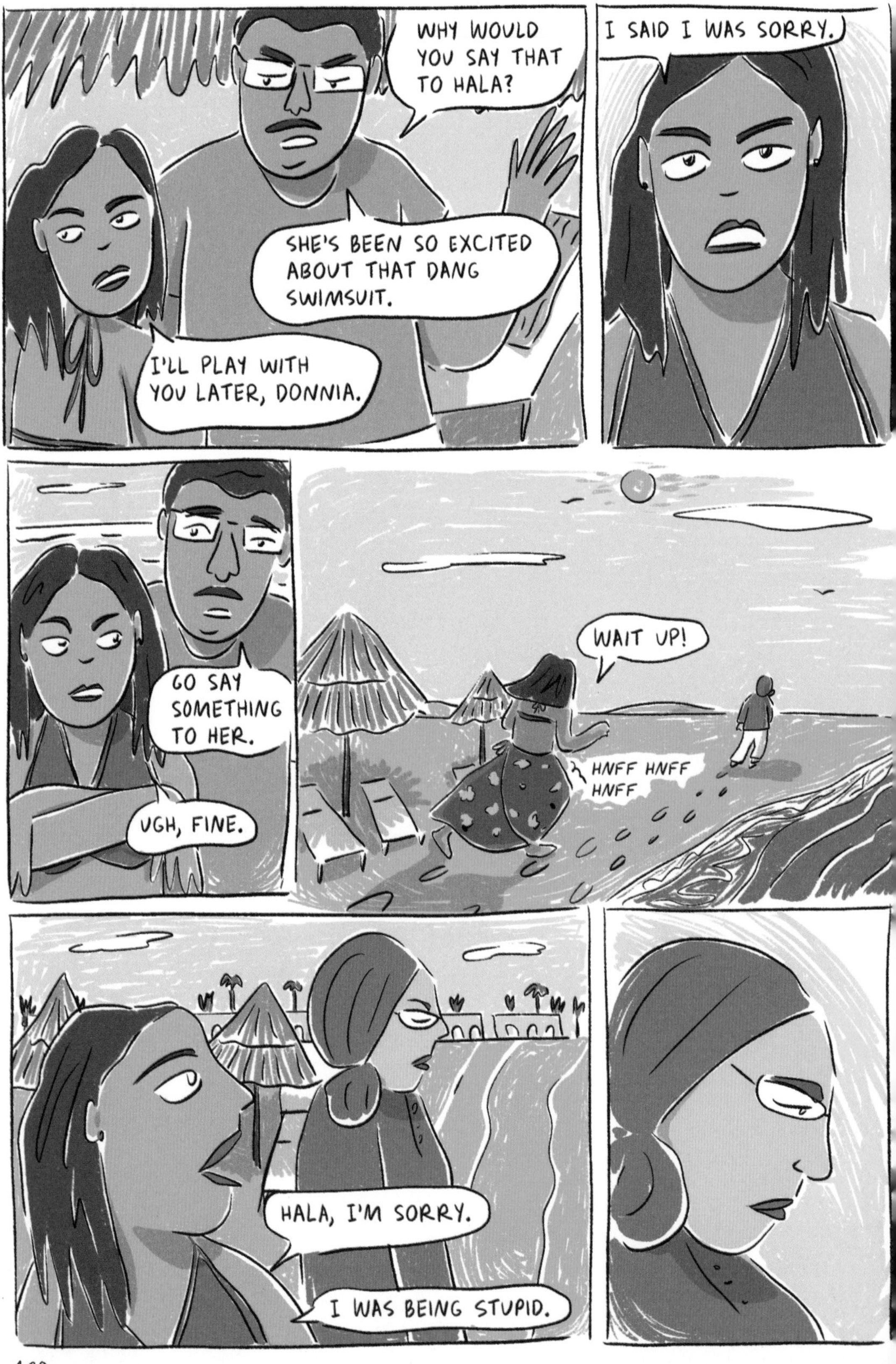
WHY WOULD YOU SAY THAT TO HALA?
SHE'S BEEN SO EXCITED ABOUT THAT DANG SWIMSUIT.
I'LL PLAY WITH YOU LATER, DONNIA.
I SAID I WAS SORRY.
GO SAY SOMETHING TO HER.
UGH, FINE.
WAIT UP!
HNFF HNFF HNFF
HALA, I'M SORRY.
I WAS BEING STUPID.

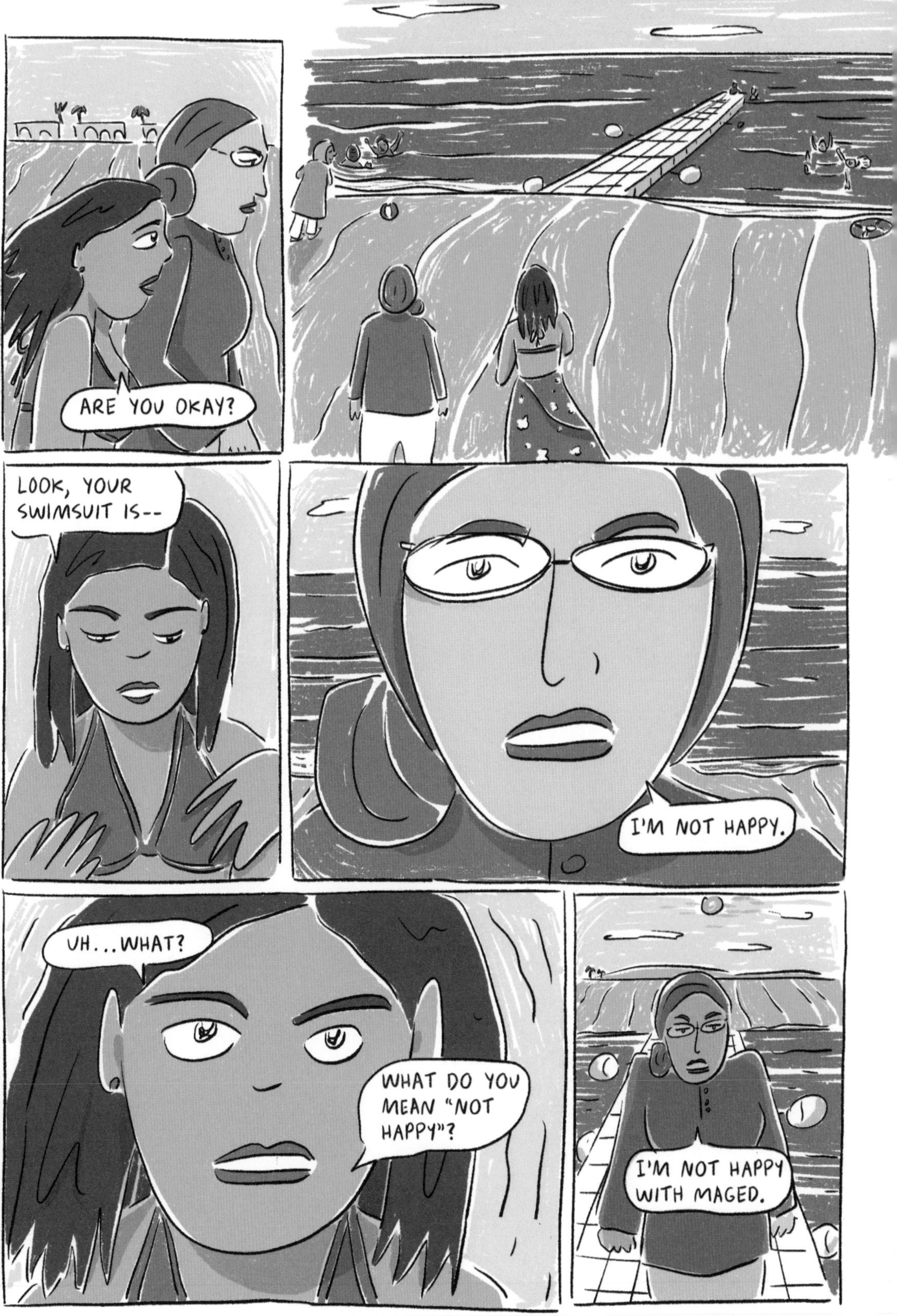
ARE YOU OKAY?
LOOK, YOUR SWIMSUIT IS--
I'M NOT HAPPY.
UH...WHAT?
WHAT DO YOU MEAN "NOT HAPPY"?
I'M NOT HAPPY WITH MAGED.

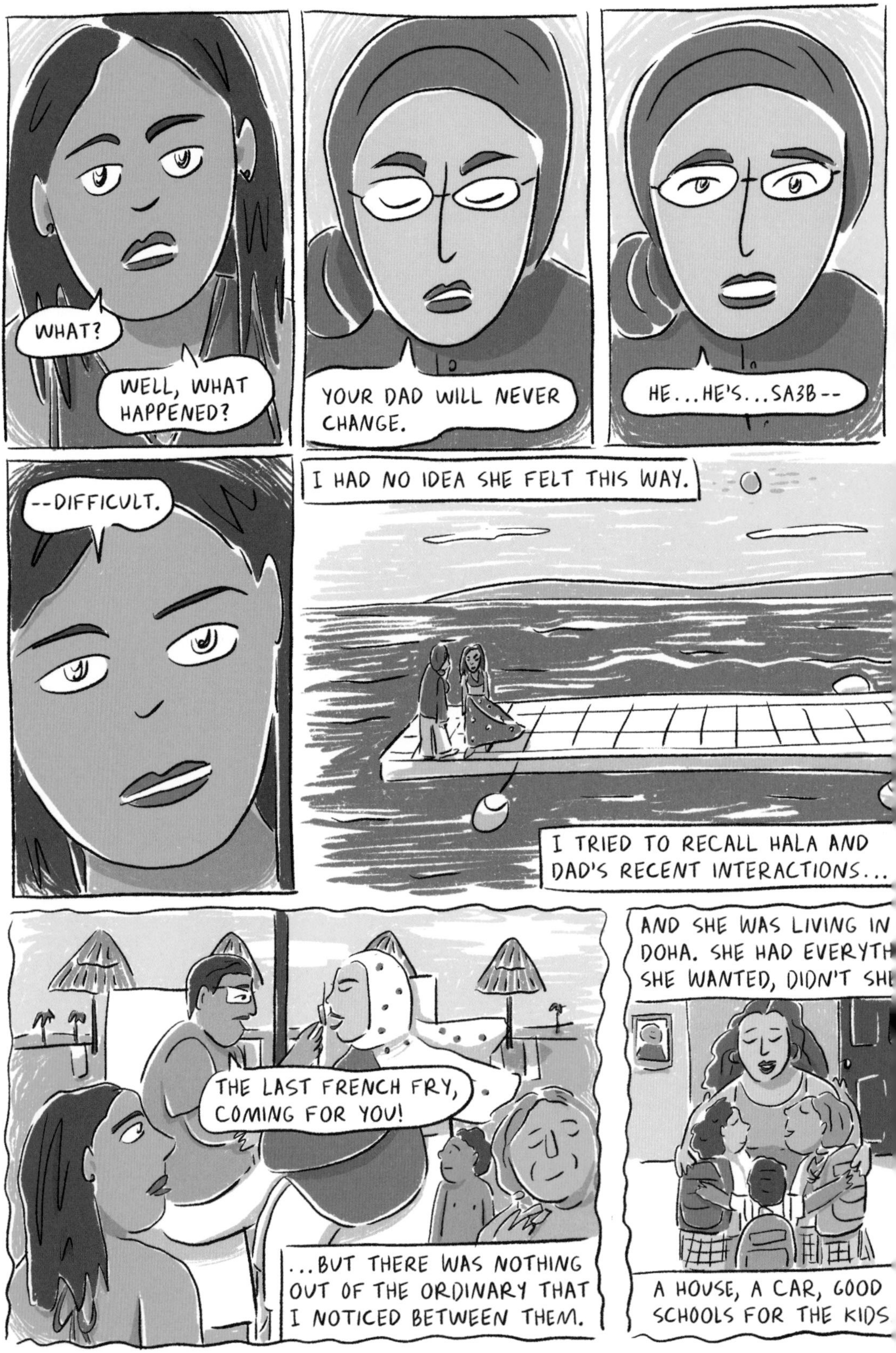
WHAT?
WELL, WHAT HAPPENED?
YOUR DAD WILL NEVER CHANGE.
HE...HE'S...SA3B--
--DIFFICULT.
I HAD NO IDEA SHE FELT THIS WAY.
I TRIED TO RECALL HALA AND DAD'S RECENT INTERACTIONS...
THE LAST FRENCH FRY, COMING FOR YOU!
...BUT THERE WAS NOTHING OUT OF THE ORDINARY THAT I NOTICED BETWEEN THEM.
AND SHE WAS LIVING IN DOHA. SHE HAD EVERYTH SHE WANTED, DIDN'T SH
A HOUSE, A CAR, GOOD SCHOOLS FOR THE KIDS

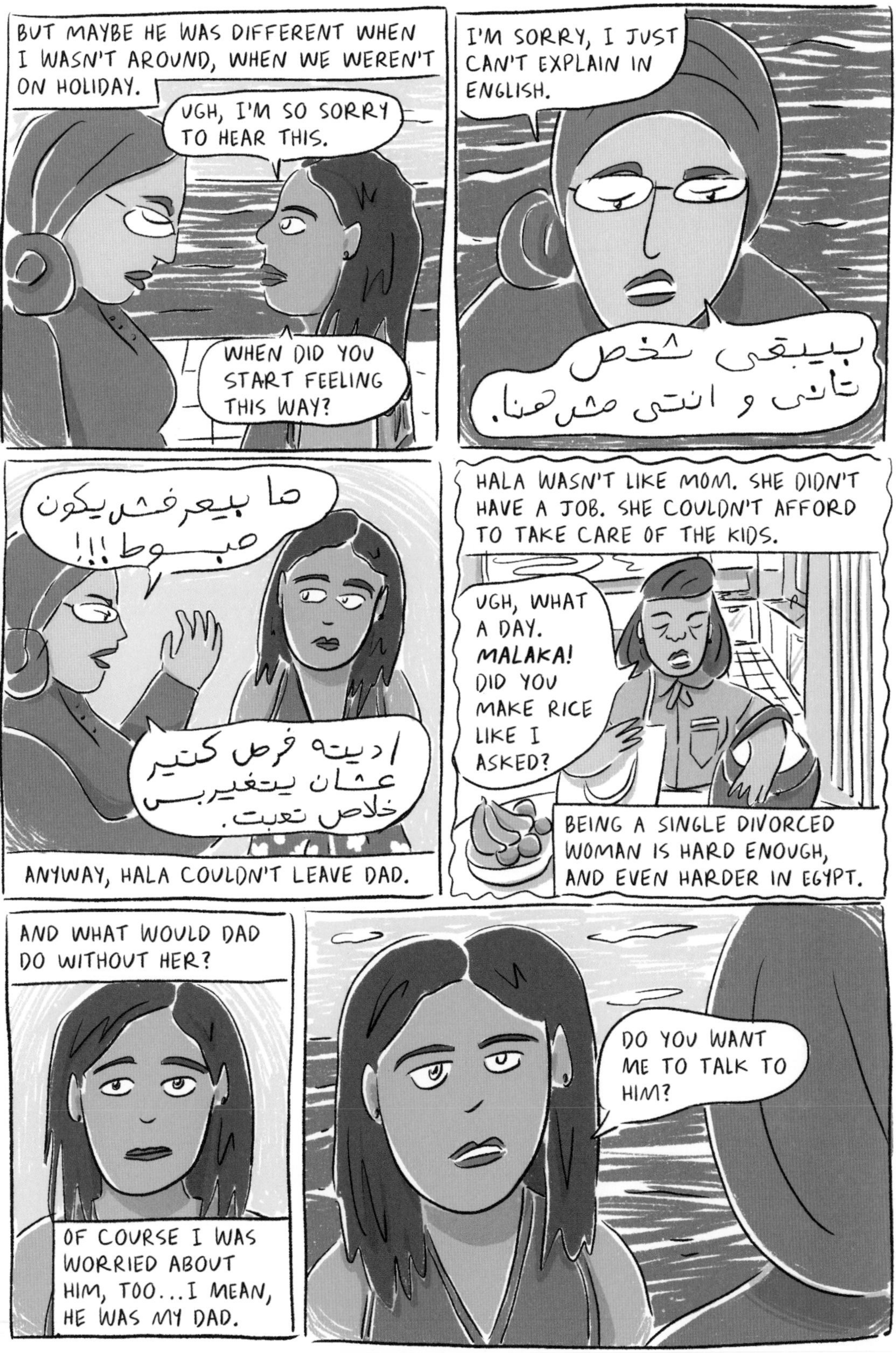
BUT MAYBE HE WAS DIFFERENT WHEN I WASN'T AROUND, WHEN WE WEREN'T ON HOLIDAY.
UGH, I'M SO SORRY TO HEAR THIS.
WHEN DID YOU START FEELING THIS WAY?
I'M SORRY, I JUST CAN'T EXPLAIN IN ENGLISH.
بيبقى شخص تاني و انتي مش هنا.
ما بيعرفش يكون مبسوط!!!
اديته فرص كتير عشان يتغير بس خلاص تعبت.
ANYWAY, HALA COULDN'T LEAVE DAD.
HALA WASN'T LIKE MOM. SHE DIDN'T HAVE A JOB. SHE COULDN'T AFFORD TO TAKE CARE OF THE KIDS.
UGH, WHAT A DAY. **MALAKA!** DID YOU MAKE RICE LIKE I ASKED?
BEING A SINGLE DIVORCED WOMAN IS HARD ENOUGH, AND EVEN HARDER IN EGYPT.
AND WHAT WOULD DAD DO WITHOUT HER?
OF COURSE I WAS WORRIED ABOUT HIM, TOO... I MEAN, HE WAS MY DAD.
DO YOU WANT ME TO TALK TO HIM?

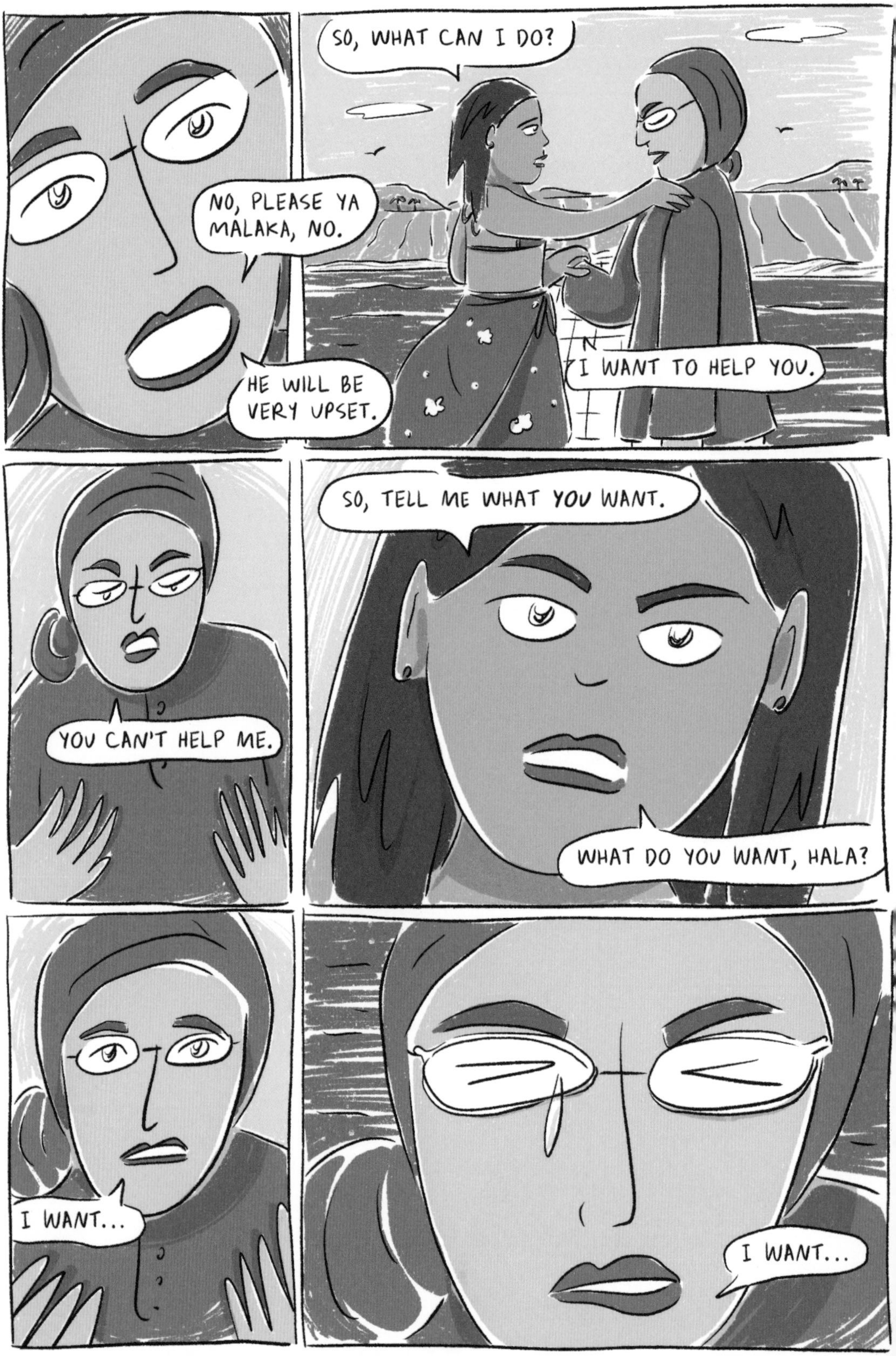
NO, PLEASE YA MALAKA, NO.
HE WILL BE VERY UPSET.
SO, WHAT CAN I DO?
I WANT TO HELP YOU.
YOU CAN'T HELP ME.
SO, TELL ME WHAT YOU WANT.
WHAT DO YOU WANT, HALA?
I WANT...
I WANT...

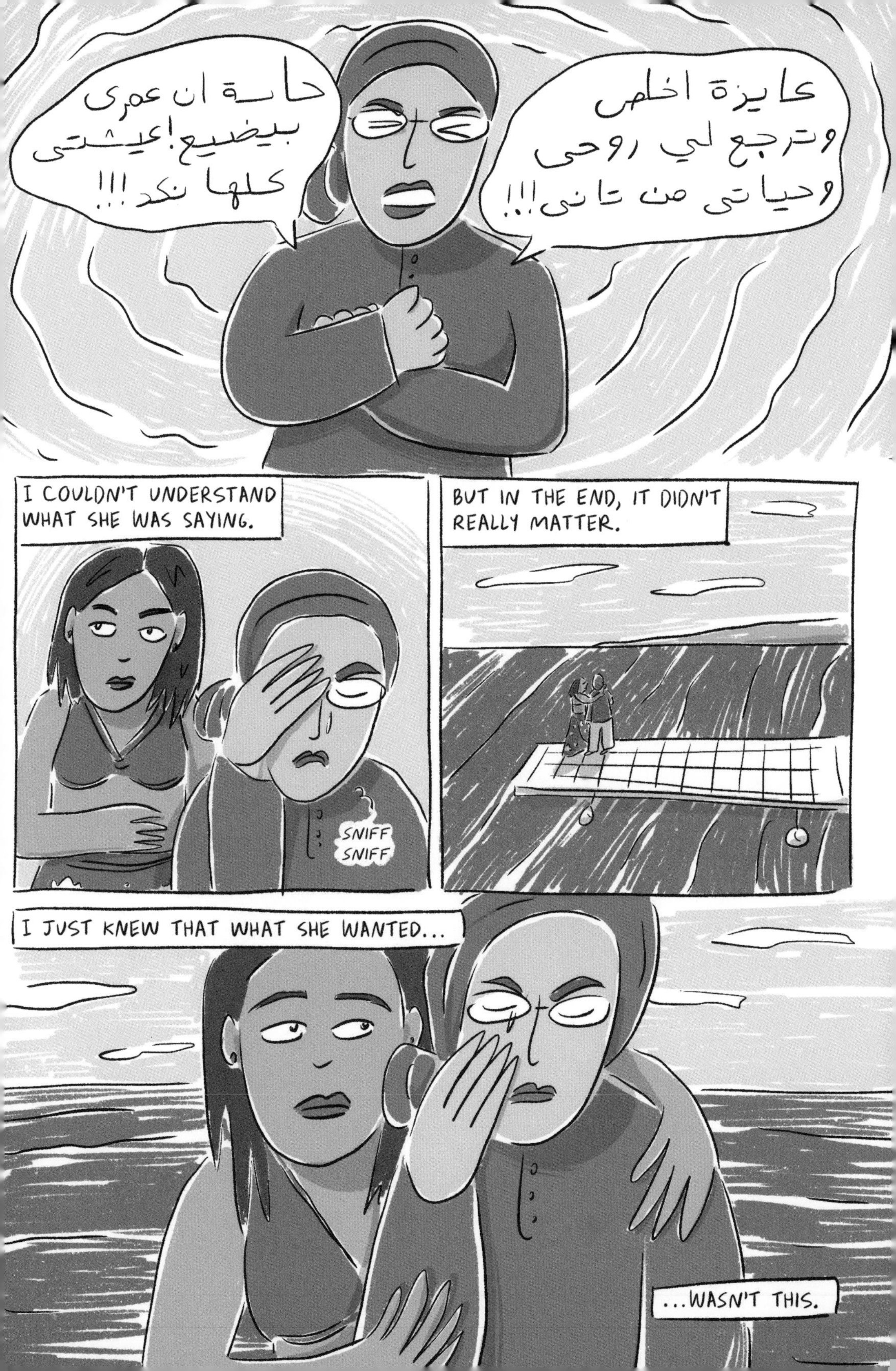
حاسة ان عمرى
بيضيع! عيشتى
كلها نكد!!!
عايزة اخلص
وترجع لي روحى
وحياتى من تانى!!!
I COULDN'T UNDERSTAND WHAT SHE WAS SAYING.
SNIFF SNIFF
BUT IN THE END, IT DIDN'T REALLY MATTER.
I JUST KNEW THAT WHAT SHE WANTED...
...WASN'T THIS.

CHAPTER 8

The Cigarette

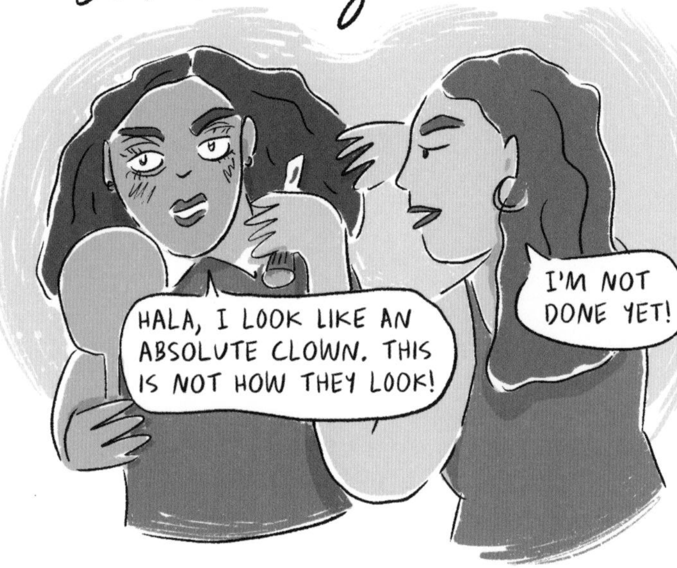

HALA, I LOOK LIKE AN ABSOLUTE CLOWN. THIS IS NOT HOW THEY LOOK!
I'M NOT DONE YET!

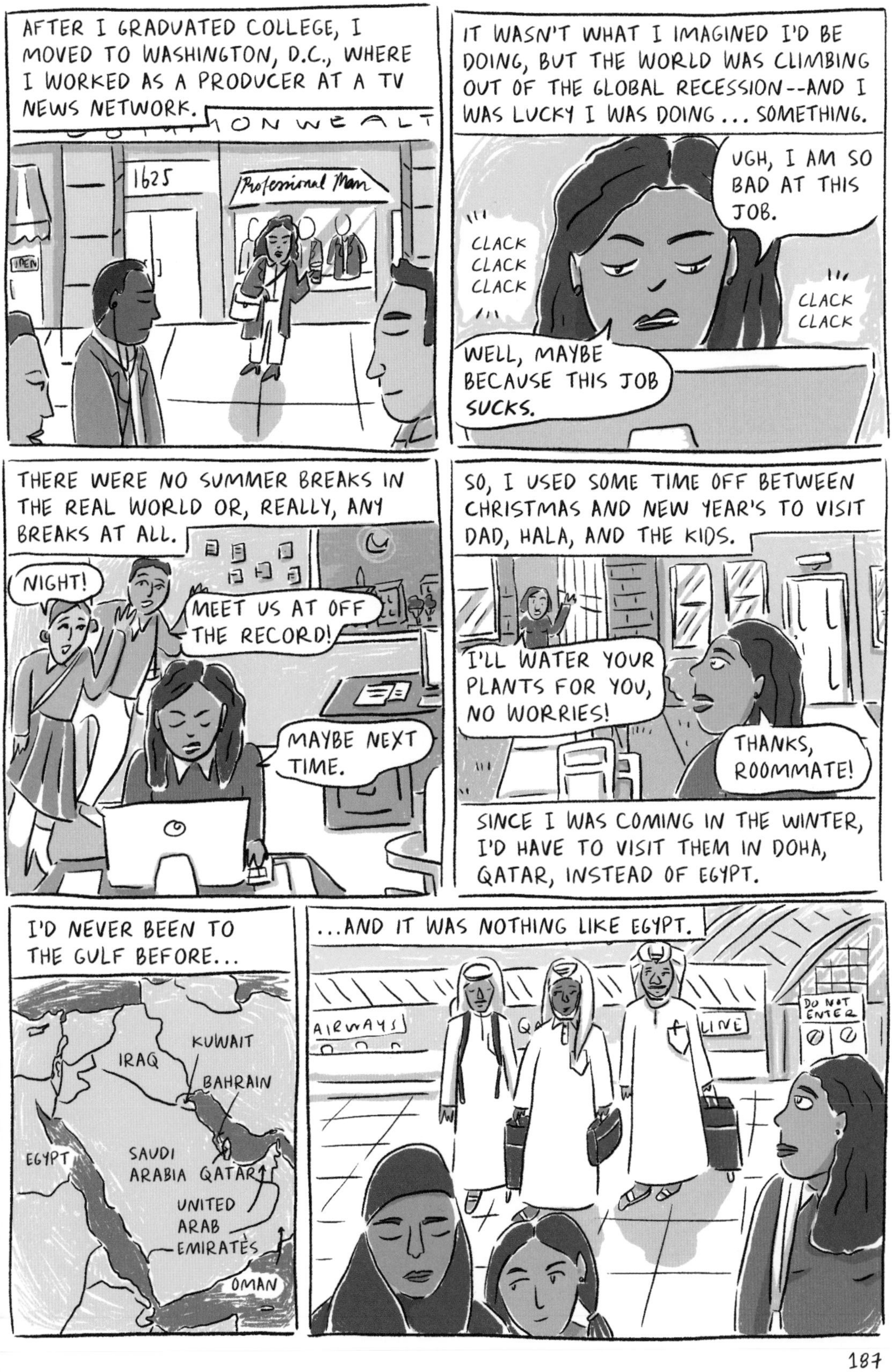
AFTER I GRADUATED COLLEGE, I MOVED TO WASHINGTON, D.C., WHERE I WORKED AS A PRODUCER AT A TV NEWS NETWORK.
1625
Professional Man
OPEN
IT WASN'T WHAT I IMAGINED I'D BE DOING, BUT THE WORLD WAS CLIMBING OUT OF THE GLOBAL RECESSION--AND I WAS LUCKY I WAS DOING... SOMETHING.
UGH, I AM SO BAD AT THIS JOB.
CLACK CLACK CLACK
CLACK CLACK
WELL, MAYBE BECAUSE THIS JOB SUCKS.
THERE WERE NO SUMMER BREAKS IN THE REAL WORLD OR, REALLY, ANY BREAKS AT ALL.
NIGHT!
MEET US AT OFF THE RECORD!
MAYBE NEXT TIME.
SO, I USED SOME TIME OFF BETWEEN CHRISTMAS AND NEW YEAR'S TO VISIT DAD, HALA, AND THE KIDS.
I'LL WATER YOUR PLANTS FOR YOU, NO WORRIES!
THANKS, ROOMMATE!
SINCE I WAS COMING IN THE WINTER, I'D HAVE TO VISIT THEM IN DOHA, QATAR, INSTEAD OF EGYPT.
I'D NEVER BEEN TO THE GULF BEFORE...
KUWAIT
IRAQ
BAHRAIN
EGYPT
SAUDI ARABIA
QATAR
UNITED ARAB EMIRATES
OMAN
...AND IT WAS NOTHING LIKE EGYPT.
AIRWAYS
DO NOT ENTER

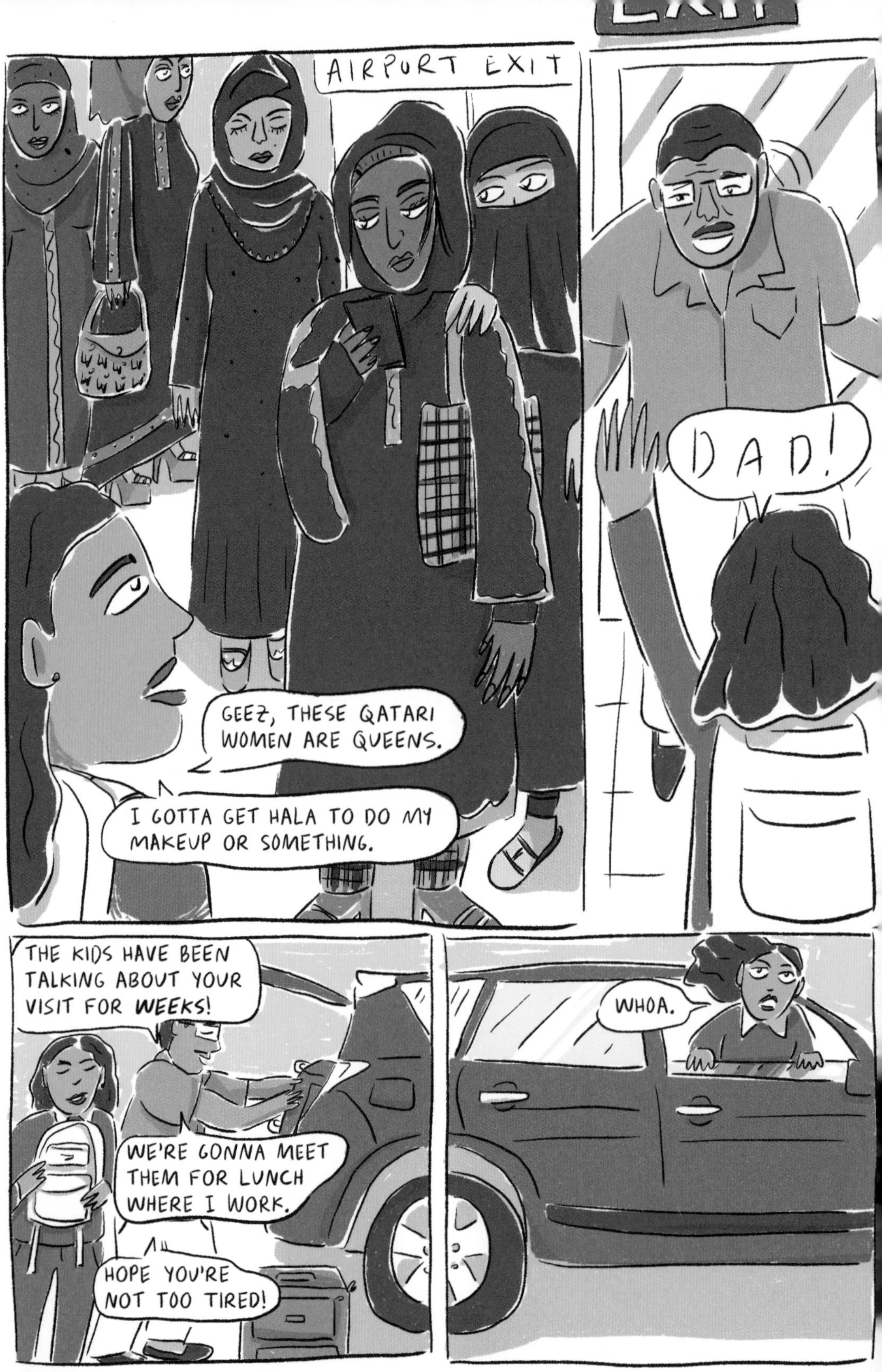
AIRPORT EXIT
GEEZ, THESE QATARI WOMEN ARE QUEENS.
I GOTTA GET HALA TO DO MY MAKEUP OR SOMETHING.
DAD!
THE KIDS HAVE BEEN TALKING ABOUT YOUR VISIT FOR **WEEKS**!
WE'RE GONNA MEET THEM FOR LUNCH WHERE I WORK.
HOPE YOU'RE NOT TOO TIRED!
WHOA.

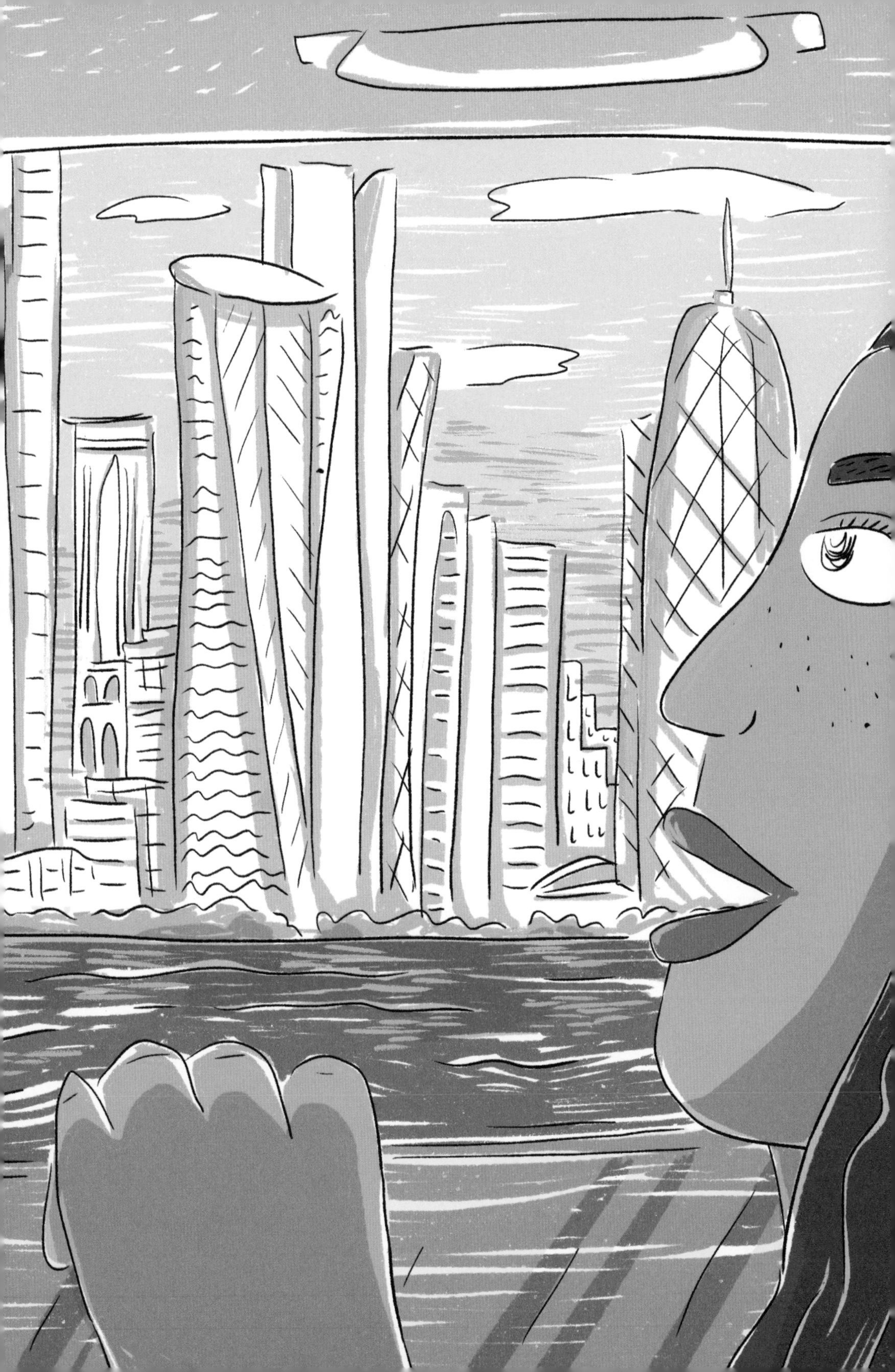

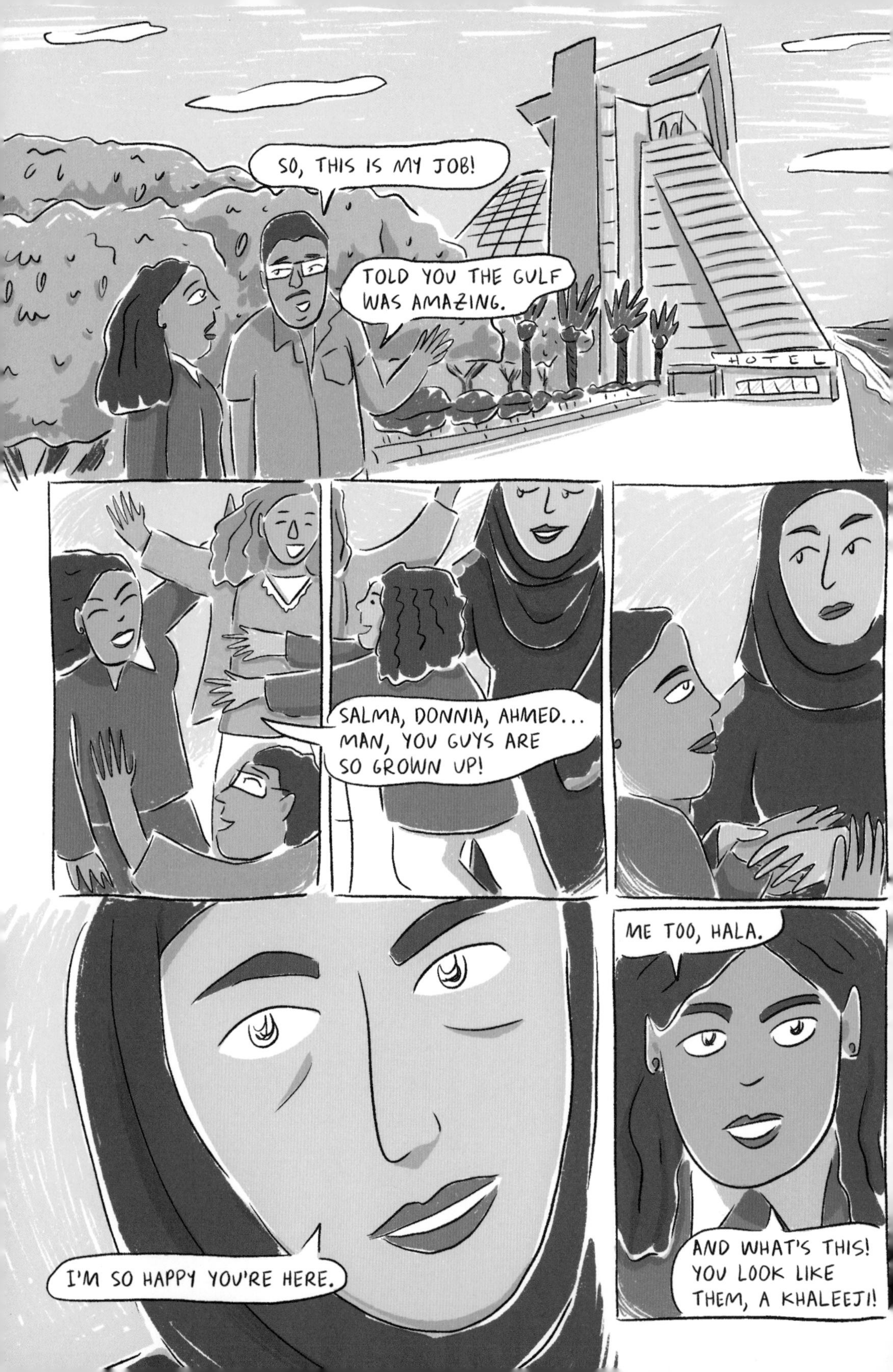
SO, THIS IS MY JOB!
TOLD YOU THE GULF WAS AMAZING.
HOTEL
SALMA, DONNIA, AHMED... MAN, YOU GUYS ARE SO GROWN UP!
I'M SO HAPPY YOU'RE HERE.
ME TOO, HALA.
AND WHAT'S THIS! YOU LOOK LIKE THEM, A KHALEEJI!

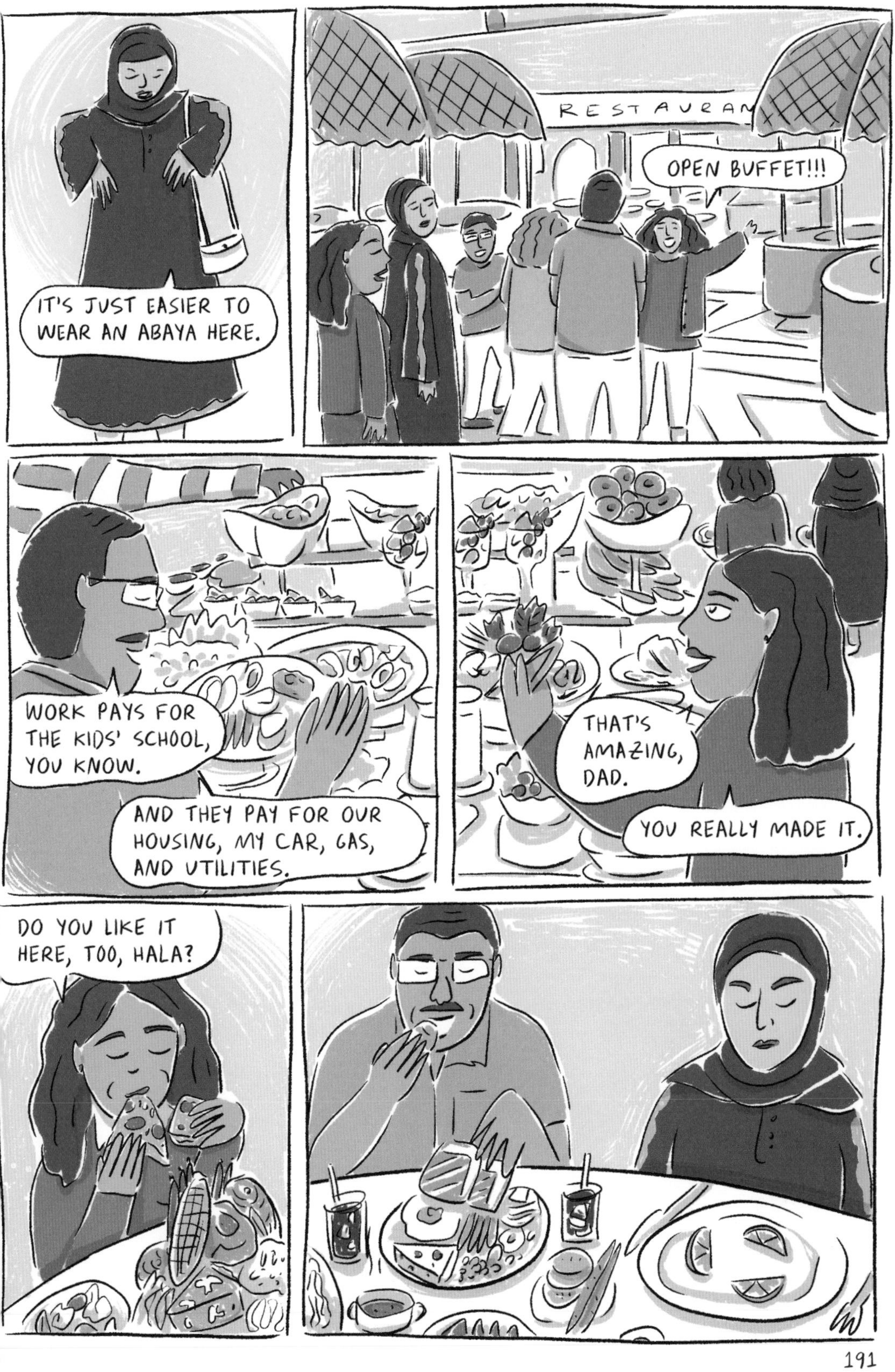
IT'S JUST EASIER TO WEAR AN ABAYA HERE.
RESTAURAN
OPEN BUFFET!!!
WORK PAYS FOR THE KIDS' SCHOOL, YOU KNOW.
AND THEY PAY FOR OUR HOUSING, MY CAR, GAS, AND UTILITIES.
THAT'S AMAZING, DAD.
YOU REALLY MADE IT.
DO YOU LIKE IT HERE, TOO, HALA?

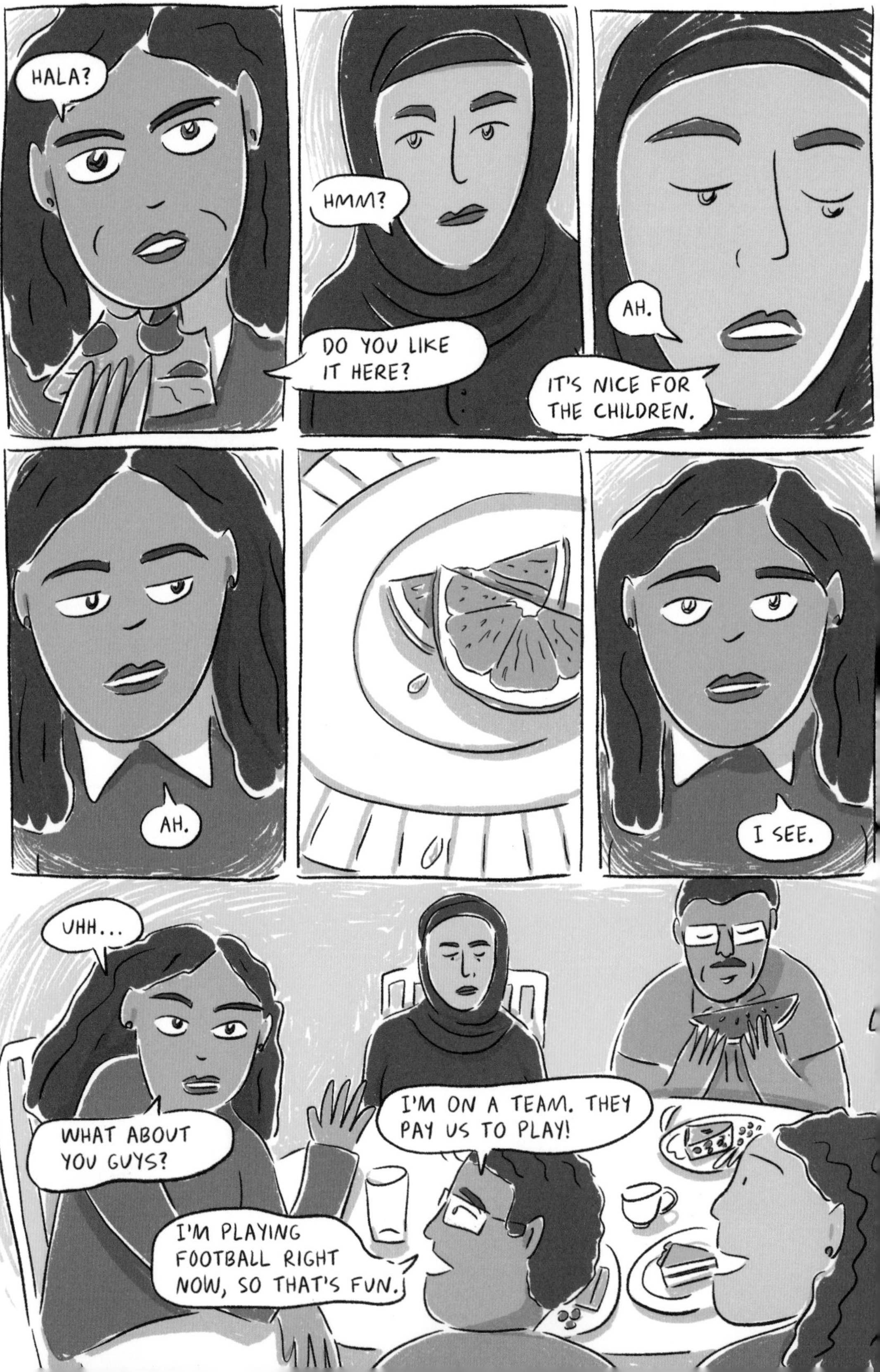
HALA?
HMM?
DO YOU LIKE IT HERE?
AH.
IT'S NICE FOR THE CHILDREN.
AH.
I SEE.
UHH...
WHAT ABOUT YOU GUYS?
I'M ON A TEAM. THEY PAY US TO PLAY!
I'M PLAYING FOOTBALL RIGHT NOW, SO THAT'S FUN.

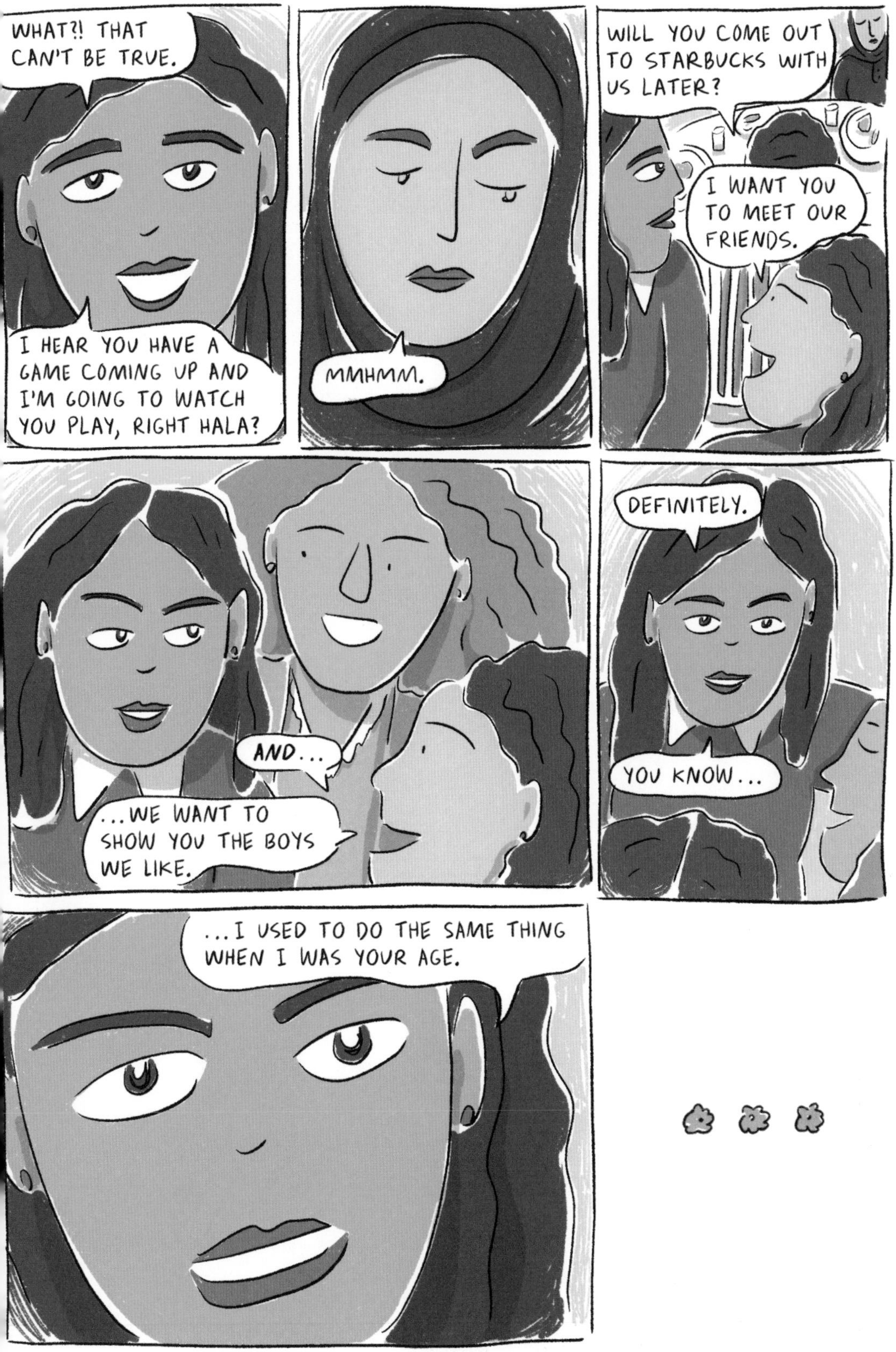
WHAT?! THAT CAN'T BE TRUE.
I HEAR YOU HAVE A GAME COMING UP AND I'M GOING TO WATCH YOU PLAY, RIGHT HALA?
MMHMM.
WILL YOU COME OUT TO STARBUCKS WITH US LATER?
I WANT YOU TO MEET OUR FRIENDS.
AND...
...WE WANT TO SHOW YOU THE BOYS WE LIKE.
DEFINITELY.
YOU KNOW...
...I USED TO DO THE SAME THING WHEN I WAS YOUR AGE.

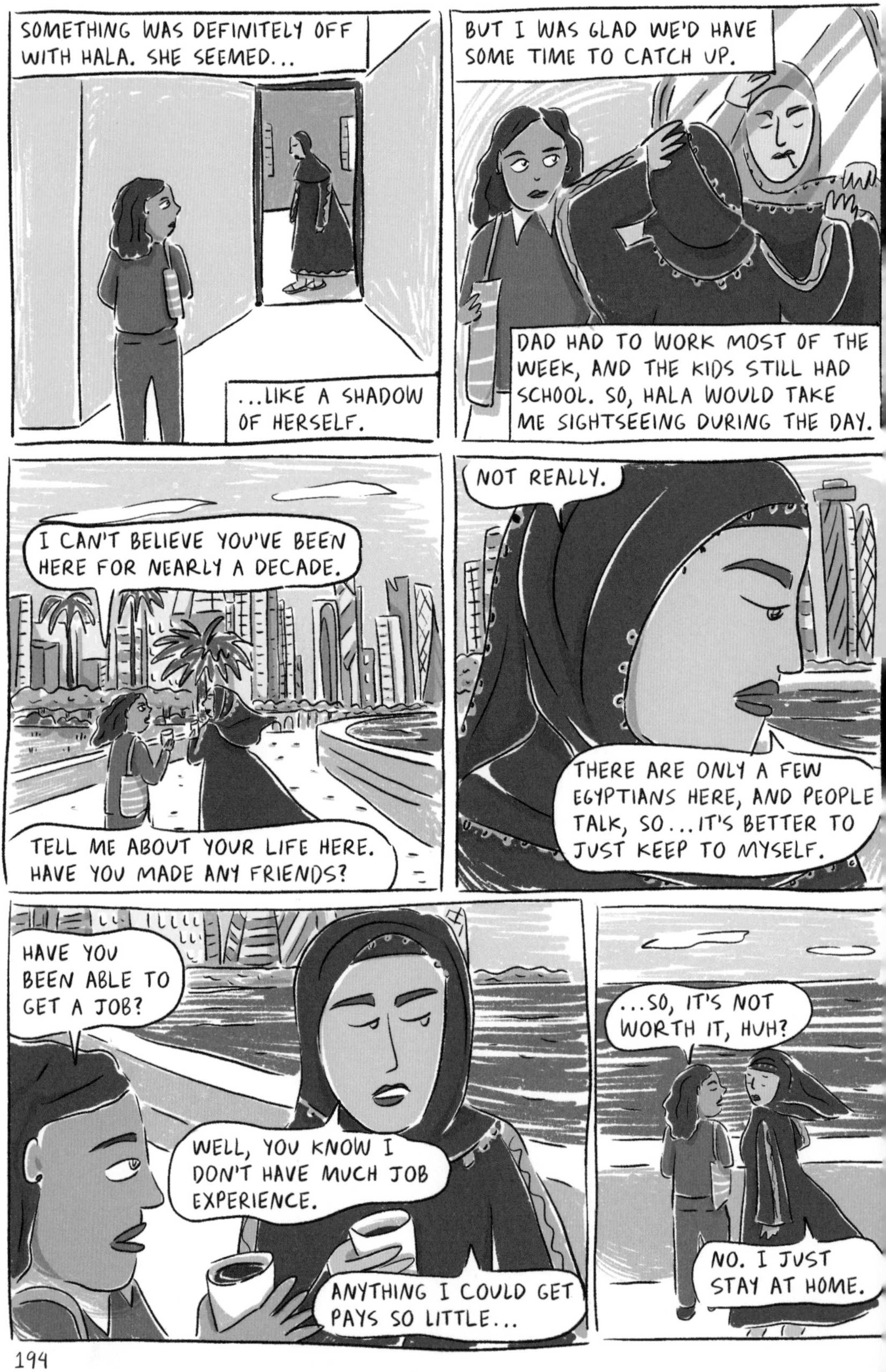

SOMETHING WAS DEFINITELY OFF WITH HALA. SHE SEEMED...
...LIKE A SHADOW OF HERSELF.
BUT I WAS GLAD WE'D HAVE SOME TIME TO CATCH UP.
DAD HAD TO WORK MOST OF THE WEEK, AND THE KIDS STILL HAD SCHOOL. SO, HALA WOULD TAKE ME SIGHTSEEING DURING THE DAY.
I CAN'T BELIEVE YOU'VE BEEN HERE FOR NEARLY A DECADE.
TELL ME ABOUT YOUR LIFE HERE. HAVE YOU MADE ANY FRIENDS?
NOT REALLY.
THERE ARE ONLY A FEW EGYPTIANS HERE, AND PEOPLE TALK, SO...IT'S BETTER TO JUST KEEP TO MYSELF.
HAVE YOU BEEN ABLE TO GET A JOB?
WELL, YOU KNOW I DON'T HAVE MUCH JOB EXPERIENCE.
ANYTHING I COULD GET PAYS SO LITTLE...
...SO, IT'S NOT WORTH IT, HUH?
NO. I JUST STAY AT HOME.

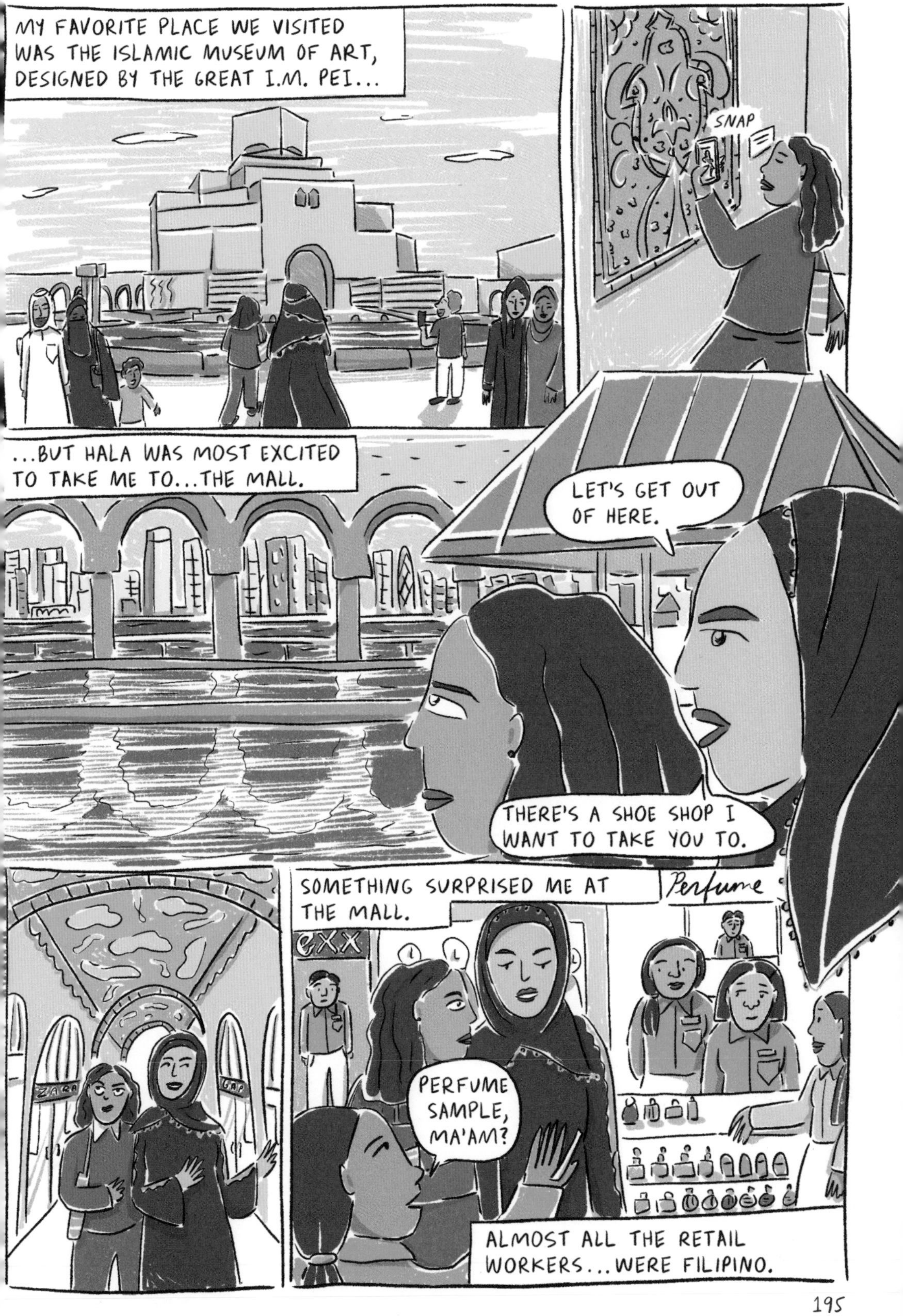

MY FAVORITE PLACE WE VISITED WAS THE ISLAMIC MUSEUM OF ART, DESIGNED BY THE GREAT I.M. PEI...
SNAP
...BUT HALA WAS MOST EXCITED TO TAKE ME TO...THE MALL.
LET'S GET OUT OF HERE.
THERE'S A SHOE SHOP I WANT TO TAKE YOU TO.
ZARA
GAP
SOMETHING SURPRISED ME AT THE MALL.
Perfume
PERFUME SAMPLE, MA'AM?
ALMOST ALL THE RETAIL WORKERS...WERE FILIPINO.

I KNEW THAT FILIPINOS LIVED AND WORKED IN THE GULF.

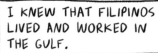

SHOE EXPRESS

SALE

ALE

SALE

I JUST DIDN'T EXPECT TO SEE SO MANY.

SUDDENLY... I HAD THIS URGE TO LET THEM KNOW I WAS FILIPINO, TOO.

SALE

OOH, THESE ARE CUTE FOR YOU, MALAKA.

UH, I DON'T REALLY WEAR HEELS.

JUST GET 'EM!

I DIDN'T GET A CHANCE TO SHARE MY FILIPINO SIDE MUCH WHEN I WAS IN THE MIDDLE EAST.

A LOT OF PEOPLE HERE ASSOCIATED FILIPINOS WITH THE LABOR CLASS. SO, I DIDN'T BRING IT UP WHEN I WAS AROUND OTHER ARABS. I DIDN'T WANT THEM TO MAKE ASSUMPTIONS ABOUT ME.

IT WAS HARD ENOUGH TRYING TO FIT IN WITH THEM AS AN EGYPTIAN AMERICAN.

BUT COULD THESE STRANGERS SEE THIS PART OF ME?

SIZE 8, PLEASE.

MAYBE THERE WAS SOME WAY I COULD MAKE IT OBVIOUS.

Cashier

SHUKRAN,* MA'AM.

SHOE EXPRESS

*THANK YOU

HERE WAS MY CHANCE.

UHHHM ...

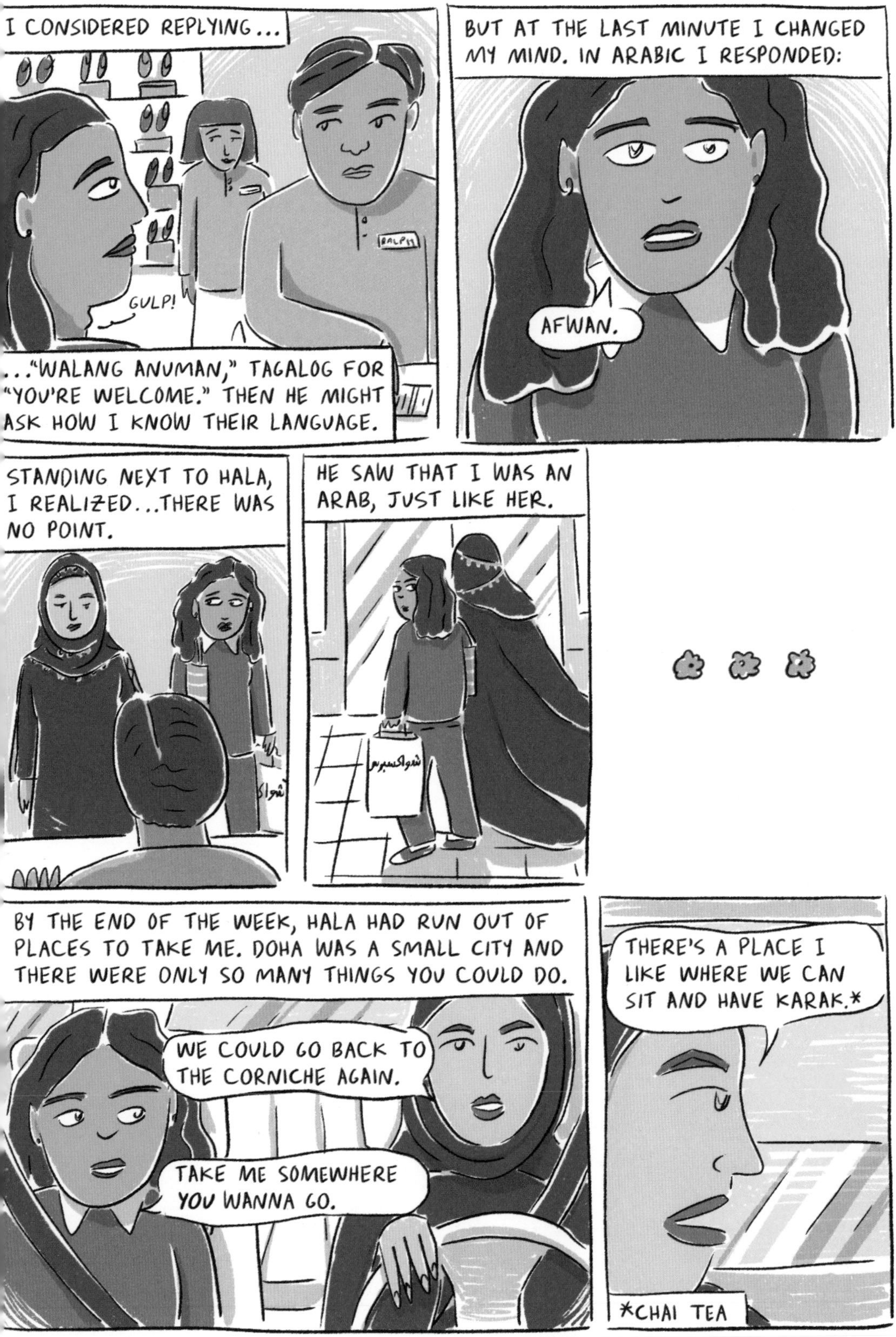
I CONSIDERED REPLYING...
GULP!
RALPH
..."WALANG ANUMAN," TAGALOG FOR "YOU'RE WELCOME." THEN HE MIGHT ASK HOW I KNOW THEIR LANGUAGE.
BUT AT THE LAST MINUTE I CHANGED MY MIND. IN ARABIC I RESPONDED:
AFWAN.
STANDING NEXT TO HALA, I REALIZED...THERE WAS NO POINT.
HE SAW THAT I WAS AN ARAB, JUST LIKE HER.
BY THE END OF THE WEEK, HALA HAD RUN OUT OF PLACES TO TAKE ME. DOHA WAS A SMALL CITY AND THERE WERE ONLY SO MANY THINGS YOU COULD DO.
WE COULD GO BACK TO THE CORNICHE AGAIN.
TAKE ME SOMEWHERE YOU WANNA GO.
THERE'S A PLACE I LIKE WHERE WE CAN SIT AND HAVE KARAK.*
*CHAI TEA

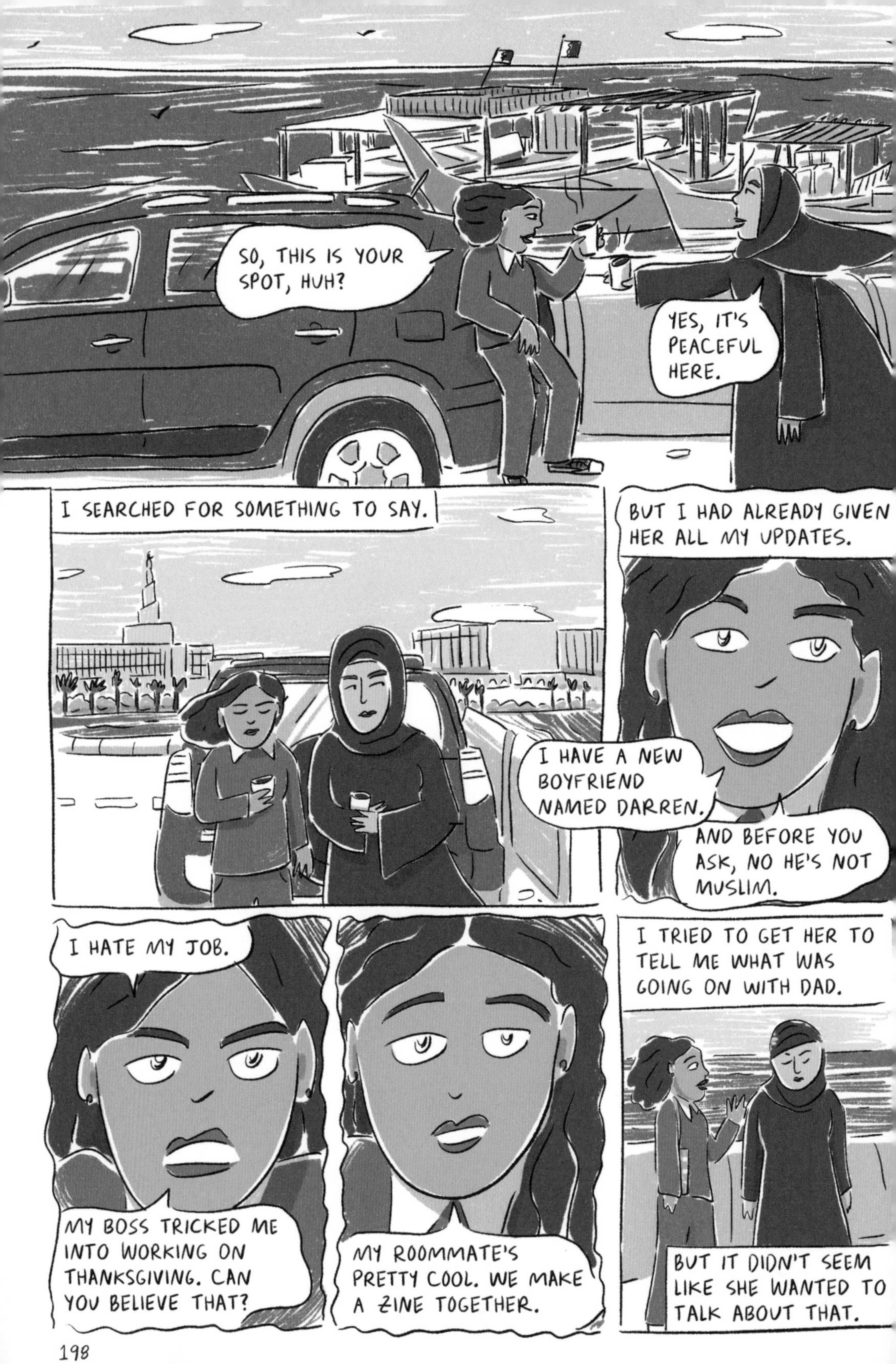

SO, THIS IS YOUR SPOT, HUH?
YES, IT'S PEACEFUL HERE.
I SEARCHED FOR SOMETHING TO SAY.
BUT I HAD ALREADY GIVEN HER ALL MY UPDATES.
I HAVE A NEW BOYFRIEND NAMED DARREN.
AND BEFORE YOU ASK, NO HE'S NOT MUSLIM.
I HATE MY JOB.
MY BOSS TRICKED ME INTO WORKING ON THANKSGIVING. CAN YOU BELIEVE THAT?
MY ROOMMATE'S PRETTY COOL. WE MAKE A ZINE TOGETHER.
I TRIED TO GET HER TO TELL ME WHAT WAS GOING ON WITH DAD.
BUT IT DIDN'T SEEM LIKE SHE WANTED TO TALK ABOUT THAT.

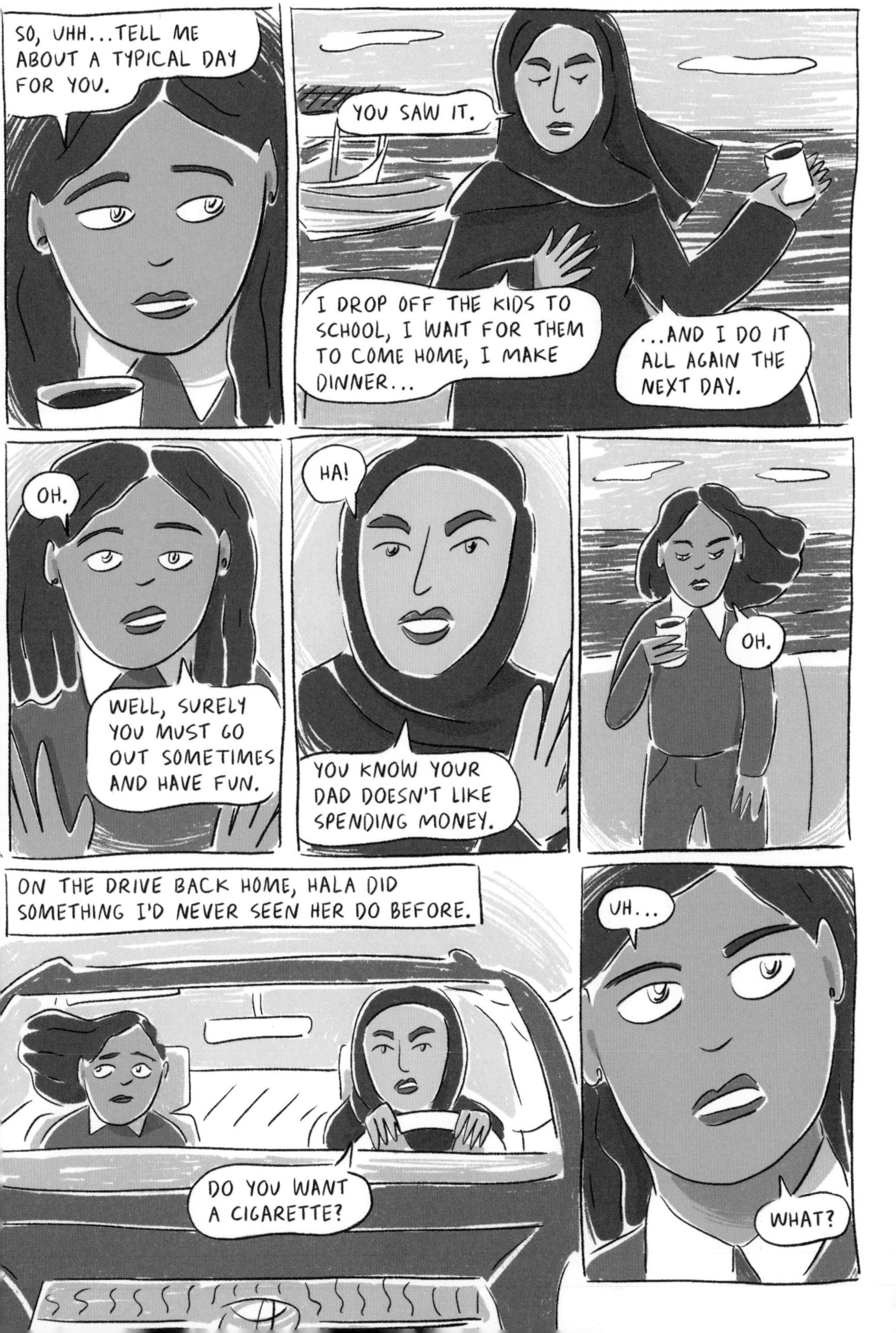
SO, UHH...TELL ME ABOUT A TYPICAL DAY FOR YOU.
YOU SAW IT.
I DROP OFF THE KIDS TO SCHOOL, I WAIT FOR THEM TO COME HOME, I MAKE DINNER...
...AND I DO IT ALL AGAIN THE NEXT DAY.
OH.
WELL, SURELY YOU MUST GO OUT SOMETIMES AND HAVE FUN.
HA!
YOU KNOW YOUR DAD DOESN'T LIKE SPENDING MONEY.
OH.
ON THE DRIVE BACK HOME, HALA DID SOMETHING I'D NEVER SEEN HER DO BEFORE.
DO YOU WANT A CIGARETTE?
UH...
WHAT?

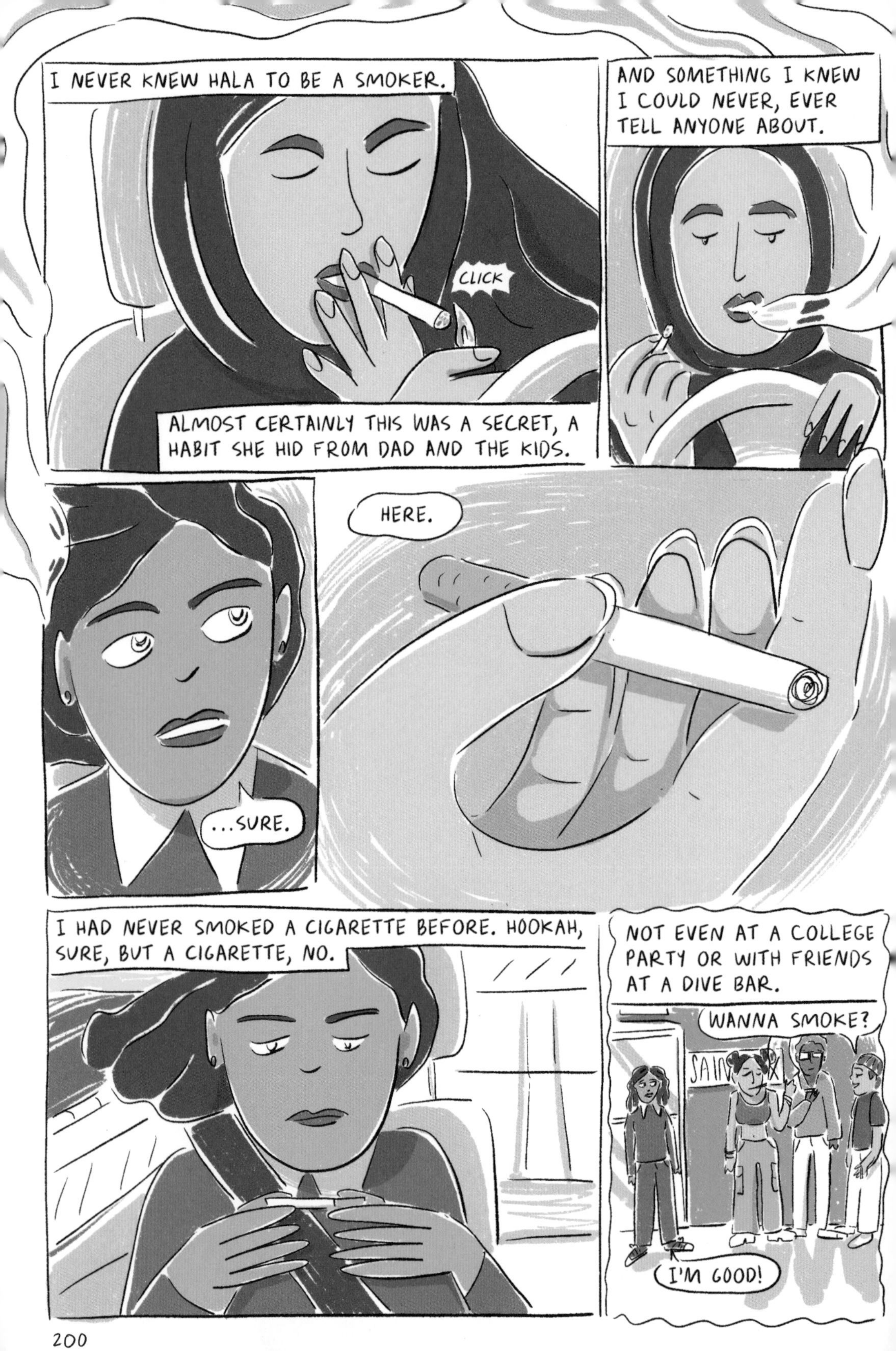
I NEVER KNEW HALA TO BE A SMOKER.
CLICK
ALMOST CERTAINLY THIS WAS A SECRET, A HABIT SHE HID FROM DAD AND THE KIDS.
AND SOMETHING I KNEW I COULD NEVER, EVER TELL ANYONE ABOUT.
HERE.
...SURE.
I HAD NEVER SMOKED A CIGARETTE BEFORE. HOOKAH, SURE, BUT A CIGARETTE, NO.
NOT EVEN AT A COLLEGE PARTY OR WITH FRIENDS AT A DIVE BAR.
WANNA SMOKE?
I'M GOOD!

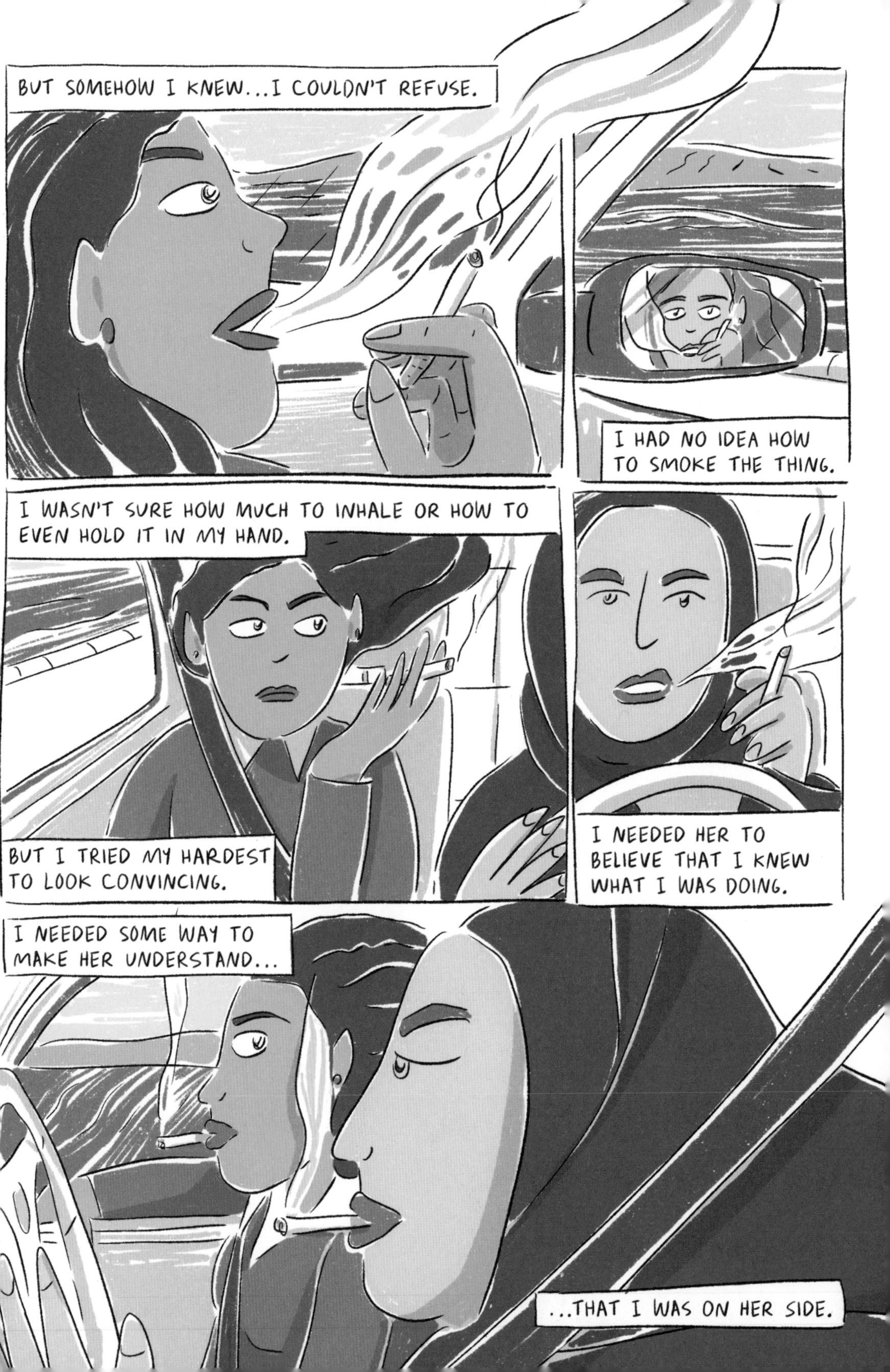
BUT SOMEHOW I KNEW...I COULDN'T REFUSE.
I HAD NO IDEA HOW TO SMOKE THE THING.
I WASN'T SURE HOW MUCH TO INHALE OR HOW TO EVEN HOLD IT IN MY HAND.
BUT I TRIED MY HARDEST TO LOOK CONVINCING.
I NEEDED HER TO BELIEVE THAT I KNEW WHAT I WAS DOING.
I NEEDED SOME WAY TO MAKE HER UNDERSTAND...
...THAT I WAS ON HER SIDE.

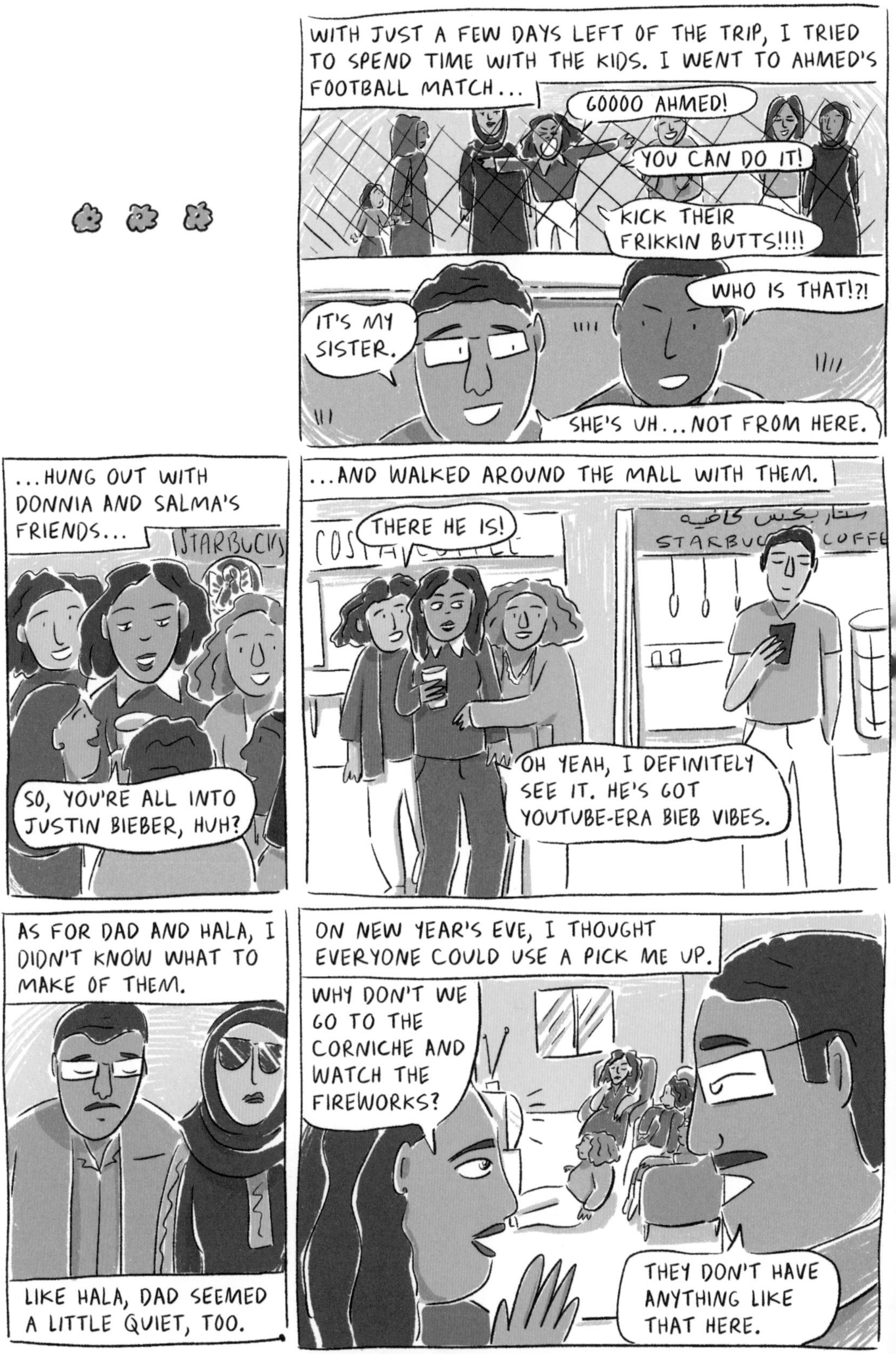
WITH JUST A FEW DAYS LEFT OF THE TRIP, I TRIED TO SPEND TIME WITH THE KIDS. I WENT TO AHMED'S FOOTBALL MATCH...
GOOOO AHMED!
YOU CAN DO IT!
KICK THEIR FRIKKIN BUTTS!!!!
WHO IS THAT!?!
IT'S MY SISTER.
SHE'S UH... NOT FROM HERE.
...HUNG OUT WITH DONNIA AND SALMA'S FRIENDS...
STARBUCKS
SO, YOU'RE ALL INTO JUSTIN BIEBER, HUH?
...AND WALKED AROUND THE MALL WITH THEM.
THERE HE IS!
OH YEAH, I DEFINITELY SEE IT. HE'S GOT YOUTUBE-ERA BIEB VIBES.
AS FOR DAD AND HALA, I DIDN'T KNOW WHAT TO MAKE OF THEM.
LIKE HALA, DAD SEEMED A LITTLE QUIET, TOO.
ON NEW YEAR'S EVE, I THOUGHT EVERYONE COULD USE A PICK ME UP.
WHY DON'T WE GO TO THE CORNICHE AND WATCH THE FIREWORKS?
THEY DON'T HAVE ANYTHING LIKE THAT HERE.

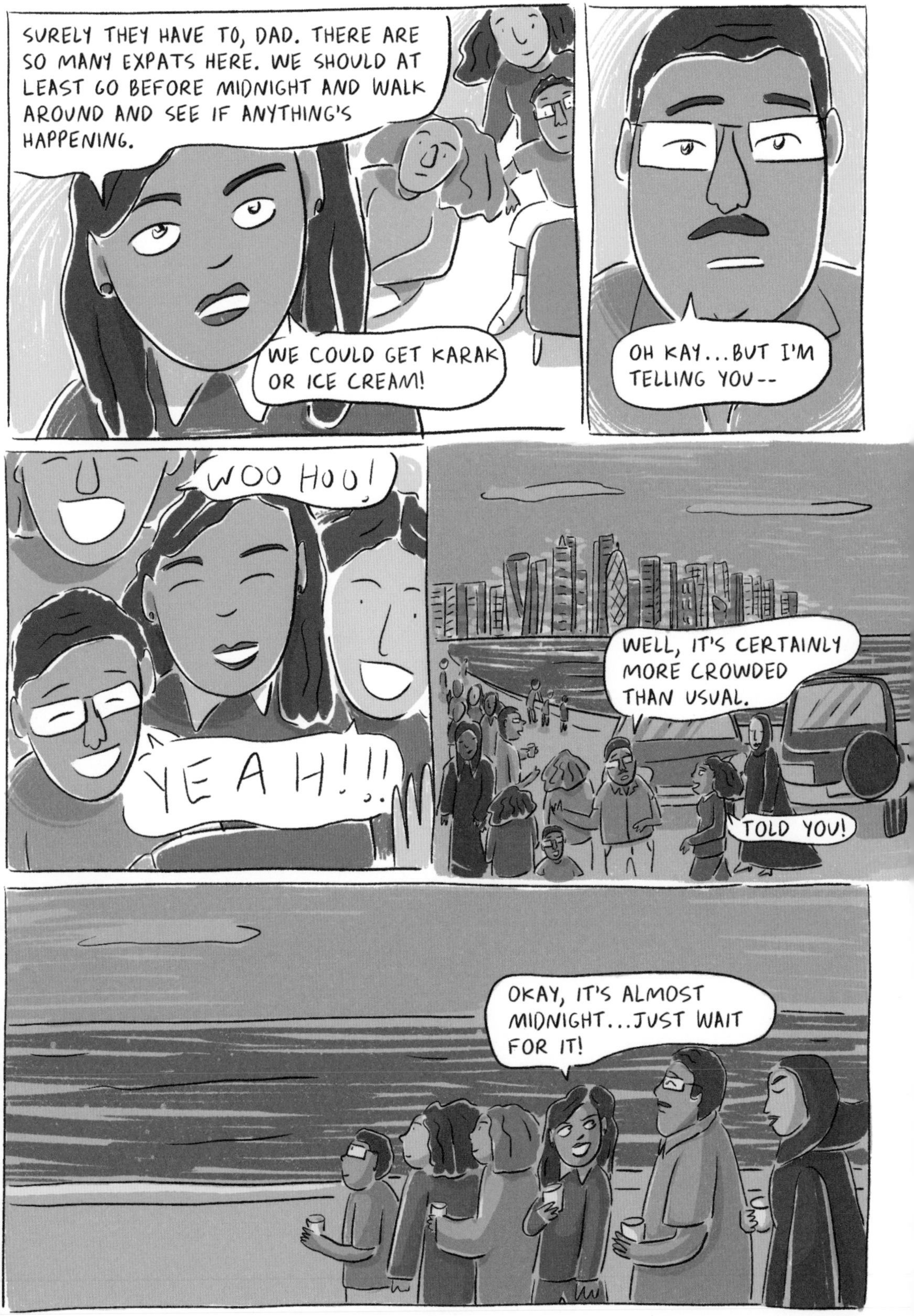

SURELY THEY HAVE TO, DAD. THERE ARE SO MANY EXPATS HERE. WE SHOULD AT LEAST GO BEFORE MIDNIGHT AND WALK AROUND AND SEE IF ANYTHING'S HAPPENING.
WE COULD GET KARAK OR ICE CREAM!
OH KAY...BUT I'M TELLING YOU--
WOO HOO!
YEAH!!!
WELL, IT'S CERTAINLY MORE CROWDED THAN USUAL.
TOLD YOU!
OKAY, IT'S ALMOST MIDNIGHT...JUST WAIT FOR IT!

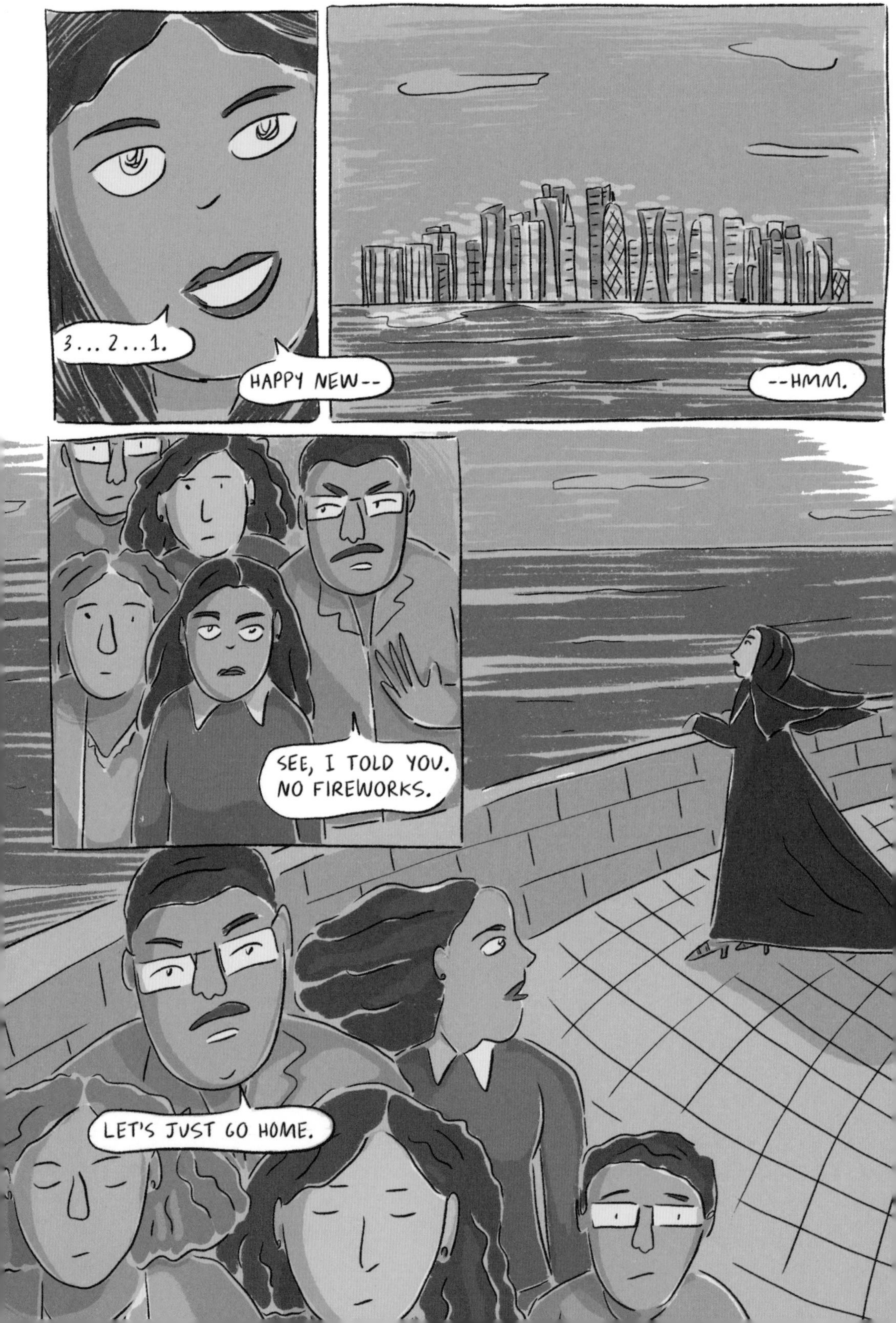
3...2...1.
HAPPY NEW--
--HMM.
SEE, I TOLD YOU. NO FIREWORKS.
LET'S JUST GO HOME.

CHAPTER 9

Hearts Forever

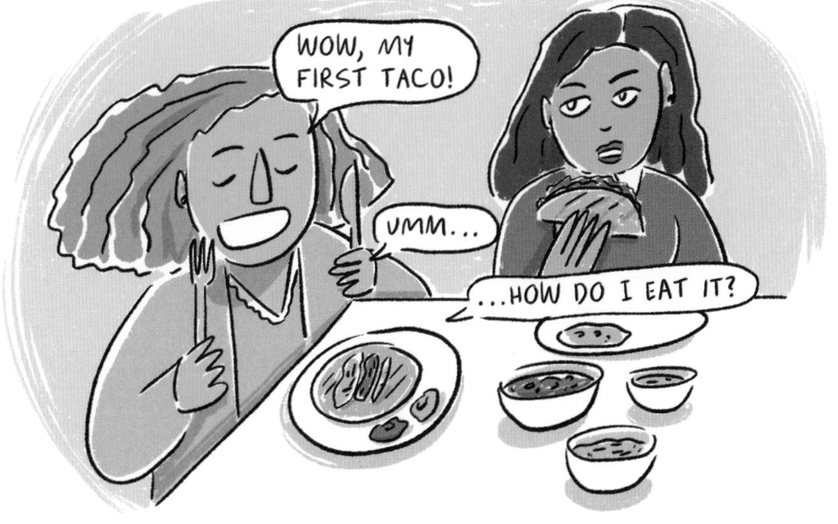
WOW, MY FIRST TACO!
UMM...
...HOW DO I EAT IT?

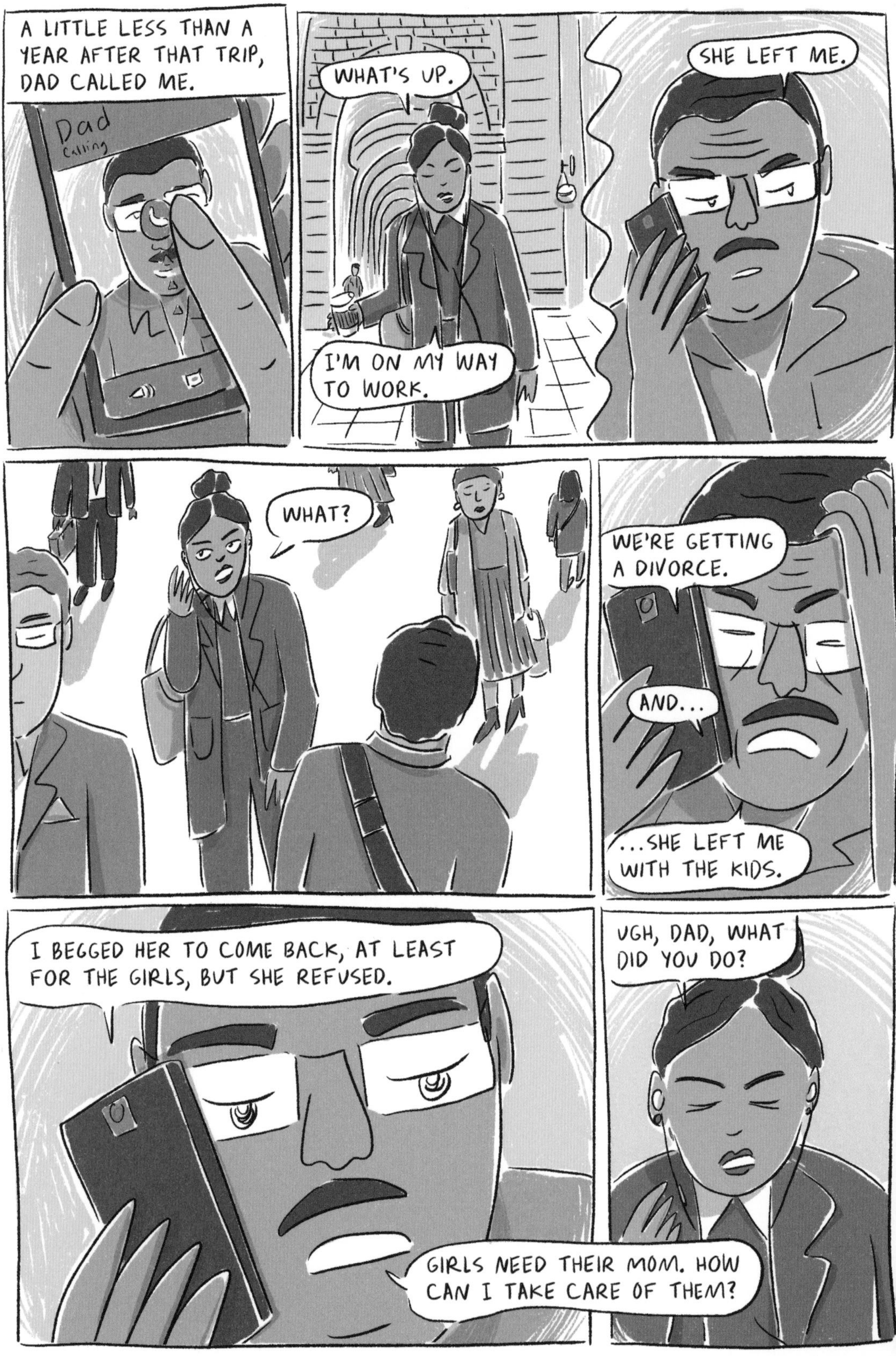
A LITTLE LESS THAN A YEAR AFTER THAT TRIP, DAD CALLED ME.
Dad Calling
WHAT'S UP.
I'M ON MY WAY TO WORK.
SHE LEFT ME.
WHAT?
WE'RE GETTING A DIVORCE.
AND...
...SHE LEFT ME WITH THE KIDS.
I BEGGED HER TO COME BACK, AT LEAST FOR THE GIRLS, BUT SHE REFUSED.
UGH, DAD, WHAT DID YOU DO?
GIRLS NEED THEIR MOM. HOW CAN I TAKE CARE OF THEM?

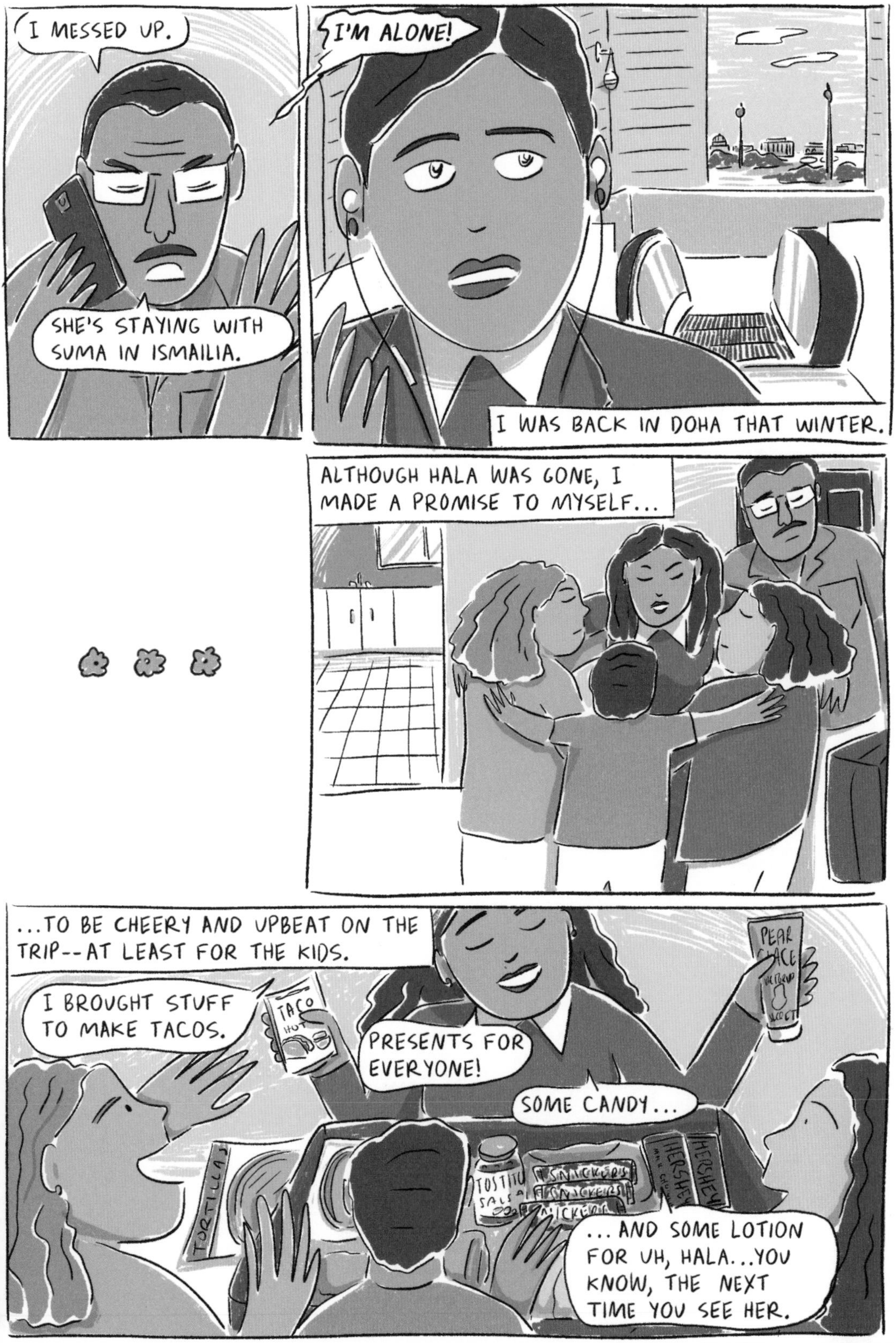
I MESSED UP.
SHE'S STAYING WITH SUMA IN ISMAILIA.
I'M ALONE!
I WAS BACK IN DOHA THAT WINTER.
ALTHOUGH HALA WAS GONE, I MADE A PROMISE TO MYSELF...
...TO BE CHEERY AND UPBEAT ON THE TRIP--AT LEAST FOR THE KIDS.
I BROUGHT STUFF TO MAKE TACOS.
PRESENTS FOR EVERYONE!
SOME CANDY...
...AND SOME LOTION FOR UH, HALA...YOU KNOW, THE NEXT TIME YOU SEE HER.
TACO
PEAR GLACE
TORTILLAS
TOSTITOS SALSA
SNICKERS
HERSHEY'S

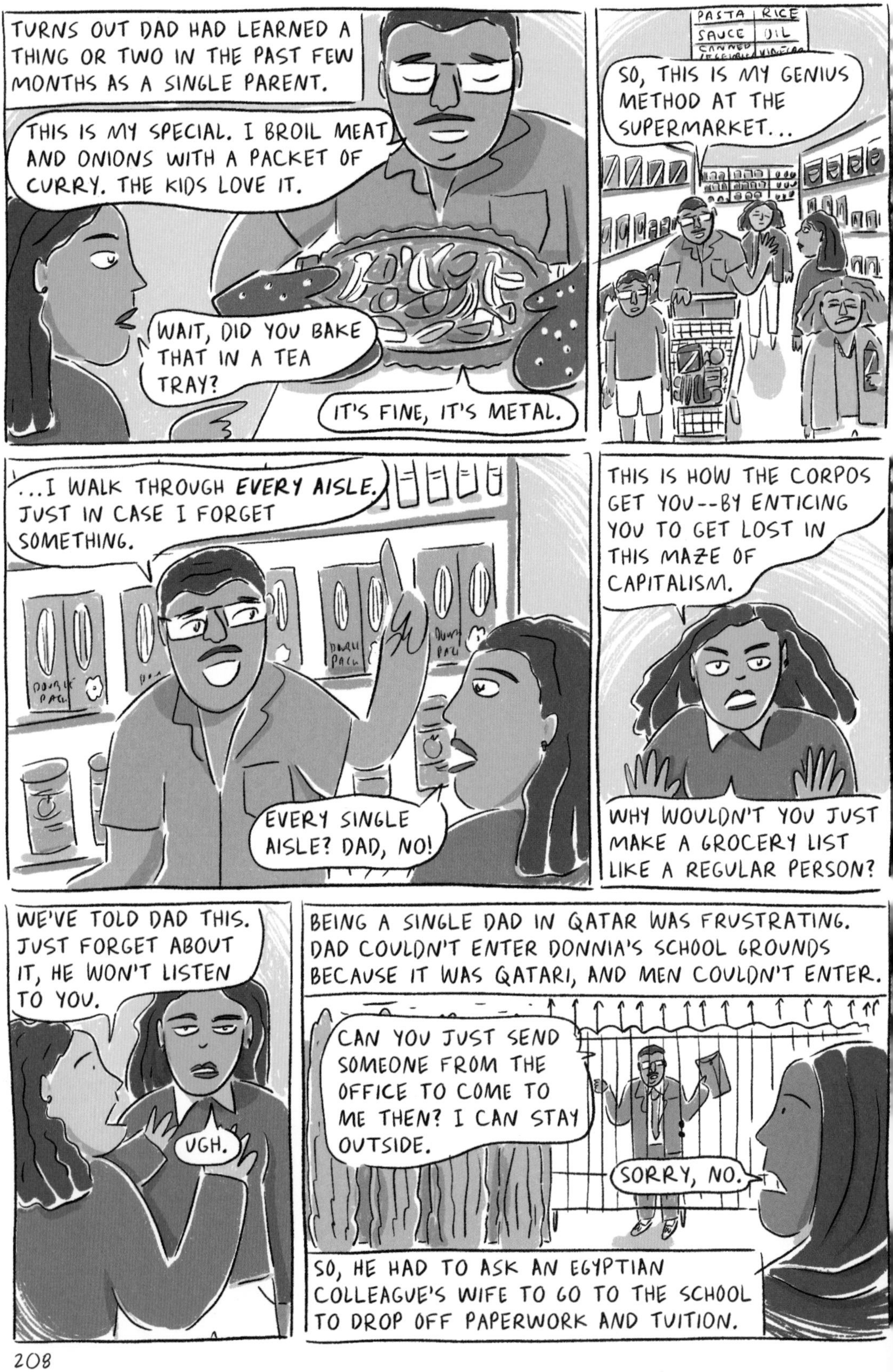
TURNS OUT DAD HAD LEARNED A THING OR TWO IN THE PAST FEW MONTHS AS A SINGLE PARENT.
THIS IS MY SPECIAL. I BROIL MEAT AND ONIONS WITH A PACKET OF CURRY. THE KIDS LOVE IT.
WAIT, DID YOU BAKE THAT IN A TEA TRAY?
IT'S FINE, IT'S METAL.
PASTA
RICE
SAUCE
OIL
SO, THIS IS MY GENIUS METHOD AT THE SUPERMARKET...
...I WALK THROUGH **EVERY AISLE.** JUST IN CASE I FORGET SOMETHING.
EVERY SINGLE AISLE? DAD, NO!
THIS IS HOW THE CORPOS GET YOU--BY ENTICING YOU TO GET LOST IN THIS MAZE OF CAPITALISM.
WHY WOULDN'T YOU JUST MAKE A GROCERY LIST LIKE A REGULAR PERSON?
WE'VE TOLD DAD THIS. JUST FORGET ABOUT IT, HE WON'T LISTEN TO YOU.
UGH.
BEING A SINGLE DAD IN QATAR WAS FRUSTRATING. DAD COULDN'T ENTER DONNIA'S SCHOOL GROUNDS BECAUSE IT WAS QATARI, AND MEN COULDN'T ENTER.
CAN YOU JUST SEND SOMEONE FROM THE OFFICE TO COME TO ME THEN? I CAN STAY OUTSIDE.
SORRY, NO.
SO, HE HAD TO ASK AN EGYPTIAN COLLEAGUE'S WIFE TO GO TO THE SCHOOL TO DROP OFF PAPERWORK AND TUITION.

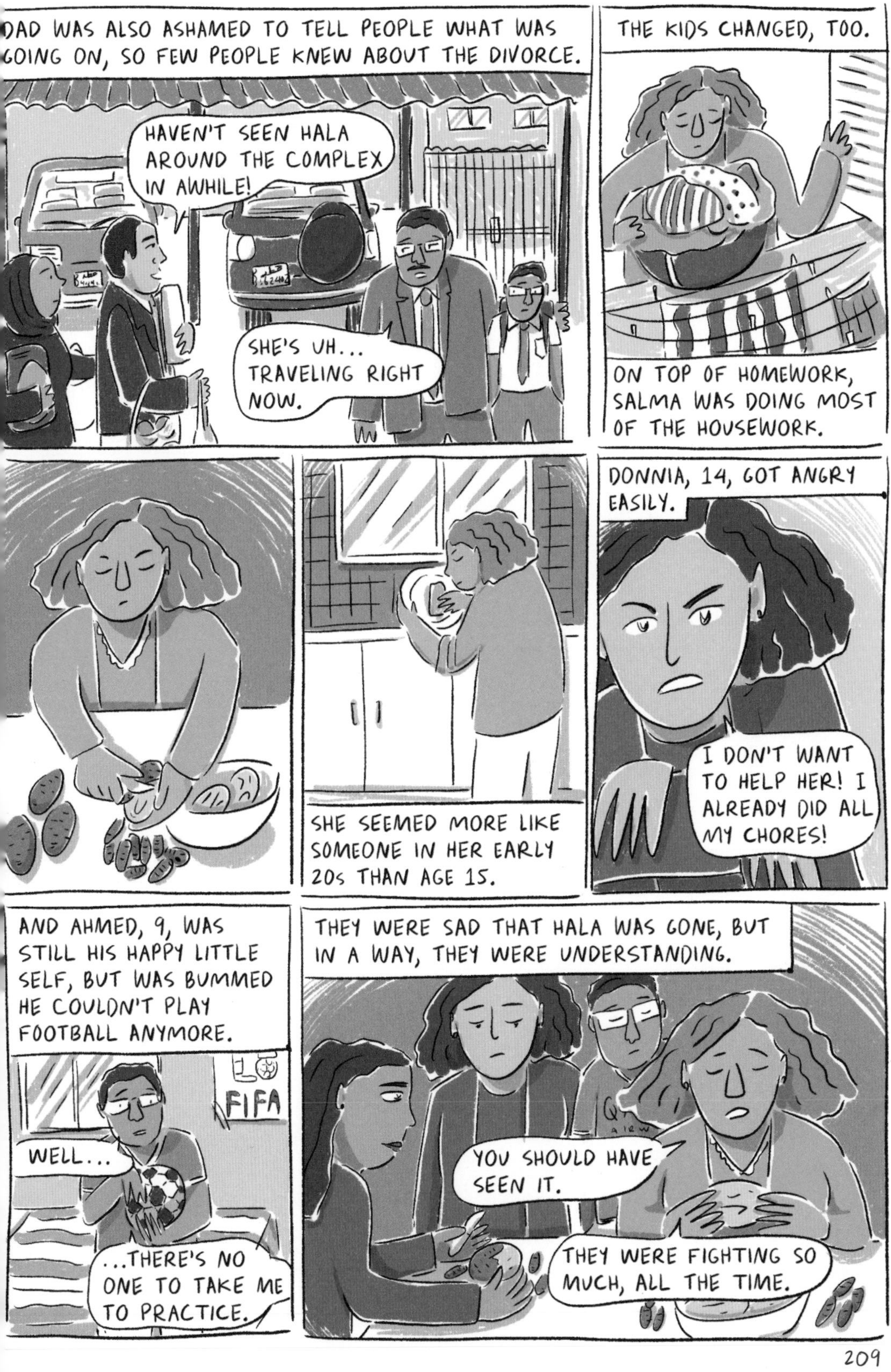
DAD WAS ALSO ASHAMED TO TELL PEOPLE WHAT WAS GOING ON, SO FEW PEOPLE KNEW ABOUT THE DIVORCE.
HAVEN'T SEEN HALA AROUND THE COMPLEX IN AWHILE!
SHE'S UH... TRAVELING RIGHT NOW.
THE KIDS CHANGED, TOO.
ON TOP OF HOMEWORK, SALMA WAS DOING MOST OF THE HOUSEWORK.
SHE SEEMED MORE LIKE SOMEONE IN HER EARLY 20s THAN AGE 15.
DONNIA, 14, GOT ANGRY EASILY.
I DON'T WANT TO HELP HER! I ALREADY DID ALL MY CHORES!
AND AHMED, 9, WAS STILL HIS HAPPY LITTLE SELF, BUT WAS BUMMED HE COULDN'T PLAY FOOTBALL ANYMORE.
FIFA
WELL...
...THERE'S NO ONE TO TAKE ME TO PRACTICE.
THEY WERE SAD THAT HALA WAS GONE, BUT IN A WAY, THEY WERE UNDERSTANDING.
YOU SHOULD HAVE SEEN IT.
THEY WERE FIGHTING SO MUCH, ALL THE TIME.

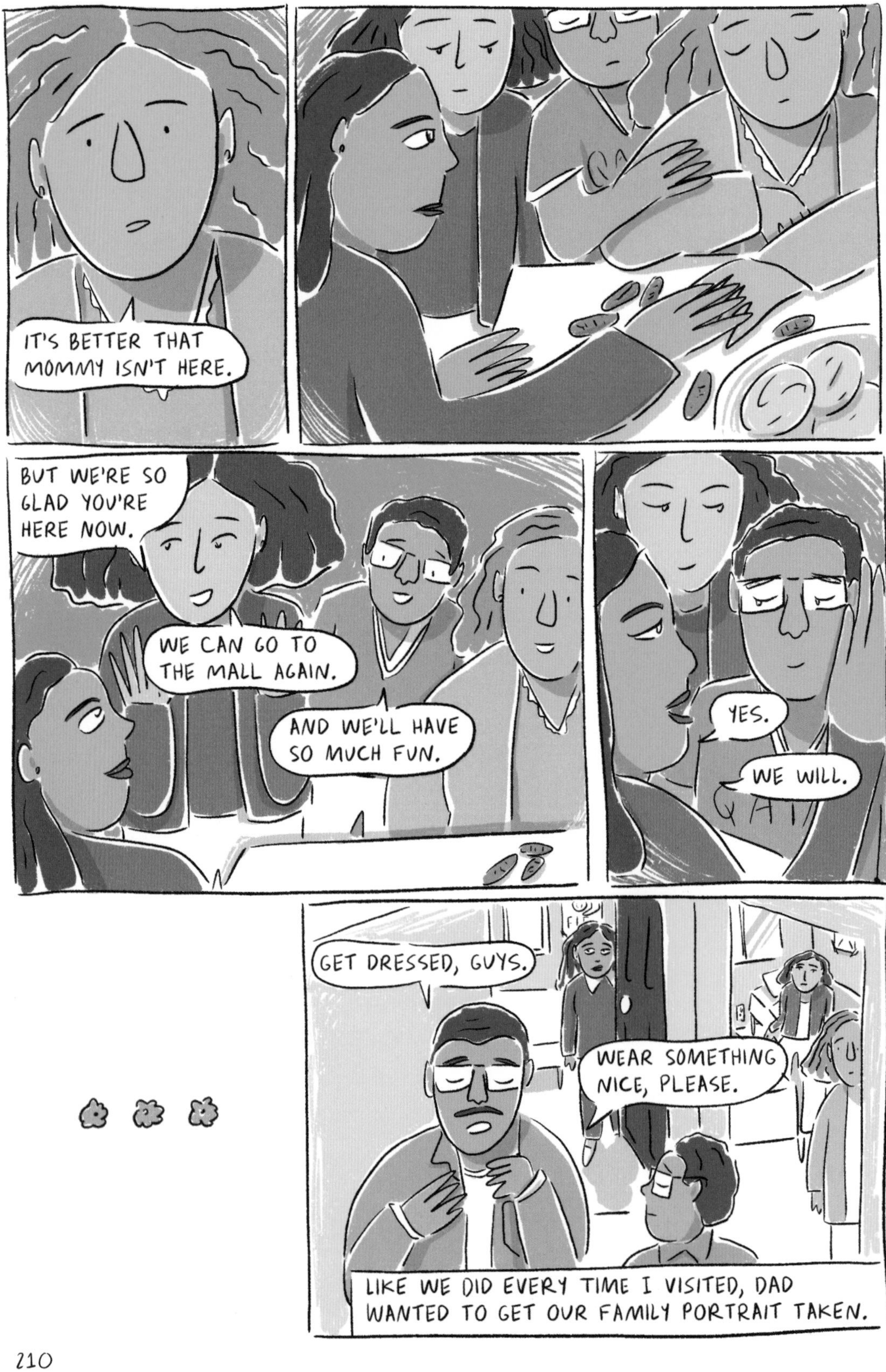
IT'S BETTER THAT MOMMY ISN'T HERE.
BUT WE'RE SO GLAD YOU'RE HERE NOW.
WE CAN GO TO THE MALL AGAIN.
AND WE'LL HAVE SO MUCH FUN.
YES.
WE WILL.
GET DRESSED, GUYS.
WEAR SOMETHING NICE, PLEASE.
LIKE WE DID EVERY TIME I VISITED, DAD WANTED TO GET OUR FAMILY PORTRAIT TAKEN.

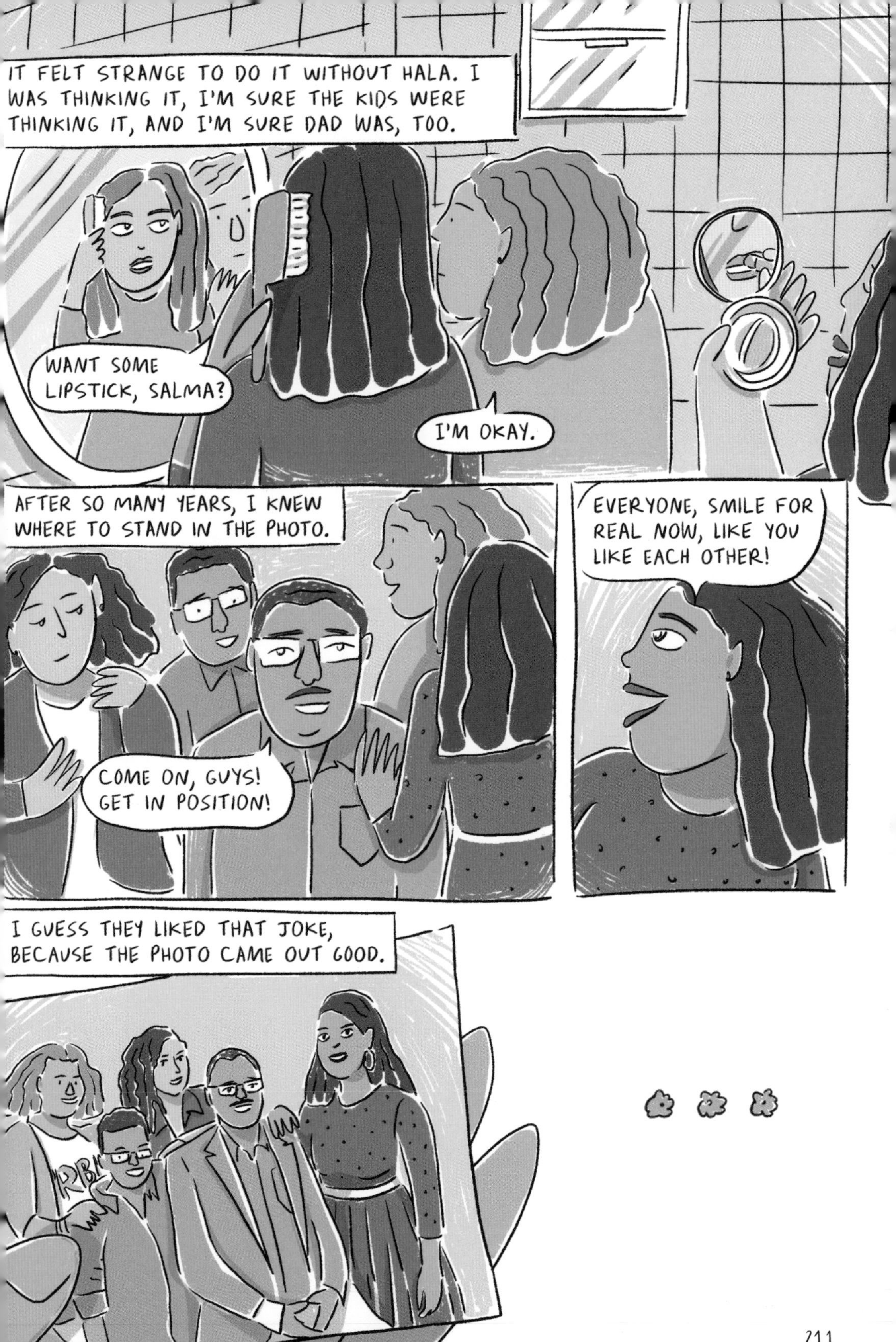
IT FELT STRANGE TO DO IT WITHOUT HALA. I WAS THINKING IT, I'M SURE THE KIDS WERE THINKING IT, AND I'M SURE DAD WAS, TOO.
WANT SOME LIPSTICK, SALMA?
I'M OKAY.
AFTER SO MANY YEARS, I KNEW WHERE TO STAND IN THE PHOTO.
COME ON, GUYS! GET IN POSITION!
EVERYONE, SMILE FOR REAL NOW, LIKE YOU LIKE EACH OTHER!
I GUESS THEY LIKED THAT JOKE, BECAUSE THE PHOTO CAME OUT GOOD.

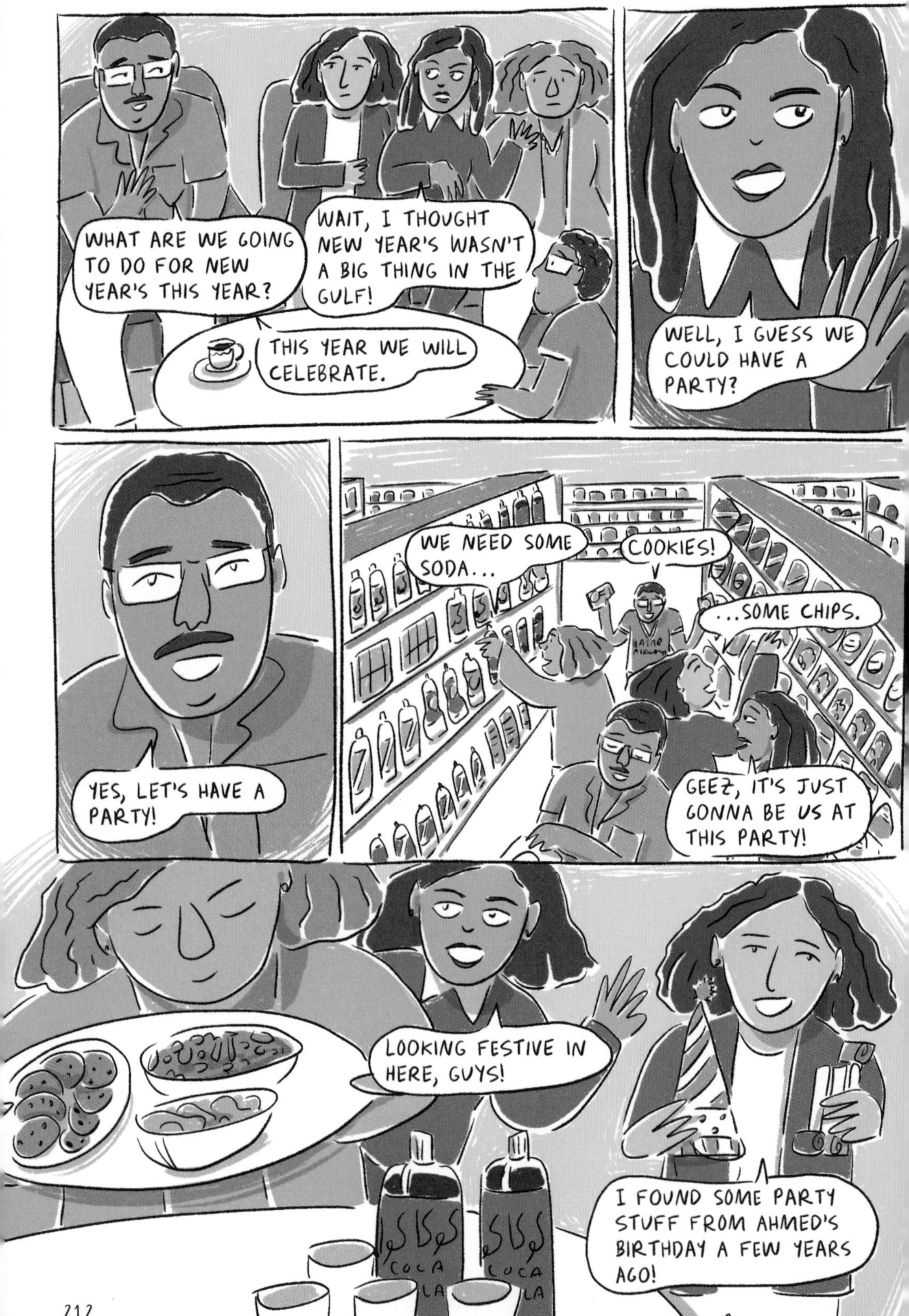
WHAT ARE WE GOING TO DO FOR NEW YEAR'S THIS YEAR?
WAIT, I THOUGHT NEW YEAR'S WASN'T A BIG THING IN THE GULF!
THIS YEAR WE WILL CELEBRATE.
WELL, I GUESS WE COULD HAVE A PARTY?
YES, LET'S HAVE A PARTY!
WE NEED SOME SODA...
COOKIES!
...SOME CHIPS.
GEEZ, IT'S JUST GONNA BE US AT THIS PARTY!
LOOKING FESTIVE IN HERE, GUYS!
I FOUND SOME PARTY STUFF FROM AHMED'S BIRTHDAY A FEW YEARS AGO!

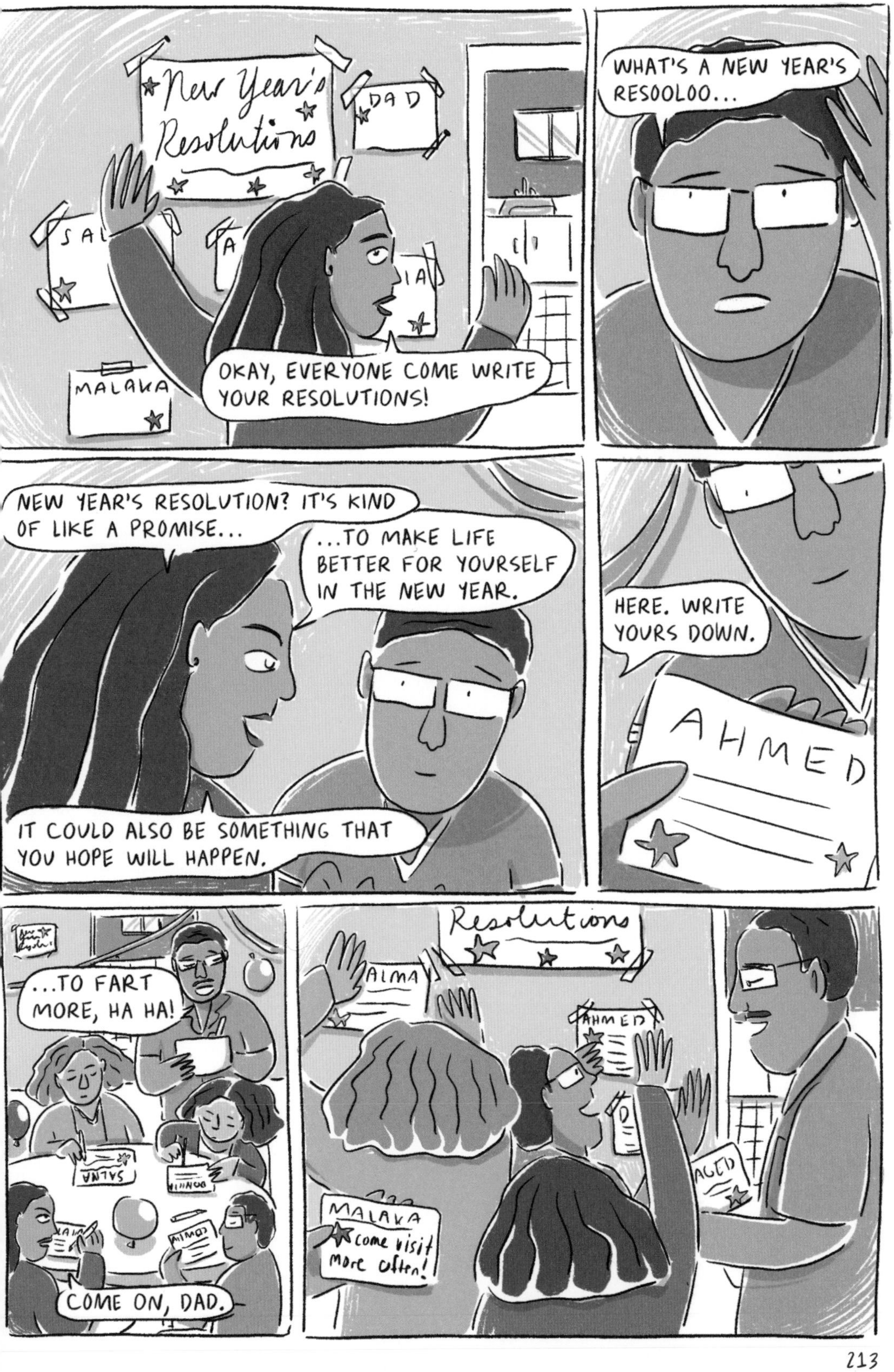
New Year's Resolutions
DAD
SA
A
IA
MALAKA
OKAY, EVERYONE COME WRITE YOUR RESOLUTIONS!
WHAT'S A NEW YEAR'S RESOOLOO...
NEW YEAR'S RESOLUTION? IT'S KIND OF LIKE A PROMISE...
...TO MAKE LIFE BETTER FOR YOURSELF IN THE NEW YEAR.
IT COULD ALSO BE SOMETHING THAT YOU HOPE WILL HAPPEN.
HERE. WRITE YOURS DOWN.
AHMED
...TO FART MORE, HA HA!
SALMA
BONNIE
COME ON, DAD.
Resolutions
ALMA
AHMED
MALAKA
come visit more often!
AGED

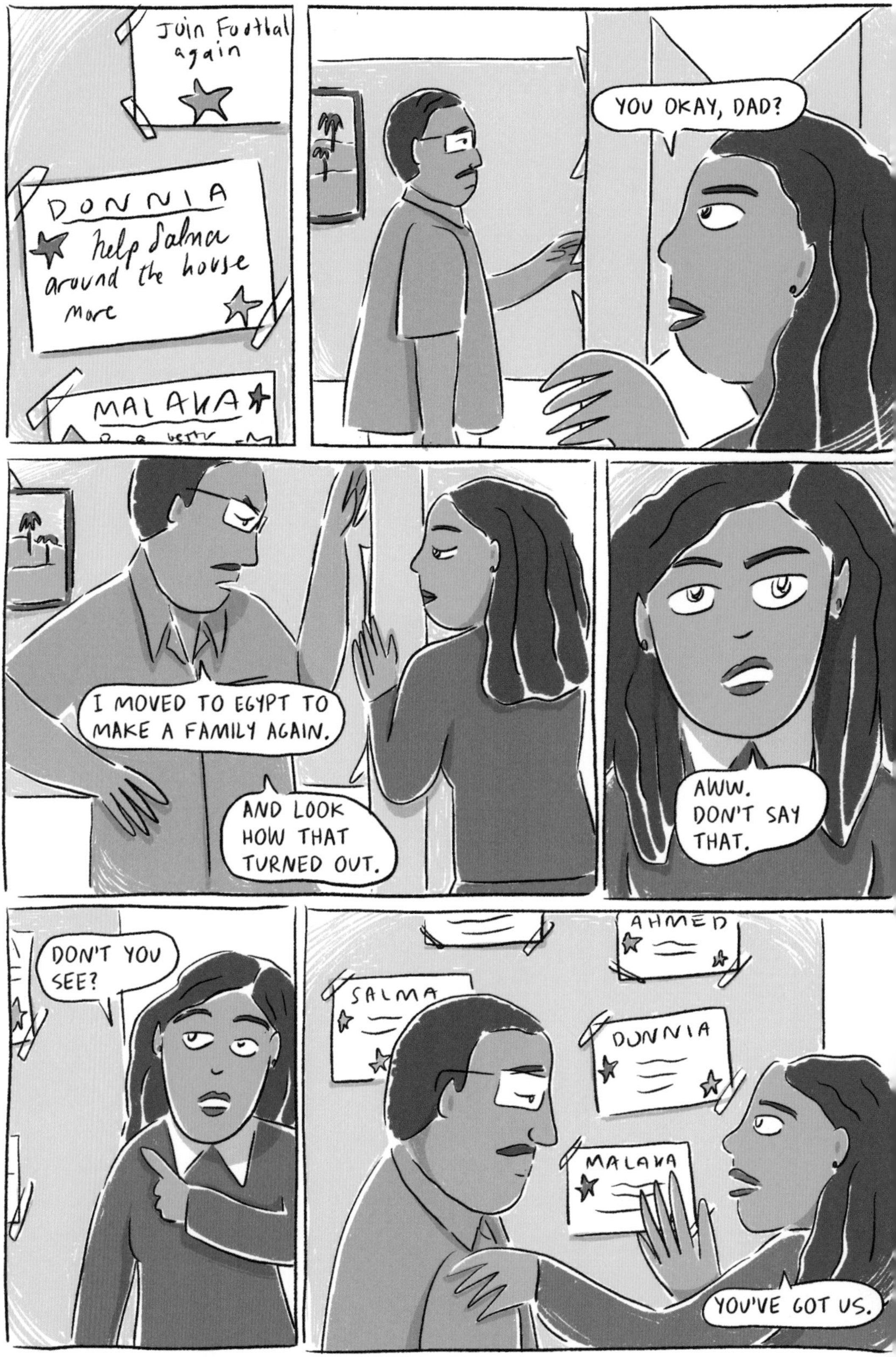

Join Football again
DONNIA
help Salma around the house more
MALAKA
YOU OKAY, DAD?
I MOVED TO EGYPT TO MAKE A FAMILY AGAIN.
AND LOOK HOW THAT TURNED OUT.
AWW. DON'T SAY THAT.
DON'T YOU SEE?
AHMED
SALMA
DONNIA
MALAKA
YOU'VE GOT US.

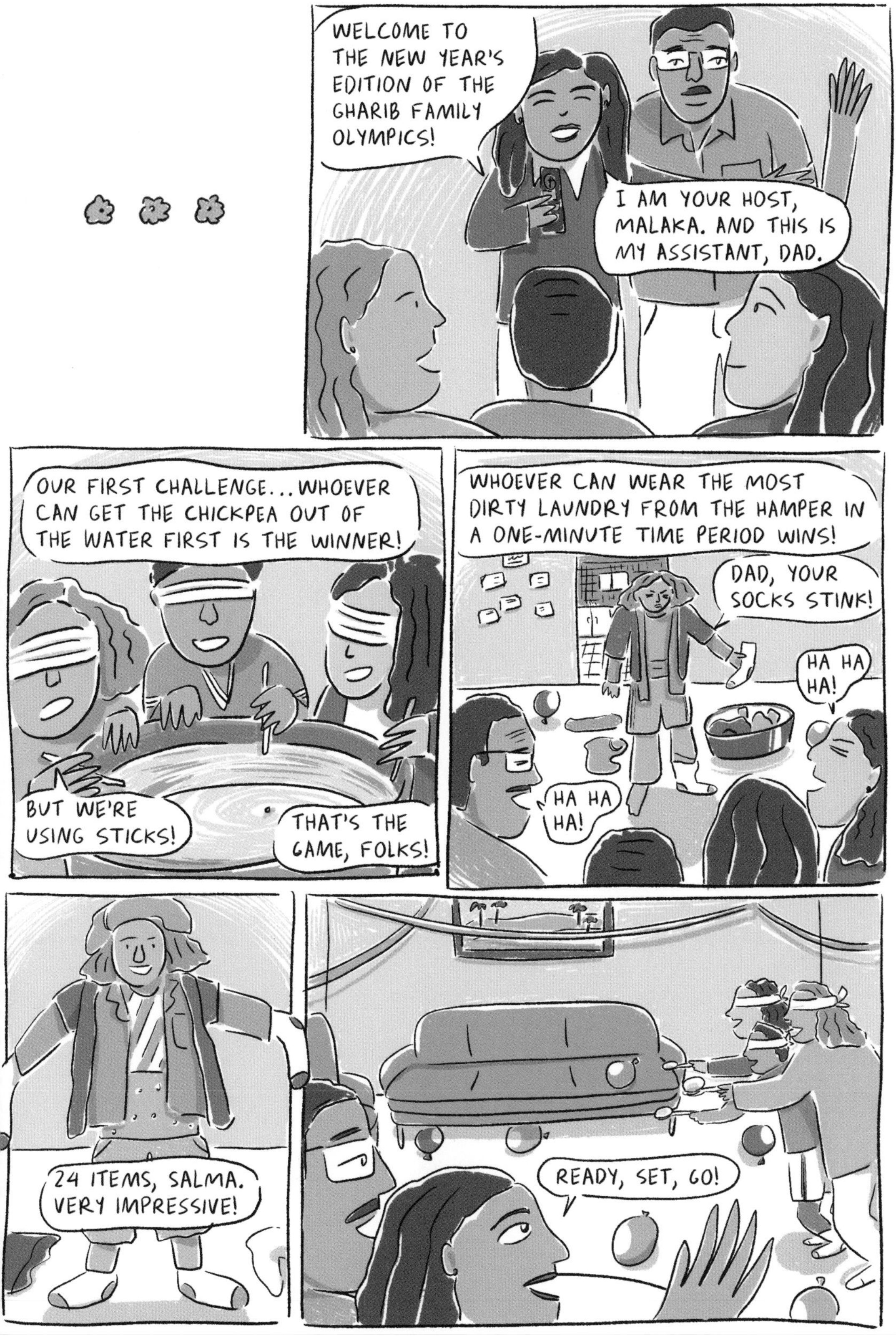
WELCOME TO THE NEW YEAR'S EDITION OF THE GHARIB FAMILY OLYMPICS!
I AM YOUR HOST, MALAKA. AND THIS IS MY ASSISTANT, DAD.
OUR FIRST CHALLENGE... WHOEVER CAN GET THE CHICKPEA OUT OF THE WATER FIRST IS THE WINNER!
BUT WE'RE USING STICKS!
THAT'S THE GAME, FOLKS!
WHOEVER CAN WEAR THE MOST DIRTY LAUNDRY FROM THE HAMPER IN A ONE-MINUTE TIME PERIOD WINS!
DAD, YOUR SOCKS STINK!
HA HA HA!
HA HA HA!
24 ITEMS, SALMA. VERY IMPRESSIVE!
READY, SET, GO!

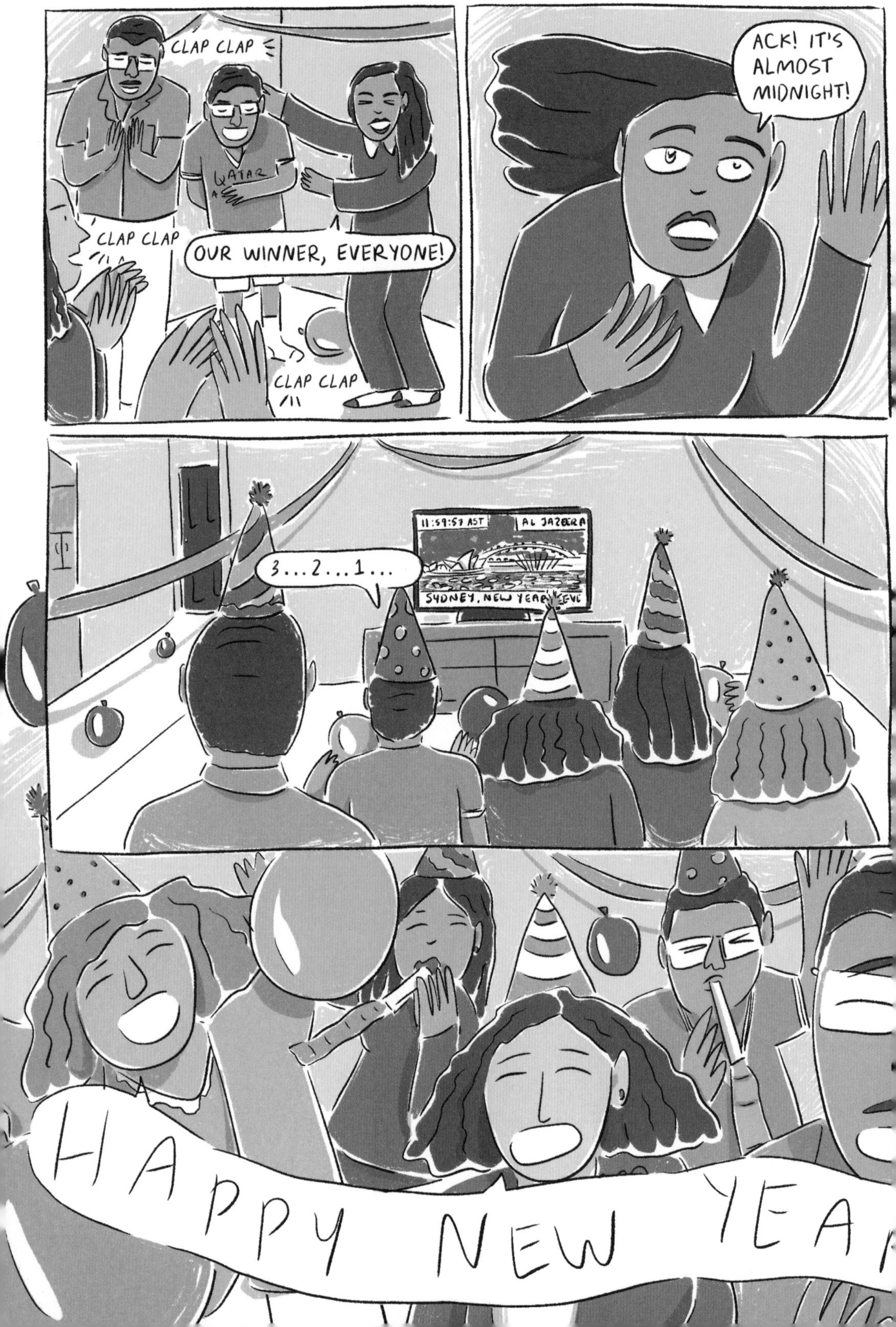
CLAP CLAP
QATAR
CLAP CLAP
OUR WINNER, EVERYONE!
CLAP CLAP
ACK! IT'S ALMOST MIDNIGHT!
11:59:57 AST
AL JAZEERA
SYDNEY, NEW YEAR'S EVE
3...2...1...
HAPPY NEW YEA

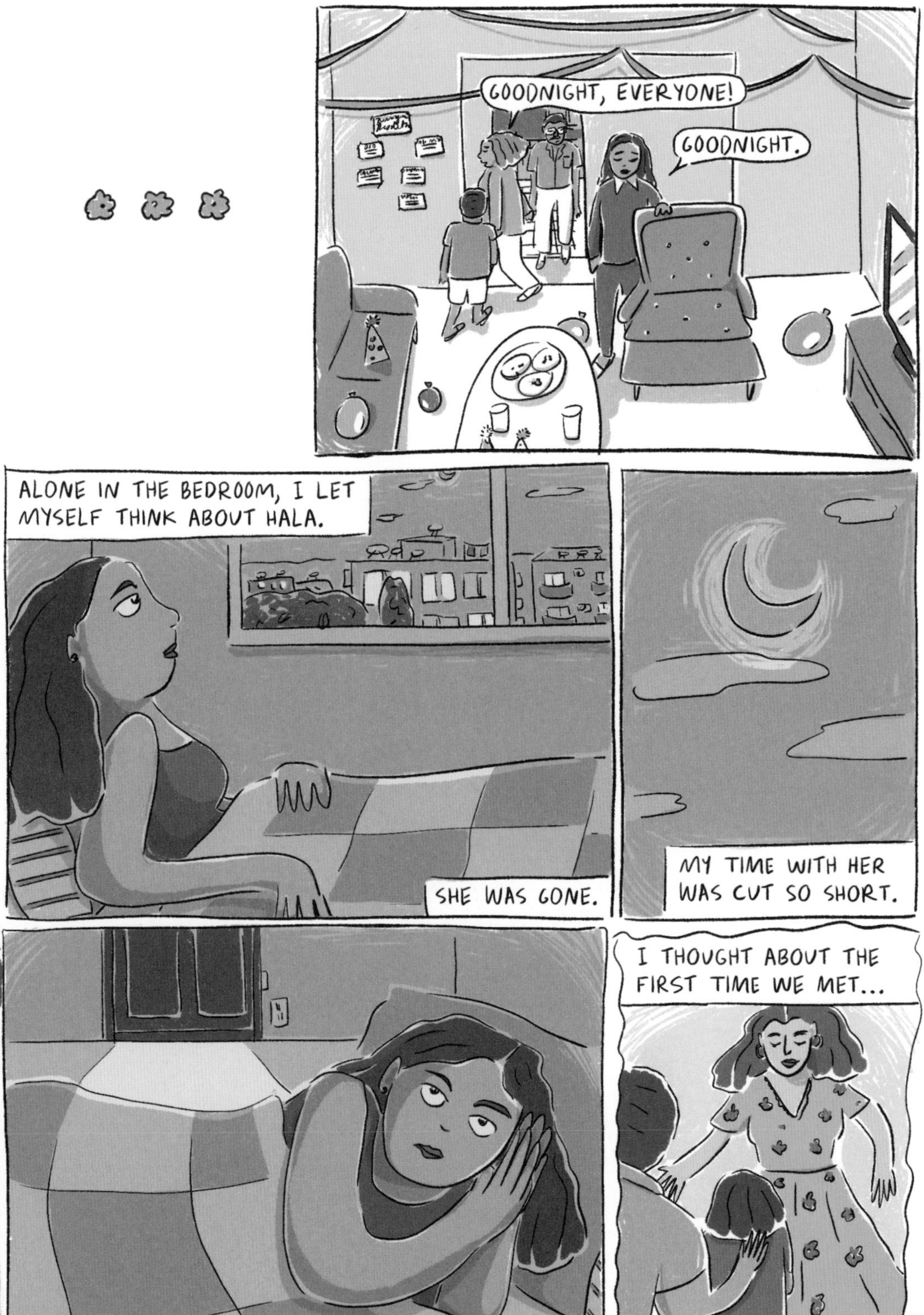
GOODNIGHT, EVERYONE!
GOODNIGHT.
ALONE IN THE BEDROOM, I LET MYSELF THINK ABOUT HALA.
SHE WAS GONE.
MY TIME WITH HER WAS CUT SO SHORT.
THE YEARS REPLAYED IN MY MIND.
I THOUGHT ABOUT THE FIRST TIME WE MET...

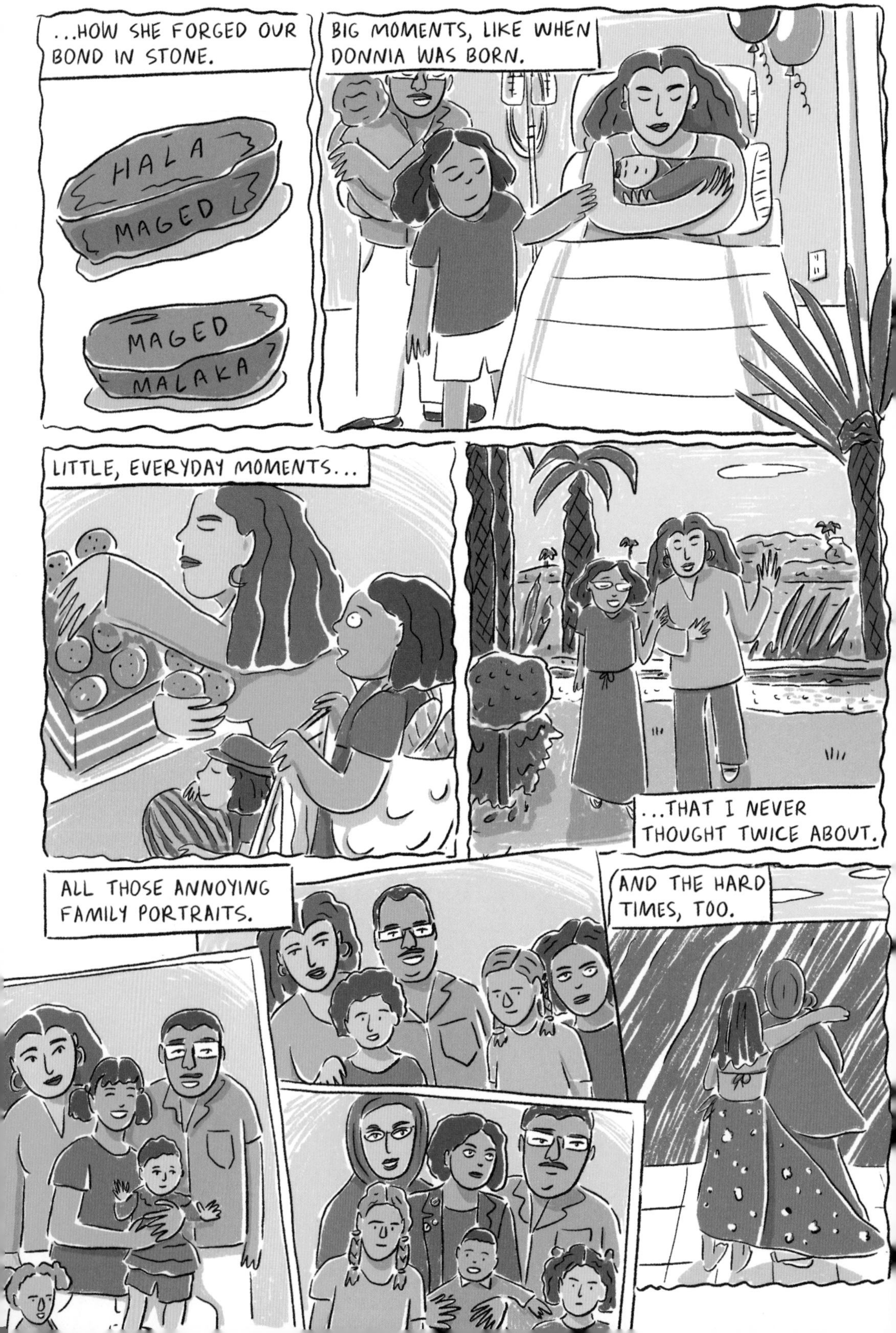
...HOW SHE FORGED OUR BOND IN STONE.
HALA
MAGED
MAGED
MALAKA
BIG MOMENTS, LIKE WHEN DONNIA WAS BORN.
LITTLE, EVERYDAY MOMENTS...
...THAT I NEVER THOUGHT TWICE ABOUT.
ALL THOSE ANNOYING FAMILY PORTRAITS.
AND THE HARD TIMES, TOO.

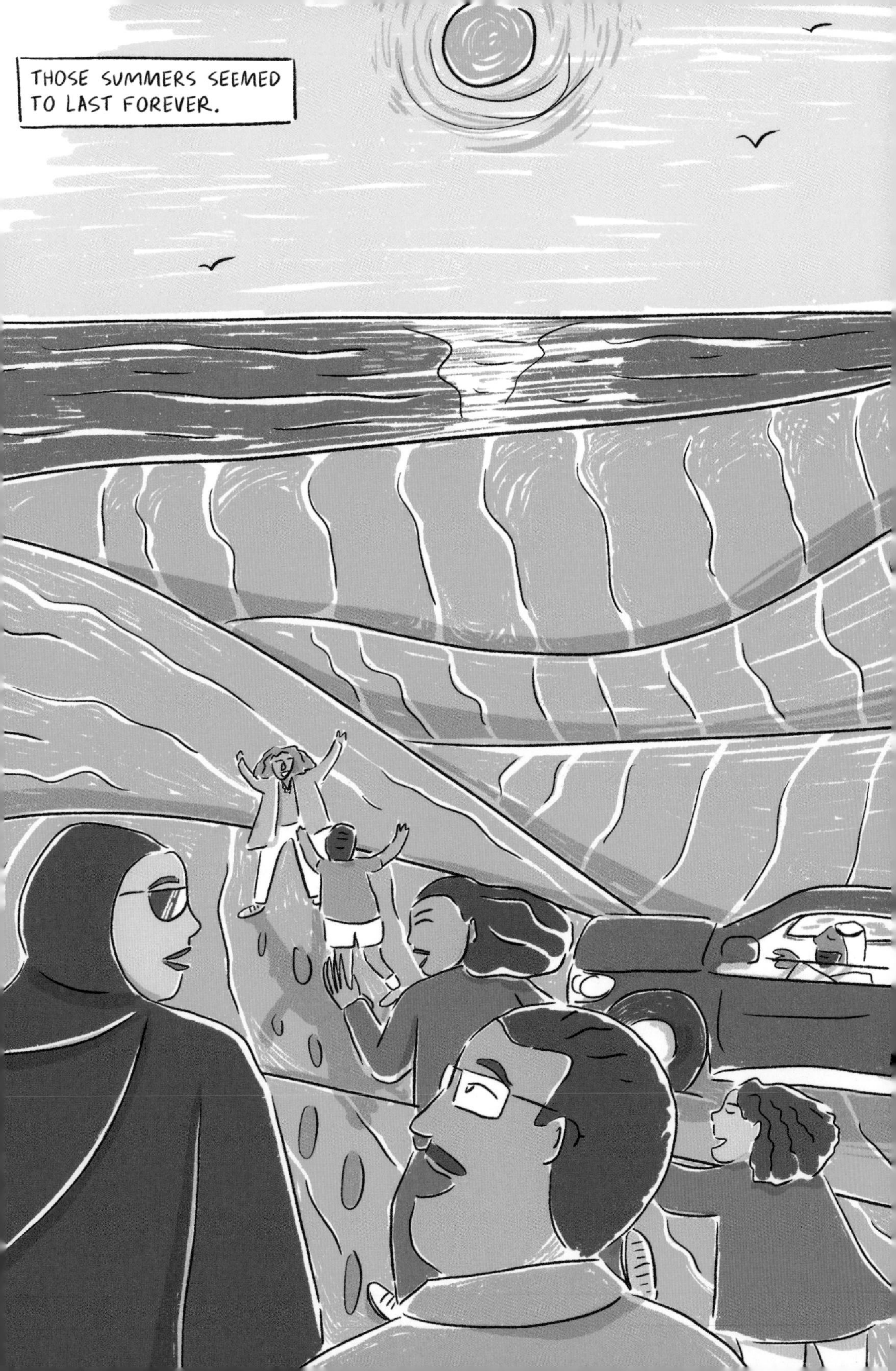
THOSE SUMMERS SEEMED TO LAST FOREVER.

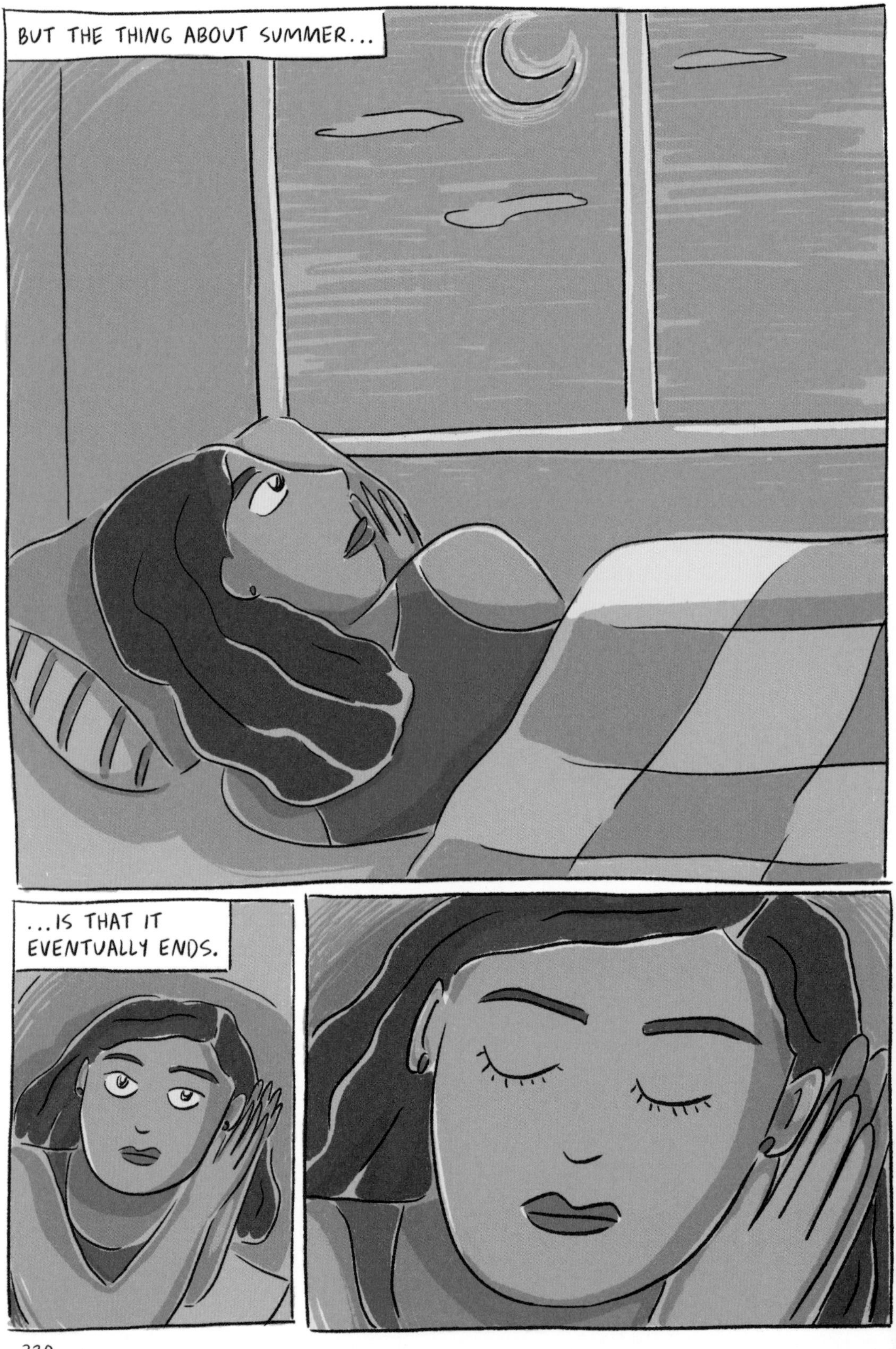
BUT THE THING ABOUT SUMMER...
...IS THAT IT EVENTUALLY ENDS.

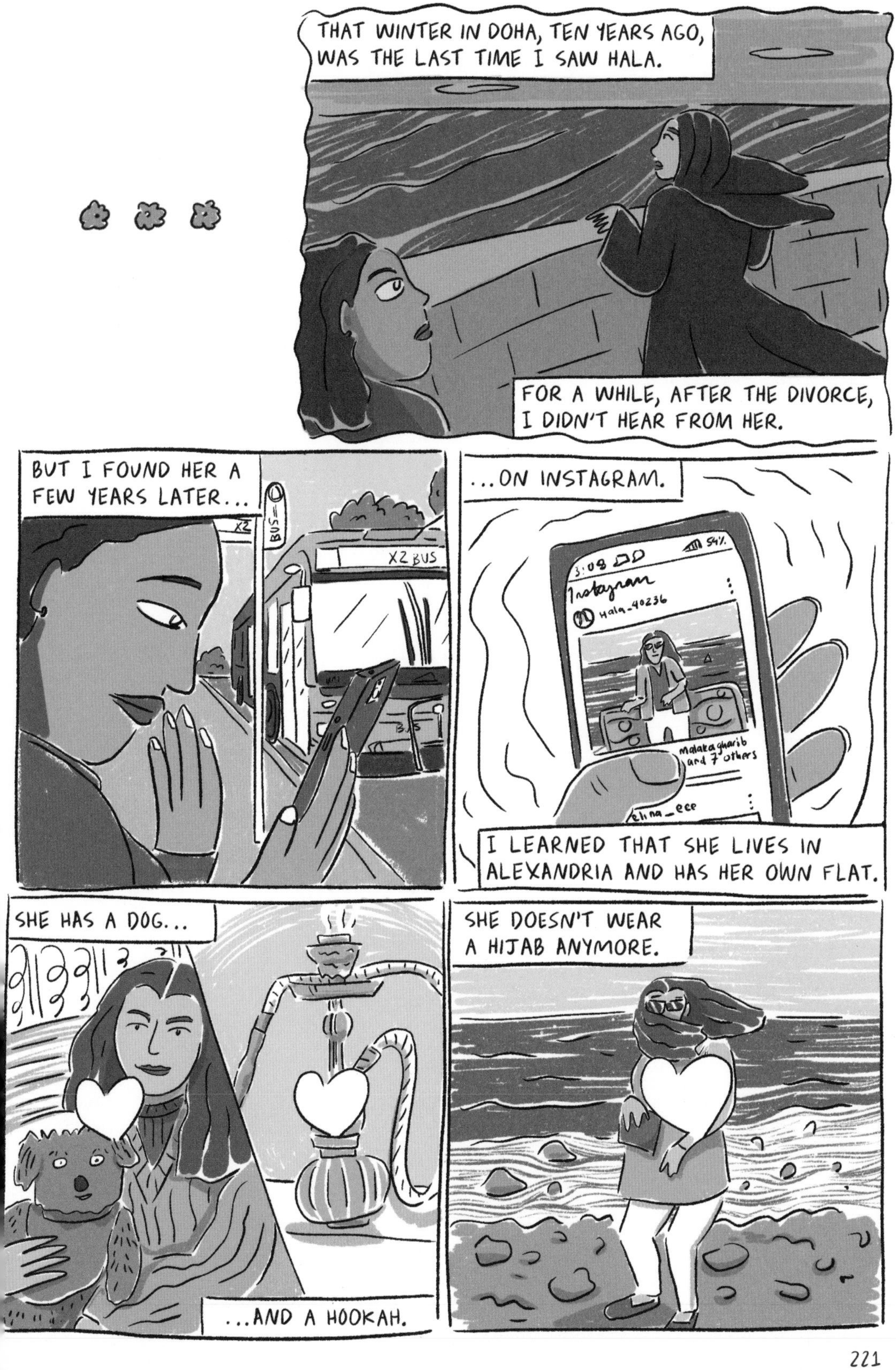
THAT WINTER IN DOHA, TEN YEARS AGO, WAS THE LAST TIME I SAW HALA.
FOR A WHILE, AFTER THE DIVORCE, I DIDN'T HEAR FROM HER.
BUT I FOUND HER A FEW YEARS LATER...
X2 BUS
...ON INSTAGRAM.
3:08
54%
Instagram
Hala_40236
malakagharib and 7 others
I LEARNED THAT SHE LIVES IN ALEXANDRIA AND HAS HER OWN FLAT.
SHE HAS A DOG...
...AND A HOOKAH.
SHE DOESN'T WEAR A HIJAB ANYMORE.

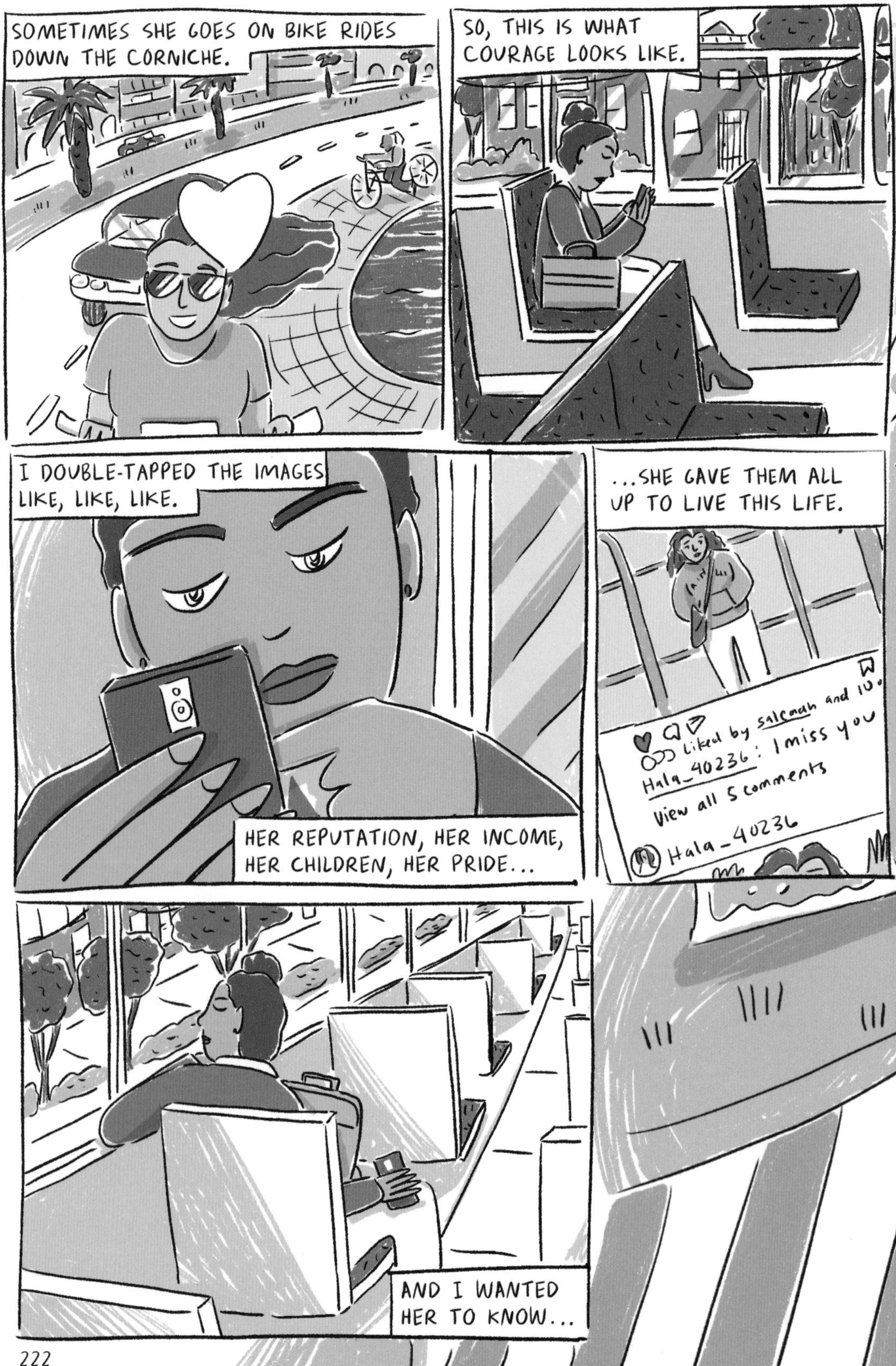
SOMETIMES SHE GOES ON BIKE RIDES DOWN THE CORNICHE.
SO, THIS IS WHAT COURAGE LOOKS LIKE.
I DOUBLE-TAPPED THE IMAGES LIKE, LIKE, LIKE.
HER REPUTATION, HER INCOME, HER CHILDREN, HER PRIDE...
...SHE GAVE THEM ALL UP TO LIVE THIS LIFE.
Liked by saleemah and 10...
Hala_40236: I miss you
View all 5 comments
Hala_40236
AND I WANTED HER TO KNOW...

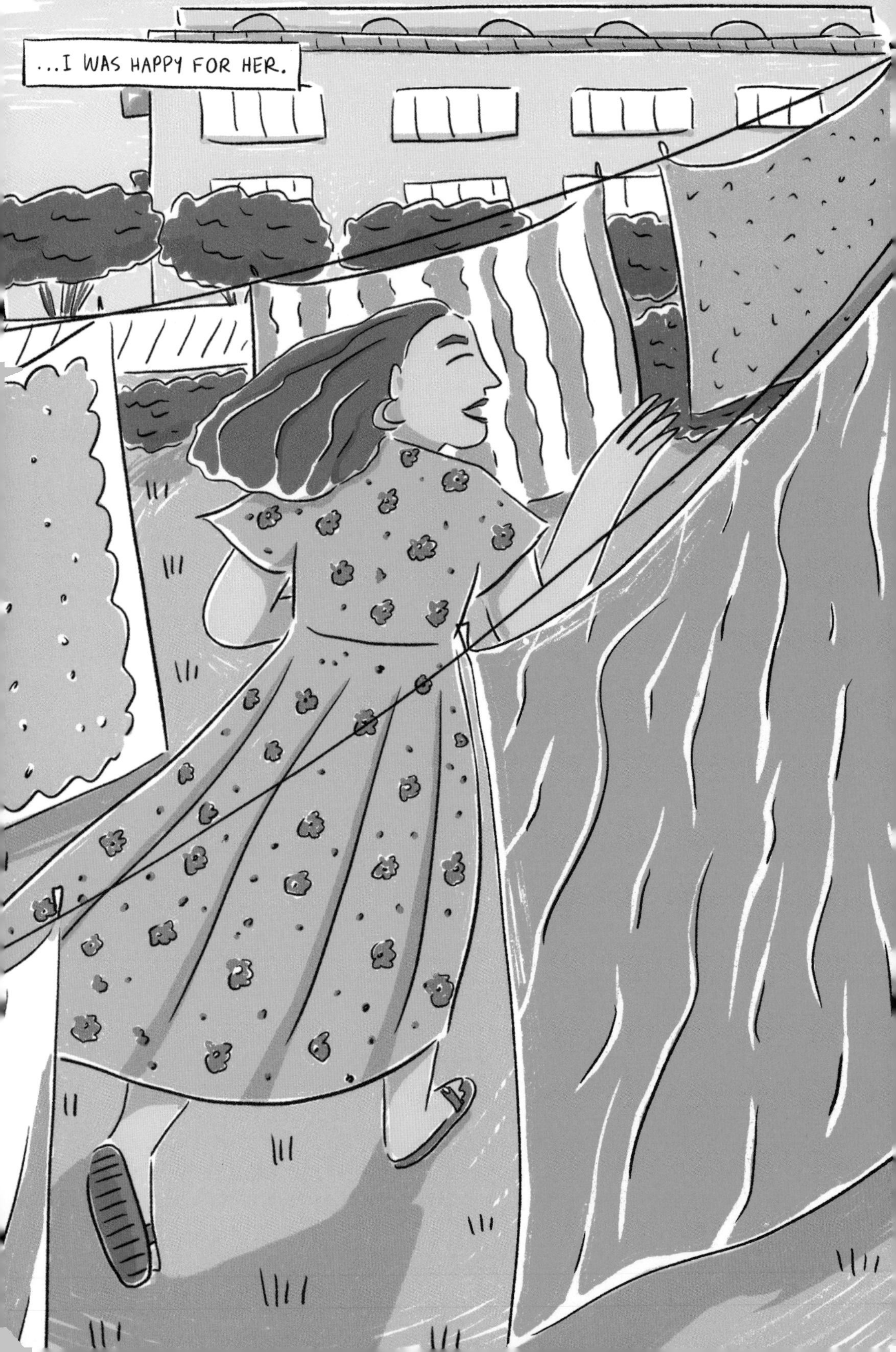
...I WAS HAPPY FOR HER.

Acknowledgments

THANK YOU TO DADDY AND HALA FOR READING EVERY DRAFT OF THE MANUSCRIPT AND WALKING THROUGH EACH CHAPTER WITH ME. TO MOMMY AND TITA PINKY FOR REMINDING ME OF TATAY'S WORDS TO JUST KEEP WRITING. TO AHMED, SALMA, AND DONNIA: THANK YOU FOR TRANSLATING THE BOOK FOR HALA AND ALLOWING ME TO WRITE ABOUT US. TO DARREN, FOR STANDING RIGHT BESIDE ME ON THIS JOURNEY AND BEING MY CHEERLEADER.

THANK YOU TO THE TEAM WHO MADE THIS BOOK POSSIBLE. TO MY EDITOR SARA NEVILLE AT CLARKSON POTTER FOR SUPPORTING THE BOOK BEFORE I EVEN KNEW WHAT IT WOULD BE ABOUT. TO BEN DE LA CRUZ FOR YOUR TREMENDOUS EDITS AND ALWAYS BELIEVING IN MY TALENT. TO RHONDA RAGAB AND SILA CONSULTING FOR THE STELLAR ARAB AND MUSLIM SENSITIVITY EDITING. TO SETH WORLEY FOR EDITING MY FIRST MANUSCRIPT. TO NURITH AIZENMAN WHO TOLD ME YEARS AGO THERE WAS A DEEPER STORY HERE TO BE TOLD. TO TOBY LEIGH FOR MAKING THE STORY COME ALIVE WITH COLOR.

THANK YOU MY AGENT DANIEL GREENBERG AT LEVINE GREENBERG ROSTAN LITERARY AGENCY, AND THE TEAM AT TEN SPEED PRESS, ESPECIALLY LISA BIESER, CHLOE RAWLINS, AND SOHAYLA FARMAN.

THANK YOU AHMAD DARWISH, RAMY GHARIB, AND OMAR ELIMAM FOR WALKING DOWN MEMORY LANE WITH ME AND LETTING ME TELL SOME AWKWARD STORIES!

THANK YOU TO MY BETA READERS DANNY HAJJAR, SUSAN MUADDI DARRAJ, DIANA ABOUALI, TAMANNA MANSURY, SUMMER THOMAD, AND KAREEM TAWFIK. YOUR PERSPECTIVES ON ARAB AND EGYPTIAN CULTURE AND ISLAM HELPED ME MORE THAN YOU KNOW.

THANK YOU TO GRACE TALUSAN, GINA APOSTOL, IHAB ZAGHLOUL, ANDREW RESTUCCIA, CLAIRE O'NEILL, JUSTIN CLARAVALL, TRENT ENGLAND, AND MICHAELEEN DOUCLEFF FOR READING EARLY DRAFTS OF THE BOOK.

THANK YOU TO ALL THOSE WHO HAVE TAUGHT ME THAT LOVE DOESN'T REALLY NEED WORDS, AND CAN APPEAR OUT OF SEEMINGLY NOTHING.